THE CULT OF HEALTH AND BEAUTY IN GERMANY

The Cult of Health and Beauty in Germany

in Germany

A Social History
1890–1930

Michael Hau

The University of Chicago Press
Chicago and London

Michael Hau is a lecturer in modern European history at Monash University in Melbourne, Australia.

The University of Chicago Press, Chicago 60637
The University of Chicago Press, Ltd., London
© 2003 by The University of Chicago
All rights reserved. Published 2003
Printed in the United States of America

12 11 10 09 08 07 06 05 04 03   1 2 3 4 5
ISBN: 0-226-31974-1 (cloth)
ISBN: 0-226-31976-8 (paper)

Library of Congress Cataloging-in-Publication Data

Hau, Michael.
    The cult of health and beauty in Germany : a social history, 1890–1930 / Michael Hau.
    p. cm.
    Includes bibliographical references and index.
    ISBN 0-226-31974-1 (cloth : alk. paper)—ISBN 0-226-31976-8 (pbk. : alk. paper)
    1. Social medicine—Germany.   2. Hygiene—Germany—History.   3. Germany—Social life and customs—History.   I. Title.

RA418.3.G3 H375 2003
306.4'61'0943—dc21

                                                                                        2002014839

CONTENTS

ILLUSTRATIONS

ACKNOWLEDGMENTS

$\mathcal{A}$ book like this is very much a collaborative work. I thank the scholars and friends who have supported this endeavor at various stages. Mitchell Ash, Kenneth Cmiel, Sarah Farmer, Laura Graham, and Susan Lawrence provided valuable criticism and support while I was at the University of Iowa. Tracy Chang, Mark Chaffee, Doug and Julie Currivan, Jason Duncan, Gesine Gerhard, Scott Grau, Ralph Lano, Marjorie Levine, Al Mask, Jason Moritz, Don Oberdorfer, and Mark Perkins were always sources of inspiration and support. Special thanks go to my Berlin friend and Iowa colleague Sierra Bruckner, who has read and critiqued the manuscript twice. Sam Smucker, Carol Lambiase, and the other friends and oganizers from Cogs/UE made the last two years at Iowa memorable ones.

David Blackbourn, Dirk Bönker, Dieter Langewiesche, Michael Hubenstorf, Wulf Kansteiner, Heikki Lempa, and Martin Roth (Deutsches Hygienemuseum) provided advice, criticism, and support at various stages of this work. I am grateful to the German Hygiene Museum and its staff for providing a pleasant and encouraging working environment during my stays in Dresden and for allowing me to use illustrations from the museum's collections. The Institut für Europäische Geschichte in Mainz has supported my research with a fellowship. My thanks go to Heinz Duchhardt, Andreas Kunz, Ralph Melville, Claus Scharf, and Martin Vogt for their help while I stayed in Mainz.

A two-year Schloeßmann postdoctoral fellowship at the Max Planck Institute for the History of Science in Berlin provided crucial support. I thank Lorraine Daston and the members of her departmental colloquium for a lively and intellectually engaging environment. Fati-Fan, Eckhardt Fuchs, Wolfgang Küttler, Jens Lachmund, Helmut Maier, Benoit Massin, Michelle Murphy, Hans Pols, Thomas Potthast, Matt Price, Helmut Puff, Skuli Sigurdsson, Claudia Stein, Fernando Vidal, and Annette Vogt gave advice and encouragement. I am also grateful for the constructive reports by the anonymous readers for the University of Chicago Press. Doug Mitchell's support as editor was invaluable.

Special thanks go to Robert Devens and Jane Zanichkowsky, whose editing helped to make the manuscript more readable.

Parts of chapter 3 were published earlier as Michael Hau, "Gender and Aesthetic Norms in Popular Hygienic Culture in Germany from 1900 to 1914," *Social History of Medicine* 12, no. 2 (1999): 271–92. Reprinted by permission of Oxford University Press.

Finally, I would like to thank Bettina Wachsmuth. Without her help, encouragement, and love I would not have finished the book.

$\mathcal{T}$he second half of the nineteenth century witnessed an increase in the living standards and the life expectancy of most Germans. At the same time, important breakthroughs in areas such as aseptic surgery and bacteriology endowed scientific medicine with symbols of diagnostic and therapeutic competence. Despite the growing prestige of the medical and life sciences, however, health and illness became important concerns for a growing number of Germans who scrutinized and disciplined their bodies in a utopian search for perfect health and beauty. During the Kaiserreich and the Weimar Republic, many Germans organized themselves into voluntary associations concerned with natural therapy and lifestyle reform. Members of the "life reform movement" *(Lebensreformbewegung)*, as it was termed, attacked the regular medical profession for its powerlessness in the face of illness and embarked on an unceasing quest for health on their own: they experimented with vegetarianism, therapeutic baths, and psychotherapies; they explored the therapeutic value of nudity and sunlight.

Supporters of the life reform movement were worried not only about the health of individuals but about the healing process *(Gesundung)* of society as a whole. They believed that modern civilization, urbanization, and industrialization had alienated human beings from their "natural" living conditions, leading them down a path of progressive degeneration that could only be reversed by living in accordance with man's and woman's nature *(naturgemäße Lebensweise)*.

Historians of the life reform movement often have focused on differences or conflicts between propagators of natural therapies and of regular medicine *(Schulmedizin)*. For instance, natural therapists and their supporters—among them a few university-trained physicians who were ostracized by their orthodox colleagues—chastised modern medicine for its inability to deliver humanity from disease and illness. They criticized regular physicians for treating patients schematically while ignoring their individual physical and spiritual constitutions. The therapies of modern medicine and modern bacteriology in particular were not only ineffective, they argued, but also dangerous. In their agitation against the smallpox vaccinations that were mandated by German law in 1874, life reformers vigorously denounced regular physicians for "poisoning" their patients. Observing this critical dynamic, some scholars have interpreted the life reform movement as a reaction against the professionalization of medicine and the divergence of professional and lay discourses about health and illness.[1] This literature, still growing, accomplishes the necessary work of examining and emphasizing the differences between regular and alternative medicine, while outlining the strategies of the antagonists in their fight for a share of the medical market.

My approach, however, is different. In this book, I examine the creation and refashioning of shared and contested values and meanings in the discourses of regular and alternative medicine. Focusing on the period between 1890 and 1930, I describe popular hygienic culture as a discursive field that was shaped by laypeople, alternative medical practitioners, and university-trained physicians. Advocates of natural therapies as well as regular physicians had to respond to the expectations and anxieties of their lay audiences when they gave hygienic advice, and it is not unreasonable to assume that to some extent they shared these expectations and anxieties. Life reformers and regular physicians thus participated in a common discourse, which emerges clearly when one considers the meanings these factions attributed to physical beauty. Aesthetic representations of the human body—such as photographs, drawings, anatomical models, and textual descriptions—made it possible for life reformers and regular physicians to visualize concepts such as health, disease, and degeneration. Like other contemporary popularizers of scientific knowledge, they used aesthetic concepts, tropes, and images in order to make their ideas visible, or *anschaulich*, for a lay public.[2]

Numerous studies of the life reform movement enriched our understanding of the Wilhelmine and Weimar periods. Most of these studies focus on specific aspects of the movement, such as the intellectual traditions of vegetarianism, aspects of nude culture, and natural therapy.[3] Examining them separately can lead to a fragmented view of life reform as a collection of distinct movements centered around different organizations and different practices. Such approaches do not always do full justice to the fluidity of boundaries between turn-of-the-century health reform concerns. People wishing to improve their personal health could choose among alternatives on the health market: they could adopt, combine, and abandon hygienic practices propagated by regular physicians and their life reform opponents. A person experimenting with natural therapies, for instance, could eventually also become an ardent vegetarian and physical culturist, only to jettison elements of this alternative lifestyle later on.

The goal of this study is to examine the various subjective social experiences that lay behind people's attempts to regain their health by reforming their lives. What was behind the constant self-scrutiny of individuals who tried to find the perfect lifestyle and therapy to help them overcome their perceived ill health? I argue that subjective experience of illness was mediated or constituted by the social experience of individuals. This is evident, for example, in the frequent complaints about nervousness among life reform supporters who were afraid that they could not keep up with their own career expectations.[4] Indeed, as Germans increasingly medicalized their professional and personal problems, anxieties about success were often at the root of concerns about health and fitness.

Medicalization, as I understand it, is the socially negotiated product of subjective social experiences, on one hand, and attempts by physicians and life reformers to explain these experiences in medical terms, on the other.[5] One of the contradictions of classical modernity during the Wilhelmine period was that medicalization emerged from the discursive space shared by scientific medicine and its life reform detractors. Germans increasingly defined their personal problems in medical terms, described them in medical language, and understood them in a medical framework.[6] At the same time, men and women turned to health advice literature for guidance concerning the management of their marriages and intimate relationships; they attempted to regain a sense of agency and assert control over their lives by means of bodily discipline and other health measures; and men in particular hoped that healthy living and natural therapies would increase their physical fitness and mental performance levels. The relation between a modern, industrializing society and the life reform movement was therefore not primarily one of modernization and protest against modernization, as some authors argue.[7] Rather, the contemporary explosion in people's attention to their health was an expression of the contradictions and tensions characteristic of the period of classical modernity.[8]

In a society that grew increasingly body-conscious, men's and women's concerns about their physical appearance were an important source of anxieties, as were concerns about the spread of venereal disease and changing gender relations. It would be a mistake, however, to explain the new body-consciousness solely in terms of anxieties, because this awareness also had a liberating effect.

For instance, physical exercise functioned as compensation for sedentary work, which was becoming increasingly common. The rejection of confining clothing and corsets, as well as the popularity of hiking, open-air exercise, and sunbathing, further signaled the casting off of oppressive traditions. Finally, the cultivation of one's body became an alternative source of social esteem for men who did not enjoy the prestige of a neohumanistic education. The joys of physical culture *(Körperbildung)* contrasted favorably with the burdensome cultivation and higher education *(Bildung)* that Wilhelmine elites acquired in the *Gymnasium,* the secondary school whose degrees gave access to universities and a number of other social privileges. In this respect, the criticism of life reformers resonated with the concerns of contemporary school reformers, who attacked Gymnasium education, with its emphasis on Greek and Latin, as outdated and impractical for people living in a modern industrial society.[9]

In terms of social class, the life reform movement was quite heterogeneous, part of the Wilhelmine and Weimar "cultural mass market" *(kultureller Massenmarkt)* in which men and women with different social backgrounds and experiences actively participated. Some of its most outspoken leaders came from the educated middle class *(Bildungsbürgertum).* Others who never enjoyed a formal higher education still felt entitled to speak and publish authoritatively on health, illness, medical therapies, and "natural" gender relations, in defiance of respectable medical specialists trained at universities. The heterogeneity of life reformers is further demonstrated by the range of attitudes toward gender relations one finds, from feminist to rabidly antifeminist; indeed, with respect to the liberties of women, life reform in general and natural therapy in particular should not be equated with a more progressive attitude than regular medicine.

The concept of hygienic culture as I use it here includes more than the therapeutic practices and dietetic prescriptions intended to keep people clean and disease-free. It also refers to the social meanings that people attributed to such hygienic practices, regimes, and notions of health and beauty. My interpretation of popular hygienic culture is indebted to the work of Mikhail Bakhtin, who has proposed a useful theoretical framework for this kind of analysis.[10] According to Bakhtin, people fashion new meanings and values from a shared social discourse based on their various social experiences. By focusing on hygienic practices and values related to norms of physical beauty, I try to show how different social groups attributed different meanings to the same practices and ideals. Men and women from both the Bildungsbürgertum and the lower middle class shared similar ideals of physical beauty, but the social uses and values attributed to these norms varied according to their social experiences. In theory, physical beauty can have as many different social meanings as there are social experiences. In this study, however, I confine myself mainly to the striking themes of hygienic advice literature and propaganda published by regular physicians and life reformers.[11]

Chapter 1 shows life reform to be an integral part of turn-of-the-century *bürgerlicher Kultur*. In accordance with recent scholarship on the German *Bürgertum*, the term *bürgerlich* (roughly translatable as "bourgeois") does not denote social class in a Marxist sense. Instead, the term refers to value orientations and cultural norms shared by different sectors of the middle classes as well as sectors of the respectable working class. Central to these shared orientations and norms was a certain goal-directedness combined with the assumption that individuals could rationally manage their own futures, a belief that found expression, for example, in people's career expectations. I argue that the experience of personal failure—or, perhaps more important, simply the *fear* of it—underpinned the contemporary obsession with health. With its promise to increase people's *Leistungsfähigkeit* (in the dual sense of ability to perform and achieve), life reform gave its supporters a sense of agency in their own future.

Chapter 2 deals with the function of aesthetic norms in popular hygienic discourse, in particular the writings of male life reformers from the Bildungsbürgertum and lower middle classes. Both groups shared aesthetic norms for the human body derived from the art of Greek antiquity (the norms of which were perceived to be timeless). Both groups claimed Bildung, in the sense of a harmonious cultivation of body, mind, and soul, but they fundamentally disagreed about how this cultivation was to be achieved. The work of the sociologist Pierre Bourdieu helps us understand this disagreement. Bourdieu has shown that subjective social experiences help form class identities and that social distinction can be expressed not only through tastes and aesthetic preferences but also through hygienic practices and attitudes toward the body.[12] Chapter 2 shows that such images, attitudes, and practices together constituted an important discursive arena for the formation of class identities and class antagonisms. Lowermiddle-class life reformers—who in Bourdieu's diction lacked economic and cultural capital (such as a thorough humanistic education)—were unable to build their social identity around material success or educational attainment. In their quest for social distinction, they therefore made a virtue out of necessity and turned to bodily discipline and a frugal lifestyle, denouncing the rich and the educated for their debauchery and physical degeneracy. Their disciplined bodies, modeled after the aesthetic ideals of Greek antiquity, thus became cultural capital and markers of distinction in relation to both the educated middle class and members of the working class who could not afford to participate in such time-consuming leisure activities.[13]

Chapter 3 shows how physicians and life reformers resorted to aesthetic concepts of the beautiful body in order to defend the traditional gender relations of the Bürgertum. But these justifications of social norms for the sexes—which appeared in popular hygienic literature at the turn of the century—were challenged by feminist critics as well as by the reality of changing relations between the sexes. The increasing participation of women in the labor market and the demands by feminists that the professions and the universities be opened to women were seen by many as threats to the traditional division of labor. For regular physicians and health reformers alike, this seemed to raise the specter of masculinized women and feminized men, and they responded by propagating "natural norms" for the sexes. Deviations from these norms were then regarded as symptoms of degeneracy expressed in outward appearance: for example, a person's lack of a clear sexual identity (a trait considered degenerate) was cast in aesthetic terms as a deviation from the eternally valid ideals of beauty that had first been formulated in Greek antiquity. As I will show, however, these same norms also provided material for feminists, who, though not denying the degeneracy of many contemporary women, blamed the deplorable state of affairs on the lack of economic and social opportunities for women.

Chapter 4 discusses the social functions of German racial discourse. In turn-of-the-century Germany, normative prescriptions concerning gender roles and sexual behavior were often conveyed in an aestheticized racial or sometimes nationalist idiom. Instead of understanding racial theories in terms of their changes over time, as historians interested in the ideological roots of Nazism have done, I try to understand racial theories in terms of the encoded messages that the authors tried to impart to their audience. For example, such theories essentialized the moral qualities of women by contrasting the sexual instincts of "exotic" or lower-class women with the sexual disinterestedness and beauty of Nordic women. One must comprehend such coded meanings in order to understand the reception of racial theories at this time. In other words, it is not enough to construct intellectual traditions; one must also grasp the social functions of racial discourses and the ways these discourses were grounded in contemporary perceptions of gender and social class.

Models of pathogenesis based on psychophysical constitution are discussed in chapter 5.[14] For life reformers and for some regular physicians, physical beauty was an indicator of a healthy constitution. Chapter 5 discusses such holistic models of constitutionalism in scientific and alternative medicine. I argue that this holism was tied to aesthetic assumptions—for instance, that a healthy and beautiful body was characterized by the harmonious and purposeful interaction of its constituent parts. Such assumptions were similar to the aesthetic assumptions of highly educated people *(Gebildeten)* in that both suggested that the human organism could be judged intuitively as a coherent whole (as one would judge a work of art). This chapter traces the development of such discourse in both forms of medicine. It also clarifies the relation between constitution-based assumptions and the acceptance of eugenics among life reformers.

Chapter 6 examines relations between regular and alternative physicians in the medical market. By accepting the constitutional approach, some regular physicians in the Weimar Republic were able to appropriate the discourse of the life reform movement in an attempt to undercut public support for alternative medicine. Physicians increasingly echoed the demands of the life reform movement. For instance, the surgeons Erwin Liek and Ferdinand Sauerbruch demanded that physicians rely less on the laboratory and instead become humane experts, taking the constitutional individuality of their patients into account and treating them holistically. The appropriation of life reform discourse was also reflected in the great hygiene exhibitions of the period, which showcased the achievements of the regular medical profession.

In chapter 7, I discuss constitutional typologies in Weimar racial science *(Rassenkunde)* and medicine. Even before World War I, life reformers from the Bildungsbürgertum had expressed their disgust with the materialism of the wealthy and the vulgarity of the masses. After the war, the works of racial scientists such as Hans F. K. Günther—which enjoyed considerable popularity among highly educated Germans—appeared to validate such concerns by racializing social conflicts within German society. I show how theories of Nordic racism reflected contemporary worries about the value of Bildung in a tight academic job market. The racism of people such as Günther appealed to the elitism of university students and graduates who had difficulties finding a place in German society that was commensurate with their expectations. As the second part of the chapter shows, even certain Weimar physicians who rejected contemporary racial theories nevertheless developed constitutional typologies based on similar holistic assumptions. Contemporary constitutional physicians elevated intuitive seeing (in the sense of Goethean *Anschauung*) to a privileged epistemological principle. This intuitive seeing was thought to be a necessary complement to the exact measurement approach in the construction of constitutional types, if not the single most important basis for such constructions.

Chapter 8 focuses on the leisure culture of the Weimar era, in particular, physical culture and nudism *(Freikörperkultur)*. The economic and social status of many Germans had suffered considerably in the course of war, revolution, and inflation, and for some people physical culture provided a way to express social distinction in the absence of this status. For propagators of physical culture and nudism, the cultivation of one's body was a sign of sincerity and authenticity—an expression of character that did not rely on deceptive appearances and clothing. With Freikörperkultur, nudity became the basis of a utopian vision, an egalitarian "people's community" *(Volksgemeinschaft)*. Many nudists claimed that political divisions and social distinctions based on economic wealth and formal educational achievements were unimportant among people who were committed to the same leisure activities.

A book dealing with body aesthetics and popular hygienic culture before 1933 raises, of course, questions about continuities with the Nazi era. Some readers might think that I am avoiding the most interesting issues by not pursuing the story into the Nazi period. But I think that it is necessary to understand periods before Nazism on their own terms in order to better understand what followed.[15]

During the entire period discussed in this book, Germans invested the human body with multiple, and at times contradictory, meanings based on their social experiences. During the Kaiserreich and during the Weimar Republic, hygienic practices and aesthetic ideals for the body were important in the formation of class, gender, and racial identities. The meanings of physical beauty were always publicly contested and rarely stable. After 1933, this would change. To be sure, leading Nazis shared the aesthetic ideals of earlier propagators of popular hygiene, but these ideals took on a much more sinister significance under the conditions of the terrorist regime that the Nazis established. During the Nazi era physical beauty represented a racial Volksgemeinschaft from which the disabled as well as religious, ethnic, and sexual minorities such as Jews, gypsies, and homosexuals were purged. The Volksgemeinschaft that was forged by the Nazis, first by means of legal, social, and cultural stigmatization of minorities and finally by mass murder, was therefore quite different from the utopian communitarian visions of many life reformers before 1933.

CHAPTER I

LIFE REFORM AS BÜRGERLICHE KULTUR

Herr Schmidt had long suffered from pain in the stomach and intestines as a result of his nervousness. Because his career as a schoolteacher was threatened by his illness, he went to a regular physician with a good reputation and was advised to eat only light, nonirritating foods. Although his pains decreased for a while, they returned and worsened so much that he turned to a specialist in stomach and intestinal ailments. The therapeutic prescriptions, consisting of medicine and diet, failed as well. When Schmidt was completely exhausted and weighed only 51 kilograms (112 pounds), he took a vacation from his job and went to a natural therapy sanatorium *(Naturheilanstalt)* in Chemnitz. After two weeks his symptoms were considerably alleviated: He could sleep again, and his stomachaches and headaches had almost disappeared, results that he attributed to the rest he had given to his irritated nerves. Schmidt felt that he was on his way back to full health with a therapy that combined water, steam baths, electricity, and massage and that stressed rest and exercise. He hoped ultimately to overcome the somatic symptoms of his nervousness, which, in his view, were caused by the emotional stress and the physical and mental overexertion demanded by his job.[1]

Schmidt's experience was characteristic of those of many people living at the turn of the century who experimented with orthodox as well as alternative therapies in their unceasing quest for health. Frequently this quest led people to become involved in one of the hygienic and therapeutic reform associations that mushroomed during that period. The membership of the German League of Natural Living and Therapy Associations *(Deutscher Bund der Vereine für natur-gemäße Lebens- und Heilweise)* grew from about 19,000 in 1889 to about 148,000 in 1914.[2] Along with some smaller groups such as the Vegetarian League and some physical culture organizations, these associations made up the bulk of what became known as the life reform movement. Life reformers called on their contemporaries to change their entire way of life. Modern people, they believed, were on a path of progressive degeneration that could only be reversed if they once again lived in accordance with human nature. Life reformers attributed illness and lack of success in their personal lives to the unhealthy living habits they had acquired as members of a highly industrialized and urbanized society. They claimed that only exercise, proper diets, and natural therapies could guarantee people a healthy, happy, and successful life.

In this chapter I first try to situate the life reform movement in the context of contemporary middle-class (in the sense of *bürgerlich,* or, loosely, "bourgeois") German culture, then discuss the attractiveness of life reform in terms of common bürgerliche value orientations and the experiences of some of its supporters. I argue that the rise of life reform can be understood in part as the expression of a growing reflexivity centered on the healthy body as a precondition for success in a competitive, modern, urbanized society; conversely, life reformers conceptualized their inability to perform in terms of illness or even degeneracy. Therefore, the movement owed its success largely to its promise to deliver adherents from professional and personal failure.

Bürgerliche Kultur and Health-Mindedness

The recent historiography of the German Bürgertum has attempted to describe the German middle classes in terms of common cultural orientations and behavioral norms that distinguished them from other social groups. When referring to these value orientations I will always use the term *bürgerlich* instead of *bourgeois,* since the latter term is loaded with Marxist assumptions concerning economic class that are misleading in this context. Jürgen Kocka has pointed out that the Bürgertum was a social formation comprised of groups that were vastly different in terms of their education, their socioeconomic status, and their relation to the means of production. During the late nineteenth century, those who would have considered themselves part of the Bürgertum included employers, civil servants, higher-level managers of large enterprises, simple clerks *(Hand-lungsgehilfen),* and independent artisans and shopkeepers, who constituted the so-called old middle class *(alter Mittelstand).*[3]

Although the wealthier and better educated of these groups certainly would have denied the lower middle classes' claims to respectability, all of them valued personal achievement and individual performance, Bildung (in the humanistic sense of a harmonious development of all aspects of one's personality), and the belief that people could determine their own futures. According to Kocka, these bürgerliche mentalities and values and their expression in the discursive styles and conventions of the Bürgertum constituted a distinct culture that served to distinguish the Bürgertum from other social groups in German society. In the late eighteenth and early nineteenth centuries, the newly emerging bürgerliche Kultur served as a common identity for groups—educated civil servants, intellectuals, and the early entrepreneurs—that had no clear place in the corporatist structure of German society.[4]

Health-mindedness was a core value for this emerging bürgerliche Kultur. From the late eighteenth century onward, middle-class writers emphasized the importance of health as a precondition for individual performance and personal achievement. Health was perceived as the product of a rational, hygienic lifestyle that stressed self-restraint and moderation in all aspects of life. The hygienic literature of the time contrasted these bürgerliche virtues with the idleness and debauchery of the nobility. It rejected the luxuries and refinements associated with the aristocracy and, like life reform literature a century later, called for a return to the simplicity of nature. This meant following dietetic rules, a regime that stressed sound nutrition, fresh air, sunlight, exercise, work, and rest as well as a balanced emotional life. Although such dietetic prescriptions were a reformulation of those of ancient Galenic medicine, they constituted a normative system for the Bürgertum that it could use to criticize the nobility.[5]

If the emphasis on rationality and healthy habits allowed the Bürgertum to create a positive identity in opposition to the aristocracy, it also, in their view, underscored differences between the responsible and thrifty middle classes and the sexually immoral, irresponsible, and filthy lower classes. As the nineteenth century progressed and the wealthy Bürgertum increasingly appropriated the conspicuous consumption patterns and other status markers of the nobility, members of the Bürgertum increasingly defined themselves in opposition to the working class instead. From the middle of the nineteenth century onward, employers tried to use factory sickness funds to inculcate regular habits and work discipline in the emerging industrial proletariat by denying workers insurance benefits if they did not follow the hygienic rules laid down in factory regulations.[6] Alfons Labisch has argued that health as a norm of the Bürgertum served to enforce social discipline by ensuring that irresponsible proletarians would become responsible industrial workers.[7]

Members of the late nineteenth-century life reform movement shared many of the value orientations and cultural premises that have been described by historians of Germany as bürgerlich—especially the emphasis on a rational lifestyle that stressed self-discipline and moderation and the value accorded to personal achievement and Bildung. Further, the membership of life reform associations was drawn predominantly from the middle classes. The movement reflected the diversity and fragmentation of these middling sectors of German society.[8] Natural therapy voluntary associations included white-collar workers, shopkeepers, small entrepreneurs, artisans, technicians, and skilled workers, as well as professionals, civil servants, and other members of the educated middle classes *(Bildungsbürgertum)*.[9]

Membership data for the Berlin local of the German Association for Rational Body Discipline *(Deutscher Verein für vernünftige Leibeszucht)* show that the vast majority of the members were from the new middle or lower middle classes: Merchants, clerks, low-level administrators, and members of modern technical professions (such as engineering) accounted for about 60 percent. About a quarter of the members, most prominent among them academic professionals and university students, had some form of higher education and might be considered Bildungsbürger.[10] Members of the new middle classes were often highly skilled, but they did not have the same neohumanistic education and schooling on which the Bildungsbürgertum's status claims rested. (As we will see in chapter 2, tensions between these groups were expressed in arguments about the role of physical culture in the cultivation of the human personality.) In marked contrast to the natural therapy movement, the physical culture associations counted no artisans and far fewer skilled workers among their members. This difference might be explained by the fact that physical culture was a rather time-consuming activity, and as such may not have appealed to artisans and skilled workers, who had physically demanding jobs and little leisure time; physical exercise was particularly attractive to people who sought compensation for sedentary work. It is also important to keep in mind that the membership structure of other physical culture associations might have been rather different—the situation in Berlin, for instance, is probably not representative of similar associations in provincial cities such as Koblenz.

In examining the social composition of the life reform movement, historians have relied mainly on the membership data published in journals, address books, and other publications of the voluntary associations.[11] This is not surprising, because these sources contain the only hard data on the social composition of the movement that we have. Yet, it is problematic to simply equate the movement with the membership of the life reform associations, which were dominated by middle-class males. For one thing, such an approach does not account for women who participated with their husbands but did not formally join an association.[12] The large number of health advice books specifically written for women is a clear indication that women were as preoccupied with their personal fitness, health, and beauty as were men, although they made up only 10 to 25 percent of the formal membership of the life reform associations for which there are data on gender composition.[13]

The numbers of people who were concerned with health reform thus exceeded the official membership of life reform associations. It is true, there were almost no representatives of the wealthy upper classes among either the leadership or the membership of such associations.[14] But that does not mean that the wealthy were not affected by the new health-consciousness. Although the upper classes rarely participated in middle-class life reform associations, they frequented expensive sanatoriums and spas whose services were difficult to afford for the middling sectors of the Bürgertum that provided the organizational backbone of the life reform movement.[15]

Although the evidence is too sketchy to permit a clear assessment of the ways in which most life reform associations' memberships changed after the turn of the century, their social basis seems to have broadened to include substantial numbers of skilled workers. The membership of the homeopathic association in Heidenheim/Brenz in Württemberg, which has been examined by the historian Eberhard Wolff, became increasingly heterogeneous in the early twentieth century. In the 1880s and 1890s the members and officials of the association were mainly recruited from the middle and lower middle classes, but after the turn of the century the share of workers—especially skilled workers *(Facharbeiter)*—increased substantially.[16] Between 1908 and 1912 the percentage of workers who were members of natural therapy associations grew from about 24 to 28 percent. The increase might be taken as a sign of what has been called the *Verbürgerlichung*—the acceptance of bürgerliche values and norms—by at least some sectors of the working class. By adopting a self-consciously healthy and rational lifestyle, workers were indeed accepting the values of the Bürgertum. If we are to better understand the relation between such bürgerliche value orientations and the wide social appeal of health reform, however, the quantitative evidence concerning the social composition of the life reform movement has to be supplemented with qualitative evidence drawn from contemporary health advice books and medical autobiographies.

Subjective Experiences of Personal Illness

In order to unearth the life reformers' subjective experiences of illness, one has to look at two different kinds of sources. In the first group are those in which regular physicians or life reformers tried to address a popular audience in public lectures, commercial health advice books, or articles in life reform periodicals. If they were to be persuasive, physicians and life reformers had to be sensitive to the potential concerns of their audiences. Although lectures and health advice books are normative sources, it is still possible to learn at least a few things about the motivations of those who turned to this movement. Life reformers who wrote popular health advice books often knew how to address prospective converts because they had similar hopes and anxieties before they became converts themselves.

An even more important source for this kind of information, however, is the medical autobiography. Many such autobiographies were written by life reformers in order to convince people of the effectiveness of an improved lifestyle. Most are merely confessionals whose authors recount their conversion to a natural lifestyle and their miraculous salvation from a supposedly life-threatening illness. A few individuals, however, have left examples that go beyond the conversion and salvation narrative to suggest complex motives and expectations. A careful interpretation reveals which subjective somatic and psychological experiences the authors regarded as pathological.

The most important common goal of participants in the life reform movement was personal health. Some adherents of natural therapies, vegetarians, and physical culturists tried to come to terms with debilitating illnesses such as tuberculosis. Life reformers also addressed contemporary fears concerning the devastating effects of venereal disease on men, women, and their families, and (as I show in greater detail in chapter 3) the assignment of responsibility for the spread of venereal disease became an issue in contemporary gender politics.[17]

Many life reformers had to come to terms with subjective experiences of personal inadequacies. Life reform discourse medicalized contemporary worries about professional success, intimate relationships, and physical beauty. Both sexes, for example, were concerned about their physical attractiveness to the opposite sex, but this issue was especially pressing for middle-class women, who were often forced to find a provider on the marriage market.[18] One of the big selling points of cures in contemporary sanatoriums was the promise of weight loss by means of dieting *(Entfettungskuren)* or weight gain by means of better nutrition *(Mastkuren)*. The ideal was a leaner, more muscular body composed not of fat but of "firm healthy flesh." The catalogue for Ziegelroth's natural therapy sanatorium in Zehlendorf promised that therapies tailored to individual needs would help people succeed in obtaining a more ideal physique: "It happens quite frequently that patients *[Kurgäste]* arriving at the same time either should lose weight or gain it; and it is the subject of frequent joking and general satisfaction how beautifully the fat vanishes in the case of the obese and how the emaciated gain weight."[19] Since life reformers as well as orthodox physicians claimed that beauty was an expression of perfect health, people had to face the additional pressures of living up to the lofty aesthetic ideals of an increasingly body-conscious society. Indeed, one of the ironies of the health-consciousness of the period was that it perpetuated the feelings of personal inadequacy that gave rise to it.

Rational, bürgerliche attitudes and value orientations implied a certain goal-directedness and desire to manage one's future. Contemporary beliefs in the possibility of rationally controlling one's own life not only fueled the market for the innumerable health, sex, and marriage advice books that gave their readers tips on the management of their personal and intimate relationships. Such attitudes also found their expression in career expectations. Because many life reformers could not change their personal circumstances—the unhappy intimate relationships, the failed social aspirations, the frustrated career expectations—they focused on their bodies, the part of their existence that they could still control and discipline. Through the control of their bodies, they hoped to regain the fitness that would enable them to succeed again in the perceived struggle for survival. The notion of a career entailed professional aspirations and social expectations for each stage of the middle-class male's life cycle; as their lives progressed, middle-class men desired and were expected to move up the occupational ladder.[20] Life reform held considerable appeal for members of the lower middle classes who dwelled at the margins of middle-class existence but nevertheless believed in the bürgerliche achievement and performance ethos—office workers, for example, and lower-level civil servants such as teachers who stood under the tight control of their superiors. At the turn of the century, clerks in dead-end jobs, for whom an independent economic existence had become increasingly illusory, and artisans, most of whom had only a precarious existence, hoped to recapture their fitness *(Leistungsfähigkeit)* and assert mastery over their own fate with a healthful lifestyle.[21]

Such people often attributed their professional and personal failures to nervousness, or "neurasthenia." A disorder of weak nerves or nervous irritability, neurasthenia exemplifies the negotiated process of medicalization that emerged from the interaction between life reformers and regular physicians and their common clientele.[22] The list of potential psychosomatic symptoms for neurasthenia was endless, as the case that began this chapter demonstrated. According to Wilhelm Erb, a psychiatrist at the University of Heidelberg, neurasthenics were the largest group of people who looked voluntarily for the help of psychiatrists. He regarded neurasthenia as a disorder caused by a predisposition in the human nervous system; symptoms included an irritability of the nervous system, he thought, which made it react to smaller-than-normal stimuli. This irritability led to weakness, tiredness, and, as Erb put it, the "inability to carry out a given mental and physical performance repeatedly and with endurance." Mental overexertion, overwork, and overburdening in one's occupation, Erb claimed, were the most frequent causes of neurasthenia, because the "struggle for survival" and the advancement of one's social position demanded the mobilization of all mental powers. This disorder, therefore, was seen to be caused by the failure to live up to the demands of one's profession or career.[23]

Patients of sanatoriums run by natural therapists often suffered from nervous disorders. In a report by the royal provincial administration *(Kreishauptmannschaft Dresden)* of the state of Saxony on the hygienic conditions in the natural therapist Friedrich Eduard Bilz's (1842–1922) Ober-Lößnitz sanatorium, the investigators maintained that most of the patients were suffering from nervous diseases and disorders. Only about 15 to 20 percent suffered from more dangerous, infectious diseases such as syphilis and tuberculosis.[24]

The complaint of neurasthenia was thus one of the staples of life reform literature. The natural therapist and physician Erwin Silber claimed that career pressures affected all classes: The merchant or clerk *(Kaufmann)* as well as the lawyer, the officer, the teacher, the scientist, the writer, the journalist, the civil servant, and the worker, tried to climb up the social ladder and struggled to stay on top (which Silber thought was even more difficult). People had to pay a high price—the ruin of their nerves—for the pursuit of happiness and the desire to get rich quickly.[25] The natural therapists Wilhelm Siegert and Franz Schönenberger, who edited the journal *Der Naturarzt (Nature's Physician)* from 1907 onwards, offered a diagnosis similar to the ones given by Erb and Silber. *Der Naturarzt* was the official organ of the League of Natural Living and Therapy Associations. Schönenberger was a university-trained physician; Siegert was a practitioner without formal medical training. In their view, it was not necessarily great personal misfortunes that devastated people's mental health but rather the countless pinpricks *(Nadelstiche)* in life, such as unsatisfying work, lack of success, disappointed hopes, thwarted ambition, and a lack of marital happiness. Men were especially subject to the pressures of examinations and job stress, mental overexertion, and lack of sleep. " 'The sclerosis of hope' *[das Veröden der Hoffnung]* as Bismarck once strikingly called it," wrote Siegert and Schönenberger, and "the feeling that one 'can never achieve anything'" heavily affected people without property and personal connections. Therefore, as they noted, clerks, low-ranking civil servants, and teachers stuck in dead-end jobs without the prospect of professional advancement were particularly affected by nervous disorders.

According to Schönenberger and Siegert, people were constitutionally predisposed to neurasthenia by an inherited weakness of the nervous system, but the abuse of alcohol and sexual indulgence exacerbated the condition. In their view, a variety of prescriptions might prevent the defects of neurasthenia from reaching the next generation: exercise, rest, air baths, economic security, a shorter workday, better wages, and regular vacations. In other words, both social improvements and the strengthening of the nervous system with a dietetic regimen might help people resist external social pressures and eliminate the predisposition altogether.[26]

Men suffered from a combination of professional and sexual anxieties that reinforced each other, as the historian Joachim Radkau has observed of nervous weakness in his examination of patient files in mental hospitals.[27] Health and sex advice manuals likewise attributed male impotence, supposedly widespread at the time, to a combination of mental overwork and sexual performance anxieties. According to the naturopathic physician August Kühner, "persistent mental occupation" was an important reason for male impotence, which explained why businessmen and people pursuing abstract sciences such as mathematics were particularly afflicted. Nervous shocks due to significant financial losses, Kühner claimed, could have the same debilitating effects on the sexual powers of men.[28]

To focus on the subjective experience of personal illness is not to deny the foundational reality of diseases. But even the experience of a life-threatening, painful, and dangerous disease (such as cancer or tuberculosis) is mediated by the subjectivity of the affected individual and by the way an individual categorizes and contextualizes his or her sickness. Whether a person sees in illness an opportunity for agency or whether she sees her fate as inevitable, for instance, will make a difference in her subjective experience of the illness. It can be argued that one of the reasons why the life reform movement was so attractive was that it allowed for agency—no matter whether the experienced states of illness were life-threatening diseases or simply feelings of personal inadequacy. People could recapture a sense of autonomy by accepting the life reform premise that they would become healthy sooner or later if they followed nature's path and adopted an improved lifestyle.

Most supporters of the movement had had contact with orthodox physicians at some point in their lives. Only after these practitioners did not meet their expectations did they turn to alternative lifestyles or therapies. The stories of those who converted to alternative medicine depict a "confessor" who undergoes several unsuccessful therapeutic attempts by highly regarded orthodox medical specialists. Then he or she is alerted to a publication by a life reformer, which in turn moves him or her to go to an alternative practitioner or to join a vegetarian or natural therapy voluntary association. The new therapy or the changed lifestyle then miraculously restores the health of the desperate patient.

In Friedrich Bilz's health advice book, one Friedrich von Hausegger reported, for example, that he became a vegetarian after he had read such vegetarian authors as Jean-Antoine Gleizé, Eduard Baltzer, and Sylvester Graham and after he had seen that a vegetarian life had brought about miraculous cures for other people. He had suffered from ailments such as lung disease and rheumatism that had consumed all his strength. After his adoption of a vegetarian lifestyle, all his symptoms—symptoms of weakness that resulted from an unhealthy lifestyle—ceased, and he was freed from his sleeplessness, headaches, dizziness, constipation, and inflammation of the throat. Bilz published this testimonial in his health advice book in order to demonstrate to his readers that a reformed lifestyle could cure even the most chronic and hopeless cases.[29]

The propagandistic character of such confessions is obvious. In reality, the decision to choose a certain kind of natural therapy or a vegetarian lifestyle usually did not lead to a permanent commitment to life reform; committed members of vegetarian organizations, for example, complained about those who gave up their new lifestyle after a short time when their health did not improve as expected. The turnover rate among the members of vegetarian voluntary associations must have been very high, since the size of local chapters fluctuated considerably.[30]

Apparently, many people experimented with a reformed lifestyle for a short time and abandoned it when they were dissatisfied, either because life reform was too ascetic for them or because they could not improve their health. In the health market of the Kaiserreich, people could choose among orthodox medicine, homeopathy, natural therapies, and vegetarianism. They could endlessly experiment with lifestyle changes until they had found the "truly natural" lifestyle. For some committed vegetarians with chronic diseases, the quest never ended, and they anxiously observed their bodies in order to detect the flaws in their diets that prevented them from experiencing that joy of ultimate health which they were convinced only a vegetarian lifestyle could give them.[31] For other people, however, life reform was only a way-station, and they returned to orthodox therapies when they were disappointed by its results. Many people might also have employed orthodox and natural therapies at the same time, or they might have employed one or the other type depending on the kind of disorders they had.

What do autobiographical confessions tell us about subjective experiences of life reformers? Louis Kuhne's health advice book, *The New Healing Science*, provides some answers.[32] This work is interesting because of the ways in which Kuhne employed his medical autobiography in order to connect with his readers. One of the most successful health guides of the period, Kuhne's advice book was published in several dozen editions in the 1890s. It was an outrageous example of medical quackery from the point of view of the regular medical profession.[33] Louis Kuhne was a carpenter's journeyman who, according to his own claims, had managed to become a factory owner in Leipzig. Kuhne had suffered from chronic ill health all his life. He had unsuccessfully sought the help of orthodox physicians before he experimented with natural therapies and discovered the natural laws on which, he claimed, his "healing science" was based. In 1883 Kuhne opened a clinic for natural therapies in Leipzig in order to spread the word of his discovery (see figures 1 and 2). He turned into a full-blown health entrepreneur who marketed his system in his books and promoted health care supplies such as bathing utensils and bandages. Kuhne's success certainly had something to do with his therapeutic system. He claimed to have simplified natural therapy by reducing the (for the layperson) bewildering array of steam baths, showers, and wet packs that were prescribed by experts in natural therapy.[34] He advised readers to adopt a vegetarian diet and take baths that were designed to purge the body of autotoxins (see chapter 5). All one needed to do was purchase a bathtub or steam bath device (see figures 3 and 4) from Kuhne's company and one could attempt self-therapy at home, guided by Kuhne's book.

Kuhne was well attuned to the worries of his audience. He tried to establish a rapport with his readers by telling them the story of his own illness. At the age

FIGURE 1. Louis Kuhne. Kuhne, *Heilwissenschaft*. Private collection.

FIGURE 2. Kuhne's International Establishment for the Healing Art Without Drugs and Surgery in Leipzig. Kuhne, *Heilwissenschaft*. Private collection.

of twenty his body failed him and he suffered from headaches and pain in the lungs. He turned to orthodox therapy but met with no success. Then he heard of a local meeting of supporters of natural therapies. He attended the meeting and his suffering was greatly reduced by following the therapeutic prescriptions given to him by one of the attending experts. He was relieved at first, but his situation worsened again. He suffered from cancer of the stomach, his lungs were partially destroyed, and he was such a nervous wreck that he could neither sleep nor work. Luckily, he claimed, by observing nature he found the scientific laws on which he could base his new healing science.[35]

By following the therapeutic regimen advocated in his guide, people would be able to rid themselves of all existing diseases. He promised, however, much more than deliverance from life-threatening diseases such as tuberculosis: The full health that people could achieve by following his regimen would in turn deliver them from *all* the obstacles they might experience in their lives. A healthy person, he claimed, always feels fine; he or she does not know anything about

FIGURE 3. Kuhne ad for bathing tubs.
Water baths and steam baths were supposed to purge the body of autotoxins.
Kuhne, *Heilwissenschaft.* Private collection.

pain or uneasiness of any kind. Therefore, a healthy man does not need to worry
about his family because he always has the strength to care for his dependents.[36]

After healing himself with his own modified version of natural therapy,
however, Kuhne found himself in a dilemma. Should he continue to operate his
profitable factory, as he had done for twenty-four years, or should he follow his
conscience and spread the gospel of his new discovery, even if that meant making material sacrifices and suffering abuse by members of the orthodox medical
profession?[37] He chose the latter, but judging from his subsequent success as a
health entrepreneur and author, the sacrifice cannot have been very great. Indeed, one has to wonder whether the story of his illness and salvation is nothing
more than a story of personal economic failure and success expressed in hygienic
terms. Kuhne, who started out as a mere carpenter's journeyman, had discovered
the ease with which, he claimed, any healthy man could provide for himself and
his family.

Kuhne addressed people who, like himself, had failed to obtain relief from
their symptoms from other medical practitioners. He knew about his potential

clients' feelings of uneasiness or personal inadequacy, and he knew that these diffuse feelings were often not taken seriously by other medical practitioners, who could offer little to alleviate them. He maintained that many of his patients who felt seriously ill had gone to other practitioners before they consulted him, only to be told that they were healthy and that their illness was just a product of their imagination.[38] Here Kuhne tapped into an important element of the modern relation between patients and physicians. Because of modern diagnostic tools and techniques such as the stethoscope, laboratory tests, and later x-rays, scientifically trained physicians had access to a diagnostic symptomology that remained hidden from their patients. Since the results of medical examinations could be interpreted independent of patient narratives about illness, physicians believed that they could increasingly disregard the subjective perceptions and experiences of their patients.[39] Kuhne, as we have seen, took such subjective feelings of illness seriously. He argued that they were signs of chronic illness caused by harmful substances that had accumulated in the body and that could result in serious and deadly diseases if left unchecked. The signs, which many of his contemporaries might have noticed in themselves at one time or another, in-

cluded lack of appetite and the inability to perform physical and mental work efficiently. He warned his readers that these and "similar symptoms" (which the reader could fill in him- or herself) were signs of chronic disease that would sooner or later develop into acute disease.[40]

In order to demonstrate the benefits of a healthy regimen, life reformers often emphasized the exceptional achievements of some of their peers. Vegetarians stressed that their diet would increase a person's physcial fitness, and in order to prove it they published the results of long-distance walking competitions won by vegetarians.[41] The clerk Karl Mann, a vegetarian, won several such competitions, even improving the German record for the eleven-mile competition. According to his own account he had been a weak child with a narrow chest because he had devoted most of his time to reading. Because of a crooked spine and short-sightedness he was declared unfit for military service, but he managed to overcome his weakness by means of vegetarianism and exercise. Although his office job demanded that he sit at a desk for nine hours at a time, he was successful in developing a muscular body, and he managed to increase his physical and mental fitness *(Leistungsfähigkeit)* to an extent that had been unimaginable when he was a high school student. Karl Mann was a model vegetarian who, for many life reformers, embodied the potential of average individuals to achieve astonishing physical and mental performance levels. Not surprisingly, he was asked to testify for life reform journals and to describe his personal health regimen. A meatless and plain diet, abstinence from alcohol and tobacco, and daily exercise, Mann promised, would educate body, soul, and mind and allow average persons to achieve "physical strength and beauty" *(Körperkraft und Formenschönheit).*[42]

Only a few, very active life reformers engaged in public exhibitions of their ailments and personal failures. Because these individuals' lives and thinking were organized entirely around the poles of "health" and "illness," they perhaps considered the story of their own suffering to be a matter of interest to the public and, thus, repressed feelings of shame that prevented others from sharing such stories with a wider audience. The public representation of one's suffering was, however, also a means for the authors to reassure themselves that their suffering was now firmly in the past and that they had found the high road to health, happiness, and beauty, as they revealed to their readers. Seen in this light, these stories dramatized failure in order to demonstrate the ultimate success of their authors and the success that converts to life reform could expect.

The medical autobiography of Richard Ungewitter, the chief propagator of nude culture during the German Empire, reveals such subjective experiences of personal failure.[43] He related that he was born in 1868 to a family that was in the Bürgertum. He attended middle school until he was fourteen. After he started an apprenticeship with a gardener, he almost collapsed as the ten-to-fifteen-hour workday strained his constitution. He attributed his weakness to being deprived of natural nutrition during his infancy (he was not breastfed) and to a lack of "toughening up" *(Abhärtung)* during his childhood because his parents were overanxious in trying to protect him from the elements. As a child, he suffered from whooping cough for several weeks each winter. He also claimed that he had suffered from diphtheria, smallpox, scarlet fever, and measles, all of which he attributed to the smallpox vaccination prescribed by German law in 1874. His throat diseases had always been treated with bitter-tasting medicine prescribed by orthodox physicians.

During his apprenticeship, he claimed, he suffered from an ulcer of the cornea of his right eye that was treated by the ophthalmologist Alfred Graefe at the University of Halle—a medical "authority," as Ungewitter ironically called him. The ulcer disappeared when he applied a harsh ointment Graefe had prescribed, but it reappeared the following year. Since Graefe's cure had been too painful, he did not consult him again, and the ulcer disappeared on its own without orthodox medical treatment. Ungewitter had a similar experience with an injury on his chin that developed into a skin rash. Again orthodox medicine failed. This time he listened to the advice of an acquaintance and tried to cauterize it with the help of tobacco juice. The rash disappeared, but it reappeared one year later, not on his chin but on his left hand. After reading Kuhne's *New Healing Science,* it dawned on him that his old diseases had not been cured but, rather, had only been suppressed and could reoccur as acute diseases at any time. Therefore, he immediately quit smoking and drinking and started a vegetarian diet that made the skin rash disappear within two weeks. Ungewitter then made what he saw as his biggest mistake: resuming his old lifestyle.

Although Ungewitter did not fall ill for several years, his wife eventually became sick, and the successful application of Kuhne's cure to her illness convinced him to subscribe to *Naturarzt* and to join the natural therapy association in Stuttgart. Finally realizing the health hazards of meat consumption, he quit eating meat entirely and refined his vegetarian diet continuously until he had renounced eggs, milk, and cooked meals as well. As a *Rohköstler,* a person who eats only raw food, he thought he had found the basis for a truly natural lifestyle. Besides that, he performed daily gymnastic exercises and worked nude at his desk, since he believed that clothing prevented the natural expulsion of autotoxins from one's body. This led to a state of absolute health, which he described euphorically:

> While I had always thought that I was healthy, my physical and mental well-being grew now in relation to the simplification of my nutrition and I have to

confess, that what I had considered as health earlier was definitely not normal. I earlier considered myself healthy, because I did not know a better state of health and had not experienced it yet. Since I have experienced neither coughing and sneezing, nor head and stomach aches, nor other indispositions for three to four years, "true" health must really be present now. The state of the feeling of absolute health, which knows neither the fear of catching a cold nor fear of becoming infected, can be called the pinnacle of physical well-being. A certain health joyfulness *[Gesundheitsfreudigkeit]* has developed, which leads to an absolute confidence in oneself, so that one can predict with absolute security that one will never be sick again. The latter can, however, only be understood by those people who have the same feeling and keep everything that might be harmful from their body.[44]

However, Ungewitter did not quite find the state of absolute health free of all indispositions, as he claimed. A bit later in his medical autobiography, he reported the return of some of his ailments after he had become a vegetarian. His throat diseases reappeared, as did the ulcer of his eye and his skin rash.[45] He interpreted these manifestations as the ultimate healing process of the body that had been suppressed by orthodox medical treatment. According to Ungewitter, diseases had to be expressed again in their acute state before they could heal. This interpretation reassured him that he finally had reached the state of true health. "Indispositions" that reappeared were, in his view at the time, only the late consequences of his unnatural lifestyle or of poisoning by drugs at an earlier stage of his life. Such occurrences could not really cloud his newfound joyful healthiness.

Ungewitter reported that his ability to perform had increased tremendously. He could now hike for ten to fourteen hours and daily perform the most strenuous mental work, achieving "impressive enduring physical and mental performances of the highest level." In his view, his astonishing development from a "weak and sickly child raised by the milk bottle to a healthy muscular man" clearly demonstrated that a body can develop normally despite a weak constitution, provided that it is supplied with the right nutrition. As proof he published photos of himself in the nude (see figure 5).

Like Ungewitter, Klara Ebert saw health reform as the only means to save her degenerate body. Ebert was a vegetarian who frequently contributed to the *Vegetarische Warte,* the official journal of the German Vegetarian League *(Deutscher Vegetarierbund).* She also wrote a medical autobiography, in which she described her long period of suffering as a young woman—headaches, typhus, and tuberculosis had weakened her constitution to the point of almost complete physical breakdown. Her conversion to a vegetarian lifestyle brought a

FIGURE 5. Richard Ungewitter demonstrating healthy development of the chest by rational body discipline after years of weakness. Richard Ungewitter, "Was energisch durchgeführte vernünftige Leibeszucht zu leisten vermag," *Kraft und Schönheit* 5 (1905): 137. Staatsbibliothek zu Berlin. Preußischer Kulturbesitz.

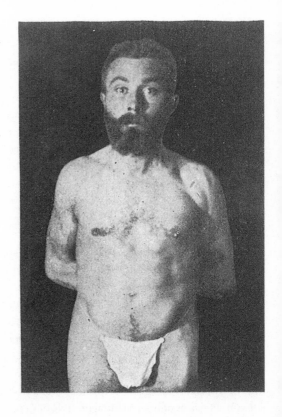

complete turnabout, making her feel saved or born again and endowing her with an incredible new strength. She cautioned her readers, however, that these successes had not come easily for her. Addressing one of the main problems of the vegetarian movement, its constantly fluctuating membership, she expressed regret that most people who became vegetarians did so for health reasons and, although their health improved at first, they gave up their new lifestyle when they became sick again. In order to encourage people who had such an experience to continue with their reformed lifestyle, she related her own experience in 1907 in an article titled "Struggle and Victory."

Before becoming a vegetarian fifteen years earlier, Ebert had been a strong believer in the medical benefits of meat consumption. Without success, she treated recurrent headaches (now attributed to her unhealthy diet) with sedative and fever-suppressing medicines (Bromide and Anti-Pyrin). When she took up her vegetarian diet, her headaches disappeared completely, but her struggle for health was far from over. One and a half years later, she experienced several grave crises, which she attributed to her ancestors, who had degenerated as a result of their unhealthy lifestyle and who passed on their degeneracy to her. First she suffered from a bad case of typhus for about six weeks; this was followed by other serious illnesses such as tuberculosis and a "lung catarrh." These illnesses initiated a period of weakness that lasted several years and brought her close to a complete breakdown several times. Although she faltered twice and started eating meat again, Ebert was proud that she never blamed her vegetarian lifestyle for these crises, as other people would have done. Instead, she explained her problems as a result of her own degeneracy and the difficulties she had in readapting to the natural lifestyle. But the resumption of her meat-eating habits was immediately punished with the return of her headaches, so she quickly returned to vegetarianism and her health was fully restored. Ebert felt that her life had begun anew. She felt physically strong as never before in her life, and her mental performance had also reached new heights.[46]

Middle- and lower-middle-class women played an important role in the fulfillment of the social aspirations of their families. Some middle-class women had to work so that their families could afford the lifestyle of a respectable family of the Bürgertum. For Ebert, health reform was also a means to keep fit in order to balance the multiple pressures of working, housekeeping, and caring for her child with her desire to lead a fulfilling and intellectually demanding life. This was all the more difficult for her because she could not afford the help of a domestic servant.[47] Her fate was not unusual for a woman of the lower middle class. Although there were "higher daughters" who sought professional fulfillment through employment, there were also middle-class women who had to work in order to supplement their family's income.[48] In order to keep their status, women often had to work secretly in addition to carrying out the traditional duties of housewife and mother; this double burden already concerned the contemporary feminist movement.[49] Failure to fulfill her supporting role in the family to her own or her husband's satisfaction might well have been the symptoms of the "general weakness of life" that left Ebert unable to perform physical and mental work for so long.[50]

Women embarking on professional careers were sometimes haunted by performance anxieties. The vegetarian physician Anna Fischer-Dückelmann maintained that the migraine attacks that she had experienced during her youth had been caused by meat consumption. For the most part, these attacks ceased when she quit eating meat, but she still considered herself a neurasthenic because she could not always cope with mental and emotional overexertion. She conceded that she ate some meat before her exams as a medical student, because the stimulation helped her perform better under stress. She did not blame vegetarianism for her nervousness, however, but claimed, like Ebert, that it was her difficulty readjusting to a natural lifestyle that was still responsible for recurring migraine attacks and the problems she had with her nerves.[51] Like Ungewitter and Ebert, Fischer-Dückelmann believed that she had overcome her personal inadequacies despite some setbacks.

How can one interpret these medical autobiographies? First of all, these accounts do not constitute objective clinical descriptions of somatic experiences. The authors had been life reformers for a very long time. Therefore, the presentation of their suffering was very selective. From a long personal history of somatic experiences they chose only those that fit into the patterns of interpretation of life reform ideology. This is especially evident in the case of Ungewitter's skin rash, which appeared on a different part of the body after it had been merely "suppressed" and not "cured." The experiences Ungewitter and Ebert had before turning to life reform are depicted as fraught with various illnesses and continuous suffering. In Ungewitter's case, the suffering was caused by his physical weakness, in Ebert's, similar weaknesses as well as serious illnesses, provided that her self-diagnosis can be trusted. In their accounts, this period of continuous suffering was followed by a time of health during which the authors still sometimes experienced serious health crises that were no longer perceived as a manifestation of their earlier sufferings. These crises were interpreted instead as negligible relics of a prior degenerate somatic state (as in Ungewitter's case) or as difficulties in readjusting to a natural lifestyle that would guarantee absolute health (as in Ebert's).

In reality the authors' lives were not characterized by the dichotomy between a time of continuous suffering and a time of complete health. In all likelihood, before and after their conversion to life reform, periods of health alternated with periods of illness. After they assumed their new lifestyle, however, the authors interpreted their illnesses differently. Health problems were now perceived not as the manifestation of a long-enduring infirmity but as difficulties of transition. This was a process of structuring experiences by means of narratives that enabled staunch supporters of life reform to deal with personal experiences of somatic and mental states that were inconsistent with the promise that a "natural" lifestyle would inevitably lead to perfect health.

The subjective experience of people who turned to life reform could nevertheless be positive, regardless of whether the new lifestyle improved their condition from an "objective" point of view. The new framework of interpreting one's somatic or psychological problems could reassure people by allowing them to see these problems as relatively insignificant distractions on the road to absolute health and happiness on which they had embarked when they had turned to life reform. The image of a degenerate modern mankind often conjured up by life reformers makes sense in this context as well. It was probably easier to perceive one's personal suffering not as an individual destiny but rather as the fate of mankind. If an individual perceived him- or herself not as different from others (as handicapped in a world of healthy people) but as someone who shared the destiny of the rest of civilization, he or she could probably cope better with his or her infirmities.

Richard Ungewitter's personal history is instructive in other ways as well. He started out as a gardener's apprentice and ended up in a dead-end job as a clerk in the office of a gardening company. Then he found his mission as a successful freelance life reform writer.[52] Although he claimed to be from a respectable middle-class family, he was most likely from the lower middle class because an apprenticeship as a gardener was hardly an acceptable career choice for a son of the established Bürgertum during the Kaiserreich. By describing his background as bürgerlich, he reflected his aspirations and claims to social respectability. The same is true for Kuhne's success story. In a sense theirs were stories of fulfilling bourgeois aspirations. Although members of the lower middle class claimed middle-class status by appropriating the cultural norms and values of the Bürgertum, such as nationalism, few actually had the economic means to move up the social ladder.[53] Because their overall economic situation was not much better than that of the better-off sectors of the working class, the specter of social decline loomed large. The claim to social standing had to rest, therefore, on the appropriation and manipulation of symbolic forms. The appropriation of a rational lifestyle stressing moderation and self-control made it possible to distance oneself from the working masses, who were perceived as irrational and immoderate.[54]

In other words, a reformed lifestyle could serve as a social marker for lower-middle-class people who wanted to set themselves apart from the working class. Life reform, however, could also be an attractive ideology for members of the Bildungsbürgertum who felt that their social status was threatened in the course of the second industrialization, characterized by the rise of new groups of wealthy bourgeois. The asceticism of life reform ideology, with its stress on the virtues of moderation and self-control, was reassuring to people who lacked the economic means to appropriate the expensive lifestyle and status markers of the new economic elite.[55]

The value orientations and aspirations associated with the Bürgertum tended to transcend the boundaries of economic class. One has to keep in mind that the membership of life reform organizations not only included people from the educated and lower middle classes but also *Facharbeiter*—members of the most prosperous sectors of the German working class. The economic circumstances of these workers made it possible for them to develop a long-term perspective for their lives instead of simply living from day to day. Skilled workers could develop social aspirations or expectations for certain stages in their lives and experience frustration if their hopes for a future that could be rationally managed went unfulfilled.[56]

The bricklayer Erdmann Lischke, for example, suffered from mental disturbances, cramps, and temporary paralysis. He attributed this to an illness from which he had not quite recovered when he resumed his work. He collapsed on the job and ended up with a total mental disturbance that was diagnosed in a university clinic as paralysis. Lischke was treated for seven months without success. Then he was brought by his relatives to a natural healer whose treatment led to a remarkable recovery within four months, enabling him to resume his work as a bricklayer in full health.[57]

Problems with his capacity for work had also troubled the iron lathe worker Langen. Langen, a vegetarian, complained that it was difficult to win working-class people over to a vegetarian lifestyle because they wrongly thought that meat consumption was indispensable for the development of physical power. In the fashion of a Bürger who complained about the uncultivated masses, he claimed that most workers' lack of education made them vulnerable to everything that so-called scientific authorities said about meat consumption. He himself experimented with a vegetarian lifestyle after a spine injury threatened to prevent him from ever returning to work. Langen claimed that his vegetarian diet helped his healing process and strengthened his weak constitution so that he could resume his work after only two and a half months. Afterwards, he continued with his new habits, even though his co-workers mocked him for not drinking and smoking. It was such mockery, he claimed, that prevented many workers from turning to a vegetarian lifestyle because they did not want to be ostracized for their bürgerliche habits of providence.[58] Among workers, an eagerness to imitate the behavior and consumption patterns of the middle classes apparently coexisted with a rejection and ridicule of such norms.[59]

Body discipline was a way to reclaim agency in an attempt to overcome personal deficiencies and attain health, social respectability, and personal success. Life reformers reassured people that they could take their fate into their own hands. This is one of the reasons why natural therapy sanatoriums offered occupational therapy in some form (such as sawing wood) for their patients. Patients could get the feeling that they actively participated in their recovery. Changes in diet, air and sun baths, and periods of physical exercise alternating with periods of rest were all meant to reassure people that there were rational regimes that could be followed in their desire to overcome their physical and mental weakness or other personal deficits such as a lack of physical attractiveness or unhappy intimate relationships (see chapter 3).[60]

Individuals could also assert agency by disciplining the mind. The editor of the natural therapy journals *Naturarzt* and *Neue Heilwissenschaft*, Reinhold

Gerling, propagated a from of psychotherapy that would enable people to overcome the challenges of their personal lives. He quite revealingly called his program "Gymnastics of the Will" *(Gymnastik des Willens)*. Gerling demanded that, in order to be successful in life, his readers train their wills by means of auto-suggestion. They would have to tell themselves to get up early, start work immediately, and not defer it. The main obstacles to success were character deficits such as slothfulness, which had to be overcome by the establishment of regular work habits. This would create a manly character and improve mental performance levels. The goal was to become "master of the self" *(Selbstbeherrschung)* because such mastery was the key to personal success. Only people with a firm character who mastered themselves, Gerling claimed, were capable of coping with failures in their personal or professional lives and, ultimately, overcoming such adversities.[61]

This chapter has tried to describe life reform in terms of rational bürgerliche attitudes and value orientations that prevailed among the German middle classes and even influenced the mentality of some workers claiming social respectability. Chapter 2 looks at a specific aspect of these value orientations and discusses the role of aesthetics and cultivation (in the sense of Bildung) in popular hygienic discourse. The goal is to show how discussions about physical beauty articulated conflicts and tensions between different sectors of the German middle classes, in particular between the educated Bildungsbürgertum and members of the lower middle classes who did not have formal higher education.

CHAPTER 2

POPULAR HYGIENIC CULTURE, CLASS,
AND AESTHETIC NORMS

The performance and achievement ethos of the Bürgertum and the difficulties
that many people experienced as they tried to live up to this ethos were among
the most striking aspects of life reform culture. However, life reform meant different things to people with different social experiences. Focusing on the social
meanings of the beautiful body in contemporary hygienic literature, this chapter
explores the *different* meanings that life reformers from the educated and the
lower middle classes attributed to the *same* shared norms for the beautiful body
and the practice of physical culture.

Life reform culture mirrored tensions between educated middle-class men
(the *Gebildeten*) and lower-middle-class men lacking Bildung. The former either held university degrees or had at least attended an elite high school such as
the Gymnasium.[1] The latter did not have formal higher education and academic
titles and therefore resented the social prestige and privileges of those who did.
To some extent these groups shared a symbolic universe, but the meanings of
these symbols were contested and constantly refashioned. Neither group questioned the ideal of a well-rounded, harmonious person, beautiful in both body
and soul, but they argued about the practices that were best suited to cultivating
such a personality. This social dynamic led to a multiplication of meanings similar to that suggested by Mikhail Bakhtin in his *Dialogic Imagination*.[2] Based on
their different social experiences, life reformers from different social back-

grounds, men as well as women, created new meanings for and reaccentuated the meanings of traditional aesthetic norms for male and female bodies (see chapters 3 and 4).

Debates about physical culture accentuated class distinctions between the Gebildeten and people without formal higher education. For the latter, the cultivated body became an alternative source of social distinction. Claiming that Körperbildung was more important than cultivation of the mind, lower-middle-class propagators of physical culture tried to subvert the claims to distinction made by the Gebildeten. Popular sciences such as physiognomics and phrenology expressed similar conflicts: Members of the educated elite, such as the philosopher Ludwig Klages, asserted their intellectual superiority, while people without higher education vented their anti-elitism and their contempt for lofty academic titles. Negative stereotypes such as that of the fat and bloated "beer philistine" *(Bierphilister)* also carried different connotations depending on their social use. Lower-middle-class people could employ such a cliché to vent their disdain for the drinking rituals associated with German academic culture (as practiced in student fraternities), but life reformers in general used it to denounce the allegedly immoral behavior of the wealthy upper classes. Before I discuss the various social uses of aesthetic ideals for the human physique, however, it is necessary to say a few words about the aesthetization of the healthy human body in contemporary medical literature.

Health and Aesthetic Norms in Contemporary Hygienic Literature

Turn-of-the-century popular hygienic literature presented an aesthetisized version of the ideal human body, as regular physicians and life reformers alike espoused the bodily norms of Greek and Roman antiquity. Regarding beauty as the expression of healthy and normal organic functioning and ugliness as a sign of disease, they offered gender-specific representations of the ideal: statues of Hercules and Apollo embodied the masculine ideals of beauty and strength, and statues of Venus gave form to the feminine ideal. These forms were believed to come closest to the formal laws determining absolute beauty that the bodies of really healthy human beings were supposed to express.

Beauty was not in the eye of the beholder; it was not something relative that depended on the taste of the individual. The external form of the body was regarded as the holistic expression of a healthy physical and mental constitution. Whether the authors were life reformers or orthodox physicians, and whether they favored constitutional models that posited hereditary or acquired dispositions toward disease (or a combination of both), in popular hygienic culture the concept of constitution was highly aesthetisized, with external physical markers signifying an individual's constitutional essence and character.

The idea that external physical characteristics expressed the constitutional essence of individuals did not emerge in the late nineteenth century. In the late eighteenth century, the Swiss theologian Johann Caspar Lavater published his *Physiognomic Fragments*, in which he developed a system for diagnosing the moral character and health of individuals based on external facial characteristics. At the same time, the Viennese physician Franz Joseph Gall developed his science of phrenology, which regarded the exterior shape of the human skull as indicative of moral and intellectual faculties. Concepts reminiscent of Lavater's physiognomy and Gall's phrenology remained part of popular medical folklore throughout the nineteenth century.[3]

In the 1850s, the Dresden anatomist and natural philosopher Carl Gustav Carus developed a comprehensive constitutional doctrine in his *Symbolik der menschlichen Gestalt* (1853). Carus distinguished first eighteen and later sixteen constitutional types that could be identified by morphological differences. Since for Carus the outward shape of the body was an expression of the inner qualities of the soul, these types represented differences in temperament and mental disposition. Carus conceived human character as the organic expression of a combination of intellectual abilities, instincts, and emotions that constituted the temperaments and mental dispositions. Drawing on concepts developed in Johann Wolfgang Goethe's theory of colors *(Farbenlehre)*, Carus constructed his constitutional typology using a process that could best be described as understanding through intuitive contemplation, which in his view revealed the essence of a person. For Carus, measurements, quantification, and analysis were not the right way to understand either the human form *(Gestalt)* or the constitutional predispositions it manifested.[4]

Carus tried to establish formal rules for arriving at an ideal type, a pure form that would symbolize a godly idea. The various constitutional types would then be deviations from this ideal norm, signifying not only differences in character but also pathological deviations. For Carus, morphology did not simply signify character type but also indicated constitutional predisposition toward diseases. For example, he argued that persons with a strong and broad head were predisposed to diseases of the brain, strokes, and melancholic disturbances, whereas those with small and narrow heads were predisposed to different forms of folly.[5] If Carus's system aimed chiefly at the intuitive understanding of differences among human character types, it also contained the beginnings of a patho-physiognomy that tried to elucidate pathological predispositions.

At the end of the century, the natural therapist Louis Kuhne propagated a similar, albeit much more simplified, system for the diagnosis of disease based on facial expressions.[6] Kuhne argued that the human body was a unified whole and that any impairment of organs or parts of the body would influence all the other elements. A body was therefore only healthy when all its parts were in their normal state and performed their assigned functions without pain or tensions. An expression of this state of health was, according to Kuhne, the normal shape of all body parts, a shape that corresponded with the human ideal of beauty.[7] Kuhne's ideals of beauty were the figures created by Greek sculptors and not the "well nourished fat bellies" that, he maintained, were wrongly regarded as "model humans" by his contemporaries.[8] According to him, disease always affected bodily form, and obesity and pathological emaciation were only the most obvious signs that a person was sick, that is, that he or she had accumulated "alien substances" in his or her body. Diseases found their expression in changes in the shape of the throat and the face, and by analyzing them, Kuhne tried to identify the organs or body parts that were most affected.[9]

Kuhne distinguished between a front, a back, and a side accumulation of alien substances depending on their distribution in the body. The accumulation, he claimed, was made manifest in different facial expressions (see figures 6, 7, and 8).[10] By reading the face, Kuhne thought, he could both discover existing diseases and recognize predispositions toward serious illness in the future. Side accumulation was the least serious, because it could be cured within a couple of

FIGURE 6. Exclusive front accumulation according to Kuhne. Kuhne, *Heilwissenschaft*, 461. Private collection.

FIGURE 7. Exclusive back accumulation according to Kuhne. Kuhne, *Heilwissenschaft*, 462. Private collection.

weeks; back accumulation was the most serious because it indicated the potential for serious mental disturbances and impending death.[11]

That Louis Kuhne, who was considered by many contemporaries to be a crank, revived the doctrine of reading facial expressions to diagnose disease might not be very surprising. But such approaches were not unusual within life reform circles. Writing in one of the most popular natural therapy compendiums, Willy Vierath maintained that human constitutional and temperamental types corresponded to certain body types. Drawing on ancient humoral-pathological vocabulary, he claimed that a sanguine temperament, for example, was the consequence of a sanguine constitution, which predisposed individuals to nervous disorders such as hysteria and neurasthenia. This constitutional type was signified by slim and tender body forms. In contrast, a choleric temperament expressed in a strong and slender frame corresponded with a choleric constitution, predisposing individuals to congestions, neuralgias, and diseases of the hepatic system. Vierath argued for physiognomics as a semiotic science—as an art of discerning internal pathological states and constitutional predispositions from the outward appearance of humans. He claimed that commonsense

FIGURE 8. Front, back, and side accumulation with a preponderance of front accumulation according to Kuhne. Kuhne, *Heilwissenschaft*, 463. Private collection.

experience could demonstrate for everybody that a high degree of "mental weakness" was revealed in a facial expression that deviated considerably from the normal state. In Vierath's view, even laypersons could interpret such physical signs.[12]

The psychiatrist Paul Julius Möbius (1853–1907) relied on external physical markers to diagnose mental states as well. Möbius did not have an appointment at a university, but he was the co-editor of *Schmidt's Jahrbücher der gesamten Medizin (Schmidt's Yearbook for All Medical Fields)*, for which he reviewed much of the international literature on clinical neurology and psychiatry. He was well known to the public because of his popular scientific tracts delineating the limited mental capabilities of women.[13] In his pathographies of famous individuals Möbius gave physiognomic theories renewed respectability by interpreting facial features of such persons as Johann Wolfgang von Goethe and pointing out signs of their deviance from normality.[14] Möbius also claimed that deviation from physical norms was a sure sign of degeneracy, and he cast degeneracy in aesthetic terms as well. Like Charles Darwin, he regarded ugliness or beauty as the basis of sexual selection. Normality was, in his view, the precondition for beauty, whereas ugliness was the most important sign of degeneracy, a warning sign of nature that told people "not [to] love this person, because united with her you will worsen the race."[15]

Quite a few contemporary physicians were moved to take sides in discussions about the prestige of neohumanistic Bildung and the value of the aesthetic ideals of classical antiquity. As the historian Dieter Langewiesche has remarked, the Bildungsbürgertum at the turn of the century experienced a decline in its cultural competence. The confidence of the highly educated—who thought that their neohumanistic Bildung made them competent judges in all fields of knowledge—was shaken by the specialization of knowledge during the late nineteenth century, the rise of the natural sciences, and the questioning, through avant-garde art, of aesthetic norms thought to be timeless.[16] Bildungsbürger often felt that their aesthetic values were denigrated by naturalist and, later, impressionist and expressionist art. In the 1890s conflicts about the nature of "true" art and obscenity and censorship were ignited. Art exhibitions and museum acquisitions were closely scrutinized by a public critical of aesthetic innovations.[17]

These cultural conflicts affected some physicians deeply. As members of the Bildungsbürgertum, they felt the need to give authoritative aesthetic advice to the public based on their expertise. In 1891, the renowned physiologist Ernst Brücke, professor emeritus at the University of Vienna and former teacher of anatomy at the Academy of Arts in Berlin, wrote a vigorous defense of these traditional aesthetic norms of beauty, which he saw as threatened by naturalist art and its obsession with ugliness. He thought it necessary to give artists authoritative medical advice about the proper aesthetic norms of the male and the female body, because the bodies of his contemporaries did not correspond to the ideal norms anymore.[18] One year later the physician Max Nordau voiced similar concerns in his notorious book *Degeneracy (Entartung)*, in which he attacked the naturalist tendencies of modern art as the product of sick and immoral minds. Nordau gave Benedict August Morel's and Cesare Lombroso's psychiatric concepts a new twist by describing degeneracy as deviance from the aesthetic norms and sensibilities of the Bildungsbürgertum.[19]

Similar concerns were shared by the life reformer Paul Schultze-Naumburg (1869–1949), a member of a respectable, educated middle-class family. His father had been an academically trained portrait painter, and Schultze-Naumburg attended the art academy in Karslruhe and made a name for himself as a cultural critic and architect in the decades before World War I. He frequently contributed articles to Ferdinand Avenarius's *Der Kunstwart,* a journal devoted to the fight against "Kitsch" and bad taste brought about by the age of industrial mass production. Schultze-Naumburg wanted to provide cultural leadership and guidance for the public at a time when bad taste and the participation of people without Bildung in public debates seemed to erode the intellectual and aesthetic authority of the Gebildeten.[20]

In his book *The Culture of the Female Body as the Basis for Women's Dress*[21] Schultze-Naumburg denounced the deleterious effects of contemporary women's clothing on the health and beauty of the female body. In chapter 3, I discuss in more detail the function of such ideals in contemporary feminist and antifeminist discourse about gender roles. Here I intend to show how hygienic prescriptions by Schultze-Naumburg and others served as a symbolic assertion of the cultural competence and leadership of the educated middle class. In his book, widely referred to in life reform journals, he argued that body aesthetics was not simply a matter of individual taste. The "aesthetic of the future" (for which he wanted to lay the foundation) should be based on the knowledge of all anatomical, biological, and motoric characteristics of the human body. Only then, he claimed, would a new physical principle for the body, one that would culminate in a new body ideal, emerge.[22]

In arguing for his body aesthetics, Schultze-Naumburg maintained that it was important to distinguish clearly between the norm and the average because the behavior as well as the appearance of the majority of the people did not correspond to the aesthetic norms he as a *Bildungsbürger* had in mind.[23] He claimed throughout his book that his aesthetic norms were also hygienic norms because they demanded a rejection of such women's fashions as tight shoes and the corset, which would damage women's internal organs and also destroy their natural and beautiful physique. These norms were constitutive of an aesthetic cultivation that would uplift mankind. In Schultze-Naumburg's view, Kultur, in the sense of aesthetic development of mind and soul, was not the cause of mankind's degeneracy, as claimed by lower-middle-class life reformers such as Richard Ungewitter, who rejected excessive cultivation as the outgrowth of modern intellectualism (see below). Kultur was the solution to all of mankind's social and hygienic problems, which were caused precisely by a lack of aesthetic cultivation in average people. Schultze-Naumburg cast himself as a Bildungsbürger, maintaining that the social question could be solved if the masses would follow the lead of people like himself and cultivate their artistic sensibilities. His aesthetic was a moral one. He insisted that it was a duty to develop and refine one's body, as it was a duty to develop and refine one's mind—for him, these could not be separated. He wrote: "One has to look at the type of those unfortunates, whose crumpled, disjointed, odd, twisted, swollen . . . , prematurely deteriorated bodies scarcely remind one of a human body in its outer appearance, in order to understand, how crumpled, disjointed, odd, twisted, and swollen . . . the thoughts produced by such bodies must be."[24]

Schultze-Naumburg argued that all disease should be regarded as a disgrace caused by a lack of cleanliness, excessive eating or drinking, forcible disfigurement of the body (by means of the corset), lack of exercise, or any other abuse of the body through indulgence. All morality was based on the conscience of the body, and true culture would lead to the unfolding of beauty and happiness, even though not all individuals and races were capable of participating in this process. In order to achieve this goal, one should follow "the conscience of one's eye." Then man would recognize by intuitive contemplation *(Anschauung)* what was beautiful and what was ugly. By educating one's eyes, one would soon realize that beauty and ugliness were other terms for good and evil.[25]

The reverse side of Schultze-Naumburg's moral aesthetic, with its mutually reinforcing metaphors of health, beauty, and morality, was the ruthless condemnation of the sick and the disabled. Such an aesthetization of health culminated in a devaluation of human life that ultimately led to the stigmatization that set the stage for the extermination of those with inherited diseases during the Nazi regime. It is therefore not surprising that Schultze-Naumburg later actively participated in the defamation of those with hereditary illnesses in his book *Kunst und Rasse,* which juxtaposed pictures of mentally ill people with paintings by modern artists (see chapter 7).

An even more influential Wilhelmine expert on body aesthetics than Schultze-Naumburg was the gynecologist Carl Heinrich Stratz. Stratz, a regular physician, shared the aesthetic ideals of the life reformers, but he rejected medical practice by people without a university medical degree. He maintained that a physician's task was to help laypersons develop an understanding of the scientific foundations of the body's aesthetics without threatening the authority of regular physicians by providing patients with unnecessary details of anatomy and physiology. In a health advice book for women, Stratz claimed that he intended to write a book that could be recommended by physicians to their female patients without turning women into half-educated quacks.[26]

In addition to his health advice book, Stratz published several other books about the beauty of female bodies that, because of their lavish use of photographs of nude females, appealed to the male voyeur at least as much as to female readers. Because the illustrations made his books expensive, Stratz's readers were most likely respectable Bürger with education and property *(Bildung und Besitz).* His works on body aesthetics are excellent examples of the way in which aesthetic representations of nature in general and of human beings in particular served as a basis for the popularization of natural scientific knowledge.[27]

Stratz's books allowed cultivated readers to appreciate the "natural" beauty of female bodies in a holistic way. In a sense, such aesthetic representations allowed people to visually experience knowledge. Although aesthetics could not convey competence in the natural sciences, it could at least create in the reader the illusion of competence. It allowed one to appreciate the body as a unified whole whose essence was expressed in its appearance. Connoisseurs of the beautiful did not have to bother with scientific knowledge that had become too complex to be judged by those who had merely enjoyed a broad neohumanistic Bildung. The appeal of Stratz's work was in part similar to the appeal of Julius Langbehn's *Rembrandt as Educator (Rembrandt als Erzieher)*, which went through dozens of editions in the 1890s, carrying the message that art was the source of a higher knowledge, a knowledge obscured by the painstaking and petty research of insignificant details carried out in laboratories at German universities.[28] Faced with contemporary attacks on the utility of neohumanistic Bildung, its defenders used visual representation as a means to convey the timeless normativity and beauty of Greek aesthetic ideals to educated laypeople irritated by specialized scholarship that tried to situate Greek art in a historical perspective.[29]

Although Stratz presented an aesthetisized version of the body in order to appeal to people with a humanistic education, his work did not lack the aura of naturalistic authority that was associated with the exact sciences. Stratz was drawing on a long tradition in Western art to establish eternally valid norms for the human body when he tried to explain his norms for beauty in terms of formal laws. The ancient Greek artist Polyklet had done so, and during the Renaissance such explanations culminated in Leonardo da Vinci's and Albrecht Dürer's efforts to establish the divine proportions manifested in beautiful human bodies.[30]

For Stratz, beauty was the expression of a scientific and divine law governing the proportions of healthy individuals of the most "advanced" races. A well-proportioned body could be reduced to a "canon," a set of formal rules from which all physical proportions could be deduced. Stratz claimed that he had to focus on the female body because as a gynecologist he did not have enough suitable material relating to males. Nevertheless, he thought that the male aesthetic was governed by similar laws.[31]

According to Stratz, a normal (meaning a healthy) body would represent the ideal of beauty. Like Schultze-Naumburg, he did not consider the average body to be normal, however. Stratz thought that in order to establish what is normal and beautiful one simply had to select individuals who were normal and beautiful:

> If we want to define the value of normality, then not the number, but rather the selection of individuals is decisive. We first have to eradicate *[ausmerzen!]* all individuals who for whatever reason have lost the claim to normality. Normal in this sense is, however, . . . beautiful. . . . Like the gaze of the artist, the gaze of the physician is hereditary. One need neither be physician nor artist, to have

both. There are however not only colorblind humans but also humans blind to
form [proportion], who lack both [the gaze of the artist and the physician] to a
smaller or larger extent, and among those are unfortunately quite a few
physicians and artists.[32]

Stratz's reasoning was tautological. His objective standard of beauty was
derived from what he had already intuitively perceived as beautiful. In order to
confirm that his intuition corresponded with the absolute norm of beauty, he
used the canon for ideal proportions established in 1896 by the Berlin physiologist and anthropologist Gustav Fritsch. Like Brücke, Fritsch extolled the perfection of "ideal-normal" male and female bodies as they were represented in the
art of classical antiquity, and he condemned artists who opted for a naturalistic
representation of the imperfect bodies of their contemporaries. He rejected
modern art, especially its impressionist and naturalist tendencies, singling out
for attack Franz von Stuck, whose paintings he saw as representative of the Munich Secession—guided by dirty fantasies rather than timeless aesthetic principles.[33]

Fritsch's canon of body proportions was founded on a "basic measure" that
he called a "modulus" from which, Stratz claimed, all the two-dimensional proportions of the human body could be derived. This modulus was the length of
the spine measured from the bottom of the nose to the upper border of the sym-
physis of the pubic bones in the anterior part of the pelvis. The division of this
modulus into four equal parts resulted in a submodulus, the length of which was
equal to the length of the line from the lower bottom of the nose to the vertex
and equal to the straight lines from the spine to the right and left shoulder
joints. One-half of a submodulus equaled the length of the straight lines from
the spine to the hip joints, and all other two-dimensional measures could be derived in a similar fashion (see figures 9 and 10).[34] Bodies whose proportions
were different from the ones suggested by Fritsch deviated from classical norms
of beauty.

Like Stratz, Fritsch argued that the "normal ideal body" represented a state
of human health that few people had attained but that could be achieved by civilized humans *(Kulturmenschen)* who adopted a hygienic lifestyle.[35] In this respect, Fritsch's views coincided with those of many life reformers, and he
actively supported some aspects of the movement such as physical culture, represented by the German Association for Rational Body Discipline. Together
with Ernst Schweninger, the former personal physician of Bismarck, Fritsch
was honorary president of this organization, which was committed to harmonious development of the human body and strengthening of the "physical constitution" of individuals and of the German *Volk.*[36] He urged his contemporaries

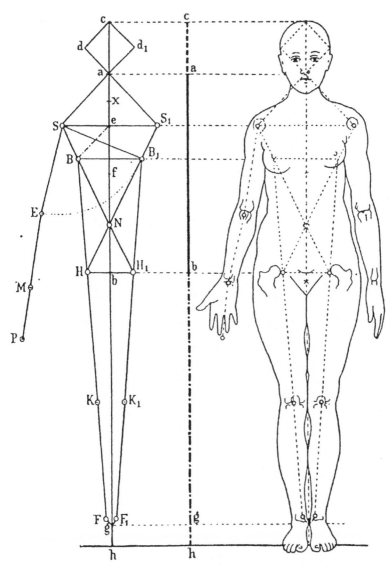

FIGURE 9. Ideal or normal female figure according to Fritsch's canon. Stratz, *Schönheit des weiblichen Körpers*, 36. Landesbibliothek Stuttgart.

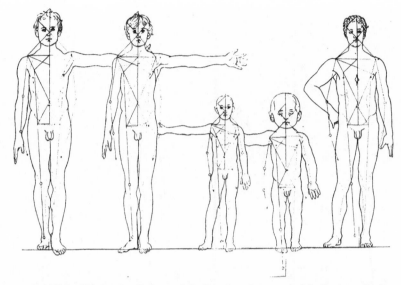

FIGURE 10. Fritsch's canon applied to male bodies of varying ages (originally drawn by the Berlin sculptor Johann Gottfied Schadow, 1764–1850). The proportions of the four infants and boys on the left do not yet correspond to the ideal norms for adults. The young adult on the right shows perfect correspondence with Fritsch's norms for the ideal or normal body. Fritsch, *Gestalt des Menschen*, table 22. Landesbibliothek Stuttgart.

to reform their lifestyles and cultivate their bodies according to Greek ideals, because he believed that this in turn would have a wholesome effect on art.

The Beautiful Body and Social Class

Life reformers agreed that physical beauty was the expression of perfect health and morality and that people should strive to achieve the ideals of physical beauty that were propagated in the contemporary medical and life reform literature. However, life reformers from the educated middle classes held different ideas about the importance of physical culture for the development of harmonious and cultivated personalities than did those from the lower middle class, although they accepted the same aesthetic ideals for the human body. These differences become most apparent if one compares the life reform journals *Beauty (Die Schönheit)* and *Strength and Beauty (Kraft und Schönheit)*. *Die Schönheit* (first published in 1903) was directed at *bildungsbürgerliche Schöngeister*, people who had the aesthetic sensibility, leisure, and money to enjoy short stories, poems, and aesthetic observations illustrated by photographs of (mainly) female nudes.[37] Articles in *Die Schönheit* emphasized the necessity of cultivating the mind and the body, and they rejected the one-sided cultivation of the body as vulgar. In contrast, *Kraft und Schönheit* (first published in 1901) appealed chiefly to people in the comparatively uncultured middle and lower middle classes who were dominant among the membership of the German Association for Rational Body Discipline. For them, the cultivation of the mind was secondary to the cultivation of the body, because a healthy body was the best guarantee of a healthy mind. Therefore there were no sophisticated discussions about art, poetry, and fine literature in this journal.

For the Gebildeten who wrote for *Die Schönheit*, spiritual culture, or *Geisteskultur*, could thrive only if the body and the mind were cultivated to approach the ideal of classical beauty. Like Schultze-Naumburg, whose work was often cited approvingly, they deplored the one-sidedness of an existence that neglected the body in favor of the mind. This call for more attention to the body could culminate in an appeal like the one by A. E. Brinkmann, who demanded that his contemporaries become more animal-like and develop an aesthetic sensuality. This was to be a refined sensuality devoid of any lust, however, an intuitive sensuality constantly created and re-created by humans in the course of their subjective perception.

Brinkmann, therefore, did not argue for an absolute and eternal standard of beauty. But he admired Hellenic culture's balancing of body and spirit, because the wonderfully developed abilities of the Greek spirit were in perfect harmony with a body of good race and beautiful growth. Although Brinkmann regretted that contemporary society supposedly lacked appreciation for the body because the intellect had overwhelmed it, he did not argue for a neglect of Geisteskultur in favor of Körperkultur. His was the position of the Bildungsbürger who resented one-sided intellectualism and tried to achieve true cultivation by means of the simultaneous and harmonious development of body, soul, and mind.[38] As Oskar Stoll, another writer for *Die Schönheit*, put it, in addition to "the beauty of the body" it was necessary to achieve "the nobility of the soul," and it was impossible to do this by means of body discipline alone. Instead, the soul had to ennoble the body, and the soul was to be cultivated by the dreams of poets and artists, which truly cultivated individuals should reflect in their very essence.[39]

Many of the Gebildeten therefore argued explicitly against the exaggerated emphasis on body culture, considering the focus on the body alone to be vulgar. The physician Johannes Grosse attacked the excesses of uneducated physical culturists who, like Richard Ungewitter, thought that nude culture and excessive training of the body were keys to human regeneration. Whereas Christianity had overemphasized the soul, Grosse claimed, people were now threatened by the accentuation of the corporeal, which made man a "feebleminded half-animal through the overgrowth of physical nude culture." This neglect of the soul and excessive emphasis on the body could only be prevented, according to Grosse, by "the heavyweight of classical cultivation" and "antique reasonableness," which developed the mind as well as the body.[40]

Schultze-Naumburg and Stratz, although they were in a sense perfect archetypes of the German Bildungsbürger, also felt they had a mission to educate the wider public about aesthetic norms for the human body. These norms also appealed to members of the lower middle class, who constituted the backbone of the membership of life reform voluntary associations. Richard Ungewitter is a case in point. He was a person without Bildung, yet he accepted the neohumanistic aesthetic concepts of the educated middle class. In doing so, however, he did not simply accept the values of the educated but criticized them at the same time: He contrasted the bodies represented in antique art with the real bodies of many of his contemporaries and maintained that these ugly, degenerate bodies were the result of a middle-class lifestyle that neglected the body in favor of intellectual work. In other words, he gave the aesthetic discourse of the Gebildeten an anti-intellectual twist. Ungewitter used the aesthetic norms of the ancient Greeks to advocate a new biological morality intended to replace conventional middle-class morality. Marriage should be based on eugenic and not on social criteria, and the one-sided preoccupation with intellectual concerns should be replaced with physical culture. In Ungewitter's view, physical culture was the key to character development.[41]

It was typical of many life reformers to assert bildungsbürgerliche aesthetic norms while rejecting intellectualism and luxuries and to prefer an ascetic health regimen that emphasized physical development instead. This combination held a special appeal for the lower middle-class members of life reform organizations, people who had neither cultivation in the form of higher formal education (Bildung) nor significant amounts of property (Besitz), the social markers of the Gebildeten. No wonder they tried to achieve true cultivation by transforming their bodies in order to approach the aesthetic ideals that had first been formulated in Greek antiquity. As Ungewitter put it: "the culture of the nude [body culture] . . . is the necessary precondition *for the true culture of all of mankind*" (der Kultus des Nackten [ist] . . . die unerläßliche Bedingung für *die wahre Kultur der gesamten Menschheit überhaupt*).[42]

Although Schultze-Naumburg saw the cultivation of the body as one precondition for a well-developed and balanced personality, he did not argue that one could exist without the other. For him, body culture was a necessary supplement to and not a replacement for the culture of the mind: Körperkultur was no substitute for Geisteskultur. For Ungewitter it was exactly that. True culture in the sense of *wahre Geisteskultur* could, in Ungewitter's view, be achieved exclusively by Körperkultur.

Articles in *Kraft und Schönheit* denounced the educated and wealthy as Bierphilister. For lower-middle-class life reformers, the Bierphilister was an academic who had a lofty title but was crippled in mind and body (see above). He was supposedly only interested in drinking and debauchery—behavior that was in sharp contrast to the ascetic and moral regimen of physical culturists. A 1905 editorial in *Kraft und Schönheit*, probably written by the editor, Gustav Möckel, attacked so-called *Bierstudenten*. The author claimed that their drinking behavior and lifestyle caused hostility and resentment in nonacademic circles, all the more so because the dominant and influential position of privileged academic professionals was incommensurate with their real contributions toward culture and progress. Neither the humanities nor the natural and technical sciences had been capable of easing the fate of mankind, and medicine had proved incapable of contributing anything positive to the health of the people. This, the author maintained, was a result of the neglect of the body, because its cultivation was a precondition for the culture of the mind. Instead, humanistic education produced nothing but physical and mental cripples who, in turn, were incapable of creating a viable culture. The German Gymnasium thus contrasted sharply with the ideal of the gymnasiums of ancient Greece, with their "noble gymnastics of the nude body."[43]

This contrast between the Gymnasium of the Wilhelmine era, the high school whose degree gave access to universities and other social privileges, with that of ancient Greece, where the entire human being was developed to the highest perfection by the cultivation of the male body, was one of the most suggestive themes in *Kraft und Schönheit*.[44] Unfortunately, according to lower-middle-class life reformers, students and academics did not possess this deep and general cultivation. Quite the contrary: As a result of their lack of exercise and excess consumption of alcohol, their bodies and minds had decayed, and whatever might still be left of their mental capacities was used up in the course of their academic work.

There was a considerable distance between the noble and harmonious figures of the Hellenic philosopher youth and contemporary university students. As the *Kraft und Schönheit* editorial pointed out, not everybody had yet realized the "truly elevated ridiculousness and comic effect of those bloated beer figures" who combined their general unfitness for military service with an exhibition of their dueling scars, the physical markers of those who were or had been members of student fraternities. Only nude culture, as it was practiced in the ancient Greek gymnasiums (which derived their name from the Greek *gymnos*, "nude") could lead to real health and cultivation.[45]

Life reformers with no higher education also gave voice to their anti-academic bent by suggesting a contrast between the "man of practical life" and the one who was more academically inclined. As the mail inspector W. Bräunlich claimed, most of the best students in high school went on to fail in practical life; the children with the strongest grades were often weak, pale, and predisposed to tuberculosis. Gustav Möckel maintained that the hard school of life was the greatest teacher and "molder of character" and much more important than formal education.[46]

Lower-middle-class life reformers were not simply critical of the one-sided intellectual development of the Bildungsbürgertum—a criticism that echoed the sentiments of contemporary school reformers as well as the emperor.[47] Life reformers' ideal of a healthy, moderate, and austere lifestyle—which, they insisted, had nothing to do with self-denial and sacrifice but rather was a joyful return to nature—provided a counter to the lifestyle and cultivation of manners that served as a social marker for wealthier sectors of the German middle classes. Life reformers from both the educated and the lower middle classes rejected the "materialism" of luxury and conspicuous consumption. They believed that indulgence in luxuries violated the moral asceticism necessary for the shaping of true character in body and mind.

Richard Ungewitter was probably the most outspoken critic of the "fake culture" of the rich. He attacked the "status arrogance" that was expressed in a lifestyle of expensive travel and fashion. Those who lived such lives saw health—the most important possession for Ungewitter—as inappropriate to their status and thought it a sign of cultivation to ostentatiously display a fashionable disease. Ungewitter accused the wealthy of creating puppets and monkeys rather than humans; in these circles dress culture was more important than body culture. He wrote: "One does not cultivate true culture of the mind but the external appearance, empty-headedness, blasé character, arrogance, and narrow-mindedness." The entire so-called cultivation of the wealthy was an expression of this attitude, with its "social slickness," the proper use of handkerchiefs, the artful handling of knife and fork, and social conventions pretending to shame.[48] Ungewitter reasoned that sexual abnormalities such as homosexuality were a problem not only of proletarian and alcoholic criminals but also of the wealthier classes of German society. The sectors of the middle class who abstained from excess alcohol, night life, mental overexertion, and sexual debauchery were free from such habits, which were the inevitable "signs of worm-eaten, decadent cultures."[49] Ungewitter's moderation was the virtue of the uneducated petit bourgeois who resented the educated and wealthy.

Such resentment was also reflected in popular physiognomic and phrenological theories. This can be seen, for example, in Louis Kuhne's contention that people whose facial expressions showed "back accumulation" of alien substances are always inferior to others, although they might possess a higher Bildung. He claimed that back accumulation was much more widespread in the higher estates, with their indulgence in luxuries.[50] If his unsophisticated audience lacked the social markers for "distinction," it could always resort to physical markers in order to compensate for them. This anti-academic bias is also mirrored in Kuhne's use of language. Although he, like Ungewitter, accepted the classical Greek norms for the human body as visual ideals, he rejected the learned pretensions of the medical establishment. Kuhne's use of a very simple and straightforward language helped establish a rapport between himself and people who lacked higher education. Kuhne also told his readers that he could have given his method a more pretentious appearance by giving it a Latin or Greek name, but he thought that the German name *Gesichtsausdruckskunde* (literally, study of facial expressions) represented most clearly the major features of his method.[51]

The contemporary popularity of physiognomy and phrenology certainly had roots that went deeper than lower-middle-class resentment and may have been in part a response to rapid social change at the turn of the century. One has to keep in mind that at the end of the Kaiserreich, every other German lived in a place where he or she was not born. Those who moved to a big city left behind the familiar class and status differences of the smaller community. It was difficult to be sure whether, for instance, a man was a "confidence man" or held a respectable social position, or whether a woman was from a respectable family or only pretending to be in order to make an advantageous marriage.

As Reinhold Gerling, editor of *Naturarzt* from 1896 to 1905, argued in a marriage advice book, men and women tended to pretend to be what they were not. Cultivation of manners and amiability were masks that hid their real character.[52] Since people were social beings who had to interact with others in different social contexts, such masks were a necessity. Only by hiding behind them could people gain the sympathy of their peers without compromising their inner selves and personal integrity.[53] Such forms of "impression management," as the sociologist Erving Goffman called it,[54] were essential for social intercourse in a modern urban space where people lived in a "plurality of life worlds."[55] Gerling devoted an entire chapter in his book *Gymnastik des Willens* to the problem of impression management, advising his readers on how to become popular.[56] Urban people had to be able to assume context-adequate roles in various social settings without compromising the inner core of their personality. At the same time, one might try to move past the masks of social convention worn by others by means of a search for markers—in the face, skull, or handwriting—that hinted at their real character. Some contemporary employers' use of graphological evaluations for prospective employees should also be seen as attempts to make social evaluations in a rapidly changing urban society.

Keep in mind that phrenology and physiognomy were multifunctional popular "sciences," appropriated for cultural criticism by the educated and uneducated alike. The philosopher Ludwig Klages saw graphology as a means to penetrate the deceptive self-presentation of his contemporaries and unveil their true character. Klages had studied chemistry in the 1890s and obtained a Ph.D., but the natural sciences were not his real love. He had taken up chemistry as a *Brotstudium*, a means to earn a living, but he was much more drawn to the arts and to the German tradition of self-cultivation. At the turn to the century he therefore turned to the humanities and philosophy and also developed a sophisticated methodology of graphological character evaluation. According to Klages, handwriting was an objectification of a person's movements. The character of human beings could be read not only from physiognomies but also from characteristic movements that expressed what was in their souls. Klages's theories found a very receptive audience in the 1920s. His popular guide *Handwriting and Character* went through more than twenty editions, but he laid the groundwork for his theory during the Kaiserreich when he edited the *Graphologische Monatshefte*.[57]

Given his great appreciation of cultivation and the arts, Klages resented the pretensions of the uneducated *Bildungsdilettanten*, who tried to convey the appearance of inner cultivation in their behavior and their displays of taste. In graphology he saw a means to penetrate the "veils of the affected gestures" of those who tried to mask their "shopkeeper's natures." These sorts of people, he claimed, were multiplying rapidly. Despite their inner "emptiness" they tried to convey the appearance of unshakable intellectual superiority by assuming an avant-garde stand on all kinds of issues. This they did with aesthetisized expressions, nicely cut suits, and the "allures of half-educated clerks." They tried to convey the impression of sophisticated and aristocratic behavior in a way that only betrayed that they were nothing more than "parvenus." In Klages's view, graphology would unfailingly unmask the people he resented most. The beautiful soul of the Bildungsbürger was expressed in all of his body movements. Therefore it was objectified in his handwriting, as was the lack of inner beauty in the writing of the social upstart.[58]

Because of their scientific pretensions, however, phrenology, physiognomy, and graphology could also be a source of satisfaction and self-esteem for those who lacked social distinctions and markers and harbored resentments against the educated. Reinhold Gerling is a case in point. He lamented several times in his books and articles that too often formal titles and formal education dictated social estimation. As one of the leading representatives of the natural therapy movement during the empire, he was a favorite target of regular physicians, whose representatives dragged him several times into court and also attacked him in a personal manner (suggesting, for instance, that he was a failed actor who had turned to natural therapy for financial gain).

In an editorial in *The New Healing Art (Neue Heilkunst)*, the other leading journal for natural therapy during the empire alongside the *Naturarzt*, Gerling complained bitterly about these personal attacks by physicians with a "doctoral hat." He defended himself, maintaining that he had had several very successful careers as an actor, theater director, stage writer, healing artist, professional speaker, and renowned teacher of rhetoric and was now a respected editor and writer. Gerling claimed that it was not his father's money but diligence that allowed him to gain the knowledge that was necessary to succeed in all these various fields. Whether all of these careers were as successful as he claimed has to be questioned, since the list of his occupations certainly does not suggest an orderly and planned life course that led directly to his calling to write about health, in which he was indeed remarkably successful. But even after he had achieved recognition, Gerling seemed to have suffered from the fact that he did not have a formal degree and title from a university. He claimed that he might have sought such a title if he had thought that titles and the "comedy of examinations" were important. But he would only appreciate people with abilities, whether they had a degree or not, and he despised corps students who appreciated their peers more than they did people with more practical training. He attacked them as "title hunters" and "pushy persons" *(Streber)* who looked for social advancement rather than cultivating their inner selves.[59]

During the Kaiserreich, academic degrees opened opportunities for social distinction that clearly separated respectable middle-class people from their lower-middle-class counterparts. One of the most obvious, and to the latter group most galling, examples of this was the so-called *Einjährigenprivileg*. Men who had advanced schooling or a higher degree and who were able to finance their own equipment and upkeep during military service were entitled to serve only one year instead of three years in the military and received the title "officer of the reserve." Bildung and Besitz thus became the bases for a state-sanctioned social distinction that excluded the uneducated and those who lacked means. In the 1860s and 1870s, leaders of the German gymnastics movement demanded that gymnasts receive the same privileges as those with Bildung and Besitz, a request that was not granted by the authorities.[60] According to leaders of the movement, whose membership consisted mainly of lower-middle-class people, the well-trained and cultivated body should be an alternative source of distinction and privilege. It is therefore not surprising that for many life reformers, the well-trained body became a source of distinction as well (see, for example, the photos of the Kaufmann Curt Behrend in figures 11 and 12). They interpreted physical characteristics and fitness in ways that subverted the claims to distinction by their social superiors. The "physical degeneration of the educated classes" was therefore a favorite topic for physical culturists.[61] The physical educator J. P. Müller, who wrote an inexpensive exercise guide for people with sedentary occupations, such as office clerks, maintained that authors of "beautiful literature" contributed to the physical, moral, and spiritual decay of contemporary youth by their encouragement of intellectual culture.[62] The editor of *Kraft und Schönheit*, Gustav Möckel, recalled with satisfaction an episode from his military service when an *Einjähriger* who was a poor gymnast lacked the courage to jump from a scaffold.[63]

Like Möckel, Gerling attacked dueling university students, whose markers of social position were in Gerling's view characteristic of people who had drowned their reason in alcohol. For him the natural markers of the body were a

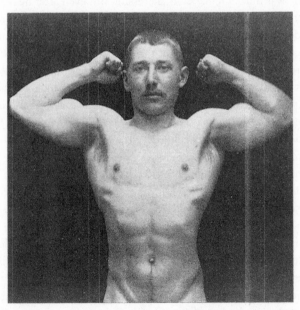

FIGURE 11. Example of good physical development: Curt Behrend. *Kraft und Schönheit* 5 (1905): 172. Staatsbibliothek zu Berlin. Preußischer Kulturbesitz.

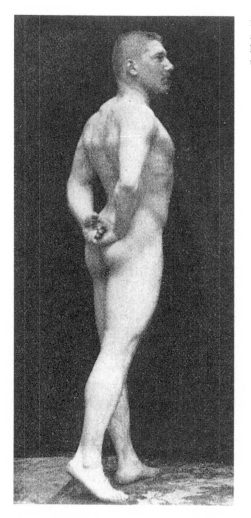

FIGURE 12. Behrend's buttocks. *Kraft und Schönheit* 5 (1905): 173. Staatsbibliothek zu Berlin. Preußischer Kulturbesitz.

more reliable external sign of the true character of individuals. It is therefore not surprising that he too turned to phrenology. In the introduction to a book he edited titled *Praktische Menschenkenntnis (Practical Knowledge of Human Character)*, Gerling related the story of a conversation he had at a party with several physicians, philologists, and theologians about Gall's phrenology. He earned nothing but unanimous and arrogant rejection. Later, however, the host told him privately that this reaction was not really surprising: "What would be the value of degrees and titles if one could prove phrenologically that an empty-head *[Hohlkopf]* was hiding behind the many degrees? The German obsession with titles does not tolerate a nude exposure *[Nacktvorführung]*, not even one of the human spirit." The man was correct, Gerling claimed, because academic titles were in reality like other bestowed titles and honors, nothing more than shining covers for empty husks. That was the real reason why some scientific circles rejected character diagnosis based on physical markers.[64]

Anti-academic resentment among these sectors of the middle class fit well with the notion, pervasive within the life reform movement, that laypeople were more competent therapeutically than university-trained physicians. Those who lacked wealth, formal degrees, and Bildung could resort to physical markers to undermine the authority of the educated or refer to the physical markers of their own body to reassure themselves of their superior inner worth or essence. Müller reminded his readers that "happiness depends on health not on titles or accumulated or inherited money."[65] Those who were active in the physical culture movement, who were mostly from a nonacademic middle-class background, could thus look with satisfaction on their disciplined bodies, remodeled after the ancient Greek ideals, and experience a sense of moral superiority in relation to beer philistines from the Gymnasium or the university. Lower middle-class people appropriated the notion of Bildung as a central characteristic of bürgerlicher Kultur. However, their notion of Bildung was a transformed one: Körperbildung was to replace Geistesbildung in the process of a harmonious cultivation of the human personality.

This chapter has examined debates about the role of physical culture in the creation of a cultivated personality. It has shown how these debates accentuated class distinctions between the Gebildeten and people without formal higher education. The Gebildeten among life reformers saw in physical education a supplement to the cultivation of the mind. Life reformers without higher education argued for the cultivated body as an alternative source of distinction. Chapter 3 will explore different kinds of social uses of aesthetic ideals for human bodies, particularly in Wilhelmine debates about gender relations.

CHAPTER 3

GENDER AND *A*ESTHETIC *N*ORMS
IN *P*OPULAR *H*YGIENIC *C*ULTURE

*P*ublic debates about gender relations, women's health, and appropriate roles
for women in society addressed some of the most contested social issues in Wilhelmine Germany. Many middle-class people regarded the separate spheres of
activity for the sexes as the result of men's and women's natural complementarity: Men, as rational human beings, were destined for the public sphere of politics and economic competition, while women were to provide a safe harbor of
intimacy and bliss for their families in their homes. Such gender norms were increasingly challenged at the turn of the century, when middle-class women
seemed to transcend their domestic sphere and found gainful employment outside their homes. In the course of rapid industrialization and urbanization
women gained employment in clerical positions in commerce and industry, and
the number of married female factory workers grew. Feminists within the Social
Democratic labor movement argued for the need to improve the situation of
working women and demanded social and political equality for the sexes. At the
same time, German feminists pushed for the full admission of women to universities and attempted to widen the range of their occupational options.[1]

Middle-class observers, among them many regular physicians and life reformers, perceived these developments as a threat to the traditional ideals of
separate spheres—ideals that were central to the identity of the German Bürgertum.[2] In their eyes, women's commitment to motherhood and domesticity
seemed to be waning. Discussions about gender relations and men's and women's

health were fueled by worries about the declining birthrate, especially among urban middle-class women. Pro-natalist critics of this development condemned the rising use of contraceptives and argued that large families from all social classes would boost the vitality of the nation. Since the lower classes reproduced at a much higher rate than the better-off sectors of German society, some physicians voiced concerns about the proliferation of "inferior stock." In the view of antifeminist male eugenicists, middle-class women's refusal to bear children contributed to the declining "quality" of the German populace.[3]

Because of the staunch opposition of the life reformers to orthodox medicine, historians have tended to assume that life reformers were more progressive than regular physicians in their attitudes toward women. This perception might have been reinforced by the life reformers' adamant rejection of unhealthful women's fashions such as the corset, even though hygienic propaganda pieces by regular physicians condemned such fashion excesses as well. But as this chapter shows, the response of the former to changing gender relations was not necessarily very different from the response of many of the latter. Antifeminists in both groups tried to defend traditional bürgerliche norms for the sexes. They denounced deviations from these norms and claimed that lack of a clear sexual identity was a sign of degeneracy that was expressed in a person's physical appearance. Many life reformers and regular physicians, therefore, raised the specter of feminized men and masculinized women by arguing that the bodies of contemporary men and women deviated from scientifically established gender norms of health and beauty.

Keep in mind, however, that life reform had considerable appeal for feminists as well. The emphasis on health had a liberating effect for women, since they could attack oppressive traditions in the name of physical fitness. The domestic, sedentary lifestyle of many middle-class women came under attack by feminists who argued that women had to be physically fit in order to have healthy offspring. They deplored the fact that women ruined their health in their efforts to attract a male provider. For feminist life reformers corset-wearing became a symbol of women's subjugation to the immoral sexual desires of men. Turn-of-the-century hygienic literature was therefore an important battleground for the conflicts between feminists and antifeminists. Both sides complained that contemporary women had ruined their health and beauty with an unhealthy lifestyle. Antifeminist men and women claimed that this was a result of women's attempts to transcend domesticity; feminist life reformers and some progressive physicians argued that it was the subjugation of the female sex that was responsible for the health problems of many women. In their view, only greater social and economic independence for women could remedy this situation. The goal of this chapter is to explore these conflicting social uses of contemporary health discourse. It concludes with a discussion of contemporary attitudes toward men's and women's sexuality.

Masculinized Men and Feminized Women

According to the historian Thomas Laqueur, nineteenth-century gender norms emerged in the eighteenth century as a response to the destruction of divinely ordained hierarchies and traditions that had been the basis for power relations between men and women. After the Enlightenment and the French Revolution, when traditional gender hierarchies came into question, the medical literature began to describe gender differences as biological, emphasizing the fundamental incommensurability of the sexes.[4] As this notion gained ground, older justifications of the social differences between the genders persisted and were sometimes cast into a modern Darwinian framework. Drawing on the German zoologist Ernst Haeckel's theory of ontogenesis as a short recapitulation of phylogenesis, some people claimed that women were inferior to men. Haeckel had argued that organisms recapitulated in their indivual development (ontogenesis) the evolutionary development of their species (phylogenesis). A few physicians, therefore, maintained that women—like children—represented a lower stage of male evolutionary development.[5]

Turn-of-the-century physicians and intellectuals reinforced such naturalistic justifications for gender inequality. In 1907 the zoologist Robby Koßmann and the physician Julius Weiß published a three-volume compendium titled *Man and Woman* whose contributors tried to give a lay audience an overview of scientific works on the biological differences and social relations between the sexes.[6] Among the authors was the Viennese medical professor Otto Großer, whose two essays explained his views on the incommensurability of the sexes by referring to the anatomical differences between men and women. To him, sexual differences were more than skin deep. They were not only reflected in the structure of the reproductive organs but extended to all parts of the human organism. He maintained that significant differences were expressed in the structure of the male and female skeleton, skull, and pelvis. He even claimed that there were characteristic differences between the male and female larynx, and he speculated about the possibility of similar differences in the morphological structure of the stomach and the lungs. He insisted that these physical differences were a reflection of the fact that throughout history, men were responsible for the acquisition of food and the defense of their family whereas women were responsible for the domestic sphere and child-rearing.[7]

Großer's position concerning appropriate gender roles was quite typical for the all-male medical professorate at German universities. His conviction that sexual differences pervaded human anatomy was part of a research paradigm that saw in anatomical details significant expressions of ontological differences between the sexes.[8] Koßmann and Weiß, as well as other male authors who contributed to the compendium, propagated rather traditional concepts of masculinity and femininity, stressing the natural differences in the anatomical structure and emotional life of men and women that necessitated the separation of the public and the domestic spheres.[9]

Uncertainty about contemporary gender relations triggered attempts by antifeminists to establish biologically sound psychological and behavioral norms for women.[10] The most famous of these attempts were those by the psychiatrist Paul J. Möbius, whose efforts to prove the physiological inferiority of women were widely publicized shortly after the turn of the century. His best-known pamphlet, titled *About the Physiological Feeblemindedness of Women*, was aimed at a popular audience.[11] Möbius wanted to develop a scientific canon that would allow people to make clear distinctions between normality, stupidity, and feeblemindedness (analogous to the canons for ideal proportions of the human body discussed in chapter 2). According to Möbius, such a canon would allow physicians to describe degeneracy as deviation from norms, but these were norms that varied according to sex, age, race, and estate (class).[12] That is to say, what was normal for men was not normal for women. A given intelligence level might define a man as feebleminded and degenerate and a woman as functional and physiologically healthy, especially since this limited intelligence would enable women to be more prolific mothers. In fact, for Möbius, healthy and fertile women had to be stupid.[13] Therefore he rejected university training for women and stressed the need to protect women against intellectualism,[14] which created "masculinized women" whose mixing of sexual characteristics was a sign of degeneracy. The increasing presence of these masculinized women in Möbius's time was, for him, a disaster because it led to a declining fertility rate and would ultimately weaken and destroy the nation.[15]

So far, historians have not been at a loss to expose the misogynist biases of the medical profession, of which Möbius was a rather extreme example.[16] Yet it would be a mistake to assume that simply because of the antagonism between regular medicine and life reform, a result of their competition in the medical market, life reformers were more sympathetic toward the emancipation of women.[17] One cannot stress often enough that the battle lines between feminists and antifeminists were by no means identical to the ones between regular physicians and life reformers. Within regular medicine, a vocal group of progressive physicians challenged ideas of female inferiority propagated by physicians such as Möbius and intellectuals such as Otto Weininger, whose book *Sex and Character* became a contemporary best-seller.[18] The dermatologist and sexual reformer Iwan Bloch, for example, urged women to develop their personalities and pursue higher education. In his view women should be able to pursue careers in business, politics, and the professions and become an integral part of public life.[19]

Regular medicine did not have a monopoly on misogyny, because some of the most vitriolic antifeminist tracts of the period were written by life reformers who argued that emancipatory desires would destroy women's health and beauty. Richard Ungewitter, for instance, took a decidedly antifeminist stand. He wanted to limit the education of women to subjects that were valuable to the practical life of housewives, excluding of course science and other disciplines that might make women the economic competitors of men. He demanded that the state introduce a compulsory service year for girls during which they would be subjected to rigorous physical exercise. The goal was to educate healthy, race-conscious mothers and not fashionable, fragile puppets.[20] Ungewitter saw women's unreasonableness (in matters such as the wearing of corsets) as the cause of their unhealthy practices and degeneracy. This resentment was clearly reinforced by his loathing of the upper classes, whom he viewed as empty-headed slaves to the fashion dictates of Paris and London.[21] He noted with satisfaction that the punishment for this behavior was inevitable; indeed, he considered the results of corset-wearing—painful or deadly childbirth and early aging—a just revenge.[22]

One would be hard pressed to find a greater misogynist than Ungewitter among regular physicians or life reformers. Yet one of the most popular health manuals of the period, Mortiz Platen's *The New Healing Method*, denounced the vanity of women in a similar, though perhaps more restrained, fashion. In Platen's view, a woman's good health was her greatest beauty, and someone who was used to seeing the creations of nature as the "epitome of perfection and beauty" would never be pleased by the appearance of a "laced-up fashion fool." Platen urged mothers to prevent their daughters from following the foolishness "sanctioned by the all-powerful goddess of fashion." Otherwise, future generations would be led down the path of decadence, and the health of the nation *(Volksgesundheit)* would be undermined. To underscore his point, Platen contrasted drawings of women having healthy and natural body forms with drawings of women whose bodies had been disfigured by a corset (see figures 13, 14, and 15). If women insisted on wearing corsets, he urged them to at least be sensible enough to purchase the affordable "health corset" that he had developed according to hygienic requirements (see figures 16 and 17).[23]

The life reformer Reinhold Gerling assumed a similar condescending attitude toward women. This is evident in the advice he gave young men for the

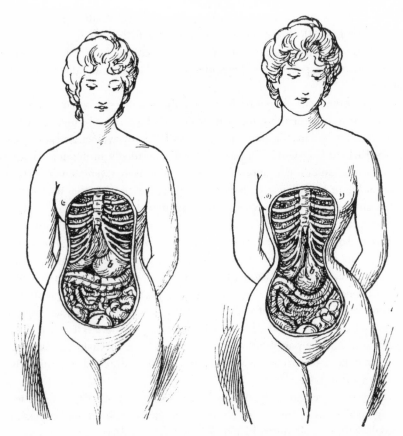

FIGURE 13. Normal position of organs compared to the position of organs impacted by corset pressure. Platen, "Weib als Gattungswesen," 195. Private collection.

choosing and treatment of their marriage partner. A good wife, he argued, should be gentle, devout, and tractable; everything else was of lesser importance. A young, loving wife should be like "soft wax in the hand of a real man"; she should be receptive, supple, and capable of cultivating herself. Men, he argued, should teach women the value of a healthy lifestyle—the importance of unrestrained breathing and regular excretions (because constipation was the cause of the bad moods of women), for example, and the hazards of the corset. If a prospective spouse disregarded such advice, Gerling maintained, the man should reconsider marriage to someone so intractable, superficial, arrogant, or strong-willed. Indeed, he advised men to leave such a woman without regret. The necessity for male dominance, according to Gerling, prohibited men from marrying for money, for "the man of a rich woman is ruined in his masculinity."

FIGURE 14. Normal female figure. Platen, "Weib als Gattungswesen," 196. Private collection.

Men who only achieved their social position through marriage were despicable; this course was not consistent with the self-made man's notion of autonomy.[24]

On the other hand, Gerling did not like the thought that women were only tractable because of their economic dependence on men. He condemned so-called marriages of convenience (*Versorgungsehen*) in which women married solely for economic security. Although middle-class men would have liked to have submissive and pliable wives, they wanted the submission to be a voluntary and internalized one. A wife's decision to accept the guidance of her husband should not follow from mundane, utilitarian concerns, for this would mean that the idealized bürgerliche private sphere of trust and intimacy would be threatened. Even a self-made man like Gerling, who as a paid endorser of health products and a successful writer was never at a loss when pursuing his own material interests, would have abhorred the thought that a woman had married him for his money. It is for precisely this reason that Gerling argued for the necessity of young women to receive improved educational and job opportunities—their decisions to marry could be based on devotion rather than economic necessity or calculation. But according to this plan, better professional opportu-

FIGURE 15. Female figure deformed by corset
use. Platen, "Weib als Gattungswesen," 197.
Private collection.

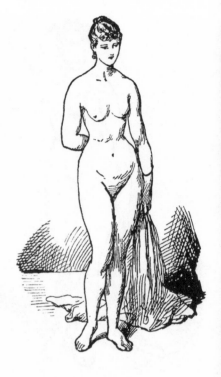

nities would lead to only temporary and transitional independence, which
would be happily abandoned for a beloved husband and the joys of motherhood.[25]

Although Platen and Gerling thought it was possible to reason with
women and convince them to abandon their errant ways and adopt a healthy
lifestyle, Ungewitter did not. Since female vanity and stupidity were not open to
the demands of reason, he argued, any female fashion would be likely to
threaten the health of offspring, unless a law could be passed that prohibited
tight corsets under penalty of whipping. Otherwise, women would continue to
follow the fashion dictates of American, English, and French "fashion monkeys." He ridiculed corset-wearing feminists who demanded political equality
and the right to vote, claiming that this would be against the natural course of
evolution, which relegated women to the home. Feminists were women without
men, and the feminist movement would inevitably destroy true femininity and
lead to the creation of "male women" *(Mannweibern)* and "female men" *(Weib-
männern).* The feminist activist Anita Augspurg, whom he saw speaking at a
meeting, was for him a "man in women's clothes! Two sexes in one person."[26]

Feminized men and masculinized women were of central concern for many

FIGURE 16. Platen's Health Corset (front). Platen, "Weib als Gattungswesen," 198. Private collection.

male health reformers and physicians, as is made clear in a popular health guide edited by F. König titled *Adviser for Healthy and Sick Days.*[27] This guide was written by regular doctors but heavily influenced by life reform concepts. It presented illustrations of ancient statues of Hercules and Apollo, with their muscular and broad shoulders and narrow hips, as ideals of masculinity. For women, the ideal was the Venus with broad hips and a well-rounded body. As did many of the other writers considered here, these authors regarded beauty—the infallible signs found in the figure and outward appearance of people—as an expression of health.[28]

One means to achieve beauty and health was exercise, the rigor of which had to be adapted to the constitution of individuals and to particular categories of people. According to König and his contributors, children should exercise moderately in order not to exhaust their bodies. This caution also applied to

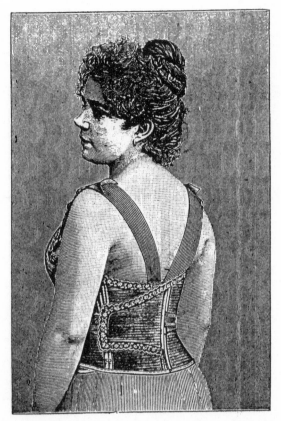

FIGURE 17. Platen's Health Corset (back). Platen, "Weib als Gattungswesen," 199. Private collection.

women, whom the authors considered to be big and wonderful children. Women should exercise only as much as necessary to gain the energy needed to conceive and bear children without danger. Exercise beyond that, the authors feared, would only lead to masculine, Herculean women.[29] They claimed that there was a beauty appropriate to each sex and that masculine-looking women were ugly. Two of the illustrations in the book depicted schematized figures in order to show prototypical beauty and ugliness in men and women (see figures 18 and 19).[30]

The prototypically ugly woman was depicted as masculinized, tall and muscular, with wide thorax and narrow hips, whereas the prototypically ugly man was shown as feminized, small and fat, with wide hips and narrow shoulders. The authors maintained that stereotypical ugliness was an unmistakable sign of disease.[31] They wrote: "Ugly is the sick and diseased human. In the same

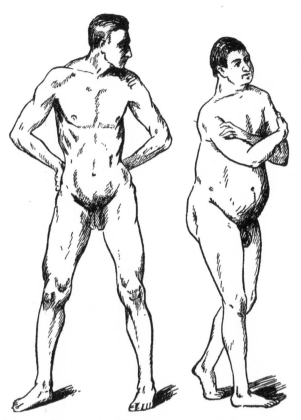

FIGURE 18. Schematic depiction of male beauty and ugliness. König, *Ratgeber,* 93. Private collection.

way in which beauty bears the stamp of a perfect harmony of all physical, mental, and spiritual functions, ugliness is the expression of all disharmony and of all physical, mental, and spiritual disturbances. Who could doubt that our comparative pictures . . . [show] that what we call beautiful and ugly can also be termed healthy and sick?"[32]

The authors hoped for a future in which science would enable the creation of beautiful people, but they claimed that the timeless standards of beauty could already be found in the art of Greek antiquity, because the old masters had known the "law of proportion" of the human body. According to the authors, the rediscovery of this law by the German professor Adolf Zeising made it possible to develop a scientific doctrine for the aesthetic judgment of figures.[33] Beauty was a function of the "golden proportion," defined as the division of a line such

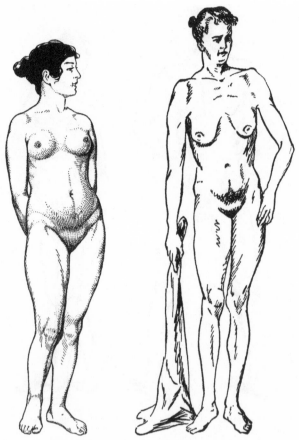

FIGURE 19. Schematic depiction of female beauty and ugliness. König, *Ratgeber*, 95. Private collection.

that the length of the shorter portion of the line relates to the longer portion in the same way that the longer portion relates to the line as a whole. In order to demonstrate the timeless validity of this aesthetic law, the authors applied it to drawings of classical male and female statues (see figures 20 and 21).[34] For them it was beyond doubt that the golden proportion was a representation of normal organic relations.[35] Note, however, that although the authors of König's health guide tried to apply the law of the golden proportion to what in their opinion were exceptionally beautiful male and female statues, they were unable to derive from this law the different standards for men (narrow hips and broad shoulders) and women (wide hips and narrow shoulders) that they had suggested earlier in their guide. Why were male proportions in women ugly and degenerate, when

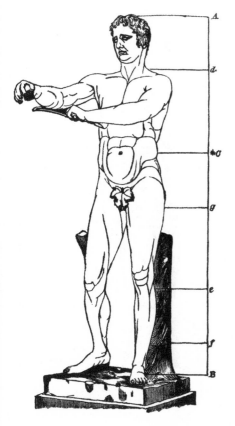

FIGURE 20. The golden proportion (male). The proportion of line AC to line CB is equal to the proportion of line CB to line AB (AC:CB = CB:AB). König, *Ratgeber*, 125. Private collection.

these same proportions represented timeless aesthetic norms for men? It seems that the authors based these gender differences on premises that they derived teleologically from the functions that they attributed to each sex: Women need to have wider hips than men because of their reproductive functions.

Other contemporary male physicians were inclined to regard physical beauty as an expression of a gender-specific telos as well. In a lecture to a southern German women's club, Hugo Sellheim, professor of obstetrics and gynecology at the University of Tübingen, argued that scientists tried to account for the charms of women in terms of women's purpose in life. Physicians were the perfect arbiters of beauty, because it was their understanding of health and disease that made them "knowledgeable in matters of beauty from a teleological point of view."[36] The aptitude of women for their natural calling was expressed in their well-developed breasts, broad hips, and erect posture. Men, Sellheim claimed, liked round and soft forms in women, their gentle, rocking ways of walking, and their childish voices.

FIGURE 21. The golden proportion (female). König, *Ratgeber*, 129. Private collection.

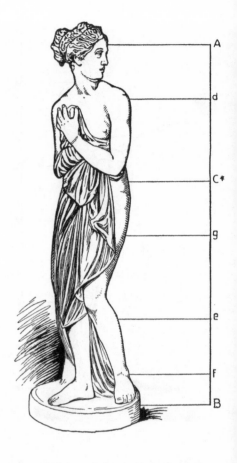

Sellheim was drawing on Ernst Haeckel's biogenetic law—that ontogenesis recapitulated phylogenetic development—in order to validate his claim that
women were inferior to men (see above).[37] Women's anatomy, in Sellheim's
view, was the result of arrested development; they were imperfect men still at the
developmental stage of children. Medical history certainly does not lack original, if at times far-fetched, examples of analogical reasoning, and Sellheim was
a master of such reasoning. Women's physical forms, he claimed, were expressions of their childlike functions. Like children, women had to grow. The only
difference was that women's growth consisted of transcending their own selves
during pregnancy. Women's beauty was thus the expression of women's ability to
create and nurture a new organism. Or as Sellheim put it: "Woman possesses
charms, man enjoys them, and the child benefits from them."[38]

Carl Heinrich Stratz, the foremost authority on Wilhelmine body aesthetics, also argued that women's beauty was an expression of their calling to motherhood. Women who transcended their traditional domestic role by accepting gainful employment would become masculinized, and this change would be evident in their external appearance. As an antidote, Stratz propagated a physiological and aesthetic dietetics for women that he called *Kallobiotik*, the doctrine that one should be beautiful and healthy, because to do so was a privilege of the "beautiful" sex.[39] According to Stratz, each human being had two lives: the life of the individual *(Einzelleben)* and the life of the race *(Gattungsleben)*. Men had a larger impact in their lives as individuals but played only a subordinate role in the Gattungsleben, whereas the individual lives of women were subordinate to their lives as propagators of the race. These differences were reflected in the anatomical structure of men's and women's bodies. Men were larger and heavier, with square body forms, stronger bones and muscles, more powerful lungs, and a greater number of red blood cells. Their skin was thicker, they had more body hair, their senses were sharper, and their active life force was stronger than that of women. Women, on the other hand, had soft skin, their body forms were well-rounded because of their fat layers, their breasts were more pronounced, and their pulse and breathing were faster than those of men. Women's active life force was weaker, although their forces of passive resistance were stronger. According to Stratz, the entire anatomical structure of men reflected the fact that their individual lives were more important than women's. Women's subordination to the Gattungsleben found its expression in their breasts, more pronounced abdomen, and wider hips.[40]

Stratz maintained, further, that the mental characteristics of the sexes corresponded to their different anatomical structures. Although men comprehended things more slowly than women, they comprehended objective facts more directly. Women, on the other hand, had a "quicker imagination," but they were not capable of distinguishing between subjective impressions and objective facts to the extent men were. Whereas men tried to achieve their goals in a straightforward way, women were easily sidetracked by their emotions and fantasies.[41]

Stratz, however, was not a political conservative but rather a liberal. When he contended that a man's soul would strive for activity and the "unfolding of power" in order to develop his individuality, he argued in the tradition of German liberalism.[42] Stratz even made the liberal-conservative dichotomy part of his complementarian dichotomy of sex characteristics. Since men were striving for individual fulfillment, man's nature was liberal, whereas women, whose lives were subordinate to the goal of propagating the race, were conservative. Men, he claimed, strove for freedom and progress; women were clinging to customs and would subordinate themselves selflessly to the demands of the race. Both groups of traits would supplement each other harmoniously, so that men and women ultimately contributed together to the higher development of the race.[43]

To Stratz's great dismay, it was difficult to find contemporary men and women who conformed physically and psychologically to the male and female ideals that he proposed. There were too many feminine men and masculine women whose existence concealed the true nature of real men and the true value of genuine women. Stratz did not reject regular employment for all women because not all women could find a husband. He even lauded the ambitions of young girls to become independent since this would give them a second option in case they could not marry. But as a rule, he claimed, long-term employment of women would harm their appearance. Their body forms would become square, their facial expressions sharp and severe, and their figure and movements masculinized. In short, the tender aura of femininity would vanish.[44] Such statements echoed the pronouncements of other contemporary physicians. The psychiatrist Albert Moll, for example, maintained that women who were inclined toward male occupations exhibited masculine movements and body forms.[45] Stratz thus expressed concerns about the blurring of traditional gender distinctions in the aesthetic idiom of the period. Deviance from behavioral norms had its expression in a deviation from aesthetic norms. Stratz implied that women could only hope to approach the ideal of perfect beauty if they complied with the traditional gender norms of the Bürgertum, which relegated women to motherhood and a place in the home. For Stratz, female beauty was thus an expression of women's essence as reproductive creatures, and the end of women's reproductive life coincided with a loss of their beauty as well as a masculinization of their body and soul. Therefore, women, Stratz claimed, would become less emotional and more rational and their body forms and facial traits would lose their roundness and became sharper after the onset of menopause.[46]

Feminist Life Reform and Women's Health and Beauty

Feminist life reformers did not dispute the degeneracy of contemporary women. They considered fashion an important factor for the deplorable constitutional weakness of women. However, many of them blamed men more than women for excesses such as the corset that led to the deterioration of women's health. Like their misogynist counterparts among regular physicians and life reformers, feminists used hygienic arguments to defend their position in contemporary gender politics. Klara Ebert, a committed feminist, was a frequent contributor to the *Vegetarische Warte (Vegetarian Observer)*, the official journal of the Deutscher Vegetarierbund (German Vegetarian League). Like Ungewitter, Ebert argued that the women's fashions of her time were unhealthy, immoral, and ugly; they were created by prostitutes who wanted to please men. Ebert denounced the corset because it contributed to the subjugation of females by stressing the sexual characteristics of women and stamping them predominantly as sexual creatures.[47]

Whereas people such as Ungewitter and Stratz tried to define women as procreative creatures who ought to subordinate all other concerns to their destiny of motherhood, Ebert demanded that women be taken seriously as "whole people" *(ganze Menschen)* and not only as sexual creatures. She maintained that the differences between men and women were only physical: if women had better occupational and educational opportunities, they would not have to prostitute themselves on the marriage market in order to find a male provider.[48] Ebert took her feminist commitment very seriously. In 1904 and 1905 she tried to organize a woman's group within the German Vegetarian League, an attempt that was doomed to failure because of the harsh opposition it met from male and female vegetarians who accused her of disturbing marital harmony by pitting men against women. Ebert's opponents argued that men and women were to be comrades with distinct but complementary marital duties as fathers and mothers and that this complementarity was threatened by power-hungry and emancipated women such as Ebert, who would contribute to the degeneration of contemporary women.[49]

Ebert had cloaked her suggestion of creating a vegetarian women's group in defensive language that stressed the need for male-female complementarity. The goal of the women's group, she claimed, was to liberate women from the "grave of the mind-numbing atmosphere" in which they were living. She argued that the vegetarian movement needed women who were personalities and not women who were just following the herd instinct. Men needed such women as comrades, administrators of their households, and mothers who would raise their children as happy, healthy, and free human beings. Ebert argued that vegetarian women had three kinds of fundamental duties. First came the duties concerning their own family. Then followed the duties concerning human society. Then came women's duties to themselves. In her view, contemporary women had a skewed conception of their familial duties, because they tried to fulfill their obligation to their husbands in "slave-like abnegation," thus neglecting the duties they had to society and to themselves.

Since women had to bear and raise children, they also had to care for themselves—"keep their body beautiful and healthy" and "elevate their spirit and cultivate everything that was beautiful, as well as the arts and the sciences." Women's care for their own bodies and minds was also necessitated by racial hygienic reasons, since, as Ebert believed, acquired characteristics would be passed on to one's offspring. Indeed, Ebert shared Nietzsche's view that society had to be saved from the "too many" *(den Vielzuvielen)* in order to create a human elite. She defended her feminist agenda by drawing on a widely shared contemporary eugenic discourse: Only independent and enlightened women who could take care of their own bodies would be able to produce healthy children and prevent degeneracy in their offspring. Ebert favored selective breeding and health reform as a means to lift up the human race.[50] Despite her appeal to hygienic values in her argument for feminist goals, antifeminist sentiment within the vegetarian movement, along with the low percentages of women in the vegetarian voluntary associations, prevented her success.[51]

While Klara Ebert acknowledged physical differences between men and women, Anna Fischer-Dückelmann maintained that even these differences were negligible. Fischer-Dückelmann was one of the first German women to obtain a medical degree, earned at the University of Zurich in the 1890s, when women were still barred from regular enrollment in German universities and medical schools.[52] Her feminist position followed in part from her outsider status as a female physician at a time when women's physical fitness for medical practice was questioned widely by male members of the profession.[53] In her extraordinarily successful book *The Woman as Home Physician* she conceded that women naturally had lighter and weaker bones than men. She maintained, however, that women had smaller and weaker muscles than men merely because of lack of exercise.[54] She refuted the theory of sex differences based on Ernst Haeckel's biogenetic law. In contrast to physicians such as Hugo Sellheim who accepted Haeckel's work, she claimed that men and women were two separate and perfect types, both clearly distinct from children. This way of thinking about the sexes could not and would not accommodate the notion of a higher and a subordinate sex.[55]

Fischer-Dückelmann argued that it was fashion which weakened women and that pressing them into confining shoes and corsets gave them a clumsy appearance when they tried to move.[56] Like Ebert, she deplored the way fashion emphasized the sexual character of women by creating an unnaturally narrow waist and thus directing attention to the breasts and the hips. Contemporary fashion was incompatible with the consciousness of the independent woman she imagined, because if women continued to stress their sexual characteristics, men would continue to value women only for their bodies and would ignore their spiritual and mental worth.[57]

Some of the activists within the German feminist movement after 1900 sought to enable women to choose their partners for reasons of sentiment rather than utility. Women such as Helene Stöcker called for a "new morality" that made personal fulfillment the criterion for the choice of a sexual partner.[58] Although the most outspoken proponents of the new morality constituted a minority of the feminist movement, they were very vocal, and they were not as isolated as they might appear at first glance. Anna Fischer-Dückelmann supported their call for marriage reform and the creation of new moral laws by women in order to make women more independent. She wanted economic independence for women so that they could choose their husbands according to their own desires, and she advocated easy divorce in cases where the emotional basis for a marriage was eroded.[59]

Whereas men's obsession with women's physical beauty can be interpreted as an expression of their concerns about changing gender roles, Fischer-Dückelmann recommended to the readers of her best-selling book the same aesthetic norms as much of the regular medical literature. In contrast to many physicians, however, she advised the same rigorous exercise for men and women. She did not fear that such exercise would lead to a masculinization of women but rather believed that it was a precondition for health and good constitution, which were in turn preconditions for a beautiful body. Diseases, on the other hand, were the result of a weakened constitution that became manifest in deviations from the timeless aesthetic norms of Greek antiquity.[60] One can see these norms at work in the following, in which she points to pictures comparing three women representing pathological fatness, pathological thinness, and the perfect ideal of healthy beauty (see figure 22).[61]

> Table No. 3 shows us a Medicaean Venus with her marvelous body forms
> and the grace of her limbs. All healthy and really beautiful women of our time
> should look similar. But where do we find women like that? We have inherited
> from our ancestors small bodies and disproportional limbs, crippled feet, short-
> sighted eyes, rounded backs, flat breasts, etc. and in addition to that there are
> the deformities which we acquire through an incorrect lifestyle. Where does
> this lead? Just look at the two deformed figures to the right and left of the
> Venus: pathological emaciation on the one side, pathological fatness on the
> other side. Deficient hair growth, sagging breasts, ugliness and deformities in
> repulsive form. Only clothes hide such figures, and only because we are not used
> to nudity, we are shocked and prone to regard such pictures as exaggerations.
> But the glance of the doctor, which penetrates the hypocritical, deceiving
> clothing covers, knows how infinitely often they can be found among the
> degenerate womanhood of today.

Feminists and antifeminists alike regarded the beautiful female body as an icon representing their own moral values, and both cast these values in hygienic

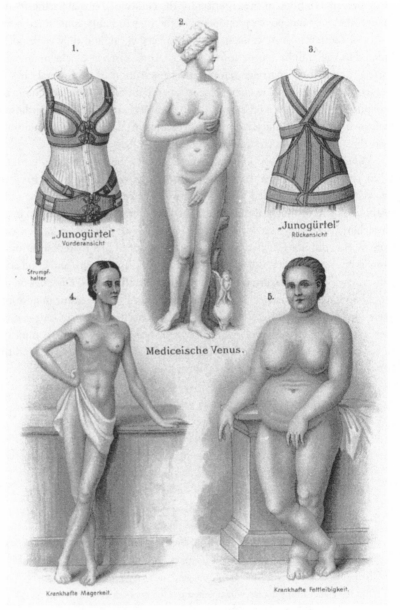

FIGURE 22. Perfect ideal, pathological thinness, and pathological fatness. Fischer-Dückelmann, *Frau als Hausärztin*, table 3. Private collection.

terms. Antifeminists saw feminine beauty as the mark of a woman who accepted her subordinate role and eventually willingly accepted a domestic role. Although writers such as Reinhold Gerling and Carl Heinrich Stratz were not categorically opposed to professional opportunities for young, not-yet-married women or women who could not find a husband, they were concerned that these opportunities might conflict with the true calling of women: domesticity and motherhood. Feminists such as Anna Fischer-Dückelmann, on the other hand, contended that health and feminine beauty were expressions of a fully developed female personality that had overcome the social obstacles to women's self-fulfillment and asserted its social and economic independence. Yet she and her adversaries were drawing on the same symbolic, neohumanistic universe: the aesthetic ideals of physical beauty from antiquity.

Hygienic Culture as a Contested Terrain: Contemporary Attitudes Toward Men's and Women's Sexuality

The fact that antifeminist and feminist life reformers both employed hygienic norms to defend their gender politics becomes further evident when one examines contemporary attitudes toward men's and women's sexuality. In their book *Sex Life and Its Aberrations*, the natural therapists Franz Schönenberger and Wilhelm Siegert revealed their ambivalence toward sexuality. They claimed that since secrecy in sexual matters only unduly incited fantasy and awakened lust, a view of sex as perfectly natural and normal would prevent immorality.[62] Siegert and Schönenberger considered both male and female sensuality and passion problematic. A husband's lust endangered his wife's reproductive health because men tended to engage in extramarital relations or visit prostitutes, thus contracting and spreading venereal disease. According to the authors, this lack of male self-control—often aggravated by alcohol consumption—led to the destruction of families via the infection of innocent wives and children and threatened the health of the entire nation.[63] As Allan M. Brandt has remarked with regard to the American context, such concerns were not necessarily a sign of incipient male feminism. Rather, they might be seen as yet another means of defining seperate spheres of gender identity. In discussions of the impact of venereal disease on families, health reformers such as Schönenberger and Siegert endorsed a traditional view of the nature and role of women. Their attacks on the immorality of men were based on a view of women as innocent, weak, and helpless.[64]

Fischer-Dückelmann also denounced male infidelity and promiscuity; for her, men who visited prostitutes were morally inferior.[65] Some feminists went even further and attacked the privacy of the physician-patient relationship because it allowed men to conceal their venereal infections from their wives. They endorsed legal penalties for those who spread venereal diseases knowingly. The physician Agnes Bluhm and the League for the Protection of Mothers demanded health certificates for all prospective married couples.[66]

The widespread fear of venereal disease certainly fueled the Wilhelmine obsession with personal health, but one should not always take contemporary statements about the omnipresent dangers of venereal diseases at face value.[67] The assignment of responsibility for the spread of venereal disease evoked powerful emotions that were harnessed by opposing parties in the gender politics of the time. Feminists campaigning against state regulation of prostitution denounced the moral double standard that was implicit in such regulation. Although in many cities prostitutes were required to register and undergo health examinations, men who visited prostitutes were not subject to such stigmatizing procedures. Women such as Anna Pappritz, who campaigned for the abolition of the regulation of prostitution, denounced promiscuous men as the main cause of the spread of venereal disease, not only among their innocent wives and children but also among prostitutes.[68] The threat of venereal disease was of course real, but so were the political uses that feminists and antifeminists made of this threat. Some feminists, for example, argued that better professional opportunities would allow women to choose their marriage partners wisely and avoid unwholesome marriages with irresponsible men.[69]

For many women, the debate about prostitution and venereal disease highlighted the lack of self-restraint and the sexual promiscuity of middle-class men. For many men, controversies about contraception brought to the fore issues concerning woman's sexuality. The existence of a growing market for contraceptives from the late nineteenth century onward raised the specter of uncontrolled female sexuality, because their use seemed to make it possible to separate sensuality from reproduction.[70] Siegert and Schönenberger, for example, were very uncomfortable with the sexual desires of women, which is why they denounced the use of contraceptives.[71] Although they considered pronounced sexual desire to be normal, if problematic, in men, they insisted that it was abnormal in women and that women who exhibited such desire had to be restrained by their husbands.[72] In this respect, their views were similar to those of many regular physicians.[73]

It is of course true that opposition to contraception cannot be simply considered antifeminist, since feminists felt ambivalent about the use of contraceptives as well. Fischer-Dückelmann, for example, was reluctant to endorse their use, even though she saw them as a necessity to limit family size. In her view, women weakened by too many births could only produce sickly and weak children. Therefore contraception had eugenic benefits, because having fewer children of a higher quality was preferable to having many that could not be properly raised and educated for lack of money.[74] Fischer-Dückelmann was worried, however, that contraceptives would make women more vulnerable to the sexual demands of their morally inferior husbands, who could more frequently demand intercourse.[75] Moderate feminists such as Anna Pappritz rejected radical feminist calls for better access to contraceptives, because such demands seemed to undermine the assumption of pre-war feminism that women were morally superior to men.[76]

In the case of many men, the hysterical condemnation of contraceptives was due to concerns that women could experience the sensual side of their sexuality without fear of unwanted consequences. Robby Koßmann therefore warned that frequent sexual intercourse with contraceptives was hazardous to the health of women. He argued that intercourse would lead to an increased supply of blood to the sexual organs of women that would only be reduced to normal levels in the course of pregnancy, birth, and breastfeeding. Such increased blood levels, he insisted, could lead to various diseases and health problems, which were punishment for the deviation from the path of nature.[77]

Many life reformers and regular physicians agreed that sexuality should remain tied to reproduction. In a popular sex advice book, the Munich hygiene professor Max von Gruber, an ardent eugenicist, argued that "untouched" women of good quality were much more interested in having children than in being sexually fulfilled. These women, he claimed, would be the best mothers and housewives. He considered contraceptives to be a threat to women's morality because they offered sexual pleasure without consequences. But in contrast to Siegert, Schönenberger, and Koßmann, von Gruber did not condemn contraceptives altogether because he believed that too-frequent pregnancies would lead to sickly and weak children.[78]

Reinhold Gerling, the editor of *Naturarzt*, initially condemned contraceptives in the strongest possible terms, warning women that contraception and lascivious sexual practices would weaken the female constitution and lead to depression, which would in turn hasten the aging process and physical decay of the face.[79] Gerling revised his position only a few years later, however, and, like Gruber, argued for contraception in order to ensure the production of quality children. To have two or three strong, healthy, and beautiful children was in his view better than to have five or six weak children who were predisposed to diseases.[80] But he left no doubt that he remained an opponent of contraception in principle, and he demanded that in cases where there were no economic or hygienic reasons for use of contraceptives the husband "provide for the repeated motherhood of his wife for her own and her husband's happiness."[81]

Men's concerns about unchained female lust were rather widespread during the period, as suggested by the resonance of Otto Weininger's book *Sex and Character*.[82] Concern about women's unleashed sexuality was also reflected in the way Siegert and Schönenberger depicted the awakening of sexual desire in young girls. They maintained that sexual desire is less pronounced in young girls than in young boys, but this is only the case as long as they are innocent: "The first lapse—and wild lust is unleashed."[83] It seems that Siegert and Schönenberger denied the very existence of what they feared: female desires that could be the basis for the independent articulation of female sexual interests. Furthermore, if women were capable of experiencing lust, whose fault was it if they did not? Accepting that women had sexual desires of their own ultimately meant the extension of the performance principle to the realm of sexuality. This was difficult to accept for male life reformers who already felt insecure about their ability to perform and achieve success in other areas of their lives.

The root of this masculine uneasiness was recognized by Johanna Elberskirchen, who argued against the notion propagated by some contemporary physicians that the female sex drive was less pronounced than the male sex drive. Writing in Koßmann's and Weiß's compendium, she refuted what she considered the confusion of men who equated the strength of the sex drive with the frequency of sexual intercourse. Women, she maintained, were selective in their choice of partners—in fact, cultivation and a deep spiritual life would make them more selective still. Then they could only be aroused by a narrow circle of men; other men were incapable of drawing out their sexual interest or, worse, were only regarded with repulsion and disgust. In other words, the notion of women's less developed sex drive was popular among men because it explained rejection in terms of innate nature rather than women's active choice. Once women were in love, Elberskirchen claimed, their sexual desire would be so strong that all social barriers would be torn down. They would long for sexual intercourse, whether married or not, and with the "entering of the male member into the vagina . . . the mere touch is already experienced as the deepest lust."[84]

Many men undoubtedly had reservations about the separation of the hedonistic aspect of sexuality from reproduction, at least as it concerned women. As customers of prostitutes, many middle-class men may have accepted such a separation as a matter of course for themselves, while preferring that their wives be simply reproductive. There were challenges to such attitudes, however, not only from feminists but also from members of the regular medical profession, who argued that the hedonistic side of sexuality was valuable in itself and an important aspect of self-expression and self-fulfillment for both sexes. One of these physicians was Iwan Bloch, a leading activist in the Society for the Fight

Against Venereal Disease. In his book *The Sexual Life of Our Time,* Bloch attempted to give a description of important trends in modern sexual behavior. Despite its rather bland appearance and lack of illustrations, the book went through nine editions within three years of its publication in 1906, totaling about 60,000 copies. It was one of the few books written by a regular physician that became a contemporary best-seller.[85]

Mixing description with prescription, Bloch proposed a new sexual ethics in which sexual desire and self-expression were no longer yoked to reproduction. He argued that love promoted the inner growth of individuals. As a monist Bloch believed that the physical side of humans could not be separated from their spiritual side. Therefore love between human beings could not be merely platonic. It needed a physical basis.[86] Bloch maintained that men and women experienced sexual lust differently: men's lust was anatomically centered in a "sexual arrow," and women were sexual from the "knees to the throat." Since their sexual feelings were not concentrated in a single point, it was more difficult to arouse women. In Bloch's view this did not mean that women were less sensual or sexual than men. Indeed, in most cases, female frigidity was feigned. Behind a veil of conventional morality, one could very often find a glowing sexuality. Or if women had difficulties in experiencing lust, that simply meant that the men they were with were incapable of triggering the complicated sexual sensibilities of women.[87]

Apparently, the extension of the performance principle into the realm of sexuality was not as threatening to Bloch as it was to many life reformers and some of his own medical colleagues. Like some contemporary feminists, Bloch argued for free love as the ideal of a life-long voluntary commitment between a man and a woman.[88] This commitment was in no need of legal or moral sanction in either a civil or a church marriage. Free love, Bloch argued, was different from what was called *Verhältnisse*—relatively short-term relationships between men and women mainly for sexual gratification.[89] According to the contemporary cliché, these were mostly asymmetric power relationships involving working girls in the big city who foolishly fell in love with middle- and upper-class men. Siegert and Schönenberger argued that such relationships were the first step toward lifelong prostitution because pregnant girls who had fallen victim to irresponsible seducers would be ostracized by judgmental people. In Siegert and Schönenberger's view, middle- and upper-class men lured naive girls into sexual relationships with the promise of marriage and destroyed the girls' reputation, thereby pushing them into prostitution. The authors depicted the lower-middle-class and working-class girls who entered such relationships as passive victims of their social superiors, with no agency or desires of their own.

They claimed that men were always the seducers of pure, untouched women; only women who had already been led astray tried to take revenge for their previous seduction by tempting men.[90]

The regular physician and cultural critic Willy Hellpach did not condemn such relationships outright. While feminists such as Helene Stöcker tried to defend the premarital sexual relationships of young women in terms of women's right to sexual fulfillment, Hellpach tried to foster an understanding of such behavior from the perspective of young men. He argued that the Verhältnis was the consequence of changing career patterns among middle-class males, who now had to postpone marriage until they were in their thirties and who therefore had to resort to extramarital relationships in order to fulfill their sexual desires. According to Hellpach, this led to a democratization of the aristocratic practice of keeping mistresses: University students who did not have the means to marry could still afford to take shop clerks and waitresses to concerts and dinners. In Hellpach's view, many of these women would find a marriage partner in this way, even though for some such relationships were simply a way station to prostitution.[91]

Bloch took a similar view of such relationships. Although he condemned them because the boundaries between wild love and prostitution were not always clear, he claimed that some of these liaisons had the potential to develop into a life-long commitment of free love. He even praised the sexual behavior of the working class as a model for the middle classes, because the working classes had already developed "noble forms of free love" among themselves. However, he condemned the promiscuity entailed by these new forms of sexual relationships as one of the main sources of venereal disease. He supported the fight against the *Verhältniswesen* because sexual gratification was more important than love in most of these short-term relationships.[92]

Did such worries about Verhältnisse reflect a fundamental change in the sexual behavior of middle-class youth? It is hard to say. Concern with sexual immorality was certainly nothing new for cultural critics from the Bürgertum, even though the moral purity movement seems to have gathered steam at the turn of the century. Unless they had firsthand knowledge, physicians and life reformers could only have diffuse suspicions about the nature of such relationships. Nevertheless, contemporary concerns can be taken as indicators of a more profound change in the ways younger people of both sexes interacted. In the case of Britain, the historian Judith Walkowitz has described how women increasingly transcended their homosocial sphere and appeared unaccompanied in public spaces such as the shopping districts of the big cities.[93] What people in Britain and in Germany were concerned about was the erosion of separate spheres for the sexes among the middle classes, a development that smacked of sexual immorality. The historian does not have to believe Willy Hellpach's claim that it was increasingly socially acceptable for unmarried middle-class women not to account for their sexual past when they married. But we can try to understand the indicators that made such a claim plausible for him: the decline of parental supervision of young women from the Bürgertum who earlier had been guarded jealously until they were married; the urban amusements that gave youth of both sexes spaces to meet; the increased participation of middle-class women in the labor force and in sports—these developments were all cited by Hellpach as evidence for a fundamental change in gender relations.[94] The anxiety-loaded image of the New Woman of the Weimar era, notorious for transcending traditional gender boundaries, was therefore already alive in the pre-war era.

This chapter has shown that life reformers were not necessarily more progressive in their attitudes toward changing gender relations than their counterparts in regular medicine. Antifeminists in both camps employed hygienic and aesthetic arguments to denounce female employment outside the home, the use of contraceptives, and the declining birthrate among middle-class women. Feminist life reformers also resorted to hygienic arguments, however, when they demanded better professional opportunities and more rights for women. In their view, it was women's dependence on men that was responsible for the degeneracy and lack of beauty of contemporary women. Debates about sexuality and appropriate gender roles for women were not limited to the sexual advice literature of the period. Such concerns were also constitutive for much of contemporary racial discourse. As chapter 4 demonstrates, notions of racial beauty did derive their meanings to some extent from Wilhelmine assumptions concerning gender and social class.

CHAPTER 4

RACIAL AESTHETICS

*A*s we have seen, gender differences were cast in an aesthetic idiom in contemporary popular hygienic literature. This chapter shows that racial differences were as well. Physicians and life reformers frequently claimed that exceptional beauty was a sign of racial superiority. Only members of the white race, they argued, could come close to the ideals of beauty of the ancient Greeks and develop the aesthetic sensibilities necessary for the creation of great works of art. Members of "lower races" could not compete with the superior beauty of the white ideal. Therefore they held different ideals of beauty, and their art reflected these aesthetic "deficits."

One example of an aesthetic construction of racial differences can be seen in König's health advice guide. Its contributors maintained that each race had its own ideal of beauty but that the beauty of whites represented an objective standard. Although there was a beauty of the sex, of the age, of the race, of the family, and of the individual, the only truly objective standard of beauty was literally embodied in the proportions of the loveliest members of the white race. According to König et al., even nonwhites had to acknowledge the greater beauty of whites. Each Negro, they claimed, would find his black female companion, with her thick lips, very attractive. But if he could choose between a beautiful white woman and a beautiful black woman, he would inevitably choose the former, because only the white woman approached the superior Aryan ideal of beauty embodied in the art of Greek antiquity.[1]

This chapter does not aim to provide an intellectual history of aesthetic racial theories at the turn of the century.[2] Nor does it examine racial theories as part of a generalized vocabulary of difference, which according to Sander Gilman was an element of Western cultural representations of Jews and blacks for at least the past two and a half centuries.[3] Although it is important to elucidate the intellectual roots of discourses about race, one also needs to look at the social and cultural dynamics that nurtured and sustained such discourses in any given period, something that has been neglected in the historiography so far. I argue that contemporary debates about aesthetics, gender, and class shaped Wilhelmine notions of race.

My goal is to demonstrate the intersection of contemporary meanings of race, class, and gender by examining the aesthetic aspects of racial discourse in turn-of-the-century popular hygienic debates.[4] I focus mainly on the work of the physician and anthropologist Carl Heinrich Stratz, the most important racial aesthete of the period. Along with some of the Gebildeten among life reformers, Stratz assumed that beauty was constituted by sexual disinterestedness. According to Stratz, only women of the most highly developed race—the Nordic race—could be truly beautiful, because they did not arouse mundane sexual interest as women from other races did. I also try to show that turn-of-the-century racial discourse was tied to assumptions about social class. Stratz and others thought that class differences within European and non-European societies could be explained by variations in the racial make-up of the classes. First, though, I offer a few words to situate Stratz's work in the context of contemporary discussions about race.

Turn-of-the-Century Debates About Race and Aesthetics

Aesthetic concepts of race were nothing new at the turn of the century. The eighteenth-century anthropologist Johann Friedrich Blumenbach, a major figure among the German intelligentsia of his time, had already used aesthetic concepts as a basis for his racial taxonomies. Blumenbach's theory of racial differences presented the bodies of non-Europeans as deviations from classical European norms of beauty represented in the art of Greek antiquity. The physician Carl Gustav Carus, mentioned in chapter 2, had also maintained that the racial inferiority of non-European peoples was reflected in their outward appearance, which deviated from the aesthetic norms of classical antiquity.[5] And the zoologist and Darwin popularizer Ernst Haeckel also espoused hierarchical concepts of racial differences.

However, the most respected late nineteenth-century German physical anthropologists were rather critical of such concepts. Rudolf Virchow and Jo-hannes Ranke, for example, represented a liberal-democratic tradition that was comparatively skeptical of racial classifications and ideologies.[6] Ranke, who accepted the notion that there was an aesthetic ideal for the human body, maintained that it would be possible to construct an aesthetic ideal for different races. But this did not mean that the European ideal was the most beautiful one. Only the melting together of all racial ideals would make it possible to establish an aesthetic ideal for all of mankind. Ranke claimed that variations in physical appearance within human races were much more important than differences between different races, and, supported by anthropological evidence, he maintained that there was no scientific proof that some human races were more highly developed than others.[7]

At the turn of the century, aesthetic concepts of race regained credence in part because of the crisis of the anthropometric tradition in physical anthropology. Anthropologists who tried to arrive at racial classifications by means of measurements of physical characteristics could not agree about which measurements really signified essential racial differences. For a long time the cephalic index, the width of the skull expressed as a percentage of its length, seemed to be the key to racial classifications, but there were no conclusive results.[8] In 1890, the absurdity of the anthropometric tradition became fully apparent when the Hungarian anthropologist Aurel von Törek made 5,371 measurements of a single skull, calculating 178 indices and more than 2,500 angles, triangles, and polygons.[9] Popularizers of racial discourse such as Stratz therefore formulated a racial aesthetic based not on quantitative precision but on intuition. According to Stratz, perfect beauty was the expression of an individual's racial constitution. Racial differences, therefore, became manifest in aesthetic differences between races. Since, in his view, reliable aesthetic judgment was ultimately based on the intuition of people with Bildung, he justified his racial classifications by referring to his intuition. This made it possible for him to evade the problems of anthropometric measurements, which by this time served to confirm intuitive perception (see also chapter 2).

Note, however, that the racialism propagated by people such as Stratz was different from the radical strands of anti-Semitism propagated by people such as Ludwig Schemann (the popularizer of Gobineau's racial theories in Germany and a man of whom Stratz thought very little) or by the radical anti-Semites organized in Theodor Fritsch's "Hammer" movement or similar groups propagating *völkisch*, or ethnic, racism.[10] One of these sects was the League of the Faithful for Rising Life *(Treubund für aufsteigendes Leben)*, a small völkisch nude culture group founded by Richard Ungewitter, a committed antifeminist and radical anti-Semite.[11] In his view, a beautiful body was a sign of a healthy racial constitution. Hence he favored a program of eugenics and racial purification based on aesthetic criteria. According to Ungewitter, nude culture would prevent the mixture of the Germanic race with alien races, since women who were exposed to the nude bodies of racially valuable Germanic males like himself would not be tempted by males from *Fremdrassen*.[12]

Stratz was also different from Houston Stuart Chamberlain, who saw the Teutons as the embodiment of cultural creativity, engaged in a racial struggle for existence with Judaism. To some extent, however, Stratz and Chamberlain held similar aesthetic assumptions. Chamberlain, son-in-law and ardent admirer of Richard Wagner, saw art as a higher source of knowledge that provided privileged access to universal truths. In his *Foundations of the Nineteenth Century* (1899) Chamberlain rejected the anthropometric tradition of German anthropology in favor of an artistic, intuitive perception of racial essences (which influenced the intuitive racism of Hans F. K. Günther more than two decades later).[13]

To be sure, Stratz shared some of the assumptions underlying the everyday anti-Semitism of his educated peers. He accepted popular, pathological, and aesthetic stereotypes about Jews. It is important to keep in mind, however, that such negative stereotypes were also shared by some Jews. Writing in 1897, Walter Rathenau, the future foreign minister of the Weimar Republic, deplored the physical deformities of the Jewish male, exhibited in his "soft weakness of form," which was an expression of his femininity. Rathenau saw this as the biological result of oppression that had to be overcome.[14] Max Nordau, the physician who in 1890 had popularized the concept of degeneracy in Germany by applying it to the negative social and cultural consequences of modernization, deplored the degeneracy of contemporary Jews as well. Nordau, who was active in the Zionist movement, called for the creation of deep-chested, powerful, and keen-eyed men, a new type of Jew that would end the decadence among Jews. Not unlike many non-Jewish life reformers, Nordau saw body discipline as a means to reverse the process of degeneracy of modern mankind and therefore called on Jews to become "muscle Jews." By strengthening their bodies, Jews would not only be able to overcome their physical weakness but would also strengthen their minds and contribute to the Zionist cause.[15]

Stratz himself was so troubled by radical anti-Semitism that he wrote a small brochure in order to refute what he regarded as its most absurd charges.[16] Contemporary European anti-Semites, Stratz claimed, depicted Jews in general as a despised people of Semitic race and mosaic beliefs, characterized by multiple infirmities such as round backs, crooked legs, and flat feet.[17] In Stratz's view, this perception was wrong. He credited Jews with laying the foundation of Western civilization and sharing Caucasian and Aryan roots with the Romanic and the Nordic races.[18] He argued that centuries of inbreeding had made European Jews defective in ways North African Jews or Europeans in general were not—besides physical deformities, they suffered disproportionally from gout, diabetes, and rheumatism. However, he maintained, one often sees sick and ugly Jews but one rather rarely sees stupid ones. Stratz tried to give negative stereotypes about Jews a positive valuation: The intelligence as well as the infirmities were the results of the Jewish struggle for survival, and Jews could contribute to the future of European culture and civilization.[19]

The fact that Stratz was not an anti-Semite (by contemporary standards) may be one of the reasons his work has almost been forgotten. It does not fit very well into accounts of racial theories that try to reconstruct the intellectual roots of anti-Semitism and Nazism. Still, it serves as an excellent example of the intersection of the discursive universes of life reformers and regular physicians, since he was accepted by both groups as an expert on body aesthetics and race. Further, Stratz was one of the most important popularizers of racial theories of the period. His books were published by the respected Ferdinand Enke company, one of the leading publishers of medical literature, and they were widely reviewed in contemporary newspapers and journals,[20] including the *Papers for People's Hygiene (Blätter für Volksgesundheitspflege)*, a popular health advice journal edited by regular physicians that sought to undercut the popularity of life reform, and the life reform journals *Die Schönheit* and *Kraft und Schönheit.* [21]

Stratz's Racial Aesthetic

Stratz served from 1887 to 1892 as a sanitary officer in the Dutch army in Indonesia, and although it is not clear how his attitudes concerning non-European women and female sexuality were shaped by his colonial experience,[22] living and traveling abroad allowed him to establish himself as an expert on the bodies of exotic women. (Indeed, his first major book was about Javanese women.)[23] As can be seen best in his turn-of-the-century work *The Racial Beauty of Woman* (a work that saw nine editions between its first appearance in 1901 and World War I), Stratz used aesthetic concepts of race and nationality to communicate his ideas about normal and healthy gender relations.

In Stratz's view, the physical characteristics of humans should only be judged holistically. The judgment of harmonious organic interconnections was in the final instance Stratz's aesthetic judgment backed up by empirical measurements made according to Fritsch's canon (see chapter 2). Stratz defined race for a given group in constitutional terms as "hereditary common properties of a specific inherited physical and spiritual habitus"; these properties distinguished one group from others with different hereditary characteristics.[24] This definition stemmed from the work of the Freiburg ethnologist and art collector Ernst Grosse, who urged research on the racial basis of cultural achievements.[25]

Stratz distinguished among three basic types of races: (1) the protomorphical races that comprised the old passive races represented by primitive peoples *(Naturvölker)*, (2) the archimorphical races, which were "the ruling, active races" represented by the civilized people *(Kulturvölker)*, and (3) metamorphical races, which had emerged from a mixture of the archimorphical races. He divided the archimorphical races further into three branches: the Mongols, or the yellow race, the so-called middle land people *(Mittelländer)*, or the white race, and the black race *(Nigritier)*. The future would belong to the tribes of these archimorphical main races, who were the bearers of modern culture and who would fight among each other for domination of the world.[26] Since Stratz thought that the white race would ultimately prevail in this struggle, he expressed confidence in the progress of European civilization—a confidence also evident in turn-of-the-century exhibitions of exotic peoples. *Völkerschauen* emphasized the distance between modern German culture and that of German colonial subjects, thereby affirming the national strength of the *Kulturnation* and presenting Germany as a contender among other imperialistic industrial nations.[27] Stratz's work was thus characteristic of a period in which confidence in the progress of the imperialistic German nation-state was coupled with cultural pessimism.

According to Stratz, the white race was the most capable and had the most perfect and beautiful individuals. Women of other races, he claimed, could still be considered beautiful and represent an ideal of racial beauty, but only if their appearance did not interfere too much with the aesthetic concept of beauty embodied in the most beautiful members of the white race. His racial typology was tied to a social Darwinist teleology that saw in the struggle for survival between different races the mechanism for the emergence of physical beauty. Although he deplored the brutality of such a struggle, he considered this brutality justified for aesthetic reasons: "Even if we see with horror how men fight each other in the solemn struggle for survival, it is a joyful feeling to recognize that from death and extermination the heavenly beauty of the human race rises to an ever newer and better shape *[Gestaltung]*."[28]

In his work, Stratz combined an evolutionary framework with a platonic morphology of ideal types. This distinguished him from nineteenth-century phylogenetic morphologists (such as the zoologist Ernst Haeckel and the comparative anatomist Carl Gegenbaur) who, relying on Darwinian concepts, tried to account for morphological characteristics of humans or animals by describing them as a result of evolution by natural selection.[29] These scientists did not resort to teleological explanations of organic forms, as did the German idealist

morphologists of the early twentieth century (see chapter 7). Stratz can be regarded both intellectually and temporally as a link between late nineteenth-
century phylogenetic morphologists and early twentieth-century idealistic
morphologists, for he saw in the phylogenesis of human forms the gradual realization of an ideal form.

Stratz tried to confirm his racial taxonomy by applying Fritsch's canon of
ideal body proportions to the bodies of women who represented different races.
Not surprisingly, he found that the proportions of female specimens of the
white race came closest to the ideal proportions codified in Fritsch's canon (see
figures 23 and 24), whereas the Mongolian and Negroid races deviated from this
norm. Women of the "yellow race" deviated from this ideal proportion because
their arms and legs were too short and their heads too large in relation to the
length of their entire bodies. According to Stratz, black women deviated because their arms and legs were too long and their heads too large in relation to
their body lengths. They also had wider shoulders than white women and narrower hips, which gave their body a more masculine appearance (see figures 25
and 26).[30]

Stratz's choice of photographs to exemplify his racial types is revealing. Although Fritsch and other anthropologists had taken great care to develop a standardized methodology for the taking of photographs,[31] Stratz's models were
not in standard poses. Further, he sometimes based his aesthetic judgment on
partially clothed models (see figure 27). Stratz's approach accorded greater credence to the intuitive gaze of the physician than to empirical measurements. If
one of his examples of a racial body type did not quite conform to his preconceived notions of that type, he dismissed it as an exception or explained the deviation as the result of racial mixture. When he was confronted with the
differing body proportions of three Zulu women (see figure 28), for example, he
maintained that one could find women with short legs and women with long
legs among all human races, even though long legs were supposed to be one of
the most important racial characteristics of black women. Commenting on the
body of a Zulu princess, whose proportions, as he admitted, came close to the
ideal body type of European women, he claimed that this woman represented a
"refined type" who must have had white ancestors.[32] Since his evidence was often based on nude photographs of exotic women that he had purchased during
his travels, he had to rely on the information provided by the sellers of these
photographs, who, he said, often lied to him about their origins. In order to
avoid being cheated, Stratz said, he only purchased photographs that accorded
with the impressions he had gained during his travels.[33] In other words, Stratz
preferred to use evidence that corroborated his theories, and he tried to attribute
conflicts to racial mixtures that might have corrupted the ideal racial type. Con-

FIGURE 23. Proportions of a Bavarian woman representing the perfect beauty of the middle-land race according to Stratz. Stratz, *Rassenschönheit*, 380. Landesbibliothek Stuttgart.

flicts with his evidence did not undermine the racial paradigm; rather, Stratz invoked this paradigm to explain away the evidence.

Stratz argued that he chose women as the basis for his racial typologies because they represented the character of a race in a purer form than men, and it was thus easier to arrive at valid racial classifications by focusing on women's bodies.[34] A man's individuality could supersede his racial character, but a woman's could not. This, however, was not the only reason for Stratz's interest in women's bodies. In an earlier work concerned with female beauty, he had claimed that he chose women as study subjects because as a gynecologist he did not have enough male material to work with.[35] There might have been a commercial reason also, since his heavily illustrated work would appeal to heterosexual male voyeurs. Since he represented himself as a Bildungsbürger who was devoted to an idealistic aestheticism, Stratz hardly would have stressed the material rewards of his endeavor—such an admission would have compromised the pretensions he shared with his educated peers and injured his credibility, since disinterestedness was thought to be a precondition for judging beauty.

FIGURE 24. Schematic representation of proportions of the same Bavarian woman. There is perfect correspondence between the ideal proportions (unbroken lines) and the woman's proportion (dotted lines). Stratz, *Rassenschönheit*, 21. Landesbibliothek Stuttgart.

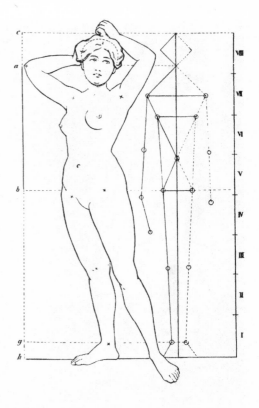

Stratz rejected, for example, aesthetic judgments of lovers because they lacked objectivity, and he maintained that beauty as the gospel of nature was too easily forgotten in an everyday life that was dominated by petty interests and prejudices.[36]

But there was probably yet another reason why Stratz focused on women in his presentations of racial differences: doing so allowed him to suggest that appropriate gender roles for women followed from the natural laws governing human evolution. As a rule, he maintained, the higher a race ranked on the evolutionary scale the more women became different from men. Beautiful and feminine women were thus the product of the same evolutionary progress that the white race had undergone. In this respect, his book on racial beauty was an extension of other works by him that reflected contemporary concerns about masculinized women. Contrasting the ideal beauty of white women with the body types of non-European protomorphical women, he depicted the latter as masculinized by claiming that their secondary sexual characteristics were less developed. They also had broader shoulders and narrower hips than European women.[37]

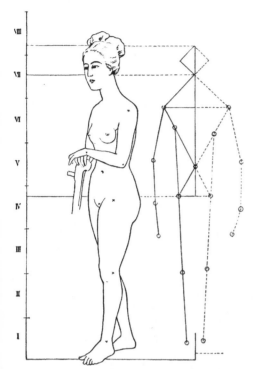

FIGURE 25. Proportions of a Japanese woman of the Mongolian race according to Stratz. The woman's extemities (dotted lines) are too short compared to the proportions representing ideal beauty. Stratz, *Rassenschönheit*, 20. Landesbibliothek Stuttgart.

There were other, more subtle messages and stereotypes concerning gender distinctions and sexual character that Stratz employed to reassure his readers and probably himself about the nature of respectable women. The message, encoded in an idiom of national and racial difference, was that white Nordic women embodied a form of beauty that was nonsensual and devoid of vulgar sexuality. The vulgar sexuality was instead projected onto women from other races and nationalities, who, as Stratz admitted, could be pretty and exert a certain sexual attraction on European men but who did not represent the true ideal of beauty of Nordic European women. Writing about Samoan women, Stratz conceded that they exerted a sensual stimulus because of their nudity and youthfulness but stated that they were not true beauties because of the admixture of too much Mongolian blood. Japanese women were not beautiful in the strict sense, either, because of their rather short legs and Mongolian facial appearance. But he considered them charming and claimed that nowhere could so many pretty girls be found as in the land of the rising sun.[38] For him, real beauty and sensuality were mutually exclusive, and Nordic women, as the embodiments of beauty, lacked the sensuality that was perceived as threatening by many contemporary males.[39]

FIGURE 26. Proportions of a
Dschagga woman of the Negroid
race according to Stratz. The woman's
extremities (dotted lines) are too long
compared to the proportions representing ideal beauty. Stratz, *Rassenschönheit*, 22. Landesbibliothek
Stuttgart.

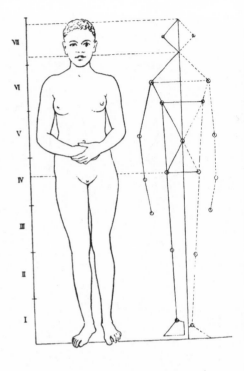

In such discourses, the observer's or artist's sexual disinterestedness was a
precondition for the aesthetic judgment. An artist or art connoisseur was believed to be unable to create or judge a representation of a beautiful woman if he
perceived her as a sexual being. Women who aroused sexual interest could therefore not serve as a standard for beauty. In an article in the life reform journal *Die
Schönheit* the artist Eduard Daelen claimed that the representation of the nude
body was the most difficult task for an artist, because it demanded the moral purity of an untainted cast of mind and feeling.[40] In Joseph Kirchner's view, any
baser sexual interest would compromise the male artist's ability to create a true
work of art. For an artist who gave in to his sexual desire and experienced his
model in a sexual way, the ideal interest in the beauty of his model was inevitably
lost—"a passionate night of love could destroy the splendor of a blossoming
woman's body."[41] For Bildungsbürger like Daelen, Kirchner, and Stratz, very
beautiful women therefore had nothing in common with "this category (of
women) . . . who look for their nightly income on the streets." In Kirchner's
view, the works of Brücke, Stratz, and Schultze-Naumburg had clearly demonstrated that "the physical throwing-away *[Wegwurf]* of a woman, the common
trade of love *[Liebeshandwerk]* is the ruin of beauty in the shortest time, and that

FIGURE 27. Japanese geisha of the Choshiu type. Stratz, *Rassenschönheit*, 113. Landesbibliothek Stuttgart.

the priestess of 'Venus vulgivaga' cannot be the seed corn from which the magnificent flower of the chaste beauty of women" flourishes. Beautiful women thus had nothing to do with the "meanness, the scum of society, [and] its most notorious swamp flowers *[Sumpfblumen]*."[42]

Stratz elaborated on a similar theme when he discussed the differences be-

FIGURE 28. Three Zulu girls with different proportions. Stratz, *Rassenschönheit*, 132. Landesbibliothek Stuttgart.

tween French and German women. He subdivided the white race into three major categories that constituted (North) African, Romanic, and Nordic subraces, with the body forms of the latter most closely approaching the ideal norms.[43] The difference between these subraces was reflected in the sensuality of French women compared to the beauty of German women. Stratz often used the categories of race and nationality interchangeably. French women supposedly tried to enhance their sexual attractiveness with the help of immoral fashions that were designed to appeal to the sexual instincts of men.[44] Stratz was referring to a pervasive contemporary cliché that associated French women with sexual immorality. French women who emphasized their sensuality to arouse men by using "poses plastiques," in which they posed in tight tricots, deviated considerably from the ideal of perfect beauty, according to Stratz. He claimed that he had examined more than three hundred photographs of such women and could find none who had a reasonably normal body. Although some of them made a pretty appearance, none was beautiful. Among more than three thousand nude photos of French artist's models, he found many women who were stocky and had legs that were too short, but he admitted that some of them were normal and beautiful.[45]

The type of sensual woman who was capable of seducing men without being beautiful was represented by the so-called *beautés du diable* (beauties of the devil)—it was no accident that through the very name this type of woman was associated with Frenchness and the Romanic race. These were women who matured very early and who radiated sexual attractiveness while they were still very young. Their sensuality and early sexual activity would bring the end of their beauty; a short blossoming was followed by early physical decay. This type of woman might be sexually attractive but did not have anything of the chaste beauty of an ideal Nordic German woman.[46]

In Stratz's view, those who did not share his and his social peers' aesthetic preferences and values had a different racial background and therefore deviated from the Nordic ideal of beauty. His descriptions of German women from the lower estates make this obvious. Stratz maintained that especially among the North German lower classes, beauty was a rarity. This notion was problematic, because his work relied on nude pictures of professional models who were recruited from the lower classes.[47] Nonetheless, he claimed that very beautiful women were usually to be found among the better classes and that working-class women often suffered from stunted development. He attributed these variations in body forms among the estates to the different racial qualities of the members of these estates. The nobility, old Bürgertum families, and the peasant estates had a higher proportion of racially valuable stock because they did not mix with others and could improve their racial qualities little by little in consecutive generations.[48]

The conception of class differences (or differences in estates, as Stratz would have put it) presented in terms of racial idioms was a theme that periodically resurfaced in Stratz's descriptions of female bodies. Writing about the bodies of Japanese women, he claimed that there were two types, the Choshiu and the Satsuma. The features of the Choshiu type were slim. Women of this type had a long trunk and a slender face that gave them a refined appearance. Women of the Satsuma type were comparatively ungainly, they had shorter and thicker legs than women of the Choshiu type, and their narrow eyelids and strong cheekbones gave them an appearance that deviated considerably from the European ideal. The Satsuma type was prominent among women workers and farmers, whereas the Choshiu type, which came closer to the European ideal, was dominant in the higher estates.[49] In Stratz's view, North Africans of lower estates often lacked beauty, since they were of mixed black and white ancestry, but among the higher estates (whose members had preserved the purity of their blood), women of classical beauty could sometimes be found. In a similar fashion, he argued that beauty representing the Nordic type was prominent among Russians from the higher circles of society, but he found traces of Mongolian ancestry in the facial features of a charming peasant girl.[50]

The racialization of class differences can be seen as an extension of earlier attempts by German anthropologists to describe class differences in terms of physical differences. In the 1880s, the liberal anthropologist Johannes Ranke, to whom Stratz repeatedly acknowledged his intellectual indebtedness, contrasted the bodies of the Bürgertum with the bodies of working-class people. He depicted class differences in terms of constitutional differences, but he did not racialize them. More important, he criticized the neglected physical constitution of the members of the Bürgertum and contrasted their one-sided mental development with what he considered to be the healthier and better-developed bodies of working-class people. Stratz turned this valuation on its head by aesthetisizing the bodies of members of the Bürgertum and racializing the difference between the lower classes and the Bürgertum. Nevertheless, this did not keep him from citing Ranke as one of his authorities.[51]

What made the naturalization of class differences as racial differences plausible to Stratz and his audience of Gebildeten, however, was not so much an anthropological tradition that examined physical differences between social classes. Rather, the association of lower-class women with the sexuality of racial "otherness" can partially be explained by the Wilhelmine encounter with the exotic. *Völkerschauen*, commercial exhibitions of "exotic peoples," were an important form of popular entertainment during the age of imperialism. Entrepreneurs such as Carl Hagenbeck and Carl Marquardt could initially claim that their shows were educational because they familiarized Germans with their new "compatriots" in the colonies. Until the late 1890s academic anthropologists such as Rudolf Virchow and Felix von Luschan certified such enterprises as authentic, because they gave them the opportunity to obtain living "specimens" for their science. However, contemporary critics soon denounced such events as a vulgar form of "a lust to look" *(Schaulust)* that had nothing to do with edifying contemplation. Their criticism was not only aimed at lower-class German women who were likely to be sexually aroused by viewing the half-naked bodies of exotic males. The masses of female spectators at such events and their behavior, characterized by the passive consumption of visual entertainment, alcohol abuse, and sexual promiscuity, embodied a rejection of Bürgertum norms of comportment and habitus.[52]

The racialization of social class made sense because of what Pierre Bourdieu has described as the different habitus of social classes. According to

Bourdieu, social identity is defined and asserted through practices and class-dependent subjective perceptions of practices that reinforce social differences and naturalize them.[53] This is also true for practices and perceptions centering on the human body. Turn-of-the-century Germans perceived eating habits, posture, body language, and speech as important signifiers of social class. Such perceptions were based on implicit assumptions of social otherness that Sander Gilman has described in his research on stereotypes about Jews. As Gilman shows, the otherness of Jews could be racialized because of contemporary perceptions and stereotypes of their physical differences and speech patterns. It was common for the accents of Eastern European Jews, their so-called *Mauscheln*, to be taken as signifiers of "natural" differences between Jews and non-Jews, despite the fact that German Jews had no such accent.[54]

The assumptions underlying such perceptions of social otherness rarely needed to be expressed explicitly. The gynecology professor Hugo Sellheim, for example, maintained that the spiritual beauty of a human being, which he saw as an expression of cultivation and social class, was transformed into muscular movements. The grace and femininity of cultivated women, for example, was expressed in their physical movements. The less spirituality women possessed, he claimed, the more physical they were. The beauty of graceful movements, he claimed, was the result of body discipline that liberated the body by making it more natural and feminine. For Sellheim, only bürgerliche control of affect—expressed in restrained physical movements and a pleasant voice—made women truly feminine. This femininity offered a pleasant contrast to the coarseness and vulgarity of lower-class women, who offended his aesthetic sensibilities with the provinciality of their Swabian dialects (Sellheim taught at the University of Tübingen).[55] He stopped short of racializing these social differences in terms of physical habitus and dialect. But since such differences could be interpreted as expressions of inherited physical and mental variations between social classes, it is not surprising that Stratz racialized class differences.

In turn-of-the-century Germany, racial discourse provided an idiom for the Protestant Bürgertum to articulate a sense of social distance from other groups. The aesthetic aspects of racial discourse are significant because aesthetic concepts of race served as an idiom for social class. In Stratz's work, Nordic women embodied the aesthetic norms and sensibilities of the Bildungsbürgertum. Therefore Stratz not only naturalized his ideal of normal, healthy, and beautiful womanhood, thus reflecting contemporary concerns about changing gender relations, but also racialized the social distinction that separated the respectable Bürgertum from the lower classes, whose women literally failed to embody the beauty characteristic of the women of higher estates.

As a review of Stratz's *Racial Beauty of Woman* in the life reform journal *Die*

Schönheit makes clear, these messages were not lost on some of Stratz's peers. Like him, the art expert Josef Kirchner, the author of the review, believed that there was an objective standard for beauty corresponding to the timeless aesthetic norms of classical antiquity. Therefore he rejected the catchphrase "individual beauty" because it only served to make the art of realists, naturalists, and impressionists socially acceptable. For Kirchner this type of art was based on representations of social inferiors: "decadent variete dancers, degenerate proletarians and robust stable maids." Renaissance artists never could have created their great works if they had relied on such models, Kirchner claimed, and he applauded Stratz for demonstrating the racial basis of beauty.[56]

Stratz's racial aesthetic was similar to the racial physiognomy of the Weimar period (see chapter 7). However, Stratz was also different from Weimar racial theorists such as Hans F. K. Günther, whose experiences were shaped by World War I and the postwar crisis. The racial theorists of the 1920s did not share Stratz's optimistic social Darwinist teleology and his confidence in the ultimate progress of Western civilization. During the war racial discourse had already conveyed a sense of hopelessness and fatalism that was absent in Stratz's work. Nevertheless, race continued to serve as a cultural idiom for social class. This is evident in an article by Karl Hutten titled "Race and Beauty" that also appeared in *Die Schönheit*.[57] Hutten maintained that concepts of beauty are determined by racial dispositions. For this reason, changes in the racial composition of a people would lead to an alteration in the prevailing concepts of beauty, which changed according to the degree of racial miscegenation. Only a race that never changed would be able to hold onto an eternally valid concept of beauty. And only a people that could preserve its racial purity would have a true style in its art. In a racially mixed people (as in the case of Germans), true art as an expression of the Volk would not exist—each individual would have a different opinion according to his or her racial disposition, and the masses would change their views like clothes without developing a genuine opinion. In Hutten's view, this racial inferiority was the reason why the masses were so easily seduced by fashions and why the degeneracy of a people due to racial mixing would lead to the corruption and decay of art by materialism, hedonism, and sensuality. Since all true art in the world could be traced to Aryan-Germanic origins, art and beauty would be doomed to death if Aryan-Germanic blood were repressed. In order to save art and beauty, Hutten advocated a racial hygiene that eliminated the unhealthy, those who did not belong to the Teutonic race. Hutten wrote this during World War I, a time when chauvinistic and racist feeling ran high, but the line of social criticism he articulated, with its racial and hygienic idiom, was not a result only of the war.

Stratz, Kirchner, and Hutten were hardly unique in their use of racial typology as an idiom for social class. After all, Count Gobineau, whose racial theories were popularized in Germany during the late nineteenth century, had already conceptualized the fall of the French aristocracy in racial terms in the 1850s. He had perceived the French Revolution as the revolt of Gallic plebeians against the Aryan-Germanic nobility.[58] From 1886 to 1894 the amateur anthropologists Otto Ammon and Ludwig Wilser measured the physical characteristics of army recruits in Baden, and Ammon was quick to conclude that social differences emerged from racial characteristics that found expression in the shape of the human skull. Because of their empirical basis, these findings had the aura of hard scientific facts, and Ammon popularized them in the contemporary press.[59] He appealed to the common sense of his readers when he wrote, "No proof is required to show that the human races and types do not only differ simply in their outer appearance, but that they are also adapted to the surroundings in their spiritual dispositions, in which they have been formed through centuries or millennia of adaptations." These differences in the "spiritual dispositions" and "mental conditions" of the races were, in his view, the basis of social stratification:

> That the higher classes are the ones which are more eager to learn, more provident, and more entrepreneurially inclined can be understood easily because due to these qualities individuals have made their way to a privileged position. Only the fact that these traits are inherited dispositions from the Teutons still has to be proven. But if we recall the mental character of the Teutons as it is related in the concurring reports of the old literature and on the other hand take into account that longheadedness was a common characteristic of *our [bürgerlichen]* ancestors and the contemporary higher estates, we will not have much doubt about that. (emphasis added)

Ammon's conceptualization of racial differences was based on distinctions between the Bürger, like himself, and the urban masses. He maintained that the thinking of the masses was fundamentally different from that of people like himself. The Teutons whom he represented as the ancestors of the higher urban estates were thus characterized by the traits and virtues of the Bürgertum. The ideals of the Teuton-Bürger emphasized the "pursuit of happiness," "free work and creativity," and "joyful enterprise and daring" *(das frohgemute Unternehmen und Wagen)*. In contrast, the masses only wanted to have peace and quiet after work and a comfortable life. He claimed that racial differences were hereditary dispositions and were the deeper cause of class divisions during the empire.

The Protestant and national liberal Otto Ammon also felt the need to racialize conflicts between Catholics and Protestants.[60] Echoing a familiar theme from the Kulturkampf against the influence of the Catholic Church in the 1870s, Ammon expressed an attitude widespread among his cohorts that the dogmatism of Catholics was incompatible with German Kultur and science. The liberal disdain for Catholicism had a class component as well because liberals were especially repulsed by the lower-class piety that found its expression in pilgrimages to the sites of Marian apparitions.[61] Ammon claimed that the results of his anthropological surveys revealed different racial backgrounds for Catholics and Protestants. The dolichocephalic (long-headed) Protestant scientists in the Scientific Association of Karlsruhe *(Karlsruher naturwissenschaftlicher Verein)* clearly demonstrated mental abilities and an independence of mind that were very different from those of the brachicephalic (broad-headed) students at Catholic seminaries, who were happily enslaved by the dogmatism of the church.[62]

Racial typologies such as the ones propagated by Ammon, Stratz, and others were based on the notion that each race had a holistic psycho-physical constitution. In the view of contemporary racial theorists, beauty was the holistic expression of a healthy Nordic constitutional type. Whether they shared such views concerning the racial basis of beauty or not, many life reformers and some physicians agreed that beauty was the expression of a healthy constitution achieved by a holistic cultivation of body, spirit, and mind. Chapter 5 examines the holistic models of health and illness that were propagated by physicians and life reformers, especially in relation to eugenic discourses of the period.

ᴄ𝑀odels of 𝑯olistic 𝑪onstitutionalism
in 𝑹egular ᴄ𝑀edicine and 𝒩atural 𝑻herapy

𝑮erman constitutional medicine was one of the most important arenas in which the discourses of regular and irregular medicine converged from the turn of the century onward. Body aesthetics and constitutional concepts in German medicine are closely related because some regular physicians as well as propagators of alternative medicine regarded physical beauty as an expression of people's constitutional health or essence. Physical beauty was the organic expression of the harmonious and purposeful interaction of the body, spirit, and mind. Such holistic assumptions were similar to the aesthetic assumptions of the Gebildeten in that the human organism, like a work of art, was to be judged intuitively as a coherent whole.[1]

These assumptions are especially evident in Carl Heinrich Stratz's constructions of constitutional and aesthetic racial types, discussed in chapter 4. But the convergence of these concepts is also apparent in the attitudes of other physicians. Gustav Fritsch and Ferdinand Hueppe, for instance, supported aspects of the hygienic lifestyle prescriptions propagated by the life reform movement. Fritsch lent his reputation as a professor who supported physical culture by becoming the honorary chair of the German Association for Rational Body Discipline.[2] As Fritsch explained in the life reform journal *Kraft und Schönheit*, the beautiful body was the "product of a rational and healthy body discipline" that improved the general constitution of individuals.[3] Hueppe, also a strong advocate of physical culture, wrote a series of articles that were read by supporters of alternative medicine as a vindication of life reform. Denouncing alcohol consumption, faulty nutrition, and lack of exercise, physicians such as Hueppe and Fritsch argued for a strengthening, or hardening *(Abhärtung)*, of the constitutions of individuals in order to counter the increasing "softness" *(Verweichlichung)* of modern mankind. Espousing Lamarckian concepts of heredity, they, like the life reformers, believed that a healthy lifestyle would improve the fitness of future generations, military and civilian. According to Paul Weindling, it was, among other things, the growing concern with the constitutional health of individuals that infused scientific medicine with a hereditarianism (that is, a view based on premises concerning the heritability of diseases) that prepared the ground for the acceptance of eugenic ideas.[4] Therefore it is well worth taking a closer look at the discourse about constitutional health in regular and alternative medicine.

The etiologic concepts of modern scientific medicine and alternative medicine are usually regarded as fundamentally different from one other. These differences can be conceived in three ways. First, scientific medicine proposes a mechanistic reductionism in which all of an organism's physiological functions or dysfunctions are reduced to chemical and physical processes in the human body. Alternative medicine, however, rejects such a reductionism in favor of a "life force" that regulates and coordinates all somatic functions. Second, scientific medicine is localistic, attributing specific diseases to pathological changes that can be localized in specific body tissues. In contrast, proponents of alternative medicine argue that life as a whole cannot be reduced to the sum of its parts; disease must be understood systemically as a disorder (or a disharmony) of the entire organism. Third, scientific medicine constructs specific disease entities from specific causes, be they pathological changes in specific tissues or specific etiologic agents, such as germs. Alternative medicine focuses on the disease as manifested in the entire organism.[5]

These conceptual distinctions are ideal typologies that capture important distinguishing features of some forms of both types of medicine. But vitalistic and holistic interpretations of physiological and pathological processes played a role not only in alternative medical theories but in some areas of orthodox medicine as well.[6] Like the defenders of natural therapies, certain orthodox medical practitioners developed concepts of individual constitutional differences in order to account for what they perceived to be individuals' varying susceptibility to disease.

From this perspective, issues concerning the political economy of the medical market, in which regular physicians battled for market share against irregular practitioners, as well as questions regarding the legitimacy of specific medical interventions (such as compulsory smallpox vaccination or serum therapy for diphtheria), should be considered analytically distinct from controversies concerning theories of disease causation.[7] Holistic medicine is *not* the equivalent of alternative medicine. Ottomar Rosenbach and Ferdinand Hueppe, for example, were two regular physicians who attacked bacteriologists such as Koch and Behring as vehemently as did members of the natural therapy movement and espoused holistic concepts of disease causation similar to, if at times more complex than, those of the natural therapists.[8] Yet these physicians were as worried as the staunchest defenders of contemporary bacteriology about issues of professional autonomy and authority in relation to a lay public that seemed increasingly less willing to accept the guidance of the regular medical profession and turned to the natural health associations in large numbers.

Neither were alternative medical theories always antireductionist. Life reformers claimed that it was important to take the entire body into account when diagnosing and treating diseases, but they nevertheless reduced all disease symptoms to a single cause or a few causes. By focusing too much on reductionism and holism as the distinguishing features of orthodox and alternative medicine, historians have tended to overlook important similarities in the etiologic concepts of the alternative health movement and some representatives of regular medicine that emerged in the late nineteenth century. In order to explore the similarities between some scientific and alternative concepts of disease causation, this chapter first discusses the resurgence of holistic constitutional concepts within turn-of-the-century scientific medicine.[9] Such approaches, with their emphasis on preventive hygiene, shaped some of the popular education efforts made during the big Dresden hygiene exhibition of 1911. The next section discusses the etiologic concepts of the life reformers who also emphasized the importance of an individual's constitution for the disease process. As I argue, this constitutionalism was at least as fertile a ground for eugenic ideas within the life reform movement as it was within scientific medicine.

Concepts of Holistic Constitutionalism
in Turn-of-the-Century Scientific Medicine

During the middle of the nineteenth century traditional holistic constitutional concepts were still prominent in German medicine. Drawing on the vocabulary of classic humoral medicine, the physician Carl Gustav Carus distinguished eighteen constitutional types that were expressed in choleric, phlegmatic, sanguinic, and melancholic temperaments or other psychological characteristics such as "mental vivacity." These were manifested in different body types that at the same time also served as signifiers for the predisposition toward different diseases (see chapter 2).[10] Such holistic conceptions of the human body were consistent with the heroic therapies of orthodox physicians at the time—especially bleeding and purging—which attempted to have an impact on the body as a whole.[11] It can be argued that this was a constitutionalism sustained by the therapeutic practice of the time. It was not yet affected by the pathological anatomy and physiology that had already begun to gain a foothold at German universities.

During the last two decades of the nineteenth century, constitutional theories within scientific medicine experienced a revival as a reaction against bacteriology. During the 1880s, the Berlin clinician Ottomar Rosenbach had already started to develop constitutional concepts of disease causation in response to what he considered the false and exaggerated claims of bacteriologists. It would be wrong to regard physicians such as Rosenbach as reactionaries simply because they were skeptical of or unenthusiastic about classical bacteriology. From the viewpoint of physicians of the 1920s, propagators of constitutional theories were pioneers of scientific progress in their own right because they had provided a much-needed corrective to the exaggerated claims of bacteriology. It is therefore small wonder that physicians such as Hueppe and Rosenbach—who during the Kaiserreich had been rather marginal to the German medical establishment—were considered to be outstanding representatives of turn-of-the-century medicine, men who had prepared the ground for the constitutional medicine of the 1920s.[12]

Rosenbach vehemently opposed bacteriology. He claimed that there was no proof for bacteriologists' contentions that certain diseases were caused by specific microorganisms as etiologic agents.[13] Microorganisms were not the primary cause of the illnesses that bacteriologists attributed to them. Since only a select number of people would contract a given disease, an individual's constitution, the ground on which an etiologic agent acted, was the decisive variable in any given disease process. Important for the disease process, he argued, was the reaction of the entire organism to an external irritant.[14] Rosenbach rejected the legitimacy of a materialistic-reductionist approach for the understanding of living organisms. He distinguished between nonliving and living molecules with a certain vital power, and he imagined that molecules that would contribute to a strengthening of an individual's immunity were such living molecules.[15] To him, medicine was an art whose practitioners had to synthesize countless observations of local symptoms in order to evaluate the vital energy of the body as a whole.[16]

Rosenbach talked in life reform terms, even though he was as worried about the expert authority of physicians as were the defenders of bacteriology. Instead of hoping for elusive specific therapies, Rosenbach argued, it was much more important to strengthen each individual's constitution using traditional dietetic approaches. Light, air, the right nutrition, and a reasonable balance between work and leisure, he claimed, were much more effective in curbing epidemics and other diseases than the vain promises of laboratory medicine. For such dietetic measures to be effective, moreover, the living conditions of the population at large had to be improved.

Some of the earliest and most forceful criticisms of bacteriology came from disenchanted followers such as Ferdinand Hueppe and Adolf Gottstein, who condemned Robert Koch's bacteriology for giving simplistic monocausal explanations of the pathogenesis of infectious diseases.[17] Adolf Gottstein (1857–1941) was a former bacteriologist and "city medical councilor" *(Stadtmedizinal-rat)* in the Berlin district of Charlottenburg. Although he had worked for some time with Robert Koch, he became an outspoken critic of bacteriologists in the 1890s.[18] Gottstein argued that the exclusively contagionist emphasis of classical bacteriology neglected the susceptibility of individuals and populations to some important diseases. In his book on epidemiology, he argued that the lowering of disease resistance by poor living conditions, catastrophes, and war did more to explain the pattern of epidemics than the mere presence of microorganisms as etiologic agents. Since these microorganisms were also present in individuals who did not become ill, Gottstein claimed that the fundamental cause of the disease was, rather, a weakened constitution. In his view, microorganisms could only unfold their pathogenic effects in the case of a nonspecific constitutional weakness.[19]

In the long run, Gottstein argued, it was more important to increase the disease resistance of human populations by strengthening their constitution—by developing *Abhärtung* and adopting a healthy lifestyle—instead of controlling the spread of contagion by isolating sick people in hospitals, a measure that he rejected for moral as well as practical reasons. Even if it were possible to control the spread of the tuberculosis bacterium, little would be won, he claimed, because another contagious disease would take the place of tuberculosis and thrive on peoples' still-weakened constitutions. Gottstein looked to improved living conditions as the solution to the problem of widespread infectious disease, but unlike some life reformers, he denied that urbanization and industrialization would lead to the progressive degeneracy of mankind. Social and economic developments were inevitable, he held; humans needed to adjust.[20] His appeal for better urban living conditions therefore went hand in hand with his demands for fitter people with healthier constitutions.

In Ferdinand Hueppe (1852–1938) classical bacteriology found another outspoken critic. Even more than Gottstein, Hueppe was at the center of bacteriological research when Robert Koch and his students made their breakthrough discoveries in the 1880s. Hueppe was the most prominent bacteriologist to break with the Koch school by formulating his own pathogenic theory, which emphasized the importance of acquired and inherited predispositions in disease causation.[21] In a presentation titled "On the Causes of Fermentations and Infectious Diseases" given during the 1893 Congress of German Scientists and Physicians, Hueppe elaborated for the first time his theory of constitutional determinants in pathogenesis. Using thermodynamics as a metaphor, he developed an energy-based theory that saw disease as a function of internal predispositions, external irritants, and external conditions. Under certain conditions, he claimed, external irritants could trigger predispositions within the body, a process that he described as the conversion of potential into kinetic energy. The effects of bacteria varied according to predisposition and external circumstances. He explicitly rejected Robert Koch's version of bacteriology, which looked only for microorganisms as specific etiologic causes.

In Hueppe's view, a given microorganism did not have a constant effect: similar symptoms could be caused by different microorganisms that triggered the same potential energy or predisposition, and differing symptoms could be caused by the same microorganisms as they acted on various tissues. Hueppe's concept of pathogenesis was thus one of a predispositional range, conceived as latent or potential energy that could be triggered by different microorganisms or irritants.[22] He did not deny the specificity of microorganisms entirely but maintained that the nature of the etiologic irritant partially determined the chemical processes in the reacting organism.[23] But since he put most of the explanatory weight on the predisposing conditions within the organism, he did away with the clear-cut concept of specificity established by classical bacteriology. Like Gottstein, Hueppe moved toward a concept of a general constitution.

Hueppe did not hesitate to draw eugenic conclusions from his constitutional concepts of etiology. He was ambivalent about the blessings of modern hygiene. On one hand he acknowledged that modern hygiene led to a lower overall mortality rate, but on the other this meant ultimately that there were more people with weaker constitutions because of the better survival chances of "minus variants." Espousing a Lamarckian concept of heredity, he saw in a healthy lifestyle with an emphasis on physical exercise one of the most important means for racial improvement. Disease resistance and mental and physical performance were all interrelated, and he claimed that physical fitness was not only compatible with mental abilities but was a precondition for them. As examples, he cited Leonardo da Vinci and Johann Wolfgang von Goethe, both of whom had combined excellent mental abilities with physical health.[24]

Stressing the importance of acquired and inherited predispositions in the etiology of diseases, Hueppe came very close to advocating dietetic regimes similar to those of the life reformers. In the development of hygienic lifestyle prescriptions using orthodox medical science, he saw a way to enhance the reputation of scientific medicine among the general public and to strengthen the professional position of regular physicians relative to "quacks" *(Kurpfuscher)* of the natural therapy movement.[25] He advocated exercise, gymnastics, and sports as means to improve the general health of individuals, and he lauded the natural therapy movement for recognizing that air, light, water, and simple nutrition were the most important factors for health and healing. Hueppe's explicit recommendation of Arnold Rikli's light and air baths *(Licht-Luft Bäder)* as a means to harden the general constitution of individuals demonstrates how far he went in accepting elements of natural therapy. Like the life reformers, moreover, Hueppe equated a healthy constitution with a beautiful body. Physical education was a means to achieve the perfect harmony of body, soul, and spirit that constituted health and beauty and that was a precondition for perfect, virtuous masculinity.[26] Physical culturists acknowledged this affinity by publishing excerpts from his book *Hygiene of Physical Exercise* in their journal *Kraft und Schönheit.*[27]

Yet Hueppe saw exercise and natural therapy as simply additions to the therapeutic and preventive measures of orthodox therapy. Unlike many life reformers, he did not deny that it was possible to fight specific predispositions with immunization. He defended, for example, the compulsory smallpox vaccination established by German law in 1874 against its life reform detractors.[28] As I argue in chapter 6, the most effective strategy of regular physicians in their conflict with the natural therapy movement was to combine holistic concepts of constitutionalism and aspects of life reform therapies, while insisting on the effectiveness of orthodox medical interventions such as vaccinations. This strategy would become even more important after World War I.[29]

Before the war, physicians who embraced constitutional approaches occupied a marginal position within the German medical establishment. In its popular hygienic education efforts the regular medical profession therefore emphasized the achievements of the bacteriological age. This was the case during the hygiene exhibitions in Dresden in 1903 and 1911, which were sponsored by the industrialist Karl August Lingner. In 1903, Lingner organized a special exhibition titled "The Fight Against Diseases of the People" that was part of the municipal exhibition that took place in Dresden during the same year. The exhibition emphasized the regular medical profession's ability to fight infectious diseases with immunizations and bacteriological therapies such as Behring's serum therapy. Opportunities for laypeople to observe preparations of real bacteria through microscopes for the first time pushed public understanding of modern bacteriology and sanitary measures such as disinfection and sterilization even further. The emphasis on bacteriology is not very surprising because Lingner had made his fortune marketing the antiseptic mouthwash Odol.[30]

The success of the 1903 exhibition encouraged Lingner to organize a huge hygiene exhibition in Dresden in 1911 that was visited by more than five million people and made a profit of one million marks.[31] This exhibition, like its Weimar successors (see chapter 6), familiarized people in an entertaining way with new advances in industry and the medical sciences. It was organized into twelve scientific divisions that were supposed to help physicians and other health professionals become acquainted with fields in which they were not specialists. There was a division for the health aspects of air, light, soil, and water, and there were additional displays concerning hygienic aspects of settlements and apartments, nutrition and food, clothing and care of the body, work, infectious diseases, children and youth, traffic, the military and the navy, tropical hygiene, and statistics. A section on heredity and "racial hygiene" stressed the importance of eugenics for the health of the nation. In addition to these scientific offerings, there were special divisions addressing a mixed audience and dealing with issues such as tuberculosis, alcoholism, venereal diseases, cancer, and dental diseases. There was also a section dealing with gymnastics and sport and a historical division that included an ethnographic display claiming to give extensive background information on hygiene and health care among "primitive peoples." The goal was to give an extensive account of all aspects of human life pertaining to health and hygiene.[32]

The core of the 1911 exhibition and of all of its successors was, however, the "popular division" *(Populäre Abteilung)*, with its exposition titled *Der Mensch*. This section showed models of human organs together with explanations of their functions, serving to acquaint the popular audience with human anatomy and physiology and to foster an understanding of man as both a work of art and a complex machine that had to be serviced with great care by scientifically trained physicians—not quacks.[33] Despite the continuing emphasis on bacteriology in the 1911 exhibition, dietetic prescriptions (not unlike the ones given by life reformers) were important as well. *Der Mensch* started out with a Herculean statue bearing the inscription "No wealth equals you, O health" (see figure 29).[34] It concluded with a section on body care that featured pictures and statues of physical exercises being performed by Etruscans, Egyptians, Greeks, and Romans. The visitor was supposed to compare the "fresh and strong figures" created by antique masters with the ones made by medieval artists. The latter, claimed the exhibition catalogue, almost always had physical deficiencies that warned against neglecting one's body in favor of the mind (since, as we have seen repeatedly, a healthy body was considered a precondition for a healthy mind).

As the catalogue explained, "The tendency of the section 'Care of the Body'

FIGURE 29. "No wealth equals you, O health." Statue in the entrance hall of the exhibition "Der Mensch" during the 1911 hygiene exhibition in Dresden. Deutsches Hygienemuseum Dresden, Bildsammlung, I. IHA 1911, Sign. 11/58, No. 1.

[Körperpflege] is to demonstrate to the visitor the fundamental importance of intensive physical care for health and also for the physical and mental performance level, in order to convince him or her to do more for his or her own body."[35] In other words, the goal of "Care of the Body" was to strengthen the general constitutional health of individuals. This becomes even more evident in the catalogue of the sports exhibition. The author claimed that it was more important to strengthen the natural resistance of the body against pathogenic influences such as microorganisms than to avoid the source of infections. Sports and exercise were not only supposed to increase individual levels of performance. Exercise could help train new generations that would be resistant to disease.[36] In contrast to the 1903 exhibition on diseases, the 1911 exhibition anticipated the emphasis on constitutional health that would characterize much of the hygienic education of Weimar exhibitions (see chapter 6). Such constitu-

tional approaches within regular medicine could serve as a basis for an appeal to a popular audience that had already become accustomed to constitutional concepts in the hygienic propaganda of the life reform movement. Some regular physicians, therefore, attempted to undercut support for the natural therapy movement by appropriating aspects of its discourse.

Life Reform Constitutionalism as Holistic Reductionism

To argue that some of the etiologic theories within scientific medicine were quite similar to the etiologic theories of the life reformers is not to try to deconstruct the differences between these two systems entirely. Most propagators of alternative therapies clearly rejected the notion of specific diseases that could either be anatomically localized or traced to specific microorganisms. Different life reformers propagated different etiologic theories. Although some of them were quite sophisticated, using elaborate theories of metabolic exchange, others relied on rather simple single-cause models. There are a few characteristics, nevertheless, that most of them have in common. I argue that these characteristics can be described in terms of a single basic structure (or metatheory), which forms a paradigm for these different etiologic conceptions.

Underlying the etiologic concepts of the life reformers was the notion of a human constitution that can be strengthened or weakened by dietetic habits. Some life reformers drew on the concept of a "life principle," or life force, which characterized early nineteenth-century systems of dietetics.[37] The Prussian physician Christoph Wilhelm Hufeland (1772–1836) argued in his *Makrobiotik* (1796) that a healthy constitution depended on a strong life force, which mediated chemical and physical processes within the body. The weakening of the life force would lead to enervation, sickness, and ultimately death. Hufeland propagated a rational and natural lifestyle, one that aimed for a stronger life force due to moderation in all things. He condemned sexual indulgence, mental overexcitement, and culinary excesses for their damaging effects on the human constitution.[38]

Similar dietetic prescriptions that stressed the importance of a rational and natural lifestyle for the prevention of disease were taken up again by life reformers during the second half of the nineteenth century. This is especially true of the works of Eduard Baltzer (1814–1887), who can be considered the founder of organized vegetarianism in Germany. Baltzer explicitly referred to Hufeland in his works.[39] What characterized most of the etiologic theories of the life reformers was what I would call their holistic reductionism. Disease symptoms, be they physical discomfort or mental difficulties, were attributed to a single un-derlying cause or a complex of a few causes. To hold both a "holistic" view and a reductionist one is not a contradiction (as the biologist Ruth Hubbard and oth-ers maintain), since alternative disease models often simply reduce various sur-face phenomena or symptoms to one underlying cause. Phenomena in these models are often constructed as dependent on a single cause such as a constitu-tion weakened by the "autotoxins" produced by an unhealthy lifestyle.[40] This becomes especially evident if one looks at the most simplistic alternative disease models, such as the one propagated by the controversial alternative healer Louis Kuhne. Kuhne argued that what modern science considered as separate disease entities were in reality but a single disease that was manifest in changing exter-nal symptoms. Nosological taxonomies (based on a systematic differentiation between disease categories) were superfluous, according to this doctrine of the "unity of diseases."[41]

Kuhne argued that all diseases had their cause in the accumulation of alien substances *(Fremdstoffe)* in the body. This accumulation was in most cases partly inherited and partly acquired through an unhealthy, immoderate lifestyle. Moderation in eating and drinking was the only way to prevent the buildup of these alien substances, and any therapy had to aim at their expulsion. Although a healthy body with a still-vigorous life force might be capable of expelling them without help, a person whose life force was already weakened by them needed some therapeutic aid in the form of a vegetarian diet, bathing, and artificially in-duced sweat, all measures that aimed at the purging of the body. The presence of alien substances in the body constituted, according to Kuhne, a chronic disease with relatively unremarkable symptoms such as the inability to perform and lack of appetite. At the same time, moreover, Fremdstoffe would predispose the body to acute illnesses. In Kuhne's view, fevers and epidemics were simply the result of the fermentation of these alien substances.[42]

Since the underlying cause of all disease manifestations was the same in this account, even relatively harmless ailments were signifiers of one's likelihood to develop a serious and possibly life-threatening disease. In a sense, each symp-tom was signifier and signified at once because it was a potential sign of innu-merable other ailments that in turn were signifiers of the original symptom. In Kuhne's system there are no stable disease entities. Any given disease can there-fore become another. According to Kuhne this happened when a crisis, which signaled the expulsion of alien substances by means of fever and sweating, was suppressed by drugs (see the discussion of the medical autobiography by the Kuhne follower Richard Ungewitter in chapter 1). The alien substances would remain in the body and accumulate further until they reappeared as even more serious diseases. Kuhne claimed that the most serious diseases, such as syphilis, tuberculosis, insanity, and cancer, were often the recurrences of fevers that had been artificially suppressed by antipyretics or other medications.[43]

Kuhne did not distinguish between somatic and mental ailments. Because each type could mutate into the other, mental and somatic conditions had to be subjected to the same form of treatments, consisting of a vegetarian diet, exercise, and water, steam, sun, or air baths. Kuhne's specialty, however, was the *Reibesitzbad*, which he recommended especially to women. It consisted of a repeated and gentle washing of the genitals, a procedure that would help expel toxins by stimulating the body's life force at the place where all the important nerves of the body were thought to converge.[44]

An article published anonymously in 1895 by a vegetarian magazine shows how such a therapy was supposed to work. The article considers the health of the German philosopher Friedrich Nietzsche, one of the great cultural heroes of the German middle class, who spent the last years of his life insane. First, the author tries to discover the cause of Nietzsche's disease by examining his biography, noting that at the age of seventeen Nietzsche suffered from disease symptoms in the form of colds, headaches, and eye pains. This was, in his view, a clear sign that Nietzsche's insanity was caused by an accumulation of "disease substances" *(Krankheitsstoffe)*. In 1868, however, Nietzsche had an accident that resulted in a wound. The wound, the author claims, might have saved Nietzsche, since it started to discharge pus. The pus contained the disease substances that had been in his body from the age of seventeen; now, the body was trying to rid itself of these substances through the wound. The author claimed that this process ought to have been enhanced by bathing and a vegetarian diet, but instead Nietzsche turned to a regular doctor who treated the wound with medical poisons, which curbed the healthy process of suppuration and chased the disease substances back into the body. There they captured Nietzsche's brain, resulting in his insanity. However, the author claimed, it was not yet too late to save Nietzsche. His caretakers only had to replace regular treatment with natural therapy and a vegetarian diet, which would lead to the natural discharge of disease substances through the intestines.[45]

The story is a good example of the holistic reductionism of alternative disease models in which all diseases, whether their symptoms were physical or mental, were attributed to a complex of a few causes or to a single cause such as the accumulation of nonspecific autotoxins. Defenders of holistic concepts in the sciences have usually rejected analytical methods by arguing that a social or natural phenomenon has a unique quality as a whole and cannot be reduced simply to the sum of its parts. Life reformers and defenders of natural therapy have sometimes argued in a similar fashion that the health of human beings has to be understood as the result of a complex and harmonious interplay of the body, spirit, and soul and that this interaction cannot be reduced to the sum of its parts. Disease, then, was regarded as a disturbance of the harmony of this complex interaction.[46]

In spite of the life reformers' claims that they understood disease as the result of a disruption in the interplay between body, spirit, and soul, I argue that the holism of most of the etiologic concepts of the life reformers was simply a way to avoid the necessity of complex analysis by reducing pathological symptoms to a single cause that could be easily understood by laypeople. Denis C. Phillips has pointed out that if all things are connected, then an elaboration and explanation of these connections—as defenders of holism demand—must precede true knowledge. Life reformers such as Louis Kuhne, of course, solved this problem by connecting all things to a single cause, which leads holism to absurdity.[47]

Even university-trained naturopathic physicians resorted to rather simplistic explanations of diseases. The vegetarian physician Heinrich Lahmann, for example, argued that the basic cause of all diseases was a constitutional disposition that he called *Dysämie*. One of the symptoms of Dysämie was the lack of beauty that he diagnosed among his contemporaries. Lahmann, who was the founder of the natural health sanatorium Weißer Hirsch in Dresden, argued that Dysämie was a deviation from the normal chemical composition of the blood, characterized by a lack of "nutritional salts" and an excess of sodium chloride as a result of a meat diet. This led to a "watering down" of the blood, which made the body susceptible to infectious diseases. In contrast to other life reformers, Lahmann did not dispute the pathogenicity of microorganisms entirely, but he claimed that if a person's nutrition were balanced and her blood composition normal, she would be immune to the pathogenic effects of microorganisms. The tubercle bacillus, for example, simply supplied the stimulus that triggered the disease in a body with an already weakened constitution.[48]

Because of the important role that constitution, either acquired or inherited, played in the etiologic theories of the life reformers, nosological taxonomies in the life reform literature were either nonexistent, as in the case of Kuhne's theory, or inherently unstable. Kuhne declared nosological systems to be superfluous because what orthodox physicians as well as laypeople perceived as different disease entities were in reality merely symptoms of the same disease. However, he claimed, he still used traditional names for diseases for the convenience of his readers.[49]

Most propagators of natural therapies did not go so far as to proclaim the unity of all diseases, as Kuhne did.[50] But since all of them maintained that an individual's general constitution played an important role in etiology, there was no clear distinction between different disease entities. This is obvious in the health dictionary published by the natural healer Friedrich Eduard Bilz.[51] Bilz, like Kuhne, was an alternative health entrepreneur who marketed health care products and ran a sanatorium for natural therapies. His health dictionary was organized according to the disease categories familiar to his readers, and different diseases were described in terms of their specific symptoms. Although Bilz did not suggest that all diseases had a single cause, his list of etiologic factors for each infectious disease was so long and his descriptions so diffuse (for example, bad blood, bad water, bad air, bad nutrition) that he cited them repeatedly as causes for different diseases. In his view, one infectious disease could be the predisposing cause for another one with, for instance, pneumonia and typhus causing a predisposition for tuberculosis. Therefore, his disease categories were also unstable. According to Bilz, it was important to strengthen the general constitution of individuals by means of a healthy lifestyle in order to prevent the *Verweichlichung* (softening) of people.[52] The cause of weak constitutions was not to be found exclusively in an unhealthy lifestyle, however. Many life reformers believed that constitutional weaknesses could be inherited. Therefore they were quite receptive to eugenic arguments.

Life Reform, Eugenics, Euthanasia

Life reformers as well as some members of the medical establishment argued that an individual's inherited or acquired constitution was a decisive factor in the genesis of infectious and other diseases. Some of the regular physicians who espoused constitutional concepts were also open to eugenic arguments. The goal of the academic racial hygiene movement during the Kaiserreich was to improve the biological quality of the German population by facilitating early marriages and large families, especially among the higher and middle classes, and by curbing the reproduction of the unfit by means of isolation and marriage restrictions. So far, historians have been concerned mainly with eugenics as an aspect of turn-of-the-century scientific medicine.[53] But supporters of natural therapies also advocated eugenic measures to reverse what they perceived as the process of degeneracy of the human race.

As Sheila Weiss has argued, German eugenics reflected middle-class prejudices in that it defined fitness in terms of social and cultural productivity while equating degeneracy with asocial behavior and the inability to contribute to society. In her view, eugenics was a managerial and technocratic attempt at a rational management of population. It sought to increase national efficiency and power in the face of the social and political problems resulting from industrialization and urbanization. Racial hygienists were, for example, concerned with the migration of healthy rural stocks to the cities, where they supposedly deteriorated biologically. They were also worried about the differential birthrates of lower and higher classes, which seemed to indicate the disproportional fertility of the unfit lower classes, who were perceived by the middle classes as a threat.[54]

In Paul Weindling's view, the emergence of German racial hygiene has to be seen in the context of a shift in German medicine from liberal principles, in which the individual's personal health was the focus of attention, to authoritarian concepts, in which personal health was subordinated to concerns about the health of collective entities such as the race or the nation.[55] All such interpretations imply that the German eugenics movement tried to offer an authoritarian and technocratic method for the control of undesirable social developments such as the differential fertility of the classes. This interpretation is correct if one only looks at the group of racial hygienists associated with the German Racial Hygiene Society, many of whom were part of the scientific establishment. These people propagated a "eugenics-from-above," mobilizing the medical establishment to develop a technocratic solution to what they perceived as the problem of the German nation's progressive degeneracy.

Eugenic theories did not appeal only to the medical establishment, however. Biological and more specific eugenic arguments were an important cultural resource for people of very different political persuasions.[56] They were employed by feminists (see chapter 3) and socialists to argue for social and political reforms. Racial hygienists sympathetic to the socialist labor movement maintained that better living conditions for the working classes would improve the health of future generations.[57] Even before the Weimar years, eugenic visions of technocratic solutions to social and hygienic problems gained currency on the Left.[58]

Given the widespread appeal of eugenic reasoning, it is not very surprising that life reformers resorted to such arguments to justify their health reform program. Their adoption of these ideas was a form of lay mobilization in which life reformers accused the regular medical profession of being helpless in the face of the progressive degeneration of modern mankind. This integration was facilitated by the fact that eugenicists had accepted to some extent the life reformers' values of physical fitness, air, sunshine, and light as preconditions for national health and racial purity.[59] In other words, the "health of the nation" and the "health of future generations" were contemporary values propagated by regular physicians and life reformers alike.

Cornelia Regin has argued that the formation of the natural therapy movement was a reaction against the authoritarianism of the regular medical profession, which was only too eager to subordinate the rights of individuals to the health of the nation. Regular physicians (among them, many liberals) supported coercive public health measures such as compulsory vaccinations that served as a rallying point for the natural therapy movement against the medical establishment. Regin also points to the natural therapy movement's opposition to the Imperial Epidemics Law, which allowed for the involuntary isolation and hospitalization of individuals who were suspected to suffer from infectious diseases. In her view, this concern with individual rights carried over into the attitudes that life reformers held toward eugenics. The movement was for the most part opposed to involuntary measures such as marriage prohibitions, because its supporters saw the cause of human decline less in degeneration of the germ plasma than in unhealthy living conditions and lifestyles.[60]

Regin's interpretation is problematic because she takes the rhetoric of natural therapy supporters at face value. Since they opposed bacteriology and its therapies, and since the epidemics law would have been a further instrument to subject them to compulsory measures justified by bacteriological theory, it is not very surprising that they vehemently rejected the law as a violation of their individual rights. Although I would not deny that this rejection of state authority was necessarily insincere, this does not mean that the natural therapy movement as a matter of principle rejected illiberal, authoritarian, and coercive measures that infringed on the rights of individuals.

Ernst Schweninger, the former personal physician of Bismarck, was one of the cultural heroes of the natural therapy movement because of his opposition to bacteriology and modern laboratory medicine. His popularity was partially due to his defense of medicine as an art that was concerned with patients as individuals. Because he had obtained the directorship of an important public hospital in Berlin despite the opposition of prominent members of the liberal medical establishment such as Rudolf Virchow, Schweninger was certainly free of any suspicion of being a liberal. Yet in an article in Maximilian Harden's journal *Die Zukunft*, Schweninger drew on the liberal discourse to attack liberals' blind faith in modern bacteriology. He argued that it was rather curious that liberals, who were usually so sensitive to violations of individual rights, were completely unconcerned about such violations by means of legal measures such as the epidemics law, which would restrict the constitutional freedom of movement of individuals in the case of an outbreak.[61] In a similar fashion, supporters of natural therapies drew on liberal discourse and championed individual rights when it served their cause in their fight against bacteriology. But that does not mean that they put the rights of individuals first and therefore rejected coercive eugenic measures as a matter of course.

Eugenics as such was not really a contested issue among life reformers, because supporters of natural therapies in general thought that it was desirable to reverse the degeneracy of modern mankind by controlling procreation and human heredity. The controversial question was whether compulsory measures were necessary to prevent those deemed hereditarily unfit from procreating. As within scientific medicine, a range of opinions on the desirability of various eugenic measures existed among supporters of natural therapy. In 1901, a writer for the natural therapy journal *Neue Heilkunst* argued that it was indeed desirable that degenerates not procreate, but the natural rights of individuals would make it impossible to pass laws that prohibited those suffering from hereditary tuberculosis or mental illness to marry. Individual liberty, the author argued, was more important than considerations concerning the improvement or deterioration of the human race. Instead of legal compulsion, the author argued for moral compulsion. It was important to instill a hygienic conscience into people that would make them abstain voluntarily from procreation if they were unfit.[62]

"Moral compulsion" was not enough in the eyes of Reinhold Gerling, the editor of the *Neue Heilkunst* and later of the *Naturarzt,* the central publishing organ of the German League of Natural Living and Therapy Associations. As early as 1896, one year after the publication of Adolf Ploetz's *Competence of Our Race and the Protection of the Weak,* one of the first influential treatises on eugenics in Germany, Gerling argued that exact scientific research had shown that certain diseases were inheritable and therefore had a negative impact on offspring.[63] It was thus necessary to demand marriage prohibitions for people with epilepsy, cancer, tuberculosis, diabetes mellitus, hypochondria, tabes dorsalis, syphilis, hemophilia, and cirrhosis of the liver. He acknowledged that his demand seemed to be excessive but argued that it would be much better to prevent the unfit from reproducing than to have them produce offspring that would "not be able to cope with the challenges of our time." It was the responsibility of the state to safeguard the health of its citizens and of the nation as a whole. Gerling rejected compulsory vaccination and the epidemics law because he rejected bacteriology and orthodox medicine, not because he wanted to defend individual rights against the state as a matter of principle. Instead, he challenged the state to adopt compulsory actions against individuals as a more effective way in order to ensure the health of society in the future.[64]

What holds true for the natural health movement also holds true for other groups within the life reform movement. In the vegetarian and nude culture literature, one can find all kinds of eugenic advice ranging from the admonition to be careful in the selection of one's marriage partner to utopian breeding schemes and even negative eugenic measures entailing the extermination of those who were too degenerate. Although some of the more extreme schemes were only very rarely advocated, few life reformers would have found something wrong with the eugenicists' utopian goal of rationalizing reproduction in order to create a society in which people could live free of disease and mental or physical impairments. Life reformers therefore advocated positive eugenic measures in order to encourage the reproduction of the fit as well as negative eugenic measures to prevent the reproduction of the unfit.

The life reformers argued that a healthy lifestyle was necessary to prevent the transmission of negative characteristics to one's offspring, because they believed that physical and mental characteristics acquired during a person's lifetime could be passed on. These Lamarckian assumptions distinguished the life reformers from mainstream eugenicists such as Alfred Ploetz and Wilhelm Schallmeyer, who accepted August Weismann's thesis of the discontinuity of germ plasma (the hereditary material) and the individual organism and denied that acquired characteristics could be passed on.[65] Weismann's concept of hard heredity, with its assumption of the inalterability of hereditary material by environmental influences, would have been impossible for life reformers to accept because they saw lifestyle changes as the key to improving the health of future generations. But their emphasis on physical and mental self-improvement by means of a healthy lifestyle was nevertheless to a certain degree in conflict with their hereditarian assumptions. When life reformers argued that civilized mankind had degenerated over the course of several generations and had cumulatively inherited constitutional predispositions toward diseases, they implicitly questioned their own dogma, which stated that a natural lifestyle could lead almost inevitably to a state of absolute and joyful health. If they put too much emphasis on the role of the inherited constitution in pathogenesis, they might undermine the willingness of people to subject themselves to their lifestyle prescriptions.

The natural therapists Wilhelm Siegert and Franz Schönenberger complained, for example, that many people used the unjustifiable excuse that a natural lifestyle could not improve their health because they were already too degenerate. In their view, this was the wrong attitude because only the dispositions toward diseases were inherited and not the diseases themselves. Even those with strong hereditary predispositions toward dangerous diseases would not necessarily become sick if they avoided aggravating their conditions with unhealthy living habits. They argued that the exaggerated fear that one was personally too degenerate only weakened the will of individuals and prevented them from living consciously healthy lives. Schönenberger and Siegert might have undermined their attempts to reassure their readers, however, by emphasizing the danger of inherited dispositions for diseases. Although they went out of their way to convince their readers that being so affected did not doom a person to disease and infirmity, they also stressed the importance of marrying a healthy partner in order to assure the health of one's offspring, and they disapproved of marriage for people suffering from epilepsy, venereal diseases, tuberculosis, or alcoholism. They argued for outright marriage prohibitions in severe cases, and even demanded that doctors be required by law to report such cases to state agencies.[66] Members of the regular medical profession were certainly not alone in their demands to have the rights of individual patients subordinated to the interests of the community.

Other life reformers argued for even stricter measures against degenerates, whom they considered to be a burden on society. The vegetarian Rudolf Franck, for example, deplored the sentimental compassion of his contemporaries. Instead of trying to contribute to the "beautification" and "purification" of life as the ancient Spartans had done when they tossed into the abyss of the Taygetos "everything" that was born sick and unable to cope with the demands of life, modern doctors attempted to prolong a painful and unhappy life at all costs, even if that meant artificial feeding and oxygen supply. Franck argued that one need not be quite as cruel as the Spartans, because one could get rid of degenerates by employing such devices as electric chairs, which would induce a quick and painless death.[67]

The editor of the *Vegetarische Warte,* the journal in which Franck's article appeared, criticized the author for going too far with his suggestions. During the empire most life reformers would not have approved of euthanasia. But the physician Gustav Selß, another editor of the journal, might not have shared such scruples. Selß was the chairman of the German Vegetarian League, and he contributed to the four volumes of Platen's health advice book, one of the most important publications of the natural therapy movement during the empire. His articles in the *Vegetarische Warte* provide another good example of how life reformers' eugenic utopia, in which mankind existed free of diseases and impairments, could lead to a compassionless and cynical attitude toward those who were considered hopelessly degenerate.

Selß complained about the dysgenic effects of altruism and compassion, a rather widespread worry of contemporary racial hygienists. The neurologist Kurt Goldstein, for example, was concerned about the potentially dysgenic effects of warfare, because the genetically most "valuable" elements of the population would be eliminated by the heroic self-sacrifice of young men.[68] Selß distinguished between legitimate compassion, the kind that could be justified by reason, and a compassion that was nothing more than sentimentality. The first form was natural and healthy, whereas the second was pathological. Compassion based on reason, he argued, would never fulfill the wishes of all sufferers. True compassion involved considering whether therapeutic actions benefited the community *(Gemeinschaft)* and not simply whether the therapy helped the sick individual. Compassion for sick or weak people who were unfit for life would only hinder the development of mankind and should therefore be curbed. Selß, himself a physician, regretted that physicians had to repress their natural compassion in favor of the unnatural kind because many people who were seeking advice from physicians were unworthy of procreation or had lives thought to be not worth living. He wrote:

> The moral conviction of the helping physician might often desire the opposite of that which his intervention brings about. His moral attitude concerning what is helpful for the people as a whole *[das Volksganze]* is even against the law. Infirm, weak and incurable people often cry for salvation. The physician can only do that if it prolongs life, but he cannot do it by shortening life. The civilized physician *[Kulturarzt]* can not always follow his true [rationally based] compassion and his feeling of what is useful. Only the savage can do this, whose natural feeling comes first and who eliminates beings who are crippled, senile and incompetent for reproduction because their lives threaten the survival of the whole. This is compassion as well, but the compassion of nature and not [the compassion] of delicate, cultured sentimentality *[Kulturverzärtelung]*. The saving extermination of life *[erlösende Lebensvernichtung]* is only allowed [in civilized societies] . . . in the form of suicide and the killing of criminals.[69]

Selß talked about the concept of "life not worth living" ten years before Karl Binding and Alfred Hoche popularized the same issue in their book *The Lifting of the Ban on the Extermination of Life Not Worth Living.*[70] The public debate about euthanasia had already started with the publication of Adolf Jost's *The Right to Die* in 1895. Before the war, advocacy of euthanasia was confined mainly to a small circle of physicians and intellectuals; only in the context of German sacrifices and defeat did such demands resonate more widely. Binding and Hoche contrasted the mass death and self-sacrifice of able-bodied young men in the trenches with the inmates of psychiatric institutions who contributed nothing to the fatherland and placed an economic burden on a German society trying to recover from the war. Even after the war, however, euthanasia did not find the support of the majority of legal and medical experts. As Michael Schwartz has argued, Weimar eugenicists tried to distance themselves from advocates of euthanasia, claiming that their own program of eugenic prevention and prenatal selection would make such discussions superfluous.[71]

Selß himself realized that his advocacy of euthanasia was problematic and in conflict with his practice as a physician. Like Siegert and Schönenberger, therefore, he tried to reassure his readers, who had probably turned to vegetarianism to improve their frail health and who might have been his patients. He maintained that he would not have become a naturopathic physician if he had not had the desire to truly help sick and infirm people. He claimed that he was capable of helping people far more often as a naturopathic physician than as an orthodox practitioner. But, he argued, one should not ignore the fact that each doctor was forced to help thousands to survive whose survival was disastrous for the community as a whole.

Here Selß faced the same dilemma that confronted Siegert and Schönenberger. On one hand, the life reform movement profited from and fostered a sense of personal degeneracy among its supporters, who hoped that they would be able to reverse this process by adhering rigidly to an alternative lifestyle. On the other, the emphasis on the gravity of people's degeneracy could discourage their hope of finding salvation from hereditary ailments. This dilemma threatened the old life reform dogma, which claimed that one had to become healthy once one left the paths of corrupting civilization and turned to a natural lifestyle.

Nevertheless, as I have shown, concern about their personal health was the main motivation for people's joining the movement, even though many life reformers argued that the importance of a healthy lifestyle was primarily its ability to hinder diseases from being passed on to the next generation. Being sick did not mean that one should give up hope, because most people were sick or degenerate in one way or another as a result of their own lifestyles or those of their ancestors. Even a weak and sickly child like Ungewitter could become a strong man. People could try to iron out physical flaws by adopting a rigid health regimen. They could therefore do something on their own. They were responsible for their own state of health; health and disease were *not* simply predetermined. Even though Louis Kuhne deplored the progressive degeneration of mankind, he nevertheless asserted that it was reversible in all but the most severe cases. By following nature's laws, people could in most cases avoid disease by strengthening their weak inherited constitutions. After a few generations were subjected to a healthy lifestyle, he claimed, a healthier and stronger human race would reemerge.[72]

After the turn of the century, however, many life reformers would have agreed that there was a certain threshold, a point at which the degeneracy of an individual had progressed so far that he or she could no longer reverse the process. This threshold was, of course, primarily a subjective one for each observer who judged individuals or groups of people and recommended negative eugenic sanctions if someone seemed to pose a threat to the people as a whole *(das Volksganze)*. For Gustav Selß, the threshold of degeneracy that defined hopeless cases was probably quite low compared to that of other life reformers, but even he rejected a strict hereditarian determinism of health and disease. He ended his article on compassion by discussing the ways in which the ill were portrayed in the contemporary press, arguing that most newspapers tried to stir the compassion of their readers when they described the fate of sick people. He condemned this practice because only in a few cases were people innocent victims of their fate. Most of the time ignorance, obstinacy, irresponsibility, and alcoholism were the reasons for people's ill health. In his view it was wrong to feel compassion for people who were themselves responsible for their infirmities, because they lacked the discipline to adopt a healthy vegetarian lifestyle.

From a strict eugenic viewpoint, however, being sick was, as such, not to be condemned. What was really reprehensible was the transmission of one's own constitutional predispositions to one's offspring. In 1904, Klara Ebert, who referred to herself explicitly as a racial hygienist, demanded that one renounce marriage if one's body was not absolutely healthy.[73] She wrote in the *Vegetarische Warte:* "There is no greater sin than contributing to the decadence of mankind. This is worse than murder, because if someone is beaten to death he does not have to suffer anymore and is relieved. If, however, one sentences sick human children to live, they have to suffer for decades. It is horrifying what kind of people have children and how these children are."[74] The goal of a healthy lifestyle was, in her view, to contribute to an uplifting of mankind according to Nietzsche's motto "Don't procreate, upgrade" *(Nicht fort sollt ihr euch pflanzen, sondern hinauf).* It is astonishing that a married woman with a child who, by her own admission, was a degenerate suffering from severe health problems (see chapter 1) could demand that people who were not absolutely healthy renounce marriage. The case of Richard Ungewitter is also very instructive in this respect. Having suffered all his life from various infirmities, with periodic relapses after he claimed to have reached the state of absolute and joyful health, he nevertheless demanded the prevention of degenerate offspring by means of marriage prohibitions and sterilizations. As candidates for such measures he listed people suffering from venereal diseases, tuberculosis, and cancer as well as alcoholics, criminals, and the insane. He argued that it was outrageous that such "trash" was allowed to procreate while the physically and mentally healthy, largely people from middle-class backgrounds, were forced to have a small number of children because the landlords in the better parts of cities disapproved of large families as renters.[75]

One could, of course, argue that neither Ebert nor Ungewitter was aware of the contradiction between what they perceived as their own degeneracies and their radical calls for negative eugenic sanctions against other degenerates. But it also seems that they wanted to reaffirm that they had become normal and healthy again. Therefore it is probably not a contradiction that Ungewitter, who admitted to inheriting a weak constitution, aggressively demanded that "weaklings" be excluded from reproduction. According to Sander Gilman, such a construction of boundaries between the sick and degenerate on one side and the healthy on the other can be reassuring for people who are themselves at risk of becoming sick, because illness then seems to threaten not oneself but only those who are perceived as hopelessly degenerate.[76] Because eugenic discourse constructed such rigid boundaries between the life reformers and people who were beyond salvation, it was attractive for those among them who were concerned that they were beyond help.

There was, however, still another reason why people such as Ungewitter, Ebert, and Selß despised those who were in their view already too degenerate to save. Life reformers saw their health as the outcome of their own responsible actions. Because they submitted to the demands of a rigorous body discipline and lived a healthy and rational lifestyle while others indulged in health-threatening luxuries and vices, their health appeared to them to be their own achievement. As part of the select minority that played by the rules that nature had established for a healthy and happy life, they could loudly condemn those who deviated from nature's law and were promptly stricken by infirmities and diseases. Since an irresponsible lifestyle not only threatened the immoral individuals who indulged in vices but also seemed to threaten future generations, harsh eugenic sanctions against such people had to be demanded. Otherwise, the immoral people would drag the morally pure with them into the abyss, leaving offspring that made life unbearable for the latter.

Eugenic measures were increasingly advocated in the life reform literature after the turn of century. Although Kuhne and others had argued that hereditary predispositions played an important role in pathogenesis, their emphasis was still on the individual's sole responsibility for his or her own health. Each individual was capable of turning his or her fate around and following nature's path to joyful health and beauty. This optimism was important for the appeal that life reform had for its followers, and this optimism continued to coexist with cultural pessimism and despair. Nevertheless, the conviction that virtually everybody could turn around his or her fate by adopting a healthy lifestyle increasingly gave way to the conviction that some people—always other people— were beyond help and constituted a threat to society by passing on their weak constitutions to the next generation. Life reformers proposed negative eugenic measures such as marriage prohibitions and sterilizations as relatively pragmatic actions to address this "problem."

Other, more fantastic schemes for the realization of eugenic utopias grew from the life reformers' plans to create communal settlements that would allow them to pursue a healthy lifestyle collectively. Although there was no shortage of plans for such schemes, in practice most failed, the only exception being the vegetarian food cooperative Eden, near Oranienburg.[77] The vegetarian Hugo

Erdmann gave the settlement idea a eugenic twist by proposing the creation of so-called health cities. Like many life reformers, Erdmann argued that the unhealthy living conditions in the big cities caused degeneracy. Since healthy rural stocks that replenished the human material in the cities were constantly depleted in the course of urbanization, the only viable solutions were not agricultural settlements but health cities, in which only people who were free from hereditary dispositions toward disease could live. These cities, he argued, should become the basis of a new biological culture based on strictly enforced hygienic norms. Alcohol and tobacco would be prohibited, and the healthy stocks that were to inhabit them should be offered economic incentives to reproduce.[78] Whether life reformers proposed relatively limited pragmatic eugenic measures against the unfit, such as marriage prohibitions, or fantastic schemes for the creation of a biological culture, they subordinated the rights of individuals to what they regarded as the interests of larger collective entities, such as the nation or the race, branding those who refused to do so as antisocial elements.

This chapter has focused on constitutional discourses propagated by physicians and life reformers during the Kaiserreich and the implications of such discourses for the acceptance of eugenics among life reformers. Leading into the Weimar era, chapter 6 shows how representatives of scientific medicine further appropriated aspects of the constitutional discourses of life reformers. The goal of some physicians was to reassert control over the medical market by co-opting and taming the natural therapy movement.

The Constitutional Convergence: Life Reform, the "Crisis of Medicine," and Weimar Hygiene Exhibitions

The war years, with their tremendous losses in human lives and health, reinforced concerns about the health of the national community. More than two million soldiers were killed, and about twice that number were wounded.[1] Many contemporaries blamed the social and economic insecurity of the postwar years on the financial burden and territorial losses imposed by the Treaty of Versailles. This does not mean, however, that the whole Weimar period was characterized by an atmosphere of cultural and economic despair. On the contrary, as soon as the immediate postwar crisis—with its revolutionary and counter-revolutionary uprisings—had subsided and the hyperinflation of 1922–23 had been overcome, the notion of modern society as technocratically, rationally manageable gained credence. "Henry Ford" and "rationalization" were contemporary buzzwords that stood for such visions of modernity.

At the same time, the expanding welfare state drew its inspiration from the perceived need for social reconstruction following the war, defeat, revolution, and inflation.[2] This is the context for contemporary calls for a "human economy" *(Menschenökonomie)* that would make rational use of human resources in order to make up for war losses. In this respect, the technocratic discourses of Weimar were a continuation of utopian visions of the war years in which machines and people were perfectly matched according to their abilities. The creators of artificial limbs for maimed soldiers, for example, developed exchangeable parts for prostheses that tried to adapt the injured to specific industrial processes, a development that the historian of technology Matt Price has described as the colonization of bodies in the service of a social vision of a rational and efficient organization of work. Already during the war, media images of wounded men with prosthetic arms and legs had tried to convey the possibility of a technological restoration of the work capacity of maimed soldiers and, by extension, of the nation.[3] Eugenics and hygienic education were also supposed to play an important role in this restoration, and the health of the nation became a central topic in the big hygiene exhibitions of the 1920s and early 1930s.

In medicine, however, the technocratic optimism of the mid-1920s was rather short-lived. Even before the Weimar Republic was hit by the effects of the Great Depression, scientific medicine witnessed its own "crisis of classical modernity."[4] Many physicians became skeptical about the promises of modern medicine and bacteriology. They saw the wide public acceptance of alternative medicine as a symptom of a "crisis of medicine."[5] Modern medicine, they worried, lost the confidence of the lay public because physicians treated their patients schematically and did not pay attention to their individual psychophysical constitutions. Regular physicians, therefore, increasingly favored holistic concepts that had been rather marginal within the scientific medical discourse of the imperial age. Some of them valued synthesis—an intuitive approach to the human organism that stressed "holistic contemplation" *(Anschauung)*—at least as much as analysis and exact "mechanistic" science.

This chapter first discusses the life reform movement and the changing medical market during the Weimar period and then explores the changing relation between the alternative health movement and the regular profession. More and more regular physicians adopted the constitutional rhetoric of the life reform movement, claiming that it was important for individuals to adopt a healthy lifestyle in order to improve their health. This was one of the reasons why the movement lost ground in the medical market. The second part of the chapter focuses on the exhibitions organized by the German hygiene museum in Dresden. Like their predecessor in 1911, some of the Weimar exhibitions attracted millions of visitors. I argue that these exhibitions reflected utopian hopes concerning the technocratic reconstruction of Germany after the war, as well as the cultural skepticism that became evident in contemporary crisis talk.

The Constitutional Convergence:
Life Reform and Regular Medicine During the Weimar Republic

During the Weimar period many elements of a reformed lifestyle found greater public acceptance than they had before the war. Local governments took over the creation of mixed-sex open-air bathing facilities for their citizens, bathing suits were less restrictive, and worries about the health-damaging effects of the corset became a thing of the past as corsets went out of fashion. There also was a growing number of loosely organized or unorganized physical culturists and nudists (see chapter 8). At the same time, participation in sports became a mass phenomenon. It has been estimated that sports and gymnastics associations together had 5.6 million members in 1925. Soccer became the period's most popular spectator sport, with tens of thousands of people attending some amateur matches. The combined membership of the soccer voluntary associations grew from 161,000 in 1913 to 780,500 in 1921.[6] The sports craze affected the middle classes and workers alike. The international worker's Olympic games held in Frankfurt in 1925 and in Vienna in 1931 drew large crowds to their events. As an alternative to bürgerlich sports the worker's sports movement stressed the communal experience of mass sports, focusing less on the celebration of individual performances.[7]

Before the Great War, German sports functionaries had stressed the importance of sports mainly for military preparedness. In the 1920s, they frequently emphasized that sports contributed to the health of the nation. Carl Diem, the general secretary of the German National Committee for Physical Exercise *(Deutscher Reichsausschuß für Leibesübungen)*, the semiofficial organization of German sports clubs, claimed that sports had important hygienic benefits in addition to contributing to military fitness. In his view, sports strenghtened the constitution of individuals by making them immune to colds, tuberculosis, and other illnesses.[8]

The fact that many regular physicians adopted the holistic and constitutional rhetoric common to life reformers is one of the most striking signs of a greater public acceptance of life reform ideas and practices. Since many physicians added natural therapies to their regular therapeutic arsenal, patients gained access to alternative therapies without becoming formal members of a natural therapy association.[9] Therefore some pre-war life reform associations had difficulty maintaining the allegiance of their supporters, and this tendency is reflected in their declining numbers. The membership of the German League of Natural Therapy Associations declined from about 148,000 shortly before the war to about 118,000 in the immediate postwar years, and the number of local chapters declined from 885 to 553 between 1913 and 1930.[10]

The period was also characterized by an accelerated fragmentation of the medical market. During the Kaiserreich it had been divided into two camps corresponding roughly to the organizations of the life reform movement and regular medicine, but the situation was much more chaotic during the Weimar years. Other groups such as the "Biochemists," proponents of a medical fad of the

1920s, appeared. Drawing on the theories of the physician Wilhelm Schüßler, biochemists attributed all diseases to an unbalanced supply of eleven basic nutritional mineral salts. The appeal of biochemistry lay in the convenience of following its simple therapeutic prescriptions. Rather than worry about a healthy lifestyle and complicated cold water therapies, one needed only to balance one's individual mineral economy by swallowing biochemical medicines, in much the same way as modern-day Americans swallow vitamins and other nutritional supplements.[11] Biochemistry seems to have been a rather short-lived phenomenon of the Weimar years, symptomatic of a diverse medical market in which a "traditional" natural therapy movement had to compete with a revived homeopathic movement, biochemists, magnetopaths, and a number of medical sects from the United States such as Christian Science and osteopathy.[12]

The fragmentation of the medical market makes it much more difficult to figure out which social groups were particularly attracted by health reform during the Weimar period. Further, Wilhelmine life reformers were much more interested in social statistics than were their Weimar successors. Although we have adequate data on the membership of life reform organizations during the Wilhelmine era (see chapter 1), there is comparatively little detailed information about the social composition of such organizations for the Weimar years.[13] In his study of a homeopathic voluntary association in Württemberg, the historian Eberhard Wolff has found that the membership structure became more heterogeneous during the Weimar years. Although members from the middle class were dominant during the Kaiserreich, workers made up half of the membership during the second half of the 1920s.[14] In 1931, about a third of the membership of natural therapy associations was composed of workers; most others were from some type of middle-class or lower-middle-class background.[15] There was not much organizational continuity between Wilhelmine and Weimar physical and nude culture associations, but the available evidence suggests that they had significantly more working-class members during the Weimar era than during the Kaiserreich (see chapters 1 and 8). In general it seems that the social appeal of a reformed lifestyle widened during the Weimar years, with health reform now affecting a greater number of workers than before the war.

In the 1920s, the dynamics of the medical market contributed to a softening of scientific medicine. There was now a noticeable change in the attitudes of many physicians toward life reform. Suddenly more and more physicians discovered that they needed to take seriously their patients' constitutional individuality (both spiritual and physical), and regular medicine appropriated themes and therapies of the natural therapy movement. Regular physicians such as Erwin Liek and Ferdinand Sauerbruch now tried to recast the nature of their expertise for a lay public. The humane expert had to combine the specialized knowledge and authority of the scientifically trained physician with the personal qualities of an empathic healer, qualities that the German alternative health movements had long demanded.

During the early years of the Weimar Republic, there was a growing appreciation of the natural therapy associations by some members of the scientific medical profession. The State Committees for Hygienic Popular Education *(Landesausschüße für hygienische Volksbelehrung)* and the National Committee for Hygienic Popular Education *(Reichsauschuß für hygienische Volksbelehrung)* were supposed to help restore the *Volksgesundheit* with hygienic education after the war. Thus, they even considered admitting natural health voluntary associations as members. Such associations had applied for membership to these committees, and a rejection of their application would have unnecessarily antagonized them.[16] The general secretary of the Saxon State Committee, Otto Neustätter, saw the possibility of instrumentalizing the associations on the behalf of the medical profession, since many of them seemed to have abandoned their staunch opposition to surgical procedures and medications. As chair of the Society for the Fight Against Quackery during the empire, Neustätter had been one of the hawks among the medical professionals who had condemned the so-called Kurpfuscher. Neustätter was supported by Carl Alexander, who also made a name for himself during the empire by attacking the natural therapy movement. The goal of regular physicians such as Neustätter (the first general secretary of the National Committee for Hygienic Popular Education) and Alexander was to tame the natural therapy movement. They conceded to natural therapy associations the right to popularize knowledge about preventive hygiene and hoped that in return they would accept the authority of the medical profession.[17]

Of course, such acceptance would have meant that the natural health movement or those of its voluntary associations that cooperated with the national or state committees for people's hygienic education would sever their ties with nonlicensed healers. Given the preference of many natural healing voluntary associations for university-trained physicians who practiced natural therapies, such a strategy had a lot to commend it from the perspective of regular physicians, especially since some increasingly realized the limited importance of scientific knowledge for therapeutic practice.[18] The leading clinician Friedrich Martius, a medical professor at the University of Rostock, approved of such a strategy in a letter to the general secretary of the Reichsausschuß. Martius argued that nineteenth-century scientific medicine with its chemical-physical materialism had contributed to a deep antagonism between scientific medicine and the "biological feelings" of the people. By acknowledging the fact that therapies could not always be derived completely from chemical and physical principles, and by emphasizing the importance of "pure experience in the biological sense," Martius argued that it might be possible to bridge the gap between the more moderate sectors of the natural therapy movement and scientific medicine by convincing supporters of natural therapy and homeopathy that the "commercial peddling of quack-cures by complete ignorants amounted to a cancer undermining the health of the people."[19]

Despite the support of leaders of the profession and veterans of the crusade against quackery, however, attempts to tame the natural health movement failed because the representatives of the German League of Physicians Associations *(Deutscher Ärztevereinsbund)* refused to cooperate in any way with natural therapy voluntary associations. Herzau, one of the representatives, successfully resisted acceptance of natural healing associations into the state committees and the national committee because such cooperation would give natural therapy added legitimacy.[20] The national committee thus became simply an agency that coordinated popular hygienic education efforts by government officials, health insurance agencies, the German Red Cross, and organizations led by regular physicians who focused on special issues, such as the German League for the Regeneration of the People (with a focus on eugenics), the Society for the Fight Against Venereal Disease, and the Central Committee for the Fight Against Tuberculosis.[21]

The most noteworthy action of the national committee was the organization of an "Imperial Health Week" *(Reichsgesundheitswoche, hereafter RGW)* in 1926, at the request of the Ministry of the Interior. During this week of hygienic propaganda, lectures by physicians, hygienic exhibitions, educational movies, and other events were organized on the local and state levels in cooperation with the state committtees and with city and county physicians.[22] Natural therapy lay associations were not explicitly excluded from participation, but the guidelines for the RGW did not list them among the organizations that could conduct events within its framework.

The Reich Ministry of the Interior and the Reichsausschuß decided that the participation of the natural healing associations would depend on their relations with regular physicians on the local level, but the ministry demanded that the associations play only a passive role, recruiting listeners for educational events; hygienic education as such would remain in the hands of university-trained physicians. The ministry feared the loss of regular physicians' support for the RGW if it officially allowed natural healing associations to participate.[23] Nevertheless, it seems that the natural therapy movement was capable of participating in some local events during the RGW. In Berlin, for example, the associations hosted a stand at the municipal hygienic fair, one of the central events of this propaganda week in the capital. One propagator of natural therapy lauded the RGW organizers' educational efforts and called for a cease-fire between the medical profession and the movement for the duration of the events. In his view, the renewed emphasis by regular physicians on the importance of a dietetic life to strengthen the constitution of individuals was very similar to what the movement had propagated for thirty years.[24]

Nevertheless, the natural therapy movement cannot be said to have triumphed during the Weimar years. The passing of the National Law for the Fight Against Venereal Disease in 1927 dealt one serious blow. This law, which broke with the principle of *Kurierfreiheit* (the freedom for everyone to practice medicine) established in 1869, made the treatment of venereal diseases by physicians mandatory and threatened irregular therapists who lacked medical approbation with stiff penalties (fines and up to one year in prison) if they did treat such diseases.[25] Although regular physicians were now increasingly willing to adopt the constitutional rhetoric of the life reform movement and some were even willing to accept natural therapy associations as junior partners in their hygienic educational efforts, they energetically fought off threats to their professional authority. This state of affairs is demonstrated by their resistance to the establishment of professorships for natural therapy, which were staffed by prominent activists in the movement during the early years of the Weimar Republic. The natural therapy movement could celebrate the installation of such chairs at the Friedrich-Wilhelm University in Berlin in 1920 and at the University of Jena in 1923 (the former going to Franz Schönenberger, a former editor of the *Naturarzt*), but these remained the only successful attempts to provide natural therapy with the legitimacy of an independent university base.[26]

Some regular physicians who were strictly opposed to lay medical practitioners nevertheless shared much of the life reformers' criticism of modern scientific medicine. The most outspoken one was the Danzig surgeon Erwin Liek. Liek's works were very popular with both physicians and laypersons who disliked the increased standardization and specialization within medicine.[27] He attributed many problems of the regular medical profession to the decline in private practice, because the majority of the German population was now covered by state-mandated health insurance.[28] In his view, this was a threat to the professional autonomy of the individual physician, who would never be adequately compensated for his unique abilities as a healing artist in a system that tried to standardize medical services and their compensation. Liek looked enviously to America, where physicians were not subject to similar constraints and had flourishing private practices.[29]

Liek's case is interesting because (like many life reformers) he criticized modern scientific medicine for not paying enough attention to the individual psychophysical constitution of patients. The physician, Liek maintained, was not to be a remote scientist in a university laboratory. He had to be an artist, capable of intuitively understanding the entire human being. The best medical scientist was usually not the best physician, for the personality of the healer was important. The art of the medical artist was his knowledge of people, which allowed him to develop a natural empathy for the sick one and his surroundings and "to build a bridge from soul to soul."[30]

According to Liek, the physician of the future had to understand the sick individual in his or her entirety and establish a relationship of trust. But this relationship was not to be a symmetrical one. Rather, confidence in the physician had to be based on an irrational trust in the physician's expertise; expertise, shrouded in secrecy and mystery, would instill belief and trust in the art of the practitioner. Since suggestion played an important part in the healing process, the physician would compromise his efficiency—his magical, priestly aura—if he shared his secrets with his patients.

Irregular practitioners could teach regular physicians much about gaining trust by fostering such mystery—namely, the art of bridging the distance between patient and healer by establishing a personal rapport without compromising the professional authority of the physician.[31] Liek's advice was not only based on his own experience as a practitioner. He also visited irregular practitioners and observed their consultations. Therefore, he could convincingly claim first-hand knowledge about the other side, which probably contributed to the popularity of his books among physicians.

Liek encountered heavy criticism from some of his colleagues, who argued that his books could provide dangerous ammunition for the defenders of the Kurpfuscher, especially since Liek explicitly argued for the integration of nonorthodox natural therapies into the therapeutic practices of scientific medicine. The editors of the *Ärztliches Vereinsblatt für Deutschland*, the journal that served as the mouthpiece of the corporate interests of the medical profession, worried that Liek's *Miracle in the Healing Science* could get into the hands of laypeople and provide arguments against regular medicine, undermining its authority even further. Liek's sympathetic reports about some so-called miracle healers in particular enraged some of his colleagues. The Heidelberg psychiatrist Hans Gruhle, for example, maintained that Liek's insights concerning suggestion were quite banal and that his defense of the "hocus-pocus" of the miracle healers could only have a negative impact on a younger generation of doctors.[32]

Erwin Liek saw in the intuitive, holistic, and empathic approach an opportunity for regular physicians to gain ground against the irregular practitioners. Nevertheless, his openness and frankness could backfire because defenders of outsider therapies drew on his arguments to attack orthodox medicine. According to an article in *Naturarzt*, Liek's work demonstrated that regular medicine and laboratory science were overrated, since they had little therapeutic value.[33] The leading homeopathic journal, the *Leipziger populäre Zeitschrift für Homö-opathie*, also interpreted Liek's book as a scathing criticism of the practices of the regular medical profession.[34]

The image of the physician as an artist with unique access to a knowledge superior to that of the university scientist was naturally appealing to the general practitioner. Other physicians, such as the university professors Alfred Gold-scheider and Hermann Kerschensteiner, stressed the necessity of reforming scientific medicine by recognizing the physical-spiritual unity of patients, but they did not want to abandon the scientific-analytical framework of regular medicine in favor of a rather uncontrolled intuitive approach that saw medicine as an art and not a science.[35] Liek himself did not argue for the abandonment of an analytical approach in medical science but stressed the importance of combining the methods. As the medical historian Eva Maria Klasen has argued, most of the internal critics of scientific medicine did not argue that one should abandon the secure scientific grounding of regular medicine but wanted to transcend a too-narrowly conceived rationalist and mechanistic attitude within the field. Analysis should not be abandoned, they thought, but supplemented by a synthetic *Gesamtschau*, an intuitive grasping of the body as a whole. The internist Louis Grote, for example, argued for a functional diagnosis that would liberate the physician from pathological concepts based on cellular pathology alone. Instead, he argued for the necessity of seeing each organ in relation to the organism as a whole and judging its performance as a "sufficiency" or "insufficiency" of its functions. He argued for a holistic and constitutional approach that took into account the patient in his psycho-physiological entirety.[36]

Many life reformers maintained that most diseases were caused by an accumulation of autotoxins in the body, and they advocated therapies that purged the body of toxic substances (see chapter 5). Such approaches also gained credence within regular medicine. In 1928, the Viennese gynecologist Bernhard Aschner published a book that advocated a "constitutional therapy" aimed at the purging of the body. In Aschner's view, diseases were caused by suppressed excretory functions, which led to an incorrect composition of the humors. He thought that bleeding and purging could help restore a healthy humoral balance, and he advocated a kind of heroic therapy in cases of high blood pressure, apoplexy, and bleeding of internal organs such as the uterus and the brain. He argued that the therapeutic effect would be achieved by the reduction of excess blood and had an "anti-dyscratic" effect due to the removal of toxins. As a gynecologist, he emphasized the importance of menstruation as a purging crisis.

This emphasis on the importance of the purging functions of the body brought him close to similar concepts within the natural therapy movement. Indeed, he cited Ernst Schweninger and the natural therapist Heinrich Lahmann as his predecessors.[37] Aschner's book was received well by advocates of natural therapies, despite its promotion of interventionist therapies that seemed to contrast with the supposedly gentle activation of the self-healing powers of the human organism. Oskar Mummert praised Aschner for his criticism of materialistic and mechanistic medicine and his defense of natural therapies.[38]

The extent to which life reform concepts shaped the hygienic propaganda of the regular medical profession can be best seen in the exhibitions mounted by the German Hygiene Museum. Martin Vogel, the scientific director of the museum, came very close to proposing the dietetic prescriptions of life reformers and natural therapists. Vogel published theoretical works concerning popular hygienic education, and he was responsible for shaping much of the proaganda of the museum.[39] Vogel was opposed to excessive meat consumption and was as staunch an opponent of alcohol consumption as any life reformer, claiming that both practices undermined the health and performance level of individuals and their offspring.[40] The nutrition exhibition that Vogel organized at the German Hygiene Museum even featured a statistical display showing the successes of vegetarians in long-distance running contests.[41] Vogel saw the human being as a whole, a view echoed by publications of the museum, which emphasized the necessity of a harmonious development of the entire human through a moderate lifestyle and physical exercise.

Propagators of natural therapies applauded regular physicians' new openness to natural therapies and healthy lifestyles. They pointed to positive remarks about natural therapies by such renowned physicians as August Bier, Hans Much, Erwin Liek, and Ferdinand Sauerbruch, who had argued that Vincenz Prießnitz's cold water therapies were an example of the contribution of the laity to medical therapy.[42] The Silesian peasant Prießnitz was the cultural hero of the movement. As early as the 1830s he had popularized therapies that were later taken up and refined by natural therapists. Nevertheless, this new appreciation of natural therapies by regular physicians was mixed, for movement supporters realized that a greater openness among practitioners of orthodox medicine could undercut support for their voluntary associations. In 1921, the twelfth federal assembly of the German League of Natural Living and Therapy Associations therefore adopted a resolution that tried to alert the public to the fundamental differences between therapy as propagated by natural therapists and that offered by regular physicians. The latter was a compromise doctrine that diluted the great heritage of the natural therapy movement with traditional regular therapies and the dispensing of drugs. According to the resolution, regular physicians were too inexperienced and therefore could not activate the natural healing powers of the organism in the way experienced naturopathic physicians could.[43]

The natural therapy advocate Paul Schirrmacher hoped that the medical profession's new emphasis on hygienic education was not designed to "take the wind out of the sails" of the movement.[44] The naturopathic physician Erwin Silber claimed in 1929 that the adoption of natural therapies by the medical profession was a superficial concession by the medical establishment to mislead the public. Regular medicine tried to misrepresent natural therapy as its own achievement and never mentioned the important contributions that the alternative health movement had made to the development of such therapies. In reality, medical practice had changed very little. There was still an overwhelming emphasis on drugs and surgery, and the natural therapy movement had still an important mission in fighting the materialistic-mechanistic spirit of regular medicine.[45] Natural therapists thus clearly saw the danger inherent in the constitutional discourse within regular medicine. Natural therapy increasingly lost its distinctiveness in the medical market of the Weimar era, and regular medicine was able to diffuse some of the contemporary discontent with the technological and mechanistic aspects of scientific medicine. These developments are also evident in the largest popular hygienic education efforts of the period: the hygiene exhibitions that took place in Düsseldorf and in Dresden in 1926, 1930, and 1931.

The Great Hygiene Exhibitions: Technocratic Hopes and Cultural Skepticism

Besides the RGW, the hygienic exhibition "Gesolei"—standing for *Gesundheit* (health), *Sozialfürsorge* (social welfare), and *Leibesübungen* (physical exercise)— was the other great popular educational effort in 1926. It was organized by the city of Düsseldorf with financial and organizational support from the state of Prussia and the national government. The German hygiene museum in Dresden provided the expertise and exhibition materials for the core exhibitions on the human organism and hygiene. The Gesolei as a whole had three major sections, in which public institutions, church and independent welfare organizations, and sports associations demonstrated the progress that Germany had made in the fields of health care, social welfare, and physical exercise. The goals of the exhibition were twofold: to give Düsseldorf, one of the cities on the Rhine most affected by the French occupation of the Rhineland, an economic boost so that it could become a center for fairs and exhibitions as it had been before the war, and to demonstrate ways in which the productivity of the nation could be raised by the improvement of its citizens' health.[46]

In the view of the organizers of the Gesolei, eugenic education of the public was important for the creation of a healthier and more efficient nation. The Gesolei, therefore, mounted exhibits demonstrating the inheritance of psychiatric disorders and the biological degeneration of criminal families. Other displays urged visitors to select a healthy marriage partner and demanded eugenic marriage certificates that attested to the health of a prospective spouse in order to guarantee the fitness of future generations.[47] This emphasis on eugenics was a reflection of the growing official recognition that the topic received in the 1920s.[48] The negative demographic impact of World War I led to the acceptance of eugenics as a rational means of management of population across the political spectrum. Before the war, government bureaucrats had been concerned mainly with the decline of the birthrate; eugenicists' concerns about the declining quality of the population had found little resonance within government circles. This would change after 1918, as several facts attest: people worried that the declining birthrate disproportionally affected the valuable segments of German society, which were more fit for the military and therefore most affected by the war losses; lectures on eugenics became a regular feature in German medical schools; public and state support for eugenics culminated in the establishment of a national eugenics institute, the Kaiser Wilhelm Institute for Anthropology, Human Heredity, and Eugenics, in 1927; and Social Democrats, liberals, conservatives, and even supporters of the Catholic center party accepted and actively promoted eugenic arguments.[49]

The qualitative and quantitative recovery of the German population after the war was a major concern of the Gesolei. As Ernst Poensgen, its director, explained, the war and reparation payments had left Germany in a situation that demanded the highest economic performance level possible, which could only be achieved by humans who were completely healthy. Therefore it was necessary to show how the workforce could be used most efficiently and how health, the basis of the working power of individuals, could be preserved and restored.[50] As deputy chair of the United Steel Works, the largest German steel concern of the 1920s, Poensgen was one of the chief propagators of company sports *(Werksport)*, which, in his view, fostered loyalty, contentment, and productivity among workers (in addition to providing exercise).[51]

At the center of the Gesolei as well as other educational efforts of the German Hygiene Museum in the 1920s was to be the "German Man" *(deutsche Mensch)* and the living conditions necessary for him to generate the effort to overcome the economic difficulties following the war without further harm.[52]

The emphasis was on a "human economy" that used human resources in the most efficient way, both for people's own good and for the good of the economy and the nation. In order to assure the most efficient use of individuals' potential and prevent people from being overtaxed and overstressed, publications of the hygiene museum insisted on the importance of choosing the right profession—one that was commensurate with one's natural abilities and talents.[53] Sections of the Gesolei, therefore, focused on the placement of youth in professions matching their physical and mental abilities; psychotechnical tests geared to assess dexterity, reaction time, and ability to concentrate; and work physiology and the most efficient use of physical labor.[54]

The Gesolei's emphasis on the viability of technocratic solutions to social and economic problems was a reflection of the rather short-lived optimism of the "Golden Twenties," the relatively quiet years of the republic after currency stabilization and before the depression. During this period, the popular imagination was captivated by the utopian promises heralded by the achievements of American civilization: Social and economic problems ultimately would be resolved by the adoption of technological innovations by private businesses. Efficient means of production such as Fordism (rationalized production processes as exemplified by Henry Ford's assembly line) and Taylorism (scientific management as propagated by Frederick Winslow Taylor in the United States) were to provide the answer to the crises of the modern business cycle. As Mary Nolan has shown, the belief in efficiency and rationalization was widely shared by people of different political persuasions, each of them emphasizing the aspects of Fordism that were most compatible with their own perceived interests.[55] Representatives of German business stressed the need to increase productivity and lower costs at the expense of wages in order to make the prices for German products more competitive on the world market. Social Democrats, on the other hand, emphasized the need to lower costs with technological innovation and increase aggregate domestic demand by lowering prices and raising workers' wages. Business and the moderate labor movement thus accepted Fordist productionism, with its emphasis on lowering costs by means of organizational and technological innovation. In contrast to labor, business representatives refused to go along with the consumerist aspect of Fordism, which saw in high wages the precondition for a prosperous economy sustained by sufficient aggregate demand.

The Social Democratic wing of the labor movement accepted aspects of rationalization, such as psychotechnics and work physiology, that had a high potential for more efficient exploitation of the labor force. Like eugenics, psychotechnics—with tests that were supposed to identify the right workers for a given job—as well as work physiology, which tried to organize the work process to prevent the tiring of workers in a monotonous work process, were seen by Social Democratic leaders as important aspects of a scientifically structured and rationally ordered ideal society whose increased efficiency would eventually benefit the workers.[56]

Even before the Great Depression, however, some criticized the promise of American civilization as shallow and alienating. Americanism was seen as one of the symptoms of the crisis of classical modernity. It deprived people of their autonomy by fragmenting the self, by reducing people to cogs in a vast technological machinery. The journalist Adolf Halfeld, who had lived for several years as a newspaper correspondent in the United States, criticized what he perceived as the dehumanizing aspects of Americanism as a social system. In America, Halfeld claimed, only success in terms of wealth mattered, and the utilitarian design of the cities demonstrated how "the majesty of purpose *(Zweck)* tyrannized the goddess of beauty."[57] Americanism, Halfeld claimed, was the feudalism of financial success, and American workers were the standardized parts of a social machinery that deprived them of their rights and subjected their inner lives to the demands of productivity with the help of psychotechnics. In Halfeld's view, psychotechnics was not part of a technocratic solution for social problems; instead it raised the "spectre of a future society . . . where card files, measurements, soul analyses and brain tests *(Gehirntestate)* take over the role of fate for the standardized individual without rights, imprisoning him or her in this or that chamber of the immense social machinery."[58] For people such as Halfeld, the psychotechnics that was celebrated in the Gesolei as a technocratic solution to Germany's quest for social and economic efficiency raised fears of alienation and loss of personal autonomy.

Such misgivings about the blessings of modern industrial society notwithstanding, there was a pronounced sense of optimism among the organizers of the Gesolei. The bad times of war, revolution, inflation, and foreign occupation seemed to be things of the past, and there was hope that the difficulties ahead could be mastered by means of technocratic rationalization. This sense was probably further enhanced by the huge success of the Gesolei, which attracted seven and a half million people.[59]

Unfortunately, there are no precise data about the social background of those who attended the big hygiene exhibitions of the 1920s and 1930s, but the very size of the crowds suggests that these events served as a form of popular entertainment that transcended class divisions. This cross-class appeal is plausible for several reasons. First, as historians have noted, forms of popular mass entertainment such as movies and spectator sports contributed to the erosion of a traditional socialist milieu in the labor movement, with its shared rituals, sports associations, and organized leisure activities.[60] In addition, such popular hygienic education was supported by many on the Left during the 1920s. The RGW, for example, was originally the brainchild of Julius Moses, the Social Democratic health spokesman.[61] Finally, there were the socialist popularizers of science. The journal *Urania*, which stressed the contribution that modern science and technology could make to a future socialist society, found a sizeable readership among socialist workers.[62] The popular science exhibits concerning hygiene therefore might have held considerable appeal for workers.

Much of the archival material about the Gesolei exhibition is lost. Illustrated catalogues still exist describing in detail the interactive displays that appealed to people's desire to have fun. Visitors could, for example, visualize the working power of the heart by generating with hand pressure a spurt of water in a transparent tube with the same amount of energy needed for each human heartbeat. According to Martin Vogel, the scientific director of the German Hygiene Museum at the time, such displays aimed for "living clarification" of the performance of the human body; this "visualization" *(Veranschaulichung)*, Vogel thought, was the key appeal to the lay public. Visitors could illuminate parts of anatomical models of human bodies by pressing a button. In one of these demonstrations, pictures of worms and intestinal parasites appeared together with the organs where those parasites could be found (see figure 30).[63] The most famous example of the practical application of Veranschaulichung was the model of the "transparent man" *(gläserner Mensch)*, first introduced to the public during the hygiene exhibition in Dresden in 1930 (see figure 31). This life-sized transparent model of a man whose inner organs could be illuminated became one of the major attractions of the German Hygiene Museum.[64] The organizers presented the gläserner Mensch as a work of art that revealed "the beauty of the forms of the body *[Formenschönheit des Körpers]* and its individual parts as an image *[Sinnbild]* of the perfect harmony that rules the laws of life."[65]

Veranschaulichung tried to bridge the gap between the gaze of the expert scientist and that of laypeople, making visible otherwise hidden physiological and psychological processes.[66] Fritz Kahn, a physician and author of popular scientific books and articles, therefore represented the functions of the human body as a factory in one of his publications.[67] The mechanisms of breathing were illustrated by way of a transport system in a modern factory, with elevators bringing oxygen to the lungs, the blood, and organs (see figure 32).[68] Another illustration compared the function of the ear to that of a car, claiming that the two were identical (see figure 33).[69] In this image, the auditory canal corresponds to the motor, in which the compressed gases (air or, in the auto, the products of internal combustion) transmit pressure to the liquid of the cochlea, or the back wheel, through the eardrum, or the flywheel. These attempts to create *Anschaulichkeit* through technological visualization were quite compatible with

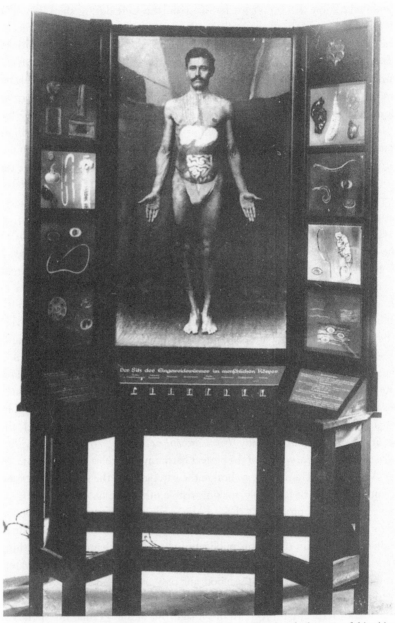

FIGURE 30. Anschaulichkeit exhibited during the Gesolei. Pushing the buttons of this object illuminated parasites along with their seat in the human digestive system. Deutsches Hygienemuseum Dresden, Bildsammlung, Fotodokumentation Städteausstellungen, Sign. 697, No. 34.

FIGURE 31. The first "gläserner Mensch," shown during the 1930 hygiene exhibition in Dresden. Deutsches Hygienemuseum Dresden, Bildsammlung, 1930, Sign. 1142 IV., fig. 15.

holistic assumptions about the purposeful interdependence of parts within a system. After a detailed discussion of the anatomy of the human skull, Kahn quoted Goethe as he warned his readers that they should not forget the spiritual bonds that animated those parts:

> Whoever wants to understand and describe the meaning of the living
> tries first to drive out the spirit,

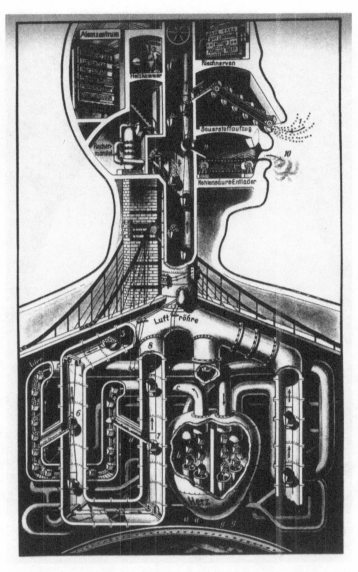

FIGURE 32. Man's breathing function. Kahn, *Leben des Menschen,* vol. 3, table 12. Landesbibliothek Stuttgart.

then he holds the parts in his hand

missing unfortunately only the spiritual bond.[70]

In keeping with holistic constitutional approaches of scientific medicine, Kahn did not want to reduce the human organism to chemical and physical

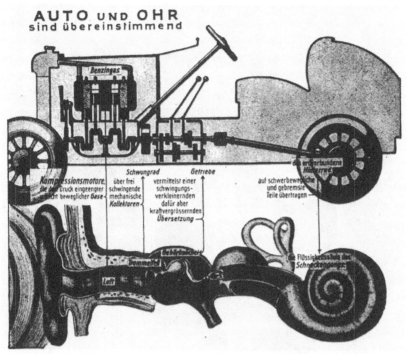

FIGURE 33. The car and the ear are identical. Kahn, *Leben des Menschen*, 4:307. Landesbibliothek Stuttgart.

processes. He believed in the intuitive gaze of an educated observer who could decipher the character of humans if he could grasp their physiognomies. In Kahn's depiction of the biological mechanisms of the sense of smell, the body is more than a machine. The illustration mirrors the social hierarchy of a modern industrial enterprise: The smell of a roast is transmitted by a pneumatic dispatch system through laboratories representing the smelling field and smelling center to the control center, representing the brain. The control center finally orders the machinist in the saliva center to release saliva (see figure 34).[71] Such technological images were organic, aesthetic representations of physiological functions; they presented such functions as the outcome of a harmonious, purposeful interaction of hierarchically ordered elements.

Organic hierarchical conceptions of the body and of human society had already been envisioned by the industrialist Lingner, the driving force behind the first international hygiene exhibition in Dresden in 1911. In 1912, Lingner claimed that the human body was the perfect organizational model for a modern enterprise.[72] During the Weimar Republic such images captured the imag-

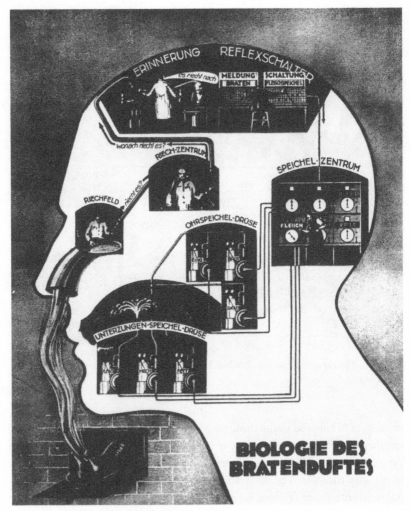

FIGURE 34. Biology of the roast smell. Kahn, *Leben des Menschen,* vol. 3, table 15. Landesbibliothek Stuttgart.

ination of life reformer Hans Surén, who used Fritz Kahn's illustrations to convey to his readers the functions of human breathing.[73]

The exhibits of the German Hygiene Museum at the Gesolei indicate that the strategy in hygienic education had shifted. Whereas in 1911 the idea had been to impress upon people the necessity of a healthy lifestyle with sometimes horrifying exhibits showing the latest stages of venereal and other diseases, the Gesolei appealed to reason rather than fear. According to the physician Schloßmann, one of its organizers, it was much more reasonable to show visitors models of the first symptoms of a disease, so that they could recognize the initial stages before it was too late. He pleaded for an exhibition that would impress its visitors with something other than fear.[74]

The concerns of the bacteriological age, however, continued to be important in the health propaganda of the Gesolei, as well as in that of the RGW that was organized during the same year. Both events emphasized avoiding the spread of infections by behaving hygienically in public: Open sneezing, coughing, and spitting in public, for instance, were to be avoided in order to prevent the spread of tuberculosis and other infectious diseases. The health propaganda of the German Hygiene Museum still enthusiastically celebrated Robert Koch for his discovery of the tuberculosis bacillus, claiming that it was Koch who had proved once and for all that tuberculosis was an infectious disease that could be cured and not a hereditary disease, as popularly believed.

Yet the issue of heredity was brought in through the back door. In contrast to classical bacteriologists, of the late nineteenth century, H. Beschorner, the author of a guide to a tuberculosis exhibition mounted by the museum, claimed that the tuberculosis bacillus was only capable of unfolding its pathogenic effects if the infected individual had a constitutional predisposition to it. Therefore, it was not surprising that children of tubercular parents also caught tuberculosis, for they were the offspring of weak and physically inferior parents.[75] To cure tuberculosis (which the author insisted was possible), he consequently recommended the entire arsenal of dietetic life reform prescriptions in order to strengthen the general constitution and increase the resistance of the body *(Abhärtung)*: air baths, light and sun baths, water cures to support the breathing of the skin, nutrition, a balance between rest, exercise, work, and leisure—all preferably under medical supervision in a sanatorium for lung diseases. This advice again demonstrates the extent to which the regular medical profession adopted aspects of the natural therapy movement.[76]

With modernization, people expressed their fears of becoming the passive objects of scientific experts; as we have seen, natural therapy supporters accused regular physicians of treating diseases rather than people. During the Gesolei, regular physicians were eager to address these anxieties, which they knew were partly responsible for the crisis of public confidence in regular medicine and the fragmentation of the medical market. Since the German Association of Natural Scientists and Physicians held its annual meeting simultaneously with the Gesolei, the occasion made it possible for well-known physicians to address a popular audience directly.

The famous surgeon and medical professor Ferdinand Sauerbruch seized this opportunity to speak to a mixed audience of physicians and laypeople about aspects of the "crisis of medicine" in a presentation titled "Healing Art and Natural Science." According to a report sent to the Reich Health Office, Sauerbruch's presentation was very persuasive, and he received tremendous applause from the audience, even though, as the reporting physician noted, his remarks were rather general and superficial. In his speech Sauerbruch alluded to popular criticism of scientific medicine. He conceded deficiencies in its therapeutic approaches partially in order to defuse attacks by defenders of alternative therapeutic systems. Sauerbruch's presentation is an excellent example of what the sociologist Pierre Bourdieu has termed a "condescension strategy."[77] Sauerbruch minimized the vast difference in status between himself and his audience and won its sympathy by addressing it on its own terms. He distinguished between the "healing art" *(Heilkunst)* and natural science and maintained that each time the natural sciences had reached a high point, medicine as a healing art had suffered. Sauerbruch claimed that there really was no such thing as medical science. There was only a "medical art," and intuition was the most important instrument of this art. Young physicians, he lamented, were incapable of giving thorough clinical examinations by evaluating their patients according to external appearance and psychological condition; instead, they wasted their time with so-called scientific examinations. Reality was constituted by the physician's experience of and feelings *(Empfindung)* about the patient, and scientific facts therefore had to be subordinated.

The human being, Sauerbruch claimed, was the greatest and most accurate physical apparatus in existence, and the physician needed intuition—a higher form of instinct—in order to grasp its complexity. Seen in this light, modern scientific medicine was harmful to the sick. Although the healing art was unthinkable without natural science, natural science had to remain the servant of the healing art and should not become its master. "It is self-evident that the presentation which culminated in the beautiful words 'Being a physician means being a servant to man' *[Arzt sein ist Dienst am Menschen]* triggered tremendous applause," the reporter to the Reich Health Office laconically remarked.[78]

The crisis of classical scientific medicine was reflected still more clearly in the International Hygiene Exhibition of 1930 in Dresden. Because the content of the core exhibition *Der Mensch* was simultaneously published as a reader for the first time, this is the best-documented of these exhibitions.[79] This work provides a superb example of the role of constitutional concepts in the health propaganda of an institution such as the German Hygiene Museum, which was committed to the interests of the regular medical profession. Like Sauerbruch, the introduction to the book stressed the necessity of understanding humans in their physical and psychological individuality. The authors, Roderich von Engelhardt and Martin Vogel, implicitly argued for the epistemological superiority of the Bildung of the educated Bildungsbürger as a privileged means to unlock the secrets of nature through intuition.[80]

Drawing on the epistemology developed by Johann Wolfgang von Goethe in his *Theory of Colors,* they claimed that biology could only be a science based on an understanding from "inside."[81] People could understand themselves and the world only through their subjectivity, because their consciousness was in fundamental correspondence with "life as it developed" *(Verlauf einer Lebenserscheinung)* and could therefore reflect life in a mirror as their own experience. Classical mechanistic natural science, Engelhardt argued, could only provide symbols for things that could not really be explained. Though necessary, science could not reveal eternal truths. Engelhardt maintained that the practitioner must intuitively grasp the orderly and purposeful organization of an organism and that this could not be done with a dissecting knife or a microscope. The object of medicine was therefore the constitution of the entire organism and its reaction to pathogenic irritants.[82]

Engelhardt did not advocate the epistemological principles of mechanistic natural science but rather an artistic, intuitive approach to understanding nature. In his contribution to the 1930 exhibition reader, he argued for the kind of *Wesensschau* (the intuitive understanding of the essence of a natural phenomenon) advocated by the contemporary philosopher and characterologist Ludwig Klages, whom he cited at length:[83] "One takes the world as an endless sign language to be deciphered by speculative immersion. One does not really observe things; instead one rather contemplates the face of things *[blickt in das Antlitz der Dinge]* and asks which pulse of life, which secret urge to build *[heimlicher Bautrieb]*, which evolution of the soul, speaks from these traits."[84]

According to Klages, a person's essence or unified character was expressed in every aspect of the body or in anything a person did. He was the leading propagator of handwriting analysis as a physiognomy of movement. Character was expressed in the "symbolism of the hand," by which Klages' epigone Engelhardt meant not only the symbolic expression of the hereditary character of human types such as race and social class but also character traits acquired in the course of a person's history. The hand as a symbol was thus a signifier of hereditary predisposition and at the same time a historical document molded by both nature and culture.[85]

The physicians who organized the hygiene exhibitions of the early 1930s shared many assumptions of leading eugenicists, and eugenics was an important aspect of the health propaganda disseminated at these events. The socialist

Rainer Fetscher, professor of hygiene at the Technical University of Dresden and, from 1926 on, director of Dresden's Marriage and Sexual Advice Clinic *(Dresdner Ehe- und Sexualberatungsstelle)* was responsible for the eugenics sections of the 1930 and 1931 exhibitions.[86] Basing his arguments on the standard textbook by Baur, Fischer, and Lenz, Fetscher emphasized the need to reverse counterselective trends in the demographic development of Germany (that is to say, inferior stocks reproducing at a faster rate than healthier stocks). He warned people to be careful in the selection of their marriage partners; they would need a healthy partner in order to produce successful offspring.[87]

But Fetscher's views about eugenics were also different in important ways from the views of other eugenicists. In contrast to Fritz Lenz, for example, who propagated a eugenics based strictly on artificial selection, Fetscher wanted to supplement selection by prescribing exercise that would strengthen peoples' constitutions. Exercise, he claimed, would contribute to self-discipline and divert the mind from luxuries and questionable forms of entertainment, which could in turn contribute to venereal diseases and alcoholism (both harmful to the germ plasma). Exercise would also make the body more resistant to infectious diseases such as tuberculosis.[88] Fetscher argued that heredity determined the mental and physical potential of an individual but that that potential could only be fully realized with education. Far from being a strict hereditarian determinist, he argued that the environment played a large role in inhibiting or fostering peoples' positive development. He attacked both the naive optimism of people who thought they could lead an unhygienic lifestyle because they had confidence in their hereditary endowment and the desperate fatalism of those who thought that their bad genes inevitably condemned them to a fate of sickness and disease.[89] Like any life reformer, Fetscher knew that a radical hereditarianism would make hygienic lifestyle prescriptions useless because it would not leave any room for hope and personal agency.

Although Fetscher stressed the importance of environmental factors in human development, he still ranked people according to their hereditary potential. In the eugenicist's meritocratic utopia, all people would realize the essence embodied in their genes, and socioeconomic standing was the result of personal achievement based on hereditary difference. The socialist Fetscher did not claim, however, that human talent was confined mainly to the educated and respectable sectors of the population. He maintained that there were "hereditarily favored" people from proletarian backgrounds who could not develop their potential because of their poverty.[90] Such claims distinguished him from Fritz Lenz, who, as a member of the conservative German National People's Party, did not conceal his classist biases.[91]

Fetscher also tried to dissociate himself from contemporary racial theories and the Nordic racism that were propagated by such conservative eugenicists as Lenz, Alfred Ploetz, and Ernst Rüdin.[92] He explicitly rejected the term "racial hygiene" in one of his publications on eugenics because he did not want to confuse eugenics with the pseudo sciences.[93] Chapter 7 discusses some of the racial theories that eugenicists such as Fetscher considered pseudo-scientific.

CHAPTER 7

CONSTITUTIONAL TYPOLOGIES:
WEIMAR RACIAL SCIENCE AND MEDICINE

As the previous two chapters have shown, eugenic thought was an important aspect of popular and expert hygienic discourses. Although the eugenicists involved in the organization of the Weimar hygiene exhibitions were very concerned with the health of the nation as it related to heredity, they tried to distance themselves from contemporary theories of Nordic racism. This was not the case, however, for other contemporary eugenicists. For example, Nordic racism was an important element of the program of Fritz Lenz, co-author of the leading eugenics textbook of the time. As the historian Sheila Weiss has shown, Lenz—who saw the Nordic race as the most talented and creative one—racialized the class bias of the conservative academic elite. He claimed that the upper class and the educated middle class had a much larger percentage of Nordic blood than the lower orders. For Lenz, the war and the revolution (with its one-sided promotion of workers' interests) were disasters, since they contributed to the "extinction of educated families—the primary standard bearers of German culture."[1]

Most Weimar racial theorists did not deny the possibility that there were exceptional, individual Nordics from a humble social background. They shared Lenz's view that educated and higher classes had the highest percentage of Nordic blood, however. According to the philologist Hans F. K. Günther and the cultural critic Paul Schultze-Naumburg, Nordics represented in their very essence the aesthetic sensibilities and cultural creativity of the educated classes.

As the historian Bernd Weisbrod has argued, the early years of the Weimar period challenged deeply ingrained moral convictions held by the middling sectors of the Bürgertum regarding the relation between personal performance and social rewards. University degrees were devalued in a tight academic job market, and the respectable Bürger, whose savings and sense of social security were destroyed in the course of inflation and postwar crisis, looked with envy at the supposed wealth of war profiteers and speculators.[2] Contemporary racial discourse tried to account for these developments, finding a particularly receptive audience among university students and academics with uncertain job prospects.

The racial theorists discussed in this chapter proposed holistic concepts of racial constitutions that posited an organic link between the physical appearance of different racial types and corresponding spiritual and mental qualities. In other words, the psychological constitution of individuals, their character and mental abilities, could be deciphered intuitively from their physical appearance. Similar epistemological assumptions are also evident in contemporary constitutional medicine.[3] Drawing on new scientific fields such as endocrinology, as well as on constitutional concepts developed during the empire, serious scientists such as the psychiatrist Ernst Kretschmer tried to formulate a theory of constitutional types that showed a connection between morphology and corresponding healthy and pathological psychological states. Here, as we have seen elsewhere, one's ability to decipher the constitutional type or essence of a person depended on *Anschauung*, the ability to "see." This Anschauung could then be supplemented with measurements that confirmed what had already been intuitively grasped.

Kretschmer's work was well received by the lay public and by physicians. His distinctions between leptosome, athletic, and pyknic constitutional types became part of German popular culture, because his theories were presented to a large public in the print media and in contemporary hygiene exhibitions. Kretschmer's constitutional typology also influenced the clinical vocabulary of the time.[4] The gynecologist Paul Mathes, for example, applied the typology to women. I show that his use of Kretschmer's work was influenced by contemporary perceptions of women's sexuality and changing gender relations.

Racial Constitutionalism

Books about racial science such as Hans F. K. Günther's *Racial Science of the German People* enjoyed considerable popularity during the Weimar period, leading historians to regard Weimar racial physiognomy as fertile ground for the growth of Nazism.[5] Although such interpretations have some plausibility, it is still worthwhile to try to understand the racial theories of the Weimar years in terms of the attraction they held for people at the time. What did a person such as Günther intend to communicate to his audience in 1922, when his book first appeared? To ask such questions is not to downplay the fact that the popularization of racial theories contributed to the rise of the radical right in Weimar Germany. Rather, an understanding of why racial theories were meaningful in their own time helps us better to understand some aspects of the rise of Nazism.

The question of which social groups were particularly attracted to certain discourses has always been problematic for historians, but there is circumstantial evidence indicating that university students and academic professionals who were worried about their futures were particularly drawn to racial discourse. Limitations on career opportunities for university graduates were exacerbated by the increase in students, whose numbers grew from 60,235 in 1914 to 87,312 in 1921 (a jump of 44 percent).[6] Hugo Iltis, a Social Democratic critic of contemporary racial thought, noted that racial theories found an audience among academics with uncertain job prospects. Believers in these theories, he claimed, derived "the right to a good position" from inborn racial qualities. Such theories allowed people to denounce more qualified competitors as "racially inferior." It was no surprise that *Rassebücher* like the one by Günther found this audience and that some publishers produced them in a "rabbit like fashion."[7]

It should also be no surprise that the *Burschenschaftlichen Blätter*, the official organ of the largest student fraternity organization of the Weimar period, recommended Günther's *Racial Science of the German People* to its readers as a work of science that showed the way to the recovery of the German Volk. Referring to the bleak job prospects of university graduates, Fritz Herbst, the author of the review, deplored the fact that "for Germany's best sons the road to . . . success remained closed" during the postwar years. Equating the creative and ruling elements of the German Volk with the Nordics, Herbst envisioned a Germany in which a purified, creative Nordic race could again play a leading social and cultural role.[8]

It is significant that the vocabulary of racial difference used by the Weimar racial theorists emphasized essential differences within the white race. Since they tried to express their dissatisfaction with developments within German society, racial theorists focused less on racial differences between Europeans and non-Europeans.[9] Günther and others racialized wealth and status distinctions among Germans by contrasting the beautiful and cultivated Nordic race with "inferior" races to which they attributed either the supposed superficiality and materialism of the wealthy or the vulgarity of the lower classes. In this respect, the contemporary discourse about race was tied to a discourse about Bildung and aesthetics. The debate about race, therefore, was very much a debate about social relations in German society.[10]

Hans F. K. Günther (1891–1968), the son of a chamber musician from Freiburg, in Baden, was neither a physician nor a biologist. He studied German and comparative linguistics and received his doctorate from the University of Freiburg in 1914. Although Günther indulged in fantasies about the heroic nature of Nordic men, he did not serve as a soldier in World War I because he was declared unfit. In 1919, after passing the Gymnasium teaching examination, he briefly taught as a substitute before he was commissioned by the extreme right-wing medical publisher Julius Friedrich Lehmann to write *Racial Science of the German People*. Günther had impressed Lehmann with his imaginative descriptions of the intuitively perceived racial physiognomies of the farmers and hikers they had encountered on a hike in the Bavarian Alps.

Even though Günther had no credentials as a natural scientist, the fact that his works were published by Lehmann, one of the most important medical publishers of the period, bestowed scientific credentials on his writings. In 1930 Günther was appointed to a professorship in social anthropology at the University of Jena, a position made possible by the Nazi presence in the state of Thuringia's coalition government.[11] Günther was worried about the decreasing value of Bildung and traditional aesthetic norms, which were challenged by mass culture and cultural avant-gardism alike. Like many other recent university graduates in the postwar years, Günther had difficulty finding a permanent position as Gymnasium teacher in the 1920s. Therefore he shared the concern of the Gebildeten that their Bildung could not provide them with a social and economic position that was commensurate with their expectations.[12]

Günther developed the image of an ideal Nordic type by contrasting it to negatively stereotyped inferior racial types, in particular the Eastern (Alpine) and the Western (Mediterranean) races. Although the names of these racial types alluded to their geographical origins, they did not primarily designate specific contemporary ethnic groups or nationalities. Günther conceived these types instead as the bearers of spiritual racial essences, which he saw at work in contemporary German society (see figures 35 and 36 for the Nordic and Eastern types).[13] At the center of Günther's racial mythology was the Nordic man—the male Bildungsbürger and soldier—whose character was marked by courageousness and an ability to make judgments and defend himself. Like any good Bürger, the Nordic man liked to be free, independent, and individualistic, and he derived his self-respect and honor from the fact that he could "prove himself in life." His urge for spiritual freedom and independence made him most likely a Protestant. Only the Nordic man was truly creative and capable of giving "the

42, 43. Bruder und Schwester aus westfälischem Uradel.

44. Braunschweig.

45. Hessen-Nassau   Adolf Fick.

46. Deutschland.

47. Westfalen. v. Zumbusch.

FIGURE 35. The Nordic or primarily Nordic race. Günther, *Rassenkunde des deutschen Volkes*, 47. Private collection.

111 a, b. Ukraine (Bez. Jekaterinoslaw). Oſtiſch. (Aufn: Dr. Lenz.)

112. Amt Bonndorf (bad. Schwarzwald). Oſtiſch. (Aufn.: Prof. Fiſcher, Freibg.)

113. Amt Neuſtadt (bad. Schwarzwald). Oſtiſch. (Aufn.: Ruf, Freibg.)

114a, b. Wolfach (Baden). (Vorwiegend)ˈ oſtiſch. (Nach Ripley, The Races of Europe.)

FIGURE 36. The eastern race. The first person is a Ukrainian; the other three are Germans from Baden, in the southwestern part of the country. Günther, *Rassenkunde des deutschen Volkes*, 76. Private collection.

masses life and movement." Thus, to recall our earlier discussion, the higher classes had more Nordic blood in their veins than the lower classes.[14] According to Günther, the racial differences between the higher and lower classes were manifest in their physiognomies. Citing the racial hygienist Fritz Lenz, Günther claimed: "No unbiased observer doubts that one can tell apart with a single gaze the [racial] type of . . . members from the higher estates from the one [of members] of the lower [estates] even if they are dressed alike."[15]

Despite theories regarding the abilities and noble character traits of the Nordic race, many of its members did not achieve the position in society that Günther believed they deserved, a position that was built into their racial constitution. To account for this failure to realize his potential, Günther explained that, despite his virtues, the Nordic man was too careless; this carelessness was then turned into a virtue, the result of the Nordic man's unwillingness to strive.[16] Strivers were characterized by a "soulless restlessness" in pursuit of material gain, which starkly contrasted with the selflessness of the Nordic. The Nordic man was thus undone in economic life by his own noble virtues, whereas the Easterner, with his pettiness and lack of nobility, was often economically more successful than his more deserving Nordic counterpart.[17] Here we have a theme that the Nazis would later use successfully in their electoral appeals to the German middle classes. As the historian Thomas Childers has shown, the Nazis played virtuosically on the theme of the illegitimate achiever (Jew or socialist), the outsider, who increasingly seemed to gain positions in the civil service and in economic life—positions that should have been given to those who considered themselves the legitimate members of the German middle classes.[18]

In his description of the Eastern race, Günther employed many contemporary anti-Semitic stereotypes, but it is important to note that in his racial taxonomy the Eastern race and the Jew occupied separate categories (for more on anti-Semitism, see below). Günther claimed that members of the Eastern race often succeeded in depriving the selfless Nordics of their independence. The cliché of the Eastern man combined the welfare cheat and the successful businessman. Whereas the Nordic man tried to achieve success on his own, the Eastern man hoped for support by the state.[19] The Eastern man was the social upstart, the businessman, the merchant; in the world he dominated, anything could be bought. Competence and ability did not count anymore. The only virtue that counted was the "cunning of the big city."[20]

The virtues of the Nordic race were also expressed in the physical beauty of its men and women. No race, Günther told his readers, could express the feminine and the masculine essences in bodily form and facial expressions as could the Nordic one. It was in this race that the anatomical differences between men and women were most pronounced.[21] The beauty of the Nordic race was asexual. It did not engender sexual feelings but was in a Kantian sense pleasing without arousing mundane interest. In his book *Race and Style*, Günther related the story of a Nordic Protestant pastor who encountered a beautiful Nordic girl working as a waitress in a tavern. The pastor was so struck by her beauty that he could not give her a tip because this would have introduced material interests into their relationship, unthinkable with a Nordic woman.[22] Like Stratz, Günther thought that Nordic women were different, that they had nothing of the sexual vulgarity that could be found among the women of other races.

In contrast, the Eastern, or Eastern-Baltic, race had neither a clear form nor evident content. It did not possess a Gestalt and was unable to create a consistent art style. Günther believed that the virtues of the Nordic race were expressed in its male body type, with its straight posture, pronounced chest, and small abdomen. This posture (chest out and belly in) was alien to the Eastern man, whose appearance was a negation of the beauty ideal of the Occident, which in turn was shaped by Nordic ideals. The body form of the male members of the Eastern race was feminine, with narrow shoulders and wide hips, and women did not possess the forms characteristic of their sex, since they were sturdy and their overall physical appearance was masculine. Both men and women of this race were lacking the clarity of form of the Nordics. The Eastern race as a whole represented feminine formlessness, since women tended to preserve the negative traits of their race longer than men, who tended to inherit the Nordic traits.[23]

This concern with form and formlessness recalls Klaus Theweleit's work on contemporary Freikorps soldiers. Although the soldiers did not express their anxieties in Günther's racial idiom, the fear of being inundated by the feminine formlessness of the masses was a recurrent theme in their writings. The officer Ernst von Salomon, for example, expressed such fears in his description of an antimilitaristic demonstration in Hamburg that he perceived as a mass of hysterical proletarian women who spat at the soldiers and attacked them with stones.[24] Günther claimed to have had a similar experience during the days of revolution, when he was once surrounded by a mob of factory workers, members of the Eastern race agitated by a communist of the same race. During this scene his gaze came to rest on the impressive figure of a Nordic wagon driver, who was not at all impressed by the hustling and bustling around him. He simply stood out from the mass because of his Nordic essence. The factory workers' complaints were like a "bleak, dirty flood that surrounded an island." The wagon driver exemplified in his posture the old Nordic Franconians as well as the quiet and stability that Günther yearned for and that had disappeared after the war.[25]

Günther's depiction of the Eastern race as lower-class mob conjured up images of the Russian as well as the German revolution.[26] Such messages were not lost on Weimar Communists, who rejected contemporary racial discourse because of its classist assumptions. The Communist newspaper *Thüringer Volksblatt*, for example, attacked Günther's inaugural lecture as a professor of social anthropology in Jena. Günther, said the paper, merely deplored the fact that the oppressive upper class was threatened by a proletarian lower class.[27]

As a Bildungsbürger with a claim to idealism, Günther thoroughly disliked relationships based on personal interests. In contrast to the selflessness and disinterestedness of the Nordics, then, he offered the "Western race"—a manipulative, dishonest race for whom life consisted of playing various roles and trying to make the right impression—a phenomenon that was exacerbated by the newly emerging Weimar mass culture.[28] (Weimar popular culture also reflected similar concerns about the eclipse of the authentic self. Contemporary debates about nudity, fashion, and cosmetics either stressed the necessity or deplored the fraudulence of self-presentation in modern market society; see chapter 8.)

Unlike members of the Nordic, Western, and Eastern races, Jews did not belong to the original European racial types, according to Günther. The Jews were a mixture of Oriental, Near Eastern, Nordic, Hamitic, and Negroid races. They were what Günther called a "race of the second order" because they were the result of mixtures of European and Asiatic races. After release from Babylonian imprisonment in 458 B.C., Günther claimed, Jewish leaders such as Ezra had realized the threat that their unique racial mixture posed to the Jews, and they created beliefs and laws that rigorously separated Jews from non-Jews. The Jewish race thus constituted a paradox: it was a pure race that emerged from racial mixture and was preserved by consequent inbreeding but, owing to its mixed origins, was "spiritually non-homogeneous."

According to Günther, Jews paradoxically were the very opposite of the pure Nordics and at the same time represented the virtues that the Nordics needed in order to guarantee the survival of their racial qualities. Their movements were soft, they looked like bad soldiers, their men were feminized and their women masculinized, but unlike Nordics, they possessed the "blood consciousness" that the Nordics still lacked. "Blood consciousness," Günther argued, created the eternal Jew by means of inbreeding. For Nordics, the image of the "eternal Jew" was a model and a threat at the same time. This diffuse image would become for Günther and a growing number of his contemporaries in the 1920s a screen onto which anything negative could be projected.[29]

It was therefore not surprising that Günther saw in the image of the Jew the source of Americanism, a spiritual attitude that subordinated all human life to profit and egoistic purposes. He resented the world of "unrestrained economic struggle" and the power of money, and he approvingly cited the Zionist Max Nordau, who had attacked wealthy Jews because they lacked the idealism to support the Zionist movement.[30] Nordau, of course, had defended the conservative aesthetic ideals of the German Bildungsbürgertum in his book *Degeneracy (Entartung)* in the 1890s. Like Günther, Nordau had constructed an irreconcilable antagonism between material self-interest and the aesthetic idealism of the Gebildeten. Whereas Nordau and other Zionists had articulated the resentment of the Gebildeten among Jews toward wealthy Jews who were not committed to the Zionist cause, Günther racialized the difference between wealthy people of "inferior" racial stock and Bildungsbürger like himself. The former were members of the Eastern race or Jews; the latter were Nordics who still had to learn to tap their potential.

Unfortunately, Günther maintained, pure Nordics were almost not to be found anymore. Most people were racial mixes, further polluted by the disintegrating and deforming attitudes of modern times. In Günther's view, impure Nordics could only be saved if they reformed themselves, and he called on his readers to gain the "will to represent their true essence." In other words, he tried to cheer up the beaten Nordic man, who only needed to realize the slumbering mental and physical potential that was inscribed into his racial constitution in order to achieve the position in society that he deserved. This was an old life reform theme cast in racialist terms. Unlike most life reformers, however, Günther did not advocate body discipline as a means of gaining renewed self-confidence. Instead, he argued for a spiritual renewal, even though he counted the love of physical exercise as one of the racial traits of the Nordics. Only through the individual will, through the rebirth of Nordic spirit and soul, through the "striving for Nordicness" *(Streben zur Nordheit)*—in contrast to striving for material rewards—could the salvation of the individual Nordic, and by implication the Nordic race and its culture, be achieved.

But in Günther's view only those with enough Nordic blood could "reinvent" themselves (to use a modern term). He estimated that about 60 percent of Germans were partially Nordic, only 10 percent having pure blood; another 20 percent were of Eastern origin and had no Nordic traits. Although he reassured his audience that they might be among the ones who could be saved, a substantial proportion of the country clearly could not.[31]

As we have seen, for Günther, the Nordic racial type was the most beautiful one. Knowing all too well that most of his contemporaries did not correspond to this ideal, he argued that physical appearance was not the most important criterion for deciding whether a person had enough Nordic blood.[32] By arguing for the relative unimportance of physical markers as a basis for deciding the Nordic identity of individuals, Günther took his own "racial science," based on his system of racial physiognomy, ad absurdum. But this was consistent in the sense that he regarded his racial types, in the tradition of German idealism, as platonic ideas or ideal types. The pure image *(Bild)* of a race was a "law," a kind of ideal measure that served as the basis for the judgment of human beings. The intuitive "image-forming gaze" *(das bildnerische Sehen)* of the observer was necessary in order to penetrate beyond the mere physical characteristics of an individual and grasp the all-important (spiritual) core of the racial essence that was tied to the body in a relation of organic interdependence. As in the aestheticizing view of the Gebildeten among life reformers, intuitive "seeing" was more important than measuring. Even though Günther gave his racial science the appearance of exactitude by introducing his readers to anthropological measuring methods, the epistemological principle of his racial science was not an analytical but a synthetic one. Analysis was to be superseded by the impressionistic gaze of intuitive Anschauung.[33]

The gaze of the racial scientist was therefore not the gaze of the natural scientist but that of the artist or the Bildungsbürger, who was capable of gaining knowledge by making a judgment based on his aesthetic preferences. Because his racial theory served as a justification of these preferences, Günther defended the value of a neohumanistic education based on exposure to the venerated texts of the ancient Greeks and Romans, which he thought should be supplemented by old Icelandic and German texts. He deplored what he considered the decline of the German language, which had become simpler and more practical, although he clung to the hope that owing to its purity and potential of expression it was still the language in which the inborn poetic talent of the (Nordic) Germans could flourish best.[34]

Some historians have tried to describe German racism as a form of "biologism." According to this concept, as developed by Gunter Mann, biology and medicine are independent of nonscientific discourses, although they infiltrate these nonscientific discourses when their categories are illegitimately applied to social phenomena.[35] In my view, this concept is not helpful for an understanding of Günther's racial science and other popular racial theories of the 1920s. The goal of Günther's racial science was the re-creation of the Nordic ideal type, and therefore Germans had to be committed to an idealistic worldview in the sense in which Plato, Kant, and Fichte had understood the term. Biology as a scientific specialty, Günther claimed, could not serve as a basis for a new worldview *(Weltanschauung)* that could mobilize people in their quest to realize the full potential of their Nordic essence.[36] By "biology" he most likely meant the anthropometric tradition of German physical anthropology, which tried to establish racial differences empirically, according to the distribution of physical characteristics in populations,[37] ignoring the spiritual element of racial characteristics in favor of analysis and exact measurement.

Günther's idealistic racial science shaped the Nordic racism of the life reformer and architect Paul Schultze-Naumburg. An admirer of Günther's work, he had difficulty coming to terms with the changed cultural environment of the Weimar period.[38] During the Kaiserreich he had been a successful architect and leading voice in debates about aesthetic and cultural issues, but during the republic, his traditional architectural aesthetic was challenged by the "New Objectivity" represented by the Bauhaus school. His list of building commissions reflects this shift: thirteen for the year 1910, but only five for the years 1918 to 1923.[39] Then, in a 1926 controversy with Walter Gropius, Schultze-Naumburg denounced modern architecture as un-German[40] and went on to claim that creativity and aesthetics had a racial basis. This racism may well have been a result of his lack of professional success during the Weimar years, since he had not resorted to such racist arguments earlier.

Contemporary society, Schultze-Naumburg claimed, was characterized by a surging flood of colorless masses who stifled everything that was excellent and outstanding. Mixing racial with eugenic categories, he argued that the families who earlier had engendered the best human beings were disappearing, while a growing number of plebeians, unable to develop any true creativity, filled the big cities with noise. The Nordic race, he asserted, was responsible for all the great cultural achievements of humanity: Not only did they create the great art of ancient Greece, they were also responsible for the artistic achievements of the Renaissance period. In Schultze-Naumburg's fantasy world, the ancient Greeks were types representing the ideal of male and female Nordic physical beauty. This was also the case with the beautiful, noble, and healthy humans of the Renaissance era, who still stood out from the layers of the ugly, sunken, and sick masses.[41]

He maintained that it was impossible for an artist to transcend his physical constitution. Since art was an expression of the constitution of the artist, and racial differences were expressed in peoples' faces and bodies, any art was an expression of the race of the artist. An artist's mental creativity bore the characteristics of his racial constitution in the same way the artist's children inherited his racial characteristics. Therefore, it was possible to deduce from the artistic production of past and present times the racial constitution of the artist and his people. "Man can do nothing else but create according to the inherent law of his physical constitution and his spirituality," Schultze-Naumburg wrote. Since art was always the expression of the very essence of human beings, harmony in artistic expression was only possible when the artist was racially pure.[42]

Any change in the racial composition of the "people's body" as a whole would therefore necessarily be reflected in the art of the period. The presentation of the degenerate, the sunken, the sick, and the physically deformed, the portrayal of idiots, prostitutes, and women with sagging breasts, and the true "hell of subhumans" that could be encountered in modern art was, in Schultze-Naumburg's view, symptomatic of the racial degeneration of the nation and its artists. He tried to substantiate his claim by comparing photographs of sick and disabled people with the paintings of modernist artists who had broken with the tradition of realistic representation and who, in his view, could evoke in those with healthy aesthetic sensibilities only feelings of nausea and disgust.[43] Similar techniques were to be used later by the Nazis in their 1937 exhibition "Degenerate Art." The Nazis juxtaposed, for example, works by such artists as Paul Klee and Oskar Kokoschka with works by inmates of mental institutions in order to make the point that modern art and modern artists were degenerate.[44]

Schultze-Naumburg was not simply a reactionary Bildungsbürger. He claimed that it was not modern technology that created the ugliness of modern cities and modern culture—technology could be beautiful and could be given an organic form that corresponded to its function. Rather, the problem with the age of the machine was that it enabled the unfit and the nonvirtuous to survive. Those whom he deemed fit—who were supposed to achieve a higher position in life—fell victim to "the two-child system," as he called it, and had fewer children than the unfit. But it was not antisocials or degenerates who presented the greatest problem to him. He was most disturbed by the masses—those who, despite never attaining the intellect or cultivation of the Gebildeten, could successfully run a business and raise children. These people were responsible for the multiplication of the uncreative, the "form- and colorless *[Gestalt- und Farblosen]*, the half and quarter humans who were lacking in beauty and were therefore not thirsting for beauty." They were the illegitimate achievers in the economic sphere. Simultaneously, the highly cultivated Nordics who alone had the potential to be beautiful in body and spirit were unable to achieve economic success and social respectability.[45]

The work of Ludwig Ferdinand Clauss, like that of Schultze-Naumburg and Günther, also embodies central aspects of the experience of the Weimar Bürgertum (the acknowledgment, for instance, of the fact that those who were supposed to succeed because of their inherent qualities often did not).[46] An influential racial theorist of the 1920s, Clauss was a student of the philosopher Edmund Husserl and used Husserl's phenomenological concepts to formulate racial theories based on a "psychological anthropology" that tried to distinguish between the behavioral styles and physiognomies of different races. According to Clauss, there was a certain behavioral and attitudinal style inscribed into each racial constitution and expressed by its bearers. These immanent styles, ideal types in the platonic sense of the term, were embodiments of psychological laws. In contrast to Günther, who did not deny that the measurements of physical anthropology had some validity, Clauss argued that these laws were not subject to objective quantitative verification. These were "laws of essence" *(Wesensgesetze)*, which had to be "seen into" in order for one to intuitively grasp the essence of a racial constitution.[47]

Clauss did not equate the Nordic race with the educated upper middle class quite as openly as Günther, Schultze-Naumburg, and Lenz did. (Whether this was due to his having a less "classist" attitude or was simply a response to contemporary denunciations of racial theories as compilations of class prejudices, it is impossible to say.) Nevertheless, a discourse on bürgerliche norms and values was central to his racial thought. For Clauss, as for Günther, the behavioral and attitudinal style of the Nordic man was the *Leistungstypus*, best translated as the "achievement and performance type." Even though the Nordic race represented norms and attitudes of the Bürgertum, he argued, it could be found among all estates. Nordics could be workers, servants, merchants, ministers, or kings— what they had in common was racial style, not social position. Racial style shaped the character and talents of a person. Clauss argued, for example, that there were talented statesmen or talented artists among all races. What distinguished them was not necessarily the greatness of their talent but the specific racial style in which it found expression. He therefore rejected the contention by the eugenicist Fritz Lenz that the Nordic race was by far the most talented race of all as unscientific.[48]

Yet the Nordic race had bürgerliche qualities that were shared by all its members, no matter how educated or wealthy. Nordic man, with his slim and trim body, was a performer who always attempted to transform his environment creatively. In this attempt he was so thorough and devoted that even the unimportant aspects of these activities reflected his achievement. "Performance" in the sense of Leistung was inscribed in the racial constitution of the Nordic man, and he always tried to give his best by working diligently and responsibly. For Clauss, the Nordic represented the values of an ideal type of autonomous Bürger; because he performed responsibly, he was an independent master in his sphere of activity, even though he might be merely a common worker. The "master-like" *(das Herrentümliche)* was thus not signified by his position within society but was inscribed into his essence. The Nordic was a master even as a servant, and he could never be a serf in the bad sense of the word: "While serving he remains a master and while serving he remains free."[49]

Corresponding to Günther's Western race was Clauss's "Middle-landic," or Mediterranean, type. Clauss called this peculiar racial style the "Presenting Type" because members of this race always tried to present themselves in the most favorable fashion; taken to the extreme, this resulted in mere posing— something that was alien to the Nordic type.[50] His readers could gain from this type of sophistry reassurance of their own worthiness. They may not have had a position in life commensurate with the inherent qualities of their racial constitution (especially when others could present themselves more effectively), but as Nordics they were the ones who deserved to be masters because their entire racial style was "master-like."

Another group that contrasted with the Nordics and corresponded somewhat to Günther's Eastern race were Clauss's "Turanians," somewhat awkwardly called the *Enthebungstypus*, because this type was "lifted above" *(enthoben)* psychological disturbances. Members of this race were born to serve and served with humility in everything they did. Turanians did not value achievement for its own sake but were content with modest success and material gain. Unlike the Nordic, the Turanian could not really fail because he never expected to achieve anything—or at least failure did not carry with it the disappointments and disturbances of the soul experienced by the Nordic.[51] The happy, easygoing Turanian, it seems, knew nothing of the vexing self-doubts of the Nordic, who was destined to succeed because of his own inborn qualities and yet always was afraid to fail.

Constitutional Typologies in Medical Science

The typological constitutionalism of the Weimar years extended beyond the racial theories of Günther, Schultze-Naumburg, and Clauss and into academic science. The Tübingen psychiatrist Ernst Kretschmer, whom I wish to discuss first, distinguished three constitutional types: the leptosome (asthenic), the pyknic, and the athletic, each of which had corresponding healthy and pathological psychological states. Although racist thinkers such as Günther and Schultze-Naumburg saw in Kretschmer's typology a corroboration of their own theories, Kretschmer denied that his constitutional types corresponded to those constructed by contemporary racial theorists. Instead he thought it more likely that the types he had identified could be found in all races, although he still considered it possible that specific constitutional types had affinities to different racial types.[52]

Kretschmer tried to synthesize some of the most recent research in endocrinology, psychiatry, and clinical medicine. He claimed that a correlation could be established between morphological types of the human body and the two basic types of psychopathology: the manic-depressive (or circular) and the schizophrenic.[53] Corresponding to these were nonpathological psychological temperaments, which Kretschmer described as predispositions to those pathological states. Temperamental predispositions were manifest in morphological types, and the examination of these physical types was the key to the question of constitutional predispositions.

Kretschmer's work was symptomatic of the crisis in scientific medicine and the life sciences in general. Analytical concepts were de-emphasized in favor of a synthetic appreciation of an organic whole. However, in his case it was not, as the historian Anne Harrington put it, "a rejection of Newton in favor of Goethe."[54] It was, rather, a supplementation of Newton with Goethe, since Kretschmer's understanding of natural science did not reject analysis and exact measurement. On one hand, he claimed that it was necessary to make careful and detailed measurements, because "aesthetic aperçus" would not be of great help, and he gave a detailed account of his method of measuring physical features. On the other, he stressed the importance of intuition and Anschauung in the process of cognition. It was necessary, he wrote, "to learn how to use our eyes, simply to see and to observe without microscope and laboratory."[55]

In Kretschmer's view, intuition had to be confirmed by measurements, but the mystique of "seeing" was elevated in his work to an epistemological principle. As shown in chapter 2, Carl Heinrich Stratz had argued twenty years earlier in a similar fashion for the importance of "the gaze of the physician" as analogous to the "gaze of the artist" in the construction of physical ideal types, thus anticipating the aesthetic epistemology of Weimar constitutionalism. In a similar fashion, Kretschmer argued that the eye was all-important. "Everything depends on the artistic, reliable training of the eye," and without a preconceived "idea and intuition of the general physique" it was impossible to arrive at biological types. Measurements could only confirm what had already been conceived intuitively and should be guided by the holistic perception of the body.[56]

Typical for Kretschmer's leptosome (or asthenic) type was thinness of the body. Variations of the asthenic type were characterized by effeminacy in the physique, a pronounced waist, wide pelvis, and a feminine lack of body hair. In physique, the athletic type, with a strong development of the skeleton, muscles, and skin, contrasted with the leptosome type. Athletic types were tall with broad shoulders, a handsome thorax, a tight and firm abdomen, and a trunk that became narrower from top to bottom. The pyknic type was of medium height with a stocky figure and a soft, wide face on a short, massive throat. Other characteristics were a considerable belly emerging from a wide, deep, and rounded thorax. (See figures 37, 38, and 39.)[57]

Kretschmer emphasized that none of these types was better than another.[58] All three constitutions were hereditarily predisposed to different diseases, and all three were valid for men and women. They were "ideal types," and between them there were many gradations. Therefore, Kretschmer claimed, it was not

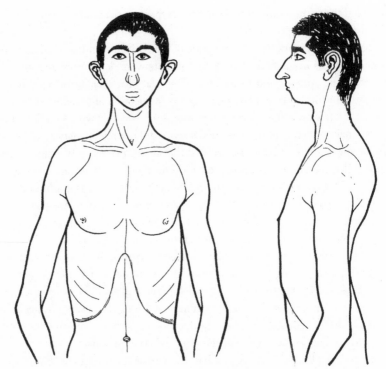

FIGURE 37. The leptosome (asthenic) type. Kretschmer, *Körperbau und Charakter*, 18, fig. 3. © Julius-Springer-Verlag.

necessary that his typology describe the types that were to be found most fre-quently but only those that most resembled the ideal. In this respect, his work resembled that of contemporary idealist morphologists. Biologists such as Adolf Naef, Karl Peter, and Wilhelm Lubosch either abandoned or de-emphasized philogenetic research in favor of the reconstruction of morphological ideal types.[59]

The leptosome and athletic types were correlated to what Kretschmer called a schizothymic temperament, that is, a constitutional predisposition to-ward schizophrenia. These types usually assumed a "strictly antithetical" posi-tion toward their environment. They had good analytical abilities, meaning that they could identify different strands in a complex flux of information, a faculty that the psychiatrist Bleuler had termed analytical or "splitting capability" *(Spal-tungsfähigkeit)*. In its uncoordinated pathological form, however, this ability constituted the clinical picture of schizophrenia. In contrast, the pyknic type most often had a zyklothymic temperament, with a predisposition toward so-called cyclical psychoses—manic-depressive disorders with their characteristic

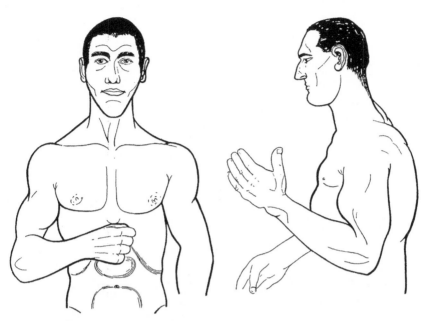

FIGURE 38. The athletic type. Kretschmer, *Körperbau und Charakter,* 23, fig. 4. © Julius-Springer-Verlag.

swings.[60] Persons with a zyklothymic temperament were characterized by cognitive patterns that were not analytical but rather were "intuitive-descriptive" *(anschaulich-beschreibend)* and thus capable of intuitively grasping the whole of a situation. Kretschmer's constitutional characterology found wide resonance in the popular press and at contemporary hygiene exhibitions (see figure 40).[61]

If Kretschmer's healthy constitutional ideal types were predisposed to different pathological states, they were nevertheless relatively stable and normal. Mixtures of different types had a greater tendency to be more imbalanced and psychopathic.[62] Kretschmer put a positive spin on such imbalanced personalities, however, by arguing that geniuses who created works of lasting value for human society were often biological bastards and psychologically unstable—in order to be creative, a genius had to be driven by inner psychological contradictions and tensions. Geniuses, he claimed, were most likely psychopaths, whereas normal and healthy people were philistines. As prominent examples of genius he cited Goethe and Bismarck.[63]

In Kretschmer's view, Goethe was the offspring of degenerates: a schizothymic father with a dry, pedantic seriousness and a zyklothymic mother with an effervescent humor bequeathed tendencies that were revealed in Goethe's artistic work. His genius was a fortunate product of degenerative predisposi-

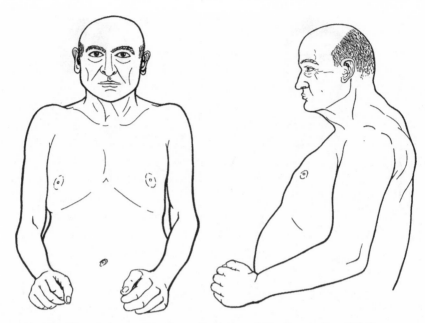

FIGURE 39. The pyknic type. Kretschmer, *Körperbau und Charakter*, 27, fig. 7. © Julius-Springer-Verlag.

tions that led to the extinction of Goethe's family within four generations. Therefore, Goethe was far from being the individual of strong mental health and inner harmony of the soul that popular folklore portrayed. Instead, he was rather fortunate in that, in contrast to some of his relatives, he found the source of genius in his pathological predispositions.[64]

In contrast to eugenicists such as Fritz Lenz, who equated talent with the social position of the upper and educated classes and who therefore favored the endogamous reproduction of these classes, Kretschmer argued that it was the transgression of class barriers that ultimately led to the creation of exceptionally talented human beings.[65] Bismarck was one example of that pattern. According to Kretschmer, Bismarck had inherited the coarse instincts of a rural nobleman from his father and fine aesthetic sensibilities with an inclination to nervousness from his bürgerlich mother, leading to emotional imbalance and spiritual lability. Only the asthenic nervousness and psychopathic imbalance of the maternal (bürgerlich!) side of Bismarck's family gave him the power to accomplish great deeds; these could never have been accomplished by a healthy and contented noble land owner.

For Kretschmer, genius was inherited, but not in a straightforward fashion. Rather, it was the result of an inheritance pattern in which psychopathological

FIGURE 40. Physique and character according to Kretschmer. Certain physical and mental predispositions are almost always correlated. Deutsches Hygienemuseum Dresden, Bildsammlung, DHM, 1930, Sign. 1142 II, No. 1.

characteristics were combined in a rare and advantageous manner. This implied, of course, that attempts to breed genius or to weed out psychopathological "minus-variants," as eugenicists liked to call those whom they regarded genetically inferior, would make little sense. Preventing the reproduction of all people who were likely to have psychopathic offspring would also eliminate the possibility of creating superior humans who were ultimately the real bearers of culture.

The greatest number of geniuses, according to Kretschmer, could be found in the regions of Germany where the "barriers of estates" had been least rigid, such as Saxony, Swabia, and the Netherlands. Those regions also featured the greatest racial mixtures in Germany, especially of the so-called Nordic and Eastern races. In contrast to Fritz Lenz and Hans Günther, who identified a single race as the bearers of culture, Kretschmer felt that the creation of geniuses owed much to the "fermenting and complementing effects of racial crossing"; Weimar racial theories were, in his view, merely an accumulation of petty prejudices. Like the crossing of constitutional types—not identical with racial types for Kretschmer—racial crossing, with its mixing of contradictory temperaments, resulted in human beings whose inner tensions predestined them for great and timeless accomplishments.[66]

Another popular constitutional typology during the Weimar years was the one developed by the French physician Claude Sigaud. Sigaud had developed his types prior to the war, and they were later introduced to a wider audience by his students Léon McAuliffe and Auguste Chaillou.[67] During the International Hygiene Exhibition of 1930, the Dresden hygienist Rainer Fetscher devoted a significant section of the popular exhibition *Der Mensch* to Sigaud's typology. Sigaud's functional constitutionalism distinguished between four basic types (see figure 41): "typus respiratorius," with its pronounced development of the thorax and all organs connected with the function of breathing; "typus muscularis," which had a strong skeleton and muscles; "typus cerebralis," which had tender limbs and looked surprisingly young—presumably because the relatively large head compared to the rest of the body produced a childlike appearance; and "typus digestivus," which had a relatively wide lower body, corresponding to the dominance of its digestive system.[68] The characteristic proportions of typus digestivus, Fetscher claimed, could be found not only in the body as a whole but also in the shape of such body parts as the hands and fingernails.

Sigaud's were normal nonpathological constitutional types, but Fetscher argued that, like Kretschmer's types, they were prone to develop corresponding pathological syndromes. The typus respiratorius was likely to become the weakling of Kretschmer's asthenic or leptosome type with its predisposition toward tuberculosis. The typus muscularis would correspond to the athletic type with predispositions toward diseases of the heart and blood vessels. The cerebral type would become an "infantile type" with pronounced infantile physical proportions and childish psychological traits. The digestive type, finally, was predisposed toward arthritis, obesity, bladder stones, and gout. The more pronounced the development of an organ system, the greater its performance level. In Fetscher's view, it was therefore not surprising that individuals with certain

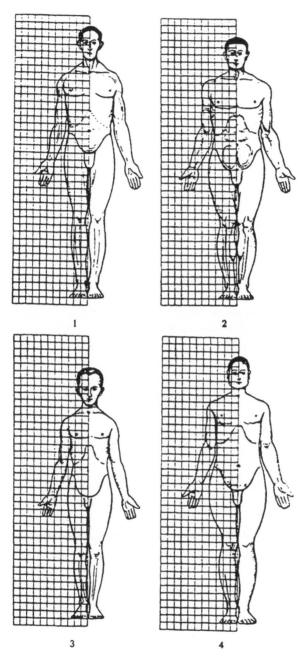

FIGURE 41. Sigaud's four constitutional types: (1) respiratorius, (2) muscularis, (3) cerebralis, and (4) digestivus. Vogel, *Der Mensch,* 344. Private collection.

constitutional types tended to be more successful in some activities than in others. The muscular type was most likely to enjoy physical activity, whereas respiratory types, given the great capacity of their lungs, would be successful long-distance runners. The cerebral type, by contrast, would avoid physical activities and concentrate instead on mental and artistic activities that were most likely to satisfy him. Finally, the hedonistic digestive type was the most sociable one.[69]

Unlike Kretschmer and Sigaud, who developed constitutional types in reference to men without applying them systematically to women, the Austrian gynecologist Paul Mathes (1871–1923) wrote directly about women.[70] In fact, his multivolume work, edited by Halban and Seitz, was the leading gynecological handbook of the time.[71] Before the war Mathes had worked on constitutional disorders of women, and in 1912 he had published a monograph on the relation of infantilism, adult women with arrested physical development, and asthenia as constitutional diseases.[72] It is therefore not surprising that Mathes was chosen to work out the implications of contemporary constitutional concepts for gynecological research and practice for Halban and Seitz's handbook. But that is not the only reason why Mathes's case is so interesting. His work is also a good example of the ways in which the construction of constitutional types was influenced by anxieties about changing gender relations.

Even more so than Kretschmer, Mathes argued for the importance of intuitive seeing as an epistemological principle, criticizing Kretschmer and others for relying too much on exact measurements in their diagnosis of constitutional types.[73] Instead, medicine was an art, and the ability to determine what was normal depended on the artistic talent of the physician.[74] An ideal type was not to be constructed from the frequency distribution of physical characteristics on a Gaussian curve. The fallacy of such a construction, he argued, could be easily discerned if one examined the distribution of the hair cover of women's lower legs. Only about one-third of all women, he maintained, did not have hair on their legs, but no woman could legitimately claim to be a fully differentiated sexual being if she had hair on her legs.

Mathes's construction of women's constitutional types was based on two arguments; one was evolutionary, and the other tried to associate the constitutional types described by Kretschmer and Sigaud with gender characteristics. The evolutionary argument was based on Mathes's assumption that the human physique was subject to a constant but nevertheless teleological transformation. He distinguished between two basic types: a "youth form" *(Jugendform)* and a "form of the future" *(Zukunftsform)* that developed from the youth form but was not yet reached. A comparatively small nose, a low brow, and a short chin were characteristics of the "youth form." The "form of the future" was characterized by an upright way of walking, comparatively broad shoulders (a precondition for the free movement of the arms), and increased dominance of the cerebrum over the interbrain. Most women, Mathes claimed, most closely resembled the youth form, most men the form of the future.[75] This theory helped account for psychological differences between men and women—since the dominance of the cerebrum was less pronounced in women than in men, women were more subject to affect and less governed by reason.[76]

The distinction between the Jugendform and the Zukunftsform also served as the basis for Mathes's attempts to apply Kretschmer's types to women, although Mathes did not deny that all of these types applied to both men and women. The pyknic type was like the feminine youth form, even though it showed good sexual differentiation, whereas the asthenic-schizoid type (Kretschmer's leptosome) showed clear signs of intersexuality. Mathes did not mention the athletic type, but one can infer that it corresponded closely to the pure form of the future. For women, Mathes claimed, this was a contradiction in terms, and he considered women who came close to it to be masculinized.[77]

Most striking in his depiction of women's constitutional types is his obsession with "intersexual types"—women who exhibited no clear sexual identity and who were psychologically torn between two competing sexual identities. He contrasted intersexual women with "Pyknika," a female ideal type who was happy with her role as a harmony-radiating companion to her husband. Pyknika was like a big child, but she was nevertheless the perfect housewife and was always quick to forgive a philandering husband. Marriage and love were no problem for her. As Mathes put it, "from her womb spring children and from her breasts springs inexhaustible nourishment."[78]

Whereas Pyknika warmed the hearts of men, the intersexual woman inflamed and blinded them with her frightening eroticism. Unsure of her own sexual identity, she was constantly on the search for men—although not for "real men," since they intimidated her. Rather, she was attracted to intersexual men who did not have a clear sexual identity themselves or, at the extreme, to other masculine women. The psychological torment of the intersexual woman was expressed in her ambivalence toward everything that was connected with her sexuality, and the gynecologist Mathes found it unsurprising that she suffered from pain during her menstruation or had difficulties during intercourse. Normally the intersexual woman wanted to obey the man she loved, but her masculine side prevented her from doing so. That made her permanently discontented and an unlikely source of emotional fulfillment for her male companions. In the author's view, it was therefore not surprising that men who had wives with a high degree of intersexuality resorted to violence; they were simply beating the man in the woman when she did not respond to her husband's wish. But the "woman in the woman," as he put it, was grateful for such treatment.[79]

Mathes's anxious construction of the intersexual woman clearly reflected concern about the crisis of the moral order in postwar Germany and Austria. Some women rejected an unambiguous gender identity by presenting an androgynous image of themselves—for example, the flapper with the boyish figure who, in his view, paid a high price for her ambiguity in terms of her inner psychological torment. The image of the flapper who supposedly longed for nothing more than to be a "real" woman was essentialized in his intersexual constitutional type. Other developments were also worrisome to people such as Mathes. Urban women from the middle and respectable working classes had fewer and fewer children so that they were better able to balance the multiple requirements of marriage, children, and work.[80] The traditional balance between men and women had been upset by the wartime employment of women and by the growing employment of women in service and clerical jobs. In addition, the new mass culture—as exemplified by the movies—was perceived by contemporary intellectuals as different as Martin Heidegger and Siegfried Kracauer as a feminine threat, in part because of the prominence of women among the audience of these new forms of entertainment.[81] In response to this prominence, the journalist Adolf Halfeld characterized women's position in the cultural sphere as a pathological manifestation of "cultural feminism" *(Kulturfeminismus)*. Leaving the enjoyment of cultural pursuits predominantly to women was unnatural, in his view, because cultivation and creativity were naturally masculine. Kulturfeminismus demasculinized men. According to Halfeld, such a development was especially evident in America, where men were reduced to providing the economic subsistence for their families, leaving cultural pursuits to their wives. This lack of masculinity was manifest in the facial physiognomy of American males: despite their pronounced physical development, the soft-featured, feminine prettiness of their faces revealed morbid defects resulting from mental inhibitions.[82]

Mathes's and Halfeld's concerns about intersexual men and women were not unique at the time. Such theories found a wide resonance among the public. According to a popular guide on character written by the physician Gerhard Venzmer, it was possible to distinguish between a (leptosome) man of thought, an (athletic) man of deeds, and a (pyknic) man of the heart, all with their corresponding physical characteristics. According to Venzmer, the man of the heart was a feminine type, but women who exhibited physical characteristics of an athletic or leptosome type were risky marriage partners because they were masculinized.[83]

Weimar constitutional discourse expressed concerns about eroding boundaries between the sexes and the social classes. Physicians such as Mathes and Venzmer were worried that women had abandoned traditional social mores.

Propagators of racial constitutionalism appealed to people with higher education who were worried about their ability to fulfill their elitist social aspirations. A history examining the social uses of aesthetic perceptions of the human body during the Weimar era would be incomplete, however, if it focused solely on such conservative and elitist impulses. As chapter 8 shows, Weimar physical culture and nudism held out a rather different promise: the vision of a utopian community in which separations between the sexes, and social distinctions based on wealth and formal education, were unimportant.

CHAPTER 8

𝒲EIMAR 𝓛EISURE 𝓒ULTURE: 𝓕REIKÖRPERKULTUR
AND THE 𝒬UEST FOR 𝒜UTHENTICITY AND 𝒱OLKSGEMEINSCHAFT

𝒜s we have seen, Weimar constitutional concepts of race and health often echoed concerns about the changing social and moral order of the postwar period. For instance, theories of Nordic racism reflected contemporary worries about the value of Bildung in a tight academic job market. Often this type of racism was an expression of the social and cultural elitism of academics who had difficulty finding a place in German society that was commensurate with their expectations. Such elitist forms of racism were rare among the Weimar life reformers who propagated nudism and *Körperkultur.* Although they frequently appealed to people who were worried about success in their professional and private lives, most of them wanted to have nothing to do with the class arrogance expressed by people such as Günther. On the contrary, the most successful life reform authors, such as Hans Surén, appealed to the anti-academic and anti-intellectual sentiment of a mass audience. Many physical culturists hoped that *Freikörperkultur* (nudism; literally, "free physical culture") as a leisure activity allowed people to transcend the "artificial" distinctions of status and wealth by creating a "people's community" of equals. Stripped of their clothes, people would present their authentic selves devoid of deceptive self-presentations. This chapter first situates physical culture and nudism in the cultural context of the Weimer period and then looks at nudists' hopes for the creation of a utopian people's community *(Volksgemeinschaft)* that might transcend the social classes.

Körperkultur and Weimar Culture

During the Weimar Republic, life reformers continued to assert that exercise and nude culture improved peoples' overall health and that life reform would save both individuals and the nation from the degeneracy brought on by the unhygienic practices and lifestyles of modern civilization. Körperkultur's goal, the holistic development of body and mind, distinguished it from other contemporary forms of exercise, such as sports.[1] In contrast to traditional gymnastics as well as the gymnastics advocated by life reformers, the goal of the various sports disciplines was to increase the performance level of individuals in specialized, competitive contests of physical exercise. Sports fragmented the human body by exercising only the skills that were necessary for high performance in a specific discipline. Physical culturists criticized this tendency; their goal was the harmonious and healthy development of the body—one that was beautiful because its physical faculties were evenly developed. (Although traditional gymnastics came closer to this holistic ideal, it was still criticized by Weimar physical culturists for its military-like drill and unnatural formalism.)[2]

Physical culture and Freikörperkultur were no longer confined to the middle and lower middle classes as they had been during the Wilhelmine era. As a result of the introduction of the eight-hour workday in many industries, workers could now participate in such time-consuming leisure activities as well. In a health guide directed at such readers, the communist Friedrich Wolf extolled the beneficial effects of sunlight, nudity, and exercise. Some of the members of the Friends of Nature *(Naturfreunde)* working-class associations were also committed to such life reform activities.[3] In addition, the physical culture school of the teacher and socialist Adolf Koch was primarily directed at working-class youths. Nevertheless, Koch's activities met with the approval of middle-class physical culturists because of some of his reformist assumptions. Koch's physical culture was remedial; it attempted to compensate for the harsh living conditions that stunted the health and physical development of working-class youths.[4]

The League for the Creation of a Free Life *(Liga für freie Lebensgestaltung)*, the most active Weimar nudist organization (at least, judging from widespread publishing and propaganda activities), prided itself on being open to all classes.[5] In its journal *Land of Light (Lichtland)*, it published data about the social background of 207 people who applied to join one of its big-city branches: Of these, 23 percent came from academic professions, 3 percent were civil servants, and 22 percent were workers; the largest group by far (at 52 percent) consisted of merchants and commercial clerical employees.[6] If these data are in any way representative of the *Liga* as a whole—and there is no way to ascertain whether they are—then even the nonsocialist nudist movement had become more socially heterogeneous than it had been in the pre-war years (see chapter 1).

In contrast to nude culture during the Wilhelmine era, when Richard Ungewitter and others early on combined rabid racism with ardent agitation for the eugenic necessity of nude culture, the nudism of the Weimar years increasingly stressed the hedonistic side of the practice. This was expressed in the titles of most nude culture journals: *Joy (Die Freude), Laughing Life (Lachendes Leben)* and *Land of Light (Lichtland)* were at no loss to celebrate the pure pleasure that could be experienced in the nature parks owned by nudist organizations. This hedonism can be understood as a rejection of old conventions and mores that seemed meaningless after the senseless slaughter of the war. As the historian Modris Eksteins has pointed out, hedonism and narcissism reached epidemic proportions in the war-weary European nations. The more meaningless the war appeared, the more people insisted that the "meaning [of life] lay in life itself, in the act of living, in the vitality of the moment."[7]

Postwar hedonism, however, implied denial of some of the consequences of the war. Although the ideal of the beautiful body was celebrated in the popular press, film, and contemporary exercise guides, the fate of the disfigured bodies of war victims was rarely discussed. War victims were represented in the paintings of George Grosz and Otto Dix, but public displays of mutilated bodies, especially faces, were considered obscene.[8] Ernst Friedrich's book *War Against War,* with its disturbing images of the mutilated faces of German war victims, went through several editions during the Weimar Republic. But when Friedrich displayed these images in the windows of his antiwar museum in Berlin, the police removed them because they caused "public offence."[9] The issue of ugly or mutilated bodies was almost never openly discussed among nudists. Only K. Lichtner, an author for the journal *Lichtland,* attacked the mindless beauty cult among nudists who rejected the presence of war invalids because they recalled the horror of war or offended their aesthetic sensibilities.[10]

What makes Freikörperkultur such an interesting movement for the historian is the role it played in larger popular hygienic subculture. The 1925 UFA movie *Ways to Strength and Beauty (Wege zu Kraft und Schönheit),* for example, urged people to reform their lives by means of exercise and a healthy lifestyle. Like physical culturists before the war, the filmmakers constructed a contrast between the ancient Greek gymnasium and the German Gymnasium. "Classic culture made perfect harmony its goal. Care for the body was as important as care for the brains. Plato and Aristotle taught in the 'Gymnasium,' the word implying the locality where gymnastics were carried out by nude men and boys," the movie claimed. The scenes that followed showed a Greek philosopher lecturing to his students in a gymnasium, while in the background young men were engaged in running, wrestling, and boxing contests. Images from a German Gymnasium followed, showing young boys crouched over their desks. The movie deplored the way people neglected their bodies in favor of book learning, and it tried to show how sedentary factory and office work stunted the physical development of modern men and women. The film fostered a sense of personal inadequacy among its viewers by contrasting neglected contemporary bodies with the beautiful figures of antique statues. "It is not sufficient for such people to study and admire the works of the ancient Greeks," the film warned before a scene showing a group of well-nourished men and women admiring an ancient statue of Venus. "We must endeavour to emulate the ancient Greeks ourselves." According to the movie, dance, gymnastics, sports, open-air exercises, and physical culture were the most important means to overcome the stunting effects of civilization and to recapture the strength and beauty of the ancient Greeks.[11] Unlike some life reformers, the movie's makers did not condemn competitive sports as one-sided. Instead, they presented both sports and physical culture as means to achieve a healthy and beautiful physique.

Similarly, the publications of the German Hygiene Museum propagated physical culture and sports as part of a leisure culture that was supposed to restore the working capacity of individuals. For instance, Wilhelm Hagen, the author of a booklet on body and sports, acknowledged that sports could lead to a one-sided, disharmonious development of the body, but he believed that balance could be attained by adding gymnastics. Thus the harmonious development of the human body exemplified by the ancient Greeks could be achieved.[12] Karl Dohrn maintained that sports would not only raise physical and mental performance levels but would pay off in the long run as well, because people who sacrificed one or two hours per day for their physical fitness would be more successful in their careers.[13]

Still, it would be wrong to emphasize only the utilitarian, economic aspects of the museum's hygienic propaganda. Rudolf Neubert, a scientific assistant at the museum, argued in a small booklet that leisure time was a basic need for humans in a modern society, who were often forced to do monotonous work that did not challenge all of their mental and physical faculties. Leisure was not simply the absence of work or a means to restore working capacity. "Leisure equaled culture," in his view, because it was also the only time during which people could develop their creativity through cultural activities (including exercise). In their leisure time, people could overcome the fragmentation of modern life and become "full humans" again. People were not on the earth to serve certain utilitarian purposes but should become "good and perfect humans [and] realize the ideal image of being human and serve the idea of mankind. It is only possible for few people to achieve this in their profession, because [the profession] leads to specialization and loneliness. Therefore, our free time has to connect us with the totality of the world."[14]

Concern about the fragmentation of humans in modern society appeared time and again in the popular hygienic literature, in mass media such as illustrated magazines, and in contemporary discourse about the legitimacy of cosmetics, cosmetic surgery, and social conventions that tried to mask a person's real character.[15] Illustrated journals such as the *Berliner Illustrierte Zeitung (BIZ)* ran articles and advertisements that stressed the importance of having a good appearance in order to impress others. Ads for cosmetics and exercise equipment underscored the importance of good looks. One article extolled the virtues of nose jobs because they enabled men as well as women to be beautiful or at least avoid making an unfavorable impression. The anonymous author argued that physical culture had become a fashion and that obesity was disappearing among the young; even in more mature people, the portly Bürger belly had disappeared. Physical culture, however, could not correct nature's excesses and malformations; these problems, and especially malformations of the nose, required plastic surgery. The article featured a picture of a man whose career chances had supposedly improved after his surgery; it stressed the importance of good appearance especially for women in modern professions.[16] Whether a woman was an actress, model, teacher, saleswoman, or domestic servant, another article claimed, she had to look young and beautiful. Cosmetic surgery could help women get rid of wrinkles and other signs of aging.[17]

These surgical forms of impression management were, however, often seen as problematic, even in a shallow illustrated weekly such as the *BIZ*, which aimed at a nonacademic mass audience. In particular, there was persistent concern that people could hide their true characters behind masks. As a remedy, *BIZ* articles extolled the virtues of physiognomy, which would allow people to decipher the "true" character of others. According to one article, the shape of the nose was the most important physical marker for character because its appearance—unlike that of the eyes or mouth—did not change, even in the course of altering facial expressions. It could not be controlled by human will. Rather, the nose was solely the expression of the spirit and personality of an individual. It would know no hypocrisy were it not for the regrettable practice of plastic surgery, especially among women.[18] A journal such as the *BIZ* thus expressed the ambiguity of modern anonymous mass society, in which people played roles in order to make a favorable impression on their peers or social superiors but also looked for reliable markers of character in others.

This was also one of the most suggestive themes in the popular writings of the philosopher Ludwig Klages. Klages argued that the living body was an expression of the human soul. His physiognomy of movements tried to uncover spiritual content in the handwriting of human beings, to discover more about people who hid their real character behind publicly performed roles.[19] For Klages, the goal of this type of physiognomy was to "liberate our impressions from the falsifying and coloring whisperings of human intentions."[20] He tried to disentangle the self-presentation of people *(Schein)* from their true being *(Sein).* Naive people, Klages claimed, could be fooled by the seemingly well-meaning and disinterested behavior of those who really only looked out for their own interests. Handwriting analysis would reveal discrepancies between the appearance and the real essence of a person, exposing, for example, a supposed friend as a shrewd and unscrupulous businessman.[21]

According to Friedrich Wendenburg, author of a health guide focusing on beauty care for the publication series of the German Hygiene Museum, a face was only beautiful when the basic trait revealed in its appearance was truthfulness. People who tried to suggest with facial expressions character traits that they did not really have (such as strength of will) lacked this truthfulness. He condemned especially the untruthful "mask of the average" that people with "average cultivation" put on for reasons of social convention. The expression of the face was the physical representation of the spirit in nature, and masking one's true character was a sin. People who knew how to read faces could see behind such masks and would inevitably arrive at the condemning judgment that such a person was inferior. Paradoxically, however, Wendenburg acknowledged that playing a role—one that expressed one's inner essence, that is—was very important. This sort of role playing, along with the practice of sports and physical culture, would lead to a unified personality:

> Also many observations have shown that the average of those who
> enthusiastically commit themselves to sports and physical exercise reject
> each artificially distorted mask *[jede Fratze]*, the aping of others, every
> unnaturalness, and inner dishonesty. It may well be that humans of this
> nature also tend to cultivate the unity of their personality through their
> inclination for physical exercise; it might also well be that physical exercise
> alone can lead to this path and goal.[22]

In a nutshell, harmony of facial expression was based on the unity of body and spirit, which could be achieved by means of body discipline. The faces of people who were completely spiritual, for example, artists who tried to give their face a romantic, enthusiastic, fantastic expression, or faces expressing suffering were in Wendenburg's view always unbalanced, pathological, and unnatural. Women who tried to achieve the highest performance in sports would have a pronounced, masculine facial type. Wendenburg alluded here to contemporary opinions that competition in sports and in professional life was masculine and that women should take jobs in which they could use their natural instincts of maternal care (such as nursing).

Conservative physicians who shared this position were hostile to the increasing participation of women in sports, seeing it as an intrusion into a male domain. The gynecologist Hugo Sellheim, already a leading expert on women's beauty during the Kaiserreich, argued that women who participated in sports would become masculinized in their physical appearance and become "viragos."[23] Wendenburg, however, did not regard masculine facial expressions in women as something unnatural or ugly; he considered it a truthful representation of character. He maintained that the bodies of women were not created to correspond to the wishes of men who demanded softness, tenderness, and flexibility. Gymnastics and dancing were important for the health of women, but, in order to increase the physical performance of women who had to balance the demands of their professional responsibilities and motherhood, so were competitive sports.[24]

Physical culturists maintained that exercise and physical culture were keys to professional and private success. Commercial health entrepreneurs tried to exploit this desire for personal success in their health propaganda. Fitness institutes such as the Lionel Strongfort Institute in Berlin-Wilmersdorf advertised their systems of physical culture in popular journals and in mailed advertisements.[25] The institute used the name of the famous and pioneering German body builder Lionel Strongfort (his real name was Max Unger and he lived from 1876 to 1967). Strongfort, the owner of several body-building schools, had already been featured in the physical culture journal *Strength and Beauty* before 1914 and had been a role model for Richard Ungewitter, who had praised his "magnificent body."[26] The Strongfort Institute managed to obtain an exhibition stand at the Dresden hygiene exhibition in 1930 and used a letter of appreciation for its participation in the event by the managing director of the German Hygiene Museum, Georg Seiring, in the advertising campaign for its correspondence courses in physical culture.

The mailed advertisements of the institute addressed the customer in the voice of Lionel Strongfort in an attempt to foster a sense of personal inadequacy among its clientele and offering its correspondence courses as a means of overcoming perceived deficiencies. The advertisements addressed men who had difficulty performing successfully in their careers or who felt insecure about their attractiveness for the opposite sex. Although the text is certainly normative, it gives some insight into the anxieties of contemporary males. In response to a customer who had ordered a booklet titled "Life Energy Through Strongfortism," a standardized letter asserted:

> The very fact that you ordered the book proves that you are aware of the deficiencies of your physical state. This book shows you what you SHOULD be; it tells you what you COULD be; it explains in a simple and open manner, what STRONGFORTISM is, what it has done for others, and what it CAN and WILL do for you.
>
> STRONGFORTISM is known as the "Science of the Normal." If you are weak, if you lack enthusiasm and mental vigor, if you are without ambition, lethargic and morose, then you are ABNORMAL. If you are too emaciated or too obese, without strength, with flabby muscles, and if you become easily tired, then you are ABNORMAL. If you suffer from disturbances and weaknesses resulting from bad habits and debauchery, then you are ABNORMAL.
>
> STRONGFORTISM teaches you how to become NORMAL. It shows you how you can free yourself from weaknesses, deficiencies, and disturbances and how you can put an end to those habits you might have that undermine your health. It strengthens your entire organism internally and externally and transforms you into a mountain of strength and endurance, full of courage and life energy, into a REAL MAN—into a NORMAL MAN.[27]

Customers of the Strongfort Institute were asked to fill out a questionnaire about their health and their body measurements. The institute would then devise an individual health and exercise regimen for each of its customers, or at least it claimed it would. Most of the questions were rather vague (Are you suffering? Do you lack will? Are you discouraged?) and suggestive (Do you aspire to better health, physical development, greater strength?). The customers could compare their physical measurements with the measurements of satisfied customers who testified about their increased health, strength, energy, and performance. Numbers (measurements of muscles), the advertisement claimed, would prove the great success of the "natural" methods of *Strongfortismus* (see figures 42 and 43). The most impressive testimonial came from one John J. Hajnos, a sailor in the U.S. navy who had earned the title "Hercules der U.S.A.-Marine" from his peers (see figure 44).

There were other testimonials from customers who had successfully finished their courses. One Richard Holdener claimed that his nervous stomach and heart problems, catarrh and back pain had all but vanished. His memory worked faster and his energy and endurance had increased tremendously. Paul Koch claimed that he had unsuccessfully tried allopathic, homeopathic, and

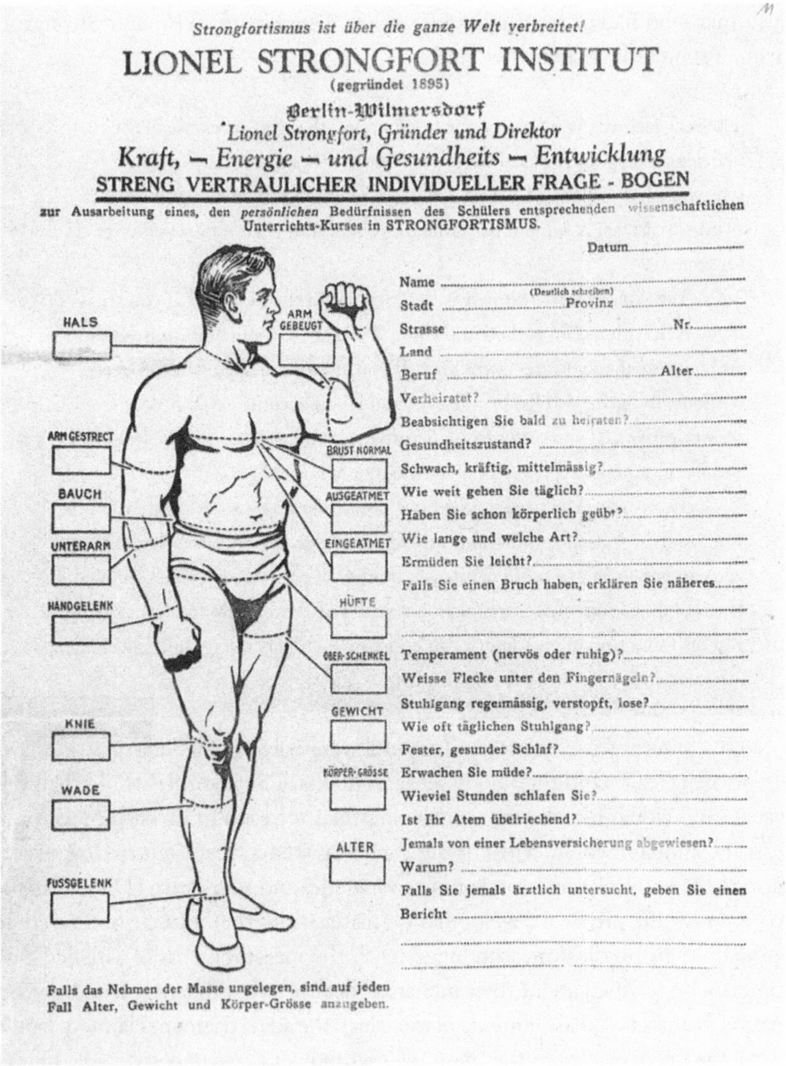

Strongfortismus ist über die ganze Welt verbreitet!

LIONEL STRONGFORT INSTITUT
(gegründet 1895)

Berlin-Wilmersdorf
Lionel Strongfort, Gründer und Direktor
Kraft, — Energie — und Gesundheits — Entwicklung
STRENG VERTRAULICHER INDIVIDUELLER FRAGE - BOGEN
zur Ausarbeitung eines, den *persönlichen* Bedürfnissen des Schülers entsprechenden wissenschaftlichen Unterrichts-Kurses in STRONGFORTISMUS.

Datum

HALS
ARM GEBEUGT
ARM GESTRECT
BRUST NORMAL
BAUCH
AUSGEATMET
UNTERARM
EINGEATMET
HANDGELENK
HÜFTE
OBER-SCHENKEL
KNIE
GEWICHT
WADE
KÖRPER-GRÖSSE
ALTER
FUSSGELENK

Name
(Deutlich schreiben)
Stadt .... Provinz
Strasse .... Nr.
Land
Beruf .... Alter
Verheiratet?
Beabsichtigen Sie bald zu heiraten?
Gesundheitszustand?
Schwach, kräftig, mittelmässig?
Wie weit gehen Sie täglich?
Haben Sie schon körperlich geübt?
Wie lange und welche Art?
Ermüden Sie leicht?
Falls Sie einen Bruch haben, erklären Sie näheres
Temperament (nervös oder ruhig)?
Weisse Flecke unter den Fingernägeln?
Stuhlgang regelmässig, verstopft, lose?
Wie oft täglichen Stuhlgang?
Fester, gesunder Schlaf?
Erwachen Sie müde?
Wieviel Stunden schlafen Sie?
Ist Ihr Atem übelriechend?
Jemals von einer Lebensversicherung abgewiesen?
Warum?
Falls Sie jemals ärztlich untersucht, geben Sie einen Bericht

Falls das Nehmen der Masse ungelegen, sind auf jeden Fall Alter, Gewicht und Körper-Grösse anzugeben.

FIGURE 42. The questionnaire of the Lionel Strongfort Institute. Archiv Deutsches Hygienemuseum Dresden.

other therapies without success. Only Strongfort's system had helped him increase his physical strength and mental vigor and enabled him to get rid of other ailments. Koch's endorsement was further designed to give renewed hope to men suffering from baldness—he claimed that he had discovered new hairs growing on his scalp (and that his gray hair had started to turn black again).

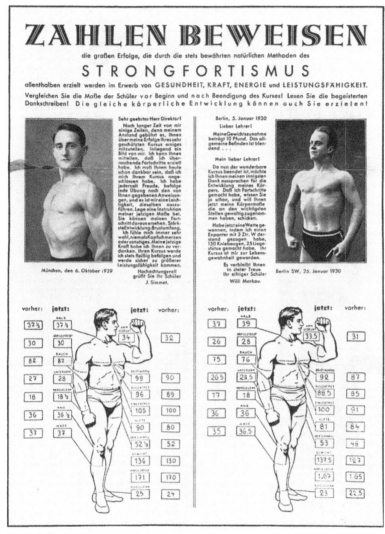

FIGURE 43. Testimonials by satisfied customers of the Strongfort Institute. Archiv Deutsches Hygienemuseum Dresden.

There is of course no way to verify whether these testimonials were genuine, but whether they are or not, they tell us a great deal about some of the anxieties that contemporary health entrepreneurs tried to exploit. They all project the masculine ideal of a male in control of all aspects of his life. As another letter from the Strongfort Institute claimed, the energy that could be acquired through the exercise system would make it possible to cope with personal disap-

HAJNOS

bekannt als

der Herkules der U.S.A.-Marine

lobt begeistert den

STRONGFORTISMUS

WUNDERBARE Erfolge erzielte John J. Hajnos durch die treue Befolgung der Methoden und Anleitungen Strongforts. Niemand, der die Geschichte von John J. Hajnos, dem Herkules der U. S. A.-Marine hört, kann noch irgend welche Zweifel über die grossen Möglichkeiten, welche STRONGFORTISMUS seinen Schülern eröffnet, hegen. Er ist einer von den Tausenden von Strongfort-Schülern, welche durch die Befolgung dieser unübertroffenen Körper-Kultur-Methode die prachtvolle Entwicklung eines kraftstrotzenden, symmetrischen Körpers erzielten.

"Sie wissen," schreibt Hajnos in einem Briefe vom Kriegsschiff 'West-Virginia' am 6. Juni 1924, "dass ich immer Ihr Schuldner bleiben werde für das, was ich Ihnen zu verdanken habe. Stets werde ich mit Verehrung zu Ihnen emporblicken, als zu meinem einzigen Lehrer, der mich zu dem gemacht hat, was ich nun bin, der allenthalben bekannte 'Herkules der U. S. A.-Marine'".

Als Hajnos die Notwendigkeit einer besseren Körper-Entwicklung zu fühlen begann, beschloss er, sich des STRONGFORTISMUS, der Wissenschaft der Körper-Kultur und Gesundheits-Förderung zu bedienen. Durch die Befolgung der Lehren des STRONGFORTISMUS konnte er seinen Körper in solcher Weise entwickeln, dass er imstande ist, ganz unglaubliche Kraftleistungen zu vollbringen, welche von Zeit zu Zeit von überall her berichtet werden, wo das Kriegsschiff ihn hinbringt, —von Australien, Hawaii, Californien, New York, etc.

Hajnos hat wiederholt sein höchstes Lob, seine tiefe Dankbarkeit für Strongfortismus zum Ausdruck gebracht und viele, die seine Leistungen bewunderten, aufgefordert, sich die Vorteile dieser erfolgreichen Kurse zu sichern.

Einige seiner Briefe sind umstehend nebst den Photos, die er beilegte, wiedergegeben. Sie sind Dokumente, welche die unbestreit baren grossen Verdienste des STRONGFORTISMUS für die innere und äussere Entwicklung des Körpers beweisen.

JOHN J. HAJNOS

Schüler des Strongfortismus, der Herkules der U. S. A.-Marine, nachdem er den Kursus beendigt hatte.

LIONEL STRONGFORT INSTITUT

gegründet 1895

LIONEL STRONGFORT, Direktor

Berlin-Wilmersdorf

FIGURE 44. John J. Hajnos, also known as "Herkules der U.S.A.-Marine." Archiv Deutsches Hygienemuseum Dresden.

pointments, failures, and lack of success because such incidents would be only worrisome if one's physical performance level was low. "All tragic conflicts of your life are caused by physical deficiencies, from which you can save yourself through STRONGFORTISM, the science of REJUVENATION," the letter claimed.[28]

The key to the control of one's life was body discipline, and the advertisement promised a new beginning to those who had already failed in personal or professional life. Success, the institute maintained, depended on a person's ability to convince and impress others. According to the institute, a well-trained body would lead to recognition and admiration by others, which in turn was important for success in professional life. Therefore, only physical exercise would give a man the perfect health he would need in the struggle for survival against other real men.

Freikörperkultur and the Vision of a People's Community

Although the Freikörperkultur movement and the health entrepreneurs of the Weimar years addressed similar concerns (rejuvenation of bodies and a restoration of mental and physical performance levels), some Weimar nudists reconciled themselves to the fact that they could not control all the aspects of their lives and tried instead to shape the aspect they could control: their leisure time. Nudism exemplified the struggle of many people to come to terms with their difficult postwar situation. Their struggle is reflected, for example, in the renewed turn toward inwardness and religiosity so characteristic of the Weimar years. Magnus Weidemann, the editor of the nude culture journal *Die Freude,* urged his readers to find religious fulfillment in the joy that permeated the German soul and the universe. The religious imagery that Weidemann used is not surprising, for he had been a Protestant pastor before he became a photographer and devoted nudist.[29] But such imagery—a reflection of the longing for salvation in a world that seemed out of control—was not untypical for the life reform movement of the time. One could probably even speak of a secular religious revival as a result of the turmoil of those early years of the Weimar Republic. This was the time when wandering prophets such as Ludwig Christian Haeusser demanded from their followers spiritual renewal, and Günther, the prophet of Nordic revival, urged people to find salvation by getting in touch with their Nordic soul.[30]

Writing in 1923, at the height of the inflation, Weidemann claimed that during the affluent pre-war years the German soul had forgotten the "joy that was her spiritual shrine." Fate, weakness, hatred, and insanity had taken away everything that had seemed necessary for happiness years ago. Since many people were impoverished, personal fulfillment could not come from material wealth but rather must be found in the German soul. According to Weidemann, people would have to quit finding fulfillment in artificial amusements, riches, and intoxication. The Protestant theologian did not reject Christianity but gave it a secular emphasis. He interpreted the life of Jesus as a metaphor for the salvation humans could find here on earth by following the example of the "archetypical man of light" *(Urbild alles Lichtmenschentums).* Jesus had drawn his spiritual strength from the solitude, beauty, and purity of nature. Through the harmonious development of his personality, Jesus had overcome all evils and had become the "son of god" in a metaphorical sense. He set an example for contemporary Germans, who could achieve perfect harmony with the universe through nude culture and sunlight.[31]

Weidemann urged his readers to achieve personal development by refashioning the spheres of their lives over which they had some control. Although he realized that it was impossible for many middle-class people to gain control over their jobs or determine their personal success, he maintained that it was essential that people try to organize their private spheres according to consistent aesthetic principles of natural simplicity. He considered this project to be among the foremost "cultural tasks" for the enlightened humans who had broken with tradition and cultivated their inner selves in a "new spirit." This was the spirit of truthfulness, which should be reflected, for example, in a simple style of clothing, in contrast to the inauthentic pretensions of the fashions that Weidemann associated with "international degeneracy." The cultivation of the soul and of the body should be expressed in everything a person did—people of the new spirit should try to actively shape their homes, their apartments, and their gardens to set a new standard of truthfulness, authenticity, and good taste. These were standards that he thought could not be achieved by the masses, who lacked the inner cultivation to make their taste and aesthetic styles a truthful expression of their "deep essence." Although the masses might try to imitate those who were truly cultivated, they were doomed to failure because they were "narrow-minded, bourgeois people" (Spießbürger) who were seduced by changing fashions.

In a sense Weidemann was rearticulating the pre-war Bildungsbürger program of cultural renewal advocated by Avenarius's Dürerbund and by Paul Schultze-Naumburg.[32] Weidemann's Die Freude was considered to be a journal for the Gebildeten among the nudists. In contrast to other journals such as Lichtland and Lachendes Leben, which tried to reach out to people from various social backgrounds, the lofty articles of Die Freude only attracted a narrow readership of "intellectuals."[33] Weidemann echoed the cultural elitism of such contemporary racial theorists as Günther and Schultze-Naumburg, but his call for cultural renewal was comparatively modest, abandoning any claims to a wider social and cultural leadership. The "cultural tasks" that Weidemann had in mind were confined to the private sphere of individuals, who were supposed to be content to exert control where they realistically could do so. They should cultivate body and mind, and they should express this cultivation in the "design" (Gestaltung) of their domestic space—which was supposed to reflect simplicity, functionality, and the unpretentious sincerity of their educated owners.[34]

Condemning the ignorance of the masses, however, was rather untypical for the Weimar nudist movement. Most physical culturists and nudists favored more egalitarian visions of society. Cheap booklets directed at a mass audience, like the ones published by Hans Surén, were free of such elitist biases. Surén was probably the most prominent popularizer of physical culture during the Weimar years and the Nazi period. Of his numerous publications on nudism and physical culture, his book *Man and Sun* was the most prominent, with more than 250,000 copies sold by 1945. The son of a Prussian captain, Surén had also pursued a military career. He was promoted to the rank of lieutenant in 1905 and soon afterward became an instructor of physical exercise at the Prussian military gymnastics institution. In 1912 he joined the German colonial troops in Cameroon, where he became a British prisoner of war in 1915. In 1919 he was retained as a member of the hundred-thousand-man Reichswehr and became the commander of the army school for physical exercise. In 1924 he quit the army and became a successful life reform author, publishing a dozen books by 1932.

Although Surén met Hitler in March 1932, he first joined the Nazi Party in May 1933 in order to pursue a career as a physical educator in the Nazi hierarchy. Within the leadership of the Reich Labor Service he became responsible for physical education, and in 1936 the *Reichsbauernführer* Walter Darré appointed him "special plenipotentiary" for the physical education of the rural population. According to Dietger Pforte, Surén's career is an example of the straight path that led the völkisch wing of the German nude culture movement into the Third Reich.[35] It would be wrong, however, to see Surén's career only from the perspective of his time in the Third Reich. Surén promoted his gymnastics system in the 1920s as a path to recovery for the German people, and he tried to disqualify gymnastics systems such as the one taught by his competitor J. P. Müller as foreign and therefore inadequate for patriotic Germans. Surén, who had spent more than three years in British captivity, could not forgive Müller for supporting the British during World War I, but the writings he published during the Weimar Republic were successful in addressing a wide audience because they did not try to cater to the völkisch fringe.[36]

Surén showed a great deal of respect for the physical education program of the socialist Adolf Koch, and although he acknowledged Richard Ungewitter as a pioneer of the nude culture movement, before 1933 his publications were free of the overt racism propagated by the rabid anti-Semite Ungewitter. Surén was an opportunist who took advantage of the Nazi takeover of power to establish himself in leadership positions as a physical educator. He succeeded in securing a position within the Nazi hierarchy not because of his völkisch credentials but because he was popular with large sectors of the German population. The Nazis had everything to gain from giving him a chance to recast his life reform message in order to accommodate Nazi views of racism. Surén obliged by selling his physical culture as "Aryan."[37]

Therefore, the works Surén published during the Weimar years should not simply be read teleologically, in light of later Nazi physical culture. To be sure, Surén himself tried to construct physical culture as part of the tradition of Nazism, but he had rather self-serving reasons for doing so. For the purposes of this work, it is more important to understand what he tried to communicate to his audience during the middle period of the Weimar era, when Nazism was still an extremist fringe movement recovering from the disaster of the Munich putsch.

Surén's writings attempted to console and reassure people who had suffered economic setbacks during the war and the inflation. This becomes especially evident in the aphoristic commentaries to his "Gymnastics in Pictures," a series of tables that depicted Surén demonstrating gymnastic exercises for different parts of the body. He argued that a beautiful body was something that everybody, even the weakest people, could successfully work toward, because everybody could overcome the debilitating effects of civilization by means of physical culture. Beauty was worth more than the buying power of money, he proclaimed to his audience, which in 1923 had just received a vivid lesson on the instability of the German currency. Physical culture, he claimed, would strengthen the character and will of individuals and make them masters in all real-life situations.[38]

Writing about the contemporary physical culture movement in Austria, Ernst Gebhard Eder has suggested that the fear of becoming déclassé, which haunted large numbers of middle-class Austrians after the war, was countered by a quest for distinction in which the shaping of one's own body according to aesthetic ideals played an important role.[39] This interpretation also applies to the German situation. In addition, there was widespread resentment of the newly rich who, according to a popular stereotype, had made a fortune illegitimately from war and inflation.[40] The nudist press made fun of Schieber (black marketeers) who were only concerned with the acquisition of wealth and who were disappointed that they could not buy physical beauty.[41] Declaring the body the key to character development, Surén's writings must have appealed to an audience that could gain distinction through neither wealth nor cultivation of the mind but was eager to justify its sense of moral superiority over war profiteers, speculators, and the newly rich. Indeed, the success and cheapness of his books suggests that they appealed to a mass audience.

Physical culture as a leisure activity that provided a self-fulfillment unavailable to people in their work lives is one of the most prominent themes running through Surén's publications. Nudists had to reconcile their quest for body discipline with the reality of life in an industrialized society. Only during their free time could men and women find self-fulfillment and refuge from the alienating world of their daily experiences in offices and factories. Surén promised his readers that they could achieve full harmony of body, reason, soul, and spirit by physical exercise and not by a one-sided training of the intellect that would only lead to materialism and egoism. Appealing to people's resentment toward those who might have achieved more in their personal lives than themselves, he argued that nudity as a display of physical prowess could silence those achievers and experts in other areas of life, making them painfully aware of their physical deficiency.[42] Surén did not specify what he meant by other areas of life, but he repeatedly referred in a derogatory manner to the cultivation of the intellect and advocated a reduction of the time children spent in school so that they would have more time for physical education. The overcrowding and mediocrity in intellectual occupations were so great, he held, that such a shift of emphasis in the education of the youth could only be beneficial to the nation as a whole.[43] (It seems that Surén could not conceal his satisfaction with the social decline of the educated middle classes that was so deplored by contemporaries such as Günther and Lenz.)

Surén further urged his audience to contemplate the meaning of personal success. Contemporaries had lost their true selves and as a result would be ruled by cold laws, wrong attitudes, and superficial social conventions. There were those whose success in professions and in sports could not be emulated by the masses of people. Full of hatred and envy, they idolized success without realizing that it was not measured by external material achievements but essentially lay within each person.[44] For Surén, success was self-fulfillment, which was not only aesthetic because it served to create a beautiful body, it was also aesthetic in that it served no mundane purpose or interest. His gymnastics did not aim at the cultivation of specialized performances, as did contemporary sports. For him the quest for records—as well as spectator sports such as soccer (a sport that in his view contributed little to harmonious physical development)—were simply the unhealthy expression of a materialist age.[45]

Surén's message was directed at men who had to come to terms with their personal inadequacies in professional or personal life. He maintained that his exercises differed from the dancing and rhythmic gymnastics that were popularized by Dora Menzler and her supporters as appropriate exercises for men and women.[46] In contrast to women, men had to develop strength, and Surén was concerned that rhythmical gymnastics could feminize men. He maintained that developing physical strength increased the sexual attractiveness of men. Therefore, he was opposed to mixing of the sexes during gymnastics exercises. Weak

FIGURE 45. Weimar nude culture 1. *Lichtland* 7, no. 13 (1930). Staats- und Universitätsbibliothek Hamburg.

FIGURE 46. Weimar nude culture 2. *Lachendes Leben* 6, no. 7 (1930): 11. Staats- und Universitätsbibliothek Hamburg.

men in particular, he argued, should not exercise or practice physical culture when women were present because he considered it inappropriate for men to display their weaknesses in front of women.[47]

Clearly, Hans Surén was very uncomfortable with the potentially discriminating feminine scrutiny of male bodies. But most other propagators of Freikörperkultur supported the free mingling of the sexes and defended the joint bathing of men and women in the socially controlled setting of the nature parks established by nude culture associations (see figures 45, 46, 47, and 48). In this respect, nudism reflected conflicts in Weimar society about the appropriate relations between the sexes. Weimar nudists were in favor of abandoning the

FIGURE 47. Weimar nude culture 3. *Lichtland* 7, no. 18 (1930). Staats- und Universitätsbibliothek Hamburg.

FIGURE 48. Weimar nude culture 4. *Lachendes Leben* 7, no. 7 (1931): 17. Staats- und Universitätsbibliothek Hamburg.

tradition of separate homosocial spheres of social intercourse in favor of a mingling of the sexes. Pre-war *Herrenpartien* (all-male gatherings) for the purpose of drinking and amusement were condemned as "petit bourgeois" *(spießig)* and contrasted with men and women jointly spending wholesome quality time together in the open.[48] Conservative attacks on mixed-sex but nonnudist family beaches were also energetically repudiated.[49] The free mingling of the sexes, the nudist Therese Mülhouse-Vogeler claimed, was a precondition for the development of "true companionship based on trust" between future marriage partners because along with their clothes men and women would also rid themselves of deceptive masks that hid their true character.[50] In addition, some propagators of nude culture refused to condemn sexual relationships between unmarried men and women because sexuality was a necessity for personal fulfillment.[51]

    The free mingling of the sexes was, however, not the only significant attraction of nude culture. Historians now debate whether the social and moral milieus that formed the backbone of the political parties in the imperial era, the working-class subculture and the Catholic milieu, found their high point during the Weimar Republic or whether these milieus were only finally destroyed when the Nazi regime created the illusion of an egalitarian people's community *(Volksgemeinschaft).*[52] A frequently recurring theme in the journals of the Freikörperkultur movement was the claim that nudism helped people transcend the boundaries between social classes. Nudity, its defenders claimed, would erase titles and other forms of social distinctions. Nudists could therefore do away with social prejudices and select their spouses based on the quality of their character and not on their social position. Nudity was seen as a certificate of authenticity. Freikörperkultur would mean that people were stripped not only of clothes but of social conventions.[53]

Nudism held out the promise of the creation of a community in which, one author argued, class hatred would be suspended, because both manual and white-collar workers would realize that material possessions were unimportant. The experience of nude bathing on Sundays would make humans free, and they would achieve true equality. They would not be reminded anymore of their own poverty and would forget the sorrows of everyday life. Envy based on social distinctions would vanish, and the German people would be welded into a "brotherly whole." Hypocritical democracy would be replaced with a noble sense of community that was in stark contrast to the class hatred that was fostered by irresponsible elements agitating among the working classes.[54] At the time, many sports and leisure associations were still organized along confessional and political lines. Many socialist workers' and bürgerliche sports associations did not yet participate in common competitions. Therefore the creation of a Volksgemeinschaft held considerable promise for people who viewed the cultural and social separatism of the Social Democratic and Communist labor movement with suspicion.[55]

"Whether one is young or old, man or woman, manual worker or thinker" was unimportant. According to many nudists, political convictions and religious beliefs did not matter as long as one was committed to the aesthetic and moral ideals of nudism.[56] They hoped to erase status barriers in order to create a community that transcended the traditional "sociability" *(Geselligkeit)* of people of the same background.[57] Nudists experienced the disintegration of the milieus that had structured leisure activities and given meaning to class identities during the Kaiserreich as a liberation. They celebrated nudism as the path to a social harmony that was to be realized as a leisure-time "people's community." The foundation of this community was a depoliticized illusion of social equality.

Nevertheless, it is important to keep in mind that the nudist movement was a multifaceted one. Some contemporary propagators of nudism did not want to abandon the class struggle. Radical socialist activists claimed that physical culture and nudism would prepare the working class for the imminent class struggle.[58] There was also a commitment to pacifism by some, a rejection of any political commitment by others, and overt sympathy with Nazism within the same sectors of the nudist movement. During the later years of the republic, there was strong and explicit criticism of the Nazi movement in the nude culture press, a tendency that was of course ruthlessly suppressed once the Nazis took power. The nudist Therese Mülhouse-Vogeler, for example, argued that the experience of the war left no other options than pacifism. Freikörperkultur, she claimed, was an affirmation of life, war its negation.[59] Herbert Zeissig, another nude culture supporter, denied that the practice of nudism implied a political commitment to pacifism. In his view everybody could become a nudist irrespective of his or her political orientation.[60]

The issue of acceptable political orientations for nudists was raised by the electoral successes of the Nazi movement in 1930. Mülhouse-Vogeler found support of the Nazis unacceptable because they were unable to understand the high moral standards of nudists and attacked Freikörperkultur as a threat to German morality. Therefore, she urged Nazi sympathizers among the nudists to reconsider whether they could support a movement that was so hostile to their own ideals.[61] This hostility troubled them, but they maintained that it was important for the nudist movement to continue its politically neutral stand and try to convince Nazi leaders that nudism was an essential part of the racial improvement of the German people.[62] It is remarkable that demands to keep the Freikörperkultur movement open to Nazism were cast in the language of political neutrality. It seems that those who considered themselves apolitical were most likely to fall for the Nazi promise that the creation of a racially based Volksgemeinschaft would heal the social and political rifts in German society.

It is important to emphasize that the vision of a people's community was not necessarily a racist one. Some nudists claimed that Freikörperkultur would not only overcome class but also racial hatred, since the German Volk was of mixed racial origins.[63] They also stressed the need for cooperation among nudists of different nationalities in order to promote world peace.[64] But for other people the vision of a Volksgemeinschaft was quite compatible with ideas of völkisch racists who demanded the exclusion of foreigners, Jews, and other minorities from the national community. During the middle years of the Weimar republic such voices were rather subdued. Josef Maria Seitz, the chairman of the League of the Friends of Light *(Bund der Lichtfreunde),* which had split from Ungewitter's League of the Faithful for Rising Life *(Treubund für aufsteigendes Leben),* championed a völkisch justification of nudism. But Seitz still preached mutual tolerance between nudists of different political persuasions and religious confessions.[65] This tolerance, however, did not mean that he disowned nationalistic chauvinism and anti-Semitism; he argued forcefully that Germans should not be forced to put up with foreign and Semitic elements.[66]

During the end of the Weimar republic such racial views became more common. In 1932, the life reform artist Fidus called for a new people's community *(Volksgemeinsamkeit)* based on the common racial origins of Germans. Fidus's voice carried weight among life reformers owing to his Art Nouveau drawings of male and female nudes. He demanded the liberation of the German Volk from dependency on foreigners and supported Nazism because he wanted a society of equals of the same race *(Art)*.[67]

The nudist and Nazi sympathizer Walter Heitsch argued that the German people was of racially mixed origin. Therefore he opposed a general exclusion of other races from nude culture. However, he maintained that such issues should be decided by each nude culture group separately, because in his view it was understandable that the presence of foreigners could be experienced as unpleasant. In contrast to elitist Nordic racists such as Günther, Heitsch downplayed racial differences among "Aryan" Germans and instead insisted on racial differences between Jews and non-Jews. Referring to Jews, Heitsch argued that German women and girls might feel depressed *(bedrückt)* if they had to show themselves without clothes to the members of another race, who, as he phrased it, "according to the views of the general public feels more sensually, and lives and thinks a little bit differently than the Aryan [race]."[68] The threat of sexual harassment and racial pollution of "Aryan" women by Jewish men was a staple of Nazi fantasies. Therefore, the exclusion of Jews from public swimming pools became a primary Nazi Party objective in many local communities after 1933.[69] This was only one sign among many that the racial vision of a people's community transcending social classes would take on a radical and sinister reality after the Nazi takeover.

CONCLUSION

*T*his work has been concerned with the various ways in which Germans invested aesthetic ideals of the human body with multiple and often contradictory meanings. Although regular physicians and life reformers, educated and lower-middle-class people, and feminists and antifeminists often used the same neo-classical icons in order to represent ideals of human health and beauty, they conveyed different messages through the various ways in which they propagated physical culture and a healthy lifestyle. For many regular physicians and male life reformers, moral propriety was a safeguard for women's beauty and health. Therefore, they expressed concern about middle-class women's transgressions into the public sphere of employment and feminist agitation during the Kaiserreich. Their feminist critics denounced women's limited professional opportunities, claiming that lack of social and economic independence was the most important reason for the deteriorating health and beauty of contemporary womanhood. They viewed the fight against figure-deforming corsets as a fight against the desires of men who tried to define women as sexual creatures.

Practices relating to the beautiful body also became important terrain for the formation of class identities. At the turn of the century, life reformers from the Bildungsbürgertum urged their male contemporaries not to neglect their bodies. Their propagation of body discipline and an ascetic lifestyle implied a rejection of the debauchery of the upper classes and the rampant materialism of a rapidly industrializing nation. They asked their educated peers to demonstrate their social distinction by the cultivation not only of their minds and souls but also of their bodies.

For other sectors of the middle classes, the turn toward Körperkultur was an alternative source of social distinction. In particular, members of the lower middle classes, such as technical, clerical and service employees, who had internalized the achievement and performance ethos of the Bürgertum, experienced very real limits to their upward mobility and social recognition. They therefore turned their attention to their bodies, an aspect of their lives that they could still master with discipline and the hard work of exercise. These endeavors also set them apart symbolically from the sectors of the working classes whose members did not have the leisure or resources to subject their bodies to a rational lifestyle regime. At the same time, lower-middle-class people resented what they perceived as the undeserved social recognition and privileges of the Bildungsbürgertum, which were based on what they saw as meaningless academic titles and diplomas. Males who did not possess any formal higher education made a virtue out of necessity and contrasted the exercises of the ancient Greek gymnasium with the intellectual exercises of physically stunted students in the Wilhelmine Gymnasium. In their view, the value and good character of a human being could not be cultivated by means of academic efforts. True character and Bildung in the sense of a harmonious balance between mind, body, and soul could only be achieved by the cultivation of one's body.

During the Weimar period, life reform and physical culture continued to reflect somewhat paradoxical and contradictory attitudes. On one hand, some practitioners of physical culture tried to reaffirm symbolically the social distinctions of the pre-war period, which had been questioned in the social disorder of the early Weimar years. On the other, most nudists claimed that their leisure activities would be the basis for transcending "unnatural" status distinctions between people from different social backgrounds, because nudity was an expression of authentic character. The weekend activities of the Weimar sunbathers thus became the model for the creation of a community free of class hatred and social divisions.

The egalitarian claims made by most nude and physical culturists contrasted with the elitist status claims of contemporary racial theorists. People such as Günther and Schultze-Naumburg tried to articulate their resentment of the erosion of social boundaries between the classes by insisting on constitutional essences that were not to be diluted by the racial (read social) mixture of Nordics with racial inferiors. Rassenkunde appealed to the concerns of university students and graduates who were worried that they could not pursue careers commensurate with their elitist aspirations. In contrast, defenders of nudism

saw in the erosion of class boundaries the dawning of a utopian "people's community." In their view, the nude body signified authenticity and truthfulness and
obliterated social distinctions and academic titles. It is important to keep in
mind that the Nazis were able to capitalize on both of these sentiments in their
successful attempt to create a political movement with broad social appeal.
Therefore, the Nazi movement itself was characterized by tensions between
elitism and egalitarianism. Such tensions were, for example, evident in conflicts
between students organized in the National Socialist German Student League
and lower-middle-class party bureaucrats. Nazi students did not want to be
subordinate to local party and SA leaders who lacked higher education.[1]

The attitudes of the elitist academics and university students who found
Günther's works meaningful, and of the nudists and physical culturists who
held utopian hopes for a harmonious Volksgemeinschaft, provided fertile ground
for the Nazi movement during the final years of the Weimar period.[2] In 1933,
people who were hostile to the labor movement welcomed the crushing of
socialist parties, unions, and worker leisure associations in the hope that such
repressive measures would remove some of the most important obstacles to
the creation of a genuine Volksgemeinschaft.[3] The Nazi leisure organization
Strength Through Joy *(Kraft durch Freude)* tapped into such communitarian
longings with its offerings of travel, sports, and educational events that were
open to all "People's Comrades" *(Volksgenossen).*[4]

During the Nazi era older meanings of the beautiful body were still invested with the intentions they had acquired in the previous years. Such meanings are rarely unambiguous, as the historian Thomas Alkemeyer has stressed in
his book on the Nazi Olympics.[5] Nevertheless, with the rise of the Nazi movement to power, the meanings of physical beauty changed significantly. It was not
merely that the Nazis dissolved or purged some life reform and nude culture associations because they considered them politically and morally suspect. Life reform associations were forced into line and nazified *(gleichgeschaltet)*. Marxists,
socialists, and especially Jews were expelled.[6]

Images of the beautiful body were no longer openly employed in symbolic
contests about class and gender identities, as they had been during the Kaiserreich and the Weimar period. They did not have the same degree of semantic
polyvalency that they had acquired in the social conflicts of these earlier, more
pluralistic, periods. Physical beauty now became the emblem of a utopian racial
community purged of stigmatized undesirables. Nazi race discourse did not
racialize perceptions of social class. After 1933, Nazi propaganda in schoolbooks
de-emphasized what the Nordic racists had claimed was the heterogeneous
racial makeup of the non-Jewish German population. Emphasizing such differ-

ences would have conflicted with their propagation of a seemingly classless people's community from which "racially undesirables," in particular Jews, were excluded by means of social, legal, and cultural stigmatization.[7]

The heroic representation of physical beauty in Nazi culture did not only serve the purpose of intimidation. The representation of the beautiful—be it in Nazi sculpture, illustrated magazines, postcards, or Leni Riefenstahl's film *Olympia*—promised Germans who were willing or able to become "worthy" members of the people's community the imaginary fulfillment of the desire of physical, spiritual, and national perfection.[8] At the same time, however, the idealization of beauty and health set the stage for the devaluation and stigmatization of people who were sick, handicapped, or non-Aryan. The Nazis considered worthless the lives of humans who, in their view, did not have the racial potential of healthy Aryans and therefore could not aspire to their lofty ideals of beauty. The annihilation of the sick and ugly in the name of health and beauty was thus an important driving force of Nazism.[9] Nowhere is the contrast between the pathological and the aesthetic more obvious than in the Nazi art exhibitions of 1937. In Munich the "pathological" art of the avant-garde shown in the exhibition "Degenerate Art" was presented in contrast to the "healthy" art shown in the "Great German Art" exhibition. Drawing on the techniques developed by Schultze-Naumburg, the former presented modern art as the product of the sick and twisted minds of "racial inferiors," whereas the latter presented works of timeless beauty as the expression of the racial essence of the German Volk.[10]

The idealization of a racially pure, harmonious people's community notwithstanding, social divisions and tangible conflicts of interest did not cease to exist in Nazi Germany, though the Nazis were masters of the symbolic resolution of such conflicts. The way the Nazis handled the conflicts between regular and alternative medicine is very instructive in this respect. On one hand, the regime created the illusion that it had fully restored the dignity, influence, and authority of the regular medical profession; on the other, it gave the supporters of natural therapies the feeling that they had overcome their reputation as illegitimate outcasts.[11]

The propagation of a "New German Healing Science" *(Neue Deutsche Heilkunde)* was in part an attempt to bring the natural therapy movement into line and reorient German medicine toward preventive medicine. This shift entailed an exclusive emphasis on the health of the "people's body" instead of on the health of individuals.[12] Germans were expected to contribute to the health of the nation by being fit and avoiding poisons such as alcohol and tobacco that would weaken the race.[13] Since official medicine adopted the rhetoric of natural therapy in its stress on preventive medicine, the old divisions between natural therapy and regular medicine seemed to have been overcome, and alternative therapies and lifestyle prescriptions were now part of the official medical system. As shown in chapter 6, attempts made during the Weimar Republic to shore up the public legitimacy of the regular medical profession by co-opting the natural therapy movement through the Committees for Hygienic Popular Education had failed. After 1933 Reich Physician Leader Gerhard Wagner succeeded in coordinating and co-opting the natural therapy associations. But this time he did so not to advance the interests of the medical profession but for the purposes of the Nazi regime—to make the German nation fit for war. Nazified natural therapy and life reform associations were supposed to further the health of the people's body by their propagation of preventive hygiene and healthy living habits. Regular medicine, however, was to keep its dominant role within the medical system, since the preventive health propaganda of natural therapy associations was subordinate to the health leadership *(Gesundheitsführung)* of regular physicians.[14] Because the military needed the scientific expertise of physicians for the planned war, the Nazis could ill afford to antagonize the regular medical profession.

Nevertheless, supporters of natural therapy and regular physicians could entertain the illusion that they profited from a "people's community" in the medical field. Although regular medicine remained the basis for scientific research as well as for most therapies, natural therapy gained in public prestige. Its practitioners received greater opportunities to publish in respectable medical journals, and they were no longer publicly attacked.[15] Healing practitioners *(Heilpraktiker)* without university training were now officially recognized, but in 1939 a prohibition against the training and approbation of new healing practitioners appeased the regular medical establishment.[16]

The Nazi attempt simultaneously to reassure the regular medical profession and life reformers could lead to a great deal of confusion with regard to such issues as compulsory vaccination. For life reformers, vaccinations had always amounted to a poisoning of people's bodies, and they devoted considerable energy to agitating against the Imperial Vaccination Law of 1874, which prescribed compulsory vaccinations against smallpox. The so-called *Impfzwang* was a highly charged symbol of the conflict between supporters of natural therapies and the regular medical profession, and the Nazis could not settle for a compromise that would satisfy both sides. Hitler's seizure of power raised hopes among some life reformers that compulsory vaccinations would be abolished as a threat to the health of the people. These hopes were fueled by prominent natural therapy sympathizers within the Nazi movement. Indeed, the circle of Nazis surrounding Julius Streicher, the *Gauleiter* (Nazi Party district leader) of Franconia, denounced vaccinations as racial blood poisoning.[17]

The Nazis working with Streicher felt emboldened in their attacks on regular medicine by a letter from an official in the Reich Chancellery to a British pastor that was published in the British antivivisectionist paper *The Abolitionist.* Ministerialrat Dr. Hans Thomsen, a foreign policy expert in the Reich Chancellery, had responded to a letter from one Reverend E. Francis Udny, who expressed concern about an article printed in the British newspaper the *Daily Express* that claimed that the German government would introduce tougher compulsory vaccination laws for a wide range of infectious diseases.[18] Thomsen explained to the pastor that "as far as I know, the German school of medicine does not believe in the practice of pouring germs and serum into people's system. Our doctors are much more willing to rely upon the natural forces of the human body normally reacting against attacks of disease, and find the force of this reaction a better proof of vitality than can be obtained by the contents of ampullae of any description." Thomsen claimed that this was basically the view of Hitler, and he gave Udny the permission to use his letter as he pleased.[19]

It is not unreasonable to assume that Thomsen indeed represented Hitler's personal views of life reform and vaccinations. Hitler led a rather ascetic life as a vegetarian who rejected smoking and alcohol, and he was also presented that way in Nazi propaganda.[20] But Thomsen's reassuring answer to Udny had some rather far-reaching and unforeseeable consequences. Udny published the letter in *The Abolitionist* of August 1933 in order to refute allegations in the British press about plans to introduce tougher vaccination laws in Germany.[21] The League of Physicians Opposed to Vaccination *(Impfgegnerärztebund)* got a hold of this article and asked Thomsen whether he had indeed written it. Thomsen affirmed that he had but asked the league not to use the article as ammunition in publications condemning compulsory vaccination. But by then it was too late; Julius Streicher's alternative health publication, *German People's Health from Blood and Soil,* had already published the article and had itself been cited in the German press. In the view of Nazis who were sympathetic to alternative medicine, this article seemed finally to vindicate them and clear up some of the confusion caused when the German states of Thuringia and Saxony had banned the journals and associations of antivaccinationists.

Faced with pressure to take a position, Rudolf Hess, the deputy of the Führer, refuted rumors that Hitler was an opponent of compulsory vaccination. Heinrich Will, the physician who edited Streicher's natural health journal, bitterly complained about the confusion. He wrote to Thomsen that although he was a convinced antivaccinationist, he was absolutely loyal to the Führer and the party, and he would end his antivaccination propaganda if he was ordered to do so. He argued that he had been emboldened to make radical attacks on compulsory vaccinations by Reich Physician Leader Wagner as well as such other prominent persons as Reich Minister of the Interior Wilhelm Frick, because they had favored a conscientious objector's clause in the national vaccination law. But by May 1934, the wind suddenly seemed to shift, and Hitler supposedly declared himself to be in favor of retaining compulsory vaccinations. Therefore, Will wanted to know whether his publication should continue with its attacks.[22]

What is one to make of this bizarre little episode involving a British pastor, German antivaccinationists, a high-ranking official in the Reich Chancellery, and apparently also people in the highest levels of the Nazi leadership? Thomsen's response to Will provides some answers. He told Will that Hitler wanted all questions regarding his position on vaccinations to receive an answer denying that Hitler was opposed to them. Thomsen tried to reassure Will that such a response did not necessarily represent Hitler's convictions; he told Will "confidentially" *(streng vertraulich)* that this decision was made for political reasons concerning the military.[23] Indeed the military seems to have taken a keen interest in the vaccination laws, as some letters of the chief of the Wehrmacht office in the War Ministry, General Walter von Reichenau, indicated in August 1935.[24] A year earlier, Hitler had gone out of his way to reassure the military that, with the elimination of the leadership of the SA, it was the sole bearer of arms in the nation, and he certainly was not about to antagonize the army concerning the issue of compulsory vaccination.

Thus, an attempt to present a favorable picture of the new Germany to the British public had backfired because it forced the Nazi leadership to make a decision about an issue that was divisive for the "people's community." The leadership had to be concerned about the potentially alienating effects such a decision could have on the alternative health movements, which they tried to instrumentalize for their own purposes. They also antagonized some of the most hard-core Nazis in Julius Streicher's circle who favored natural therapy. They resolved this dilemma with the ritualistic creation of an image of reconciliation between orthodox medicine and natural therapy. In 1935, the "New German Healing Science" propagated by Wagner promised to overcome the conflict between orthodox and alternative medicine by creating a new medicine that would integrate principles of natural therapy into a new biological healing science.[25] With this act, natural therapy gained in public prestige and its supporters were reassured, even though a key policy decision such as the retention of compulsory vaccination amounted to a rejection of one of the most sacred principles of the life reformers.

This symbolic conflict resolution might have worked for some people, but not for a die-hard life reformer such as Richard Ungewitter. Ungewitter, a committed Nazi and anti-Semite, was bitterly disappointed. For him National Socialism was the völkisch life reformer's utopia: All policy decisions were to be made with a view to the health and racial purity of the people as a whole; the individual counted for nothing. The practice of vaccination and the provaccination propaganda of the regime threatened his utopia. In a 1938 memorandum to Hitler, Göring, Frick, and other leading Nazis, Ungewitter denounced vaccination as an attempt by Jewish physicians to destroy the German race by means of blood poisoning, and he expressed his disbelief that the National Socialist state could let this happen.[26] Whether Ungewitter ever received a response is not known.

Ungewitter's totalitarian vision of a society that subordinated the rights of individuals to the health of the Volkskörper was realized, but it was not his own version of a hygienic utopia. Regular physicians, not life reformers, were entrusted with the task of purifying and beautifying the German Volk in the Nazi extermination programs. Such visions proved much more compatible with modern scientific medicine than Ungewitter could have imagined.

Introduction

1. Robert Jütte, *Geschichte der alternativen Medizin: Von der Volksmedizin zu den unkonven-*
tionellen Therapien von heute (Munich: Beck, 1996); Cornelia Regin, *Selbsthilfe und Gesundheitspoli-*
tik: Die Naturheilbewegung im Kaiserreich, 1889–1914 (Stuttgart: Steiner, 1995); Gunnar Stollberg,
"Die Naturheilvereine im Deutschen Kaiserreich," *Archiv für Sozialgeschichte* 28 (1988): 287–305;
Claudia Huerkamp, "Medizinische Lebensreform im späten 19. Jahrhundert: Die Naturheilbewegung in Deutschland als Protest gegen die naturwissenschaftliche Universitätsmedizin," *Viertel-*
jahresschrift für Sozial- und Wirtschaftsgeschichte 73 (1986): 158–82. On smallpox vaccination in
Germany, see Claudia Huerkamp, "The History of Smallpox Vaccination in Germany: A First
Step in the Medicalization of the General Public," *Journal of Contemporary History* 20 (1985): 617–
35. On the divergence of lay and professional discourses in German medicine, see Jens Lachmund
and Gunnar Stollberg, *Patientenwelten: Krankheit und Medizin vom späten 18. bis zum frühen 20.*
Jahrhundert im Spiegel von Autobiographien (Opladen: Leske & Budrich, 1995).

2. Andreas W. Daum, *Wissenschaftspopularisierung im 19. Jahrhundert: Bürgerliche Kultur,*
naturwissenschaftliche Bildung und die deutsche Öffentlichkeit, 1848–1914 (Munich: Oldenbourg,
1998), 29, 309–23.

3. For the most concise overview of the life reform movement in turn-of-the-century Germany, see Wolfgang R. Krabbe, *Gesellschaftsveränderung durch Lebensreform: Strukturmerkmale*
einer sozialreformerischen Bewegung im Deutschland der Industrialisierungsperiode (Göttingen: Vandenhoek & Ruprecht, 1974). On specific aspects of this very heterogeneous movement, see Diethart
Kerbs and Jürgen Reulecke, eds., *Handbuch der deutschen Reformbewegungen, 1880–1933* (Wuppertal: Hammer, 1998). On natural therapy, see note 1. On vegetarianism, see Eva Barlösius,
Naturgemäße Lebensweise: Zur Geschichte der Lebensreform um die Jahrhundertwende (Frankfurt:
Campus, 1997); Hans-Jürgen Teuteberg, "Zur Sozialgeschichte des Vegetarismus," *Vierteljahres-*
schrift für Sozial- und Wirtschaftsgeschichte 81 (1994): 33–65; Judith Baumgartner,

Ernährungsreform—Antwort auf Industrialisierung und Ernährungswandel: Ernährungsreform als Teil der Lebensreformbewegung am Beispiel der Siedlung und des Unternehmens Eden seit 1893 (Frankfurt: Lang, 1992); Walter M. Sprondel, "Kulturelle Modernisierung durch anti-modernistischen Protest: Der lebensreformerische Vegetarismus," *Kölner Zeitschrift für Soziologie und Sozialpsychologie* supp. 27 (1986): 314–30. On nude culture, see Arnd Krüger, "There Goes This Art of Manliness," *Journal of Sport History* 18 (1991): 135–58; Ulf Erdmann Ziegler, *Nackt unter Nackten: Utopien der Nacktkultur, 1906–1942* (Berlin: Nishen, 1990); Giselher Spitzer, *Der deutsche Naturismus: Idee und Entwicklung einer volkserzieherischen Bewegung im Schnittpunkt von Lebensreform, Sport und Politik* (Ahrensburg bei Hamburg: Czwalina, 1983); Janos Frecot, Johann Friedrich Geist, and Diethart Kerbs, *Fidus, 1868–1948: Zur ästhetischen Praxis bürgerlicher Fluchtbewegungen* (Munich: Rogner & Bernhard, 1972).

4. On the social and cultural significance of the discourse on nervousness, see Joachim Radkau, *Das Zeitalter der Nervosität: Deutschland zwischen Bismarck und Hitler* (Munich: Hanser, 1998).

5. Historians have tended to describe the medicalization process as the result of health care professionals' attempts to sustain the labor force and discipline industrial workers. Although such an approach points to an important part of the relation between the medical profession and the working class, it is too simplistic to assume that discipline and compliance with hygienic norms are imposed from centers of authority. Frevert takes her concept of medicalization from Michel Foucault, but she abandons Foucault's discourse analysis and instead stresses physicians' and factory owners' imposition of social discipline on industrial workers through health insurance schemes. Ute Frevert, *Krankheit als politisches Problem, 1770–1880: Soziale Unterschichten in Preussen zwischen medizinischer Polizei und staatlicher Sozialversicherung* (Göttingen: Vandenhoek & Ruprecht, 1983), 15ff. See also Alfons Labisch, "Homo Hygienicus: Soziale Konstruktion von Gesundheit," in *Momente der Veränderung*, ed. Franz Wagner (Berlin: Springer, 1989), 115–38.

6. Peter Conrad, "Medicalization and Social Control," *Annual Review of Sociology* 18 (1992): 209.

7. Krabbe, *Lebensreform*, 13ff.; Sprondel, "Kulturelle Modernisierung," 315ff.

8. This ambiguous character of modernity has been much emphasized in recent historiography. See, e.g., Thomas Rohkrämer, *Eine andere Moderne? Zivilisationskritik, Natur, und Technik in Deutschland, 1880–1933* (Paderborn: Schöningh, 1999); David Blackbourn, *The Long Nineteenth Century: A History of Germany, 1870–1918* (Oxford: Oxford University Press, 1998), chap. 8. See also Geoff Eley, ed., *Society, Culture, and the State in Germany, 1870–1930* (Ann Arbor: University of Michigan Press, 1997).

9. On the conflicts about the teaching of Greek and Latin in German secondary schools, see Suzanne L. Marchand, *Down from Olympus: Archaeology and Philhellenism in Germany, 1750–1970* (Princeton: Princeton University Press, 1996), 133–42.

10. Mikhail Bakhtin, *The Dialogic Imagination*, ed. Michael Holquist and Caryl Emerson (Austin: University of Texas Press, 1981).

11. For this reason I have omitted the discussion of important movements that might have shaped contemporary meanings of physical beauty. A thorough examination of the German gymnastics and dance movements, for example, is beyond the scope of this book. On German modern dance, see Karl Toepfer, *Empire of Ecstasy: Nudity and Movement in German Body Culture, 1910–1935* (Berkeley: University of California Press, 1997); Susan A. Manning, *Ecstasy and the Demon: Feminism and Nationalism in the Dance of Mary Wigman* (Berkeley: University of California Press, 1993).

12. Pierre Bourdieu, *Distinction: A Social Critique of the Judgment of Taste* (Cambridge: Harvard University Press, 1984), 179, 190–93.

13. Ibid., 175.

14. Keep in mind that regular medicine was a rather heterogeneous phenomenon and that the distinction between regular and alternative practitioners cannot be based on a single, unambiguous criterion. Regular physicians who were quite hostile toward the natural therapy movement could also be skeptical about the claims of modern bacteriology. For the purposes of this study, I regard as regular physicians those who received their training in a university medical school and who were opposed to the natural therapy movement because its representatives condoned or supported the practices of lay practitioners. On the other hand, I regard as irregular practitioners university-trained physicians who actively participated in the natural therapy movement, as well as lay practitioners.

15. Such discontinuities are, for example, emphasized by Atina Grossmann in her work on sexual reform during the Weimar period. Grossmann argues that although many reformers on the left used eugenic arguments, it would be a mistake to draw simplistic continuities between their work and the repressive population policies of the Nazis. See Atina Grossmann, *Reforming Sex: The German Movement for Birth Control and Abortion Reform, 1920–1950* (Oxford: Oxford University Press, 1995). Historians of the German welfare state have also warned against inferring continuities between the Weimar and the Nazi periods that are too simplistic: Young-Sun Hong, *Welfare, Modernity, and the Weimar State, 1919–1933* (Princeton: Princeton University Press, 1998); David Crew, "The Ambiguities of Modernity: Welfare and the German State from Wilhelm to Hitler," in *Society, Culture, and the State in Germany, 1870–1930*, ed. Geoff Eley (Ann Arbor: University of Michigan Press, 1997), 319–44.

Chapter One

1. Lehrer Schmidt, "Magenkatarrh oder Nervosität?" *Naturarzt* 22 (1894): 16f.

2. Gunnar Stollberg, "Die Naturheilvereine im deutschen Kaiserreich," *Archiv für Sozialgeschichte* 28 (1988): 289; Cornelia Regin, *Selbsthilfe und Gesundheitspolitik: Die Naturheilbewegung im Kaiserreich (1889–1914)* (Stuttgart: Steiner, 1995), 50.

3. Jürgen Kocka, "Bürgertum und Bürgerlichkeit als Probleme der deutschen Geschichte vom späten 18. zum frühen 20. Jahrhundert," in *Bürger und Bürgerlichkeit im 19. Jahrhundert*, ed. Kocka (Göttingen: Vandenhoek & Ruprecht, 1987), 21–63; Jürgen Kocka, "Bürgertum und bürgerliche Gesellschaft im 19. Jahrhundert: Europäische Entwicklungen und deutsche Eigenarten," in *Bürgertum im 19. Jahrhundert: Deutschland im europäischen Vergleich*, ed. Kocka (Munich: dtv, 1988), 11–79. For a short review of the literature on the Bürgertum, see Utz Haltern, "Die Gesellschaft der Bürger," *Geschichte und Gesellschaft* 19 (1993): 100–134.

4. Kocka, "Bürgertum und Bürgerlichkeit," 42–48; Kocka, "Bürgertum und bürgerliche Gesellschaft," 26–33.

5. Ute Frevert, *Krankheit als politisches Problem, 1770–1880: Soziale Unterschichten in Preussen zwischen medizinischer Polizei und staatlicher Sozialversicherung* (Göttingen: Vandenhoek & Ruprecht, 1984), 28–36. On the emergence of such bürgerliche virtues before the Kaiserreich, see Manuel Frey, *Der reinliche Bürger: Entstehung und Verbreitung bürgerlicher Tugenden in Deutschland, 1760–1860* (Göttingen: Vandenhoek & Ruprecht, 1997).

6. Frevert, *Krankheit als politisches Problem*, 207–19.

7. Alfons Labisch, "Homo Hygienicus: Soziale Konstruktion von Gesundheit," in *Medizin: Momente der Veränderung*, ed. Franz Wagner (Berlin: Springer, 1989), 115–38; Alfons Labisch, "Hygiene ist Moral—Moral ist Hygiene: Soziale Disziplinierung durch Ärzte und Medizin," in *Soziale Sicherheit und soziale Disziplinierung: Beiträge zu einer historischen Theorie der Sozialpolitik,*

ed. Christoph Sachsse and Florian Tennstedt (Frankfurt: Suhrkamp, 1986), 265–85. For arguments along similar lines, see also Gerd Göckenjan, "Medizin und Ärzte als Faktor der Disziplinierung der Unterschichten: Der Kassenarzt," in Sachsse and Tennstedt, 286–303; Paul Weindling, "Hygienepolitik als sozialintegrative Strategie im späten Deutschen Kaiserreich," in *Medizinische Deutungsmacht im sozialen Wandel des 19. und frühen 20. Jahrhunderts,* ed. Alfons Labisch and Reinhard Spree (Bonn: Psychiatrieverlag, 1989), 37–55. These approaches point to important aspects of relations between the state, employers, physicians, and the working classes. However, they share the implicit assumption that discipline and health-consciousness are imposed from above and cannot explain the motivation of people who voluntarily disciplined their lives and their bodies in a quest for health and fitness.

8. On the fragmentation of the middle classes, see Thomas Nipperdey, *Deutsche Geschichte 1866–1918,* vol 1, *Arbeitswelt und Bürgergeist* (Munich: Beck, 1990), 253–60, 374–89; Michael Stürmer, *Das ruhelose Reich: Deutschland, 1866–1918* (Munich: Siedler, 1983), 60ff.

9. In 1908 and 1912, skilled workers comprised about 25 percent of the membership of the German League of Natural Therapy Associations; the rest was recruited from various sectors of the middle classes. The largest group were artisans, who constituted about 30 percent of the membership. Another sizable group consisted of economically independent merchants, shopkeepers, factory owners (7–9 percent), and clerical and managerial employees *(Privatbeamte und unselbständige Kaufleute),* who made up about 9 percent. Teachers and civil servants were represented with about 3 percent and 7 percent, respectively. Regin, *Selbsthilfe und Gesundheitspolitik,* 77–82; Stollberg, "Naturheilvereine im Kaiserreich," 294. I am talking mainly about the so-called bürgerliche Lebensreformbewegung. There were also organizations of life reformers that were explicitly socialist, such as the *Verband Volksgesundheit,* but their membership was much smaller than that of the nonsocialist organizations. For the Kaiserreich, see Bernhard Herrmann, *Arbeiterschaft, Naturheilkunde und der Verband Volksgesundheit, 1880–1918* (Frankfurt: Lang, 1990).

10. The data are all based on the lists of new members of the Berlin local, which were published for the years 1903 to 1908 in the journal *Kraft und Schönheit.* Of the 626 people who joined the Berlin local during this time, 464 (74 percent) were men and 162 (26 percent) were women. For 402 (87 percent) of the men, occupation could be determined. The largest occupational group was the rather ambiguous category of *Kaufmann,* with about 20 percent. This category could include independent merchants, shopkeepers, managers, or clerks. However, "Kaufmann" was often the high-sounding self-designation of socially ambitious clerks, who wanted to downplay their dependent status as employees. Contemporary career advice books directed at prospective clerical and administrative employees in the new corporate bureaucracies referred to them by that name. See Jürgen Kocka, *Die Angestellten in der deutschen Geschichte 1850–1890* (Göttingen: Vandenhoek & Ruprecht, 1981), 131, esp. n. 55. Another 19 percent of the male members of the Berlin local worked in some other form of clerical or administerial job as *Bureaubeamte,* clerks, accountants, or secretaries, whereas 16 percent were technicians, engineers, or architects. Eight percent were skilled workers such as typesetters. Five percent were either high-level managers or factory owners, and 3 percent were public school teachers *(Volksschullehrer).* Eleven percent were university students, 7 percent were in academic professions (physicians, lawyers and gymnasium teachers), 5 percent were civil servants, and another 7 percent claimed to be artists or writers. If one counts students, civil servants, and professionals as well as the artists and the writers as members of the Bildungsbürgertum—which is of course problematic, because occupational self-designations such as "artist" or "writer" might reflect social aspirations rather than reality—then up to 30 percent of members of the Berlin local were from the ranks of the Gebildeten. Occupations were listed for only 52 (32 percent) of the 162 female members. Most of the women worked in jobs that would become increasingly feminized during the period. The largest group (35 percent) were from the lower

middle classes and worked in clerical and service sector jobs (for example, as saleswomen). Twenty-one percent were teachers. Another 17 percent claimed to practice some form of art as a painter, singer, or writer.

11. German vegetarians were from a social background similar to that of Berlin physical culturists. Turn-of-the-century address books show that the supporters of vegetarianism worked in varied fields. In 1898, about 21 percent of vegetarians listed in the address book were Kaufmänner, 6 percent clerical or managerial employees *(Privatbeamte)*, 14 percent teachers, 8 percent civil servants, 5 percent physicians or natural therapists, 4 percent factory owners, 15 percent artisans, and 9 percent technicians or skilled workers. Barlösius, *Naturgemäße Lebensführung*, 109–12, 129–44, 164–71.

12. Regin, *Selbsthilfe und Gesundheitspolitik*, 98.

13. Only about 10 percent of the formal membership of vegetarian voluntary associations consisted of women, but 25 percent of vegetarians listed in vegetarian address books were female. Barlösius, *Naturgemäße Lebensführung*, 106–8; Krabbe, *Lebensreform*, 140. About a quarter of the members of the Berlin local of the German Association for Rational Body Discipline were women. See note 10.

14. Regin, *Selbsthilfe und Gesundheitspolitik*, 70–91, 96f.; Barlösius, *Naturgemäße Lebensweise*, 136.

15. See, e.g., the study by Fuhs on the city of Wiesbaden: Burkhard Fuhs, *Mondäne Orte einer vornehmen Gesellschaft: Kultur und Geschichte der Kurstädte, 1700–1900* (Hildesheim: Olms, 1992), 303–7, 431. On the eve of World War I, sanatoriums catering to the wealthy charged ten to sixteen marks per day for treatment, board, and lodging. Römpler's sanatorium in Göbersdorf (Silesia) charged between ten and twelve marks per day, Ziegelroth's natural therapy sanatorium in Zehlendorf between ten and sixteen marks. Fuhs, *Mondäne Orte*, 431; *Katalog Dr. Ziegelroth's Sanatorium Zehlendorf bei Berlin* (Berlin, n.d.). This was a lot, especially if one considers that patients often stayed there for at least a month. In 1912, 52 percent of all Prussian taxpayers had an annual income of less than 900 marks. Gerd Hohorst, Jürgen Kocka, and Gerhard A. Ritter, eds., *Sozialgeschichtliches Arbeitsbuch II: Materialien zur Statistik des Kaiserreichs, 1870–1914* (Munich: Beck, 1975), 106.

16. Eberhard Wolff, *Gesundheitsverein und Medikalisierungsprozess: Der homöopathische Verein Heidenheim/Brenz zwischen 1886–1945* (Tübingen: Vereinigung für Volkskunde, 1989), 91–96.

17. [Dr. med.] Katz, "Die Geschlechtskrankheiten und ihre Behandlung," in *Die neue Heilmethode: Lehrbuch der naturgemäßen Lebensweise, der Gesundheitspflege und der naturgemäßen Heilweise*, ed. Moritz Platen (Berlin: Bong, 1907), 4:130–80.

18. Osmar Tränkner, "Die Schönheitspflege vom hygienischen Standpunkt," in *Die Neue Heilmethode*, ed. Platen, 4:333f.

19. *Katalog Dr. Ziegelroth's Sanatorium*, 12. *Entfettungskuren* and weight gain were also selling points for the Bühlau sanatorium near Dresden and the Frankenstein sanatorium near Rumburg, in Bohemia: *Luftkurort und Sanatorium Bühlau bei Weißer Hirsch*, (Bühlau, n.d.), 16; *Santorium Frankenstein bei Rumburg: Physikalisch-diätetische Kuranstalt ersten Ranges* (Rumburg, 1912), 27ff. The ideal body in contrast to the emaciated and the obese was also the subject of health guides of the period (see figure 22).

20. On the importance of career expectations and aspirations for Bürgertum males in the second part of the nineteenth century see Heinz Gerhard Haupt, "Männliche und weibliche Berufskarrieren," *Geschichte und Gesellschaft* 18 (1992): 143–60.

21. On the situation of clerical employees, see Kocka, *Angestellte*, 81f.; Nipperdey, *Deutsche Geschichte*, 374–77. For a balanced assessment of the precarious social situation of many artisans

during the empire, see David Blackbourn, "Handwerker im Kaiserreich: Gewinner oder Verlierer?" in *Prekäre Selbständigkeit: Zur Standortbestimmung von Handwerk, Hausindustrie und Kleingewerbe*, ed. Ulrich Wengenroth (Stuttgart: Steiner, 1989), 7-21. For a slightly earlier period see Shulamit Volkov, *The Rise of Popular Antimodernism in Germany: The Urban Master Artisans, 1873-1896* (Princeton: Princeton University Press, 1978).

22. Joachim Radkau, *Das Zeitalter der Nervosität: Deutschland zwischen Bismarck und Hitler* (Munich: Hanser, 1998), 215ff.; Joachim Radkau, "Die wilhelminische Ära als nervöses Zeitalter, oder: Die Nerven als Netz zwischen Tempo- und Körpergeschichte," *Geschichte und Gesellschaft* 20 (1994): 211-41, esp. 223f.; Anson Rabinbach, *The Human Motor: Energy, Fatigue, and the Origins of Modernity* (New York: Basic, 1990), 153-63, esp. 160.

23. Wilhelm Erb, *Über die wachsende Nervosität unserer Zeit* (Heidelberg: Hörning, 1893), 10-23. See also Friedrich Martius, *Über Nervosität* (Hamburg: Verlags Anstalt und Druckerei AG, 1894), 27-32.

24. Bilz's sanatorium eventually lost its license because of the maltreatment of a female patient with syphilis and because patients with dangerous infectious diseases were not kept separate from those with nervous disorders. BA Berlin-Lichterfelde 1501, No. 9135, 6 October 1911. See also 1501, No. 9136, 9 January 1914.

25. [Dr. med.] Silber, "Die Nervennot unserer Zeit," *Naturarzt* 37 (1909): 4-10.

26. Franz Schönenberger and Wilhelm Siegert, *Lebenskunst—Heilkunst: Ärztlicher Ratgeber für Gesunde und Kranke* (Zwickau: Förster & Borries, 1906), 209f., 1039, 1076, quotation on 232.

27. Radkau, *Zeitalter der Nervosität*, 71.

28. August Kühner, *Die Liebe: Ihr Wesen und ihre Gesetze*, 3d ed. (Berlin: Wilhelm Möller, 1903), 164f. Kühner also dealt with this issue in his contribution to Moritz Platen's health advice book, one of the most succesful health manuals of the period: "Das Geschlechtsleben und seine Störungen," in *Die neue Heilmethode*, ed. Platen, 4:3-65, esp. 48, 55.

29. Friedrich Eduard Bilz, *Das neue Naturheilverfahren: Lehr- und Nachschlagebuch der naturgemaesssen Heilweise und Gesundheitspflege*, 31st ed. (Leipzig: Bilz, n.d.), 1122-26.

30. Krabbe, *Lebensreform*, 136f.; Barlösius, *Naturgemäße Lebensweise*, 182.

31. See, e.g., "Woran liegt's?" *Vegetarische Rundschau* (1886): 365-68, in which an unknown vegetarian discusses the flaw in his diet that was responsible for his inability to achieve. See also Karl Lentze, "Was kann der einzelne zur Verbreitung des Vegetarismus tun?" *Vegetarische Warte* (1897): 2.

32. Louis Kuhne, *Die neue Heilwissenschaft oder die Lehre von der Einheit der Krankheiten und deren darauf begründete arzneilose und operationslose Heilung*, 35th ed. (Leipzig: Louis Kuhne, 1898).

33. According to the regular physician Carl Reissig, who wrote a muckraking account of the practices of quacks during the empire, Kuhne was merely a carpenter who had set aside his plane in order to enrich medical science. Carl Reissig, *Medizinische Wissenschaft und Kurpfuscherei*, 2d ed. (Leipzig: Vogel, 1901), 85.

34. Kuhne, *Neue Heilwissenschaft*, 8.

35. Ibid., 2ff.

36. Ibid., 13.

37. Ibid., 4ff.

38. Ibid., 99ff.

39. Jens Lachmund, *Der abgehorchte Körper: Zur historischen Soziologie der medizinischen Untersuchung* (Opladen: Leske & Budrich, 1997), 235ff., 247-60; Jens Lachmund and Gunnar Stoll-

berg, *Patientenwelten: Krankheit und Medizin vom späten 18. bis zum frühen 20. Jahrhundert im Spiegel von Autobiographien* (Opladen: Leske & Budrich, 1995), 208f., 217–23. See also Stanley Reiser, *Medicine and the Reign of Technology* (Cambridge: Cambridge University Press, 1979).

40. Kuhne, *Neue Heilwissenschaft*, 22.

41. See, e.g., "Tabellarische Zusammenstellung der bedeutendsten Märsche der Jahre 1905, 1906 and 1907," *Vegetarische Warte* (1908): 131f. "Sechs Sieger," *Die Neue Heilkunst* 10 (1898): 114. The article proudly reports that six vegetarians finished first in a long-distance walking competition.

42. See Karl Mann, "Meine Lebensweise: Leibeserziehung für Wettkämpfer," *Kraft und Schönheit* 2 (1902): 26–29, 379.

43. For the following, see Richard Ungewitter, *Diätetische Ketzereien: Die Eiweisstheorie mit ihren Folgen, als Krankheitsursache und ihre wissenschaftlich begründete Verabschiedung* (Stuttgart: Ungewitter, 1908), 210ff.

44. Ibid., 214f.

45. Ibid., 220.

46. Klara Ebert, "Kampf und Sieg," *Vegetarische Warte* (1907): 273f.

47. Klara Ebert, "Frauengruppe des Deutschen Vegetarierbundes: Neue Tafeln," *Vegetarische Warte* (1904): 465ff.

48. Marion A. Kaplan, *The Making of the Jewish Middle Class: Women, Family, and Identity in Imperial Germany* (Oxford: Oxford University Press, 1991), chap. 6.

49. Barbara Greven-Aschoff, *Die bürgerliche Frauenbewegung in Deutschland, 1894–1933* (Göttingen: Vandenhoek & Ruprecht, 1981), 49ff., 62ff.; Ute Frevert, *Frauengeschichte: Zwischen bürgerlicher Verbesserung und neuer Weiblichkeit* (Frankfurt: Suhrkamp, 1986), 117f.; Ann Taylor Allen, *Feminism and Motherhood in Germany, 1800–1914* (New Brunswick: Rutgers University Press, 1991), 163–71.

50. Klara Ebert, "Kampf und Sieg," *Vegetarische Warte* (1907): 273f.

51. Anna Fischer-Dückelmann, "Meine Stellung zum Vegetarismus," *Naturarzt* 24 (1894): 372–77.

52. Ungewitter, *Diätetische Ketzereien*, 210.

53. On changing patterns of nationalist mobilization, see Thomas Rohkrämer, *Der Militarismus der "kleinen Leute": Die Kriegervereine im deutschen Kaiserreich, 1871–1914* (Munich: Oldenbourg, 1990); Geoff Eley, *Reshaping the German Right: Radical Nationalism and Political Change After Bismarck* (Ann Arbor: University of Michigan Press, 1991).

54. Nipperdey, *Deutsche Geschichte 1866–1918*, 1:374–81.

55. Klaus Vondung, "Zur Lage der Gebildeten in der Wilhelminischen Zeit," in *Das wilhelminische Bildungsbürgertum*, ed. Vondung (Göttingen: Vandenhoek & Ruprecht, 1976); Janos Frecot, "Die Lebensreformbewegung," in ibid., 20–33, 138–52.

56. Gunnar Stollberg, "Health and Illness in German Workers' Autobiographies from the 19th and Early 20th Centuries," *Social History of Medicine* 6 (1993): 261–76.

57. Erdmann Lischke, "Kurberichte: Paralyse, Geistesstörung, Krämpfe," *Die Neue Heilkunst* 3 (1891): 60.

58. Th. Langen, "Gibt die vegetarische Kost einem Arbeiter genügend Kraft?" *Vegetarische Warte* (1913): 6f.

59. This tension was also reflected in the level of alcohol consumption on the job: James S. Roberts, *Drink, Temperance, and the Working Class in Nineteenth Century Germany* (Boston: Allen

& Unwin, 1984), 110ff. On the worker culture, see Lynn Abrams, *Workers' Culture in Imperial Germany: Leisure and Recreation in the Rhineland and Westphalia* (London: Routledge 1992). The socialist labor movement also encouraged workers to accept bürgerliche values and norms such as Bildung and physical fitness: Vernon L. Lidtke, "The Socialist Labor Movement," in *Imperial Germany: A Historiographical Companion*, ed. Roger Chickering (Westport: Greenwood, 1996), 272–302, esp. 293f.

60. The catalogues for Ziegelroth's and Frankenstein's sanatoriums, cited above, stressed such an active collaboration of patients in their cures. Besides exercise and air and sun baths, Frankenstein offered its patients occupational therapy such as woodcutting and sawing.

61. Reinhold Gerling, *Die Gymnastik des Willens: Praktische Anleitung zur Erhöhung der Energie und Selbstbeherrschung* (Berlin: Möller, 1905), 155–216.

Chapter Two

1. *Bildung* in the sense of higher education (such as university degrees) was with a few exceptions still limited mainly to men, as were many of the debates in life reform journals concerning the social privileges of Bildung. For many male life reformers Bildung was a masculine ideal. Feminists, however, demanded that women should also have access to higher education and cultivate their personalities (see chapter 3).

2. Bakhtin writes about a centrifugal multiplication of meanings, a heteroglossia based on the differing social experiences and intentions of multiple voices that find expression in the modern novel. Mikhail Bakhtin, *The Dialogic Imagination*, ed. Michael Holquist and Caryl Emerson (Austin: University of Texas Press, 1981), 67f., 271f.

3. Michael Shortland, "The Power of a Thousand Eyes," *Criticism* 28 (1986): 379–408; Barbara M. Stafford, John La Puma, and David L. Schiedermayer, "One Face of Beauty, One Picture of Health," *Journal of Medicine and Philosophy* 14 (1989): 213–30; Barbara M. Stafford, *Body Criticism: Imaging the Unseen in Enlightenment Art and Medicine* (Cambridge: MIT Press, 1991), 84–118.

4. Gerhard Kloos, *Die Konstitutionslehre von Karl Gustav Carus besonderer Berücksichtigung der Physiognomik* (Basel: Karger, 1951), 35–60, 83. The scope of this work does not permit an examination of the differences between Carus's and Goethe's approaches to morphology. On Carus see Wolfgang Genschorek, *Carl Gustav Carus: Arzt, Künstler, Naturforscher* (Leipzig: Hirzel, 1978). On Goethe's morphology see Timothy Lenoir, "The Eternal Laws of Form," in *Goethe and the Sciences: A Reappraisal*, ed. Frederick Amrine, Francis J. Zucker, and Harvey Wheeler (Dordrecht: Reidel, 1987), 17–28.

5. Kloos, *Konstitutionslehre*, 83, 93.

6. For a more in-depth discussion of the etiological theories of the life reformers see chapter 5.

7. Louis Kuhne, *Die neue Heilwissenschaft oder die Lehre von der Einheit aller Krankheiten und deren darauf begründete, einheitliche, arzneilose und operationslose Heilung*, 35th ed. (Leipzig: Louis Kuhne, 1898), 9ff.

8. Louis Kuhne, *Gesichtsausdruckskunde: Lehrbuch einer neuen Untersuchungsart zur Erkennung der Krankheitszustände*, 30th ed. (Leipzig: Louis Kuhne, [ca. 1904]), 31f.

9. Kuhne, *Neue Heilwissenschaft*, 16ff.

10. Ibid., 461ff.

11. Kuhne, *Gesichtsausdruckskunde*, 14, 73f.

12. Willy Vierath, "Die Physiognomik und ihre Bedeutung für die Erkennung der

Krankheiten" and "Die Körperformenkunde als Hilfsmittel zur Erkennung von Krankheiten und Krankheitsanlagen," in *Neue Heilmethode*, ed. Platen, 3:793–806, 814–23.

13. Francis Schiller, *A Möbius Strip: Fin-de Siècle Neuropsychiatry and Paul Möbius* (Berkeley: University of California Press, 1982), 5f., 79.

14. Paul Julius Möbius, *Über das Pathologische bei Goethe* (Munich: Matthes & Seitz, 1982), esp. 194–99.

15. Paul Julius Möbius, *Über Entartung* (Wiesbaden: Bergmann, 1900), 112.

16. Dieter Langewiesche, "Bildungsbürgertum und Liberalismus im 19. Jahrhundert," in *Bildungsbürgertum im 19. Jahrhundert*, ed. Jürgen Kocka (Göttingen: Vandenhoek & Ruprecht, 1987), 4:108–13; Rüdiger vom Bruch, "Kunst- und Kulturkritik in führenden bildungsbürgerlichen Zeitschriften des Kaiserreichs," in *Ideengeschichte und Kunstwissenschaft*, ed. Ekkehard Mai, Stephan Waetzold, and Gerd Wolandt (Berlin: Mann, 1983), 313–47.

17. The critical public included Emperor Wilhelm II himself, whose rather traditional taste found its physical expression in Berlin's Siegesallee, with its sculptures illustrating the history of the Hohenzollern dynasty. On the aesthetic cultural wars in imperial Germany see Robin Lenman, *Die Kunst, die Macht und das Geld: Zur Kulturgeschichte des kaiserlichen Deutschland, 1871–1981* (Frankfurt: Campus, 1994), chap. 1; Maria M. Makela, *The Munich Secession: Art and Artists in Turn-of-the-Century Munich* (Princeton: Princeton University Press, 1990); Peter Paret, *The Berlin Secession: Modernism and Its Enemies in Imperial Germany* (Cambridge: Harvard University Press, 1980).

18. Ernst Brücke, *Schönheit und Fehler der menschlichen Gestalt* (Vienna: Braumüller, 1891).

19. Max Nordau, *Entartung*, 2d ed. (Berlin: Duncker, 1893). Nordau dedicated his work to Cesare Lombroso and explicitly thanked him for the intellectual stimulation Lombroso provided. On Nordau, see also George Mosse, "Max Nordau, Liberalism and the New Jew," *Journal of Contemporary History* 27 (1992): 565–81.

20. Norbert Borrmann, *Paul Schultze-Naumburg, 1869–1949* (Essen: Bacht, 1989). On the *Kunstwart* and its fight against Kitsch, see Jennifer Jenkins, "The Kitsch Collection and the 'Spirit of the Furniture,'" *Social History* 21 (1996): 123–41.

21. Paul Schultze-Naumburg, *Die Kultur des weiblichen Körpers als Grundlage der Frauenkleidung* (Jena: Diederichs, 1905).

22. Ibid., 10ff.

23. Ibid., 4.

24. Ibid., 146.

25. Ibid., 146ff.

26. Carl Heinrich Stratz, *Die Körperpflege der Frau: Physiologische und ästhetische Diätetik für das weibliche Geschlecht*, 5th ed. (Stuttgart: Enke, 1918), viif.

27. Other contemporary popularizers of scientific knowledge, such as Bruno Wille and Wilhelm Bölsche, stressed the aesthetic aspects of nature as a harmonious, interconnected whole. Andreas W. Daum, *Wissenschaftspopularisierung im 19. Jahrhundert: Bürgerliche Kultur, naturwissenschaftliche Bildung, und die deutsche Öffentlichkeit, 1848–1914* (Munich: Oldenbourg, 1998), 309–23.

28. On Julius Langbehn, see Fritz Stern, *Kulturpessimismus als politische Gefah: Eine Analyse nationaler Ideologie in Deutschland* (Munich: dtv, 1986), 128. Some Bildungsbürger celebrated art as a way to free humans from the burdens of critical thinking in an increasingly complex modern world. The *Deutsche Rundschau*, a political and cultural magazine that addressed the highly edu-

cated, gave voice to such sentiments. In an article titled "The Essence of Art," Heinrich Bulle argued that in the modern age of the natural sciences art would deliver people from the "agony of unsatisfied thinking" and therefore constitute a "deliverance from intellect." Only art could stimulate people in such a way as to "exclude the critical work of the intellect" and produce a "harmonious overall mood of the entire human." Vom Bruch, "Kunst- und Kulturkritik," 338.

29. Marchand, *Down from Olympus,* 142–51.

30. For a short recapitulation of these body norms from the perspective of the traditional art historian, see Max Steck, "Albrecht Dürer als Kunsttheoretiker," in *Vier Bücher von der menschlichen Proportion* (Dietikon-Zürich: Stocker, 1969), 50–65.

31. Carl Heinrich Stratz, *Die Schönheit des weiblichen Körpers,* 2d ed. (Stuttgart: Enke, 1899), 3.

32. Ibid., 79.

33. Gustav Fritsch, *Unsere Körperform im Lichte der modernen Kunst* (Berlin: Carl Habel, 1893), 4f. See also Gustav Fritsch, *Die Gestalt des Menschen: Mit Benutzung der Werke von E. Harless und C. Schmidt für Künstler und Anthropologen dargestellt* (Stuttgart: Neff, 1899), 93ff., 147. On the Munich Secession see Makela, *Munich Secession.*

34. Stratz, *Schönheit des weiblichen Körpers,* 36; Fritsch, *Gestalt des Menschen,* table 22.

35. Fritsch, *Gestalt des Menschen,* 147.

36. *Kraft und Schönheit* 2 (1902), 14ff. Carl Heinrich Stratz, Gustav Fritsch, and Ferdinand Hueppe were contributors to life reform journals despite the stand they took against natural therapy because it was not practiced by university-trained physicians. See, e.g., Stratz's "Die normal-ideale Gestalt," *Kraft und Schönheit* 2 (1902): 7f., in which he explained Fritsch's canon.

37. For more information on *Die Schönheit* as a journal that addressed the Gebildeten, see Janos Frecot, "Die Schönheit: Mit Bildern geschmückte Zeitschrift für Kunst und Leben," *Fotogeschichte* 15 (1995): 37–46.

38. A. E. Brinkmann, "Körperschönheit und Kultur," *Die Schönheit* 6 (1909): 147–54, 206–13.

39. Oskar Stoll, "Leben in Schönheit," *Die Schönheit* 3 (1906): 593–601.

40. Johannes Grosse, "Nacktheit," *Die Schönheit* 9 (1912): 320–32, quotations on 322 and 324.

41. Richard Ungewitter, *Die Nacktheit in entwicklungsgeschichtlicher, gesundheitlicher, moralischer und künstlerischer Beleuchtung* (Stuttgart: Ungewitter, 1920), 80–85; Ungewitter, *Diätetische Ketzereien,* 1f.

42. Ungewitter, *Nacktheit,* 96 (emphasis in original).

43. "O Academia," *Kraft und Schönheit* 5 (1905): 345–50.

44. This theme is also reflected in the following articles: Wilhelm Spohr, "Altertum und Gegenwart in der Wertung des Menschenkörpers," *Kraft und Schönheit* 3 (1903): 191ff.; Max Thielert, "Vollkommene Gesundheit—vollkommene Schönheit," *Kraft und Schönheit* 5 (1905): 313ff. In 1925, the UFA movie *Ways to Strength and Beauty (Wege zu Kraft and Schönheit)* picked up on the same theme (see chapter 8).

45. "O Academia," *Kraft und Schönheit* 5 (1905): 348ff. Some fraternities required their members to demonstrate their manly character by participating in dueling rituals called *Mensur.* In these nonlethal sword duels, students tried to hit their opponent's face. The resulting scars marked the students as members of an elite fraternity, and this was one way for educated middle-class males to demonstrate their respectable social status. Ute Frevert, *Ehrenmänner: Das Duell in der bürgerlichen Gesellschaft* (Munich: dtv, 1995), 182–95. For a different interpretation see Kevin McAleer, *Dueling: The Cult of Honor in Fin de Siècle Germany* (Princeton: Princeton University

Press, 1994). McAleer sees dueling as a sign of the aristocratization of the German Bürgertum, which abdicated its own social ambition in favor of submitting to the dominant values of the aristocracy. On the student subculture that was criticized in this editorial, see also Konrad Jarausch, *Students, Society, and Politics in Imperial Germany* (Princeton: Princeton University Press, 1982), 243ff.

46. W. Bräunlich, "Regeneration und Jugenderziehung," *Kraft und Schönheit* 10 (1910): 19f.; Gustav Möckel, "Die menschliche Dreieinigkeit: Körper, Seele und Geist," *Kraft und Schönheit* 7 (1907): 141. The theme of the man of practical life versus the academic also surfaces in Reinhold Gerling's writings: Gerling, *Gymnastik des Willens*, 162f.

47. Emperor Wilhelm II's remark at the 1890 school conference that "we need a strong generation" was the front page motto of the journal *Kraft und Schönheit*.

48. Richard Ungewitter, *Nackt: Eine kritische Studie* (Stuttgart: Ungewitter, 1921), 47f.

49. Ibid., 70f.

50. Kuhne, *Gesichtsausdruckskunde*, 80.

51. Ibid., 26.

52. Reinhold Gerling, *Was muß der Mann vor der Ehe von der Ehe wissen? Ein Ratgeber für Verlobte*, 4th ed. (Oranienburg: Orania, 1904), 54.

53. Gerling, *Gymnastik des Willens*, 228.

54. Erving Goffmann, *The Presentation of Self in Everyday Life* (Garden City, N.Y.: Doubleday, 1959).

55. Anthony Giddens, *Modernity and Self-Identity: Self and Society in the Late Modern Age* (Stanford: Stanford University Press), 83.

56. Gerling, *Gymnastik des Willens*, 216–28.

57. On Ludwig Klages's life and work, see Rohkrämer, *Moderne*, 162–211; Friedbert Holz, "Ludwig Klages," *Neue Deutsche Biographie* 11, 700–702.

58. Ludwig Klages, "Nachtrag zur Theorie des Schreibdrucks" (1903), in *Ludwig Klages Sämtliche Werke*, ed. Ernst Frauchiger et al. (Bonn: Bouvier, 1971), 8:128ff.

59. *Die Neue Heilkunst* 17 (1905): 185ff.

60. Michael Krüger, *Körperkultur und Nationsbildung: Die Geschichte des Turnens in der Reichsgründungsära* (Schorndorf: Hofmann, 1996), 210, 276–83, 426f. By the second half of the nineteenth century the gymnastics movement had lost its attractiveness for men from upper-middle-class families. In 1869, 60 percent of the members of its associations were artisans, 28 percent were clerks or merchants, and only 11 percent had jobs that required academic training. Krüger, *Körperkultur*, 48–56. Unfortunately, there is not really a comprehensive cultural history of the German gymnastics movement after 1890 because historians were mainly concerned with the political significance of the gymnastics movement in the process of nation-building in the decades before and after 1870–71. In 1864, German and Austrian gymnastics associations had about 167,000 members, of whom about 105,000 were practicing gymnastics. By 1869, these numbers had declined to about 128,000 and 80,000, respectively. Of the latter, 30,000 were between fourteen and twenty. By 1895 membership numbers rose again to 529,925, but the reasons for this development are not systematically explored in the historiography of the gymnastics movement. Svenja Goltermann, *Körper der Nation: Habitusformierung und die Politik des Turnens, 1860–1890* (Göttingen: Vandenhoeck & Ruprecht, 1998), 217f.

61. "Physische Degeneration der gebildeten Klassen," *Kraft und Schönheit* 7 (1907): 97f.

62. J. P. Müller, *Mein System: 15 Minuten täglicher Arbeit für die Gesundheit*, 12th ed. (Leipzig: Grethlein, n.d.), 7. On J. P. Müller, see Hans Bonde, "I. P. Muller: Danish Apostle of Health," *International Journal of the History of Sport* 8 (1991): 346-69.

63. Gustav Möckel, "Die menschliche Dreieinigkeit: Körper, Seele und Geist," *Kraft und Schönheit* 7 (1907): 143.

64. Reinhold Gerling, ed., *Praktische Menschenkenntnis* (Oranienburg: Orania, 1911), 5.

65. Müller, *Mein System*, 9.

Chapter Three

1. Ute Frevert, *Frauen-Geschichte: Zwischen bürgerlicher Verbesserung und neuer Weiblichkeit* (Frankfurt: Suhrkamp, 1986), 91, 152. According to Frevert, the number of women working in industry and commerce grew by about 60 percent between 1895 and 1907. For details on the German feminist movement, see ibid., 104-28; Ute Gerhard, *Unerhört: Die Geschichte der deutschen Frauenbewegung* (Reinbek bei Hamburg: Rowohlt, 1990); Barbara Greven-Aschoff, *Die bürgerliche Frauenbewegung in Deutschland, 1894 -1933* (Göttingen: Vandenhoek & Ruprecht, 1981), 44, 69; Jean Quataert, *Reluctant Feminists in German Social Democracy, 1885-1917* (Princeton: Princeton University Press, 1979). On the feminization of the clerical work force see Carole Elizabeth Adams, *Women Clerks in Wilhelmine Germany: Issues of Class and Gender* (Cambridge: Cambridge University Press, 1988), 11-5.

2. C. Adams, *Women Clerks,* 27f. For the argument that polarized gender identities were constitutive of the identity of the Bürgertum, see Ute Frevert, *Bürgerinnen und Bürger: Geschlechterverhältnisse im 19. Jahrhundert* (Göttingen: Vandenhoek & Ruprecht, 1988), 11-6. On aspects of the antifeminist backlash at the turn of the century see Ute Planert, *Antifeminismus im Kaiserreich: Diskurs, soziale Formation und politische Mentalität* (Göttingen: Vandenhoeck & Ruprecht, 1998); John C. Fout, "Sexual Politics in Wilhelmine Germany," *Journal of the History of Sexuality* 2 (1992): 409-13; James C. Albisetti, *Schooling German Girls and Women: Secondary and Higher Education in the Nineteenth Century* (Princeton: Princeton University Press, 1988), 178-203.

3. On contemporary debates about the birthrate, see Anna Bergmann, *Die verhütete Sexualität: Die medizinische Bemächtigung des Lebens*, 2d ed. (Berlin: Aufbau, 1998), 43-49; Paul Weindling, *Health, Race, and German Politics: Between National Unification and Nazism* (Cambridge: Cambridge University Press, 1989), 241-69. On eugenics, see chapter 5.

4. Thomas Laqueur, *Making Sex: Body and Gender from the Greeks to Freud* (Cambridge: Harvard University Press, 1990), 154ff., 193-227. See also Londa Schiebinger, *The Mind Has No Sex? Women in the Origins of Modern Science* (Cambridge: Harvard University Press, 1989), chaps. 7 and 8; Karin Hausen, "Die Polarisierung der Geschlechtscharaktere: Eine Spiegelung der Dissoziation von Erwerbs- und Familienleben," in *Sozialgeschichte der Familie in der Neuzeit Europas*, ed. Werner Conze (Stuttgart: Klett, 1976), 363-93.

5. Cynthia Eagle Russett, *Sexual Science: The Victorian Construction of Womanhood* (Cambridge: Harvard University Press, 1989), 49-77.

6. Robby Koßmann and Julius Weiß, eds., *Man und Weib: Ihre Beziehungen zueinander und zum Kulturleben der Gegenwart* (Stuttgart: Union Deutsche Verlags-Gesellschaft, 1907).

7. Otto Großer, "Der menschliche Körperbau," in *Mann und Weib*, ed. Koßmann and Weiß, vol. 1, pt. 1, 41-51; Otto Großer, "Der Körperbau des Weibes (verglichen mit dem des Mannes)," in ibid., vol. 1, pt. 2, 1-43.

8. See the following article in the *Journal for Morphology and Anthropology:* W. Pfitzner,

"Sozial-anthroplogische Studien II: Der Einfluß des Geschlechts auf die anthroplogischen Charaktere," *Zeitschrift für Morphologie und Anthropologie* 3 (1901): 485–575.

9. See, e.g., Robby Koßmann, "Die Sonderung der Geschlechter," in *Mann und Weib*, ed. Koßmann and Weiß, vol. 1, pt. 1, 1–40, esp. 1:39 f.; Julius Weiß, "Das Gefühlsleben des Weibes," in ibid., vol. 1, pt. 2, 288–302. A similar position was also taken by male contributors who were not physicians. See, e.g., the article by the law professor Friedrich Zahn, "Berufstätigkeit und Ehe," in ibid., 2:212–50, esp. 2:219 ff.

10. Esther Fischer-Homberger, "Krankheit Frau," in *Leib und Leben in der Geschichte der Neuzeit*, ed. Arthur E. Imhof (Berlin: Duncker & Humblot, 1983), 215–29.

11. Paul J. Möbius, *Über den physiologischen Schwachsinn des Weibes*, 9th ed. (Halle: Marhold, 1908).

12. Paul J. Möbius, *Über Entartung* (Wiesbaden: Bergmann, 1900), 95–123, esp. 103 ff.

13. Möbius, *Physiologischer Schwachsinn*, viii, 3–16.

14. Ibid., 30 f.

15. Ibid., 16, 28 ff.

16. Katrin Schmersahl, *Medizin und Geschlecht: Zur Konstruktion der Kategorie Geschlecht im medizinischen Diskurs des 19. Jahrhunderts* (Opladen: Leske & Budrich, 1998).

17. Cornelia Regin seems to assume that life reformers had more tolerant attitudes concerning sexuality and women's issues than did regular physicians. Regin, *Selbsthilfe und Gesundheitspolitik: Die Naturheilbewegung im Kaiserreich (1889–1914)* (Stuttgart: Steiner, 1995), 216–29.

18. Otto Weininger, *Geschlecht und Charakter* (Leipzig: Braumüller, 1903). On Weininger, see Chandak Sengoopta, *Otto Weininger: Sex, Science, and Self in Imperial Vienna* (Chicago: University of Chicago Press, 2000).

19. Iwan Bloch, *Das Sexualleben unserer Zeit in seinen Beziehungen zur modernen Kultur*, 9th ed. (Berlin: Louis Marcus, 1909), 87 f. Bloch was a member of the Berlin Society for Sexual Science and Eugenics, a progressive physician's organization that advocated sexual and social reform. Its founder was the liberal psychiatrist Albert Eulenburg, who campaigned against the theory of the deficient sexuality of women. On progressive sexual reformers within the ranks of the regular medical profession, see Weindling, *Health, Race, and German Politics*, 102 ff.

20. Richard Ungewitter, *Nacktheit und Kultur*, 2d ed. (Stuttgart: Ungewitter, 1913), 136 ff.

21. Ibid., 104–11.

22. Richard Ungewitter, *Die Nacktheit in entwicklungsgeschichtlicher, gesundheitlicher, moralischer und künstlerischer Beleuchtung* (Stuttgart: Ungewitter, 1920), 24.

23. Moritz Platen, "Das Weib als Gattungswesen," in *Die neue Heilmethode*, ed. Platen (Berlin: Bong, 1907), 4:194–201, quotations on 199 f. Platen's health advice compendium sold more than 600,000 copies before 1913.

24. Gerling, *Was muß der Mann vor der Ehe von der Ehe wissen? Ein Ratgeber für Verlobte*, 4th ed. (Oranienburg: Orania, 1904), 39, 48–67, quotations on 51 and 53.

25. Reinhold Gerling, *Freie Liebe oder bürgerliche Ehe?* (Oranienburg: Orania, 1904), 22. Gerling tried to cash in on his popularity as life reform author by endorsing questionable dietary supplements and cosmetic products while he was still editor of the *Naturarzt*. The controversy erupting over his commercial engagement led to his resignation as editor in 1906. Gerling declared the commercial sale of life reform products as "materialized idealism" and maintained that good products needed to be advertised. Regin, *Selbsthilfe und Gesundheitspolitik*, 191 f.

26. Richard Ungewitter, *Nackt: Eine kritische Studie* (Stuttgart: Ungewitter, 1921), 86–93; quotations, 92.

27. F. König, ed., *Ratgeber in gesunden und in kranken Tagen*, 16th ed. (Leipzig: Meyer, [ca. 1910]).

28. Ibid., 8–15, with drawings of several Greek statues representing beauty and health.

29. Ibid., 38.

30. Ibid., 93, 95.

31. Ibid., 89–96.

32. Ibid., 96.

33. Zeising (1810–1876) formulated his aesthetic theory in his *Neue Lehre von den Proportionen des menschlichen Körpers* (Leipzig, 1854). For information on Zeising, see N. Wecklein, "Adolf Zeising," *Allgemeine Deutsche Biographie* 55, 404–11.

34. König, *Ratgeber*, 125, 129.

35. Ibid., 123–36.

36. Hugo Sellheim, *Die Reize der Frau und ihre Bedeutung für den Kulturfortschritt* (Stuttgart: Enke, 1909), 11.

37. Russett, *Sexual Science*, 49–57.

38. Sellheim, *Reize der Frau*, 14.

39. Carl Heinrich Stratz, *Die Körperpflege der Frau: Physiologische und ästhetische Diätetik für das weibliche Geschlecht*, 5th ed. (Stuttgart: Enke, 1918), viii.

40. Ibid., 1f.

41. Ibid.

42. Ibid., 2. On German liberalism see Dieter Langewiesche, *Liberalismus in Deutschland* (Frankfurt: Suhrkamp, 1988).

43. Stratz, *Körperpflege der Frau*, 3f. Note, however, that such essentialist premises were also shared by feminists, who argued for increased opportunities for women based on their roles as educators and mothers of children. Essentialist arguments enabled women, for example, to advocate increased recognition of motherhood by the state during a time when there was much public concern about the declining birthrate. Demands for extended mandatory maternity insurance for working women and an end to the legal discrimination against illegitimate children, as proposed by the League for the Protection of Mothers, thus became part of contemporary feminist agitation that subverted traditional attitudes toward unwed mothers. Ann Taylor Allen, *Feminism and Motherhood in Germany, 1800–1914* (New Brunswick: Rutgers University Press, 1991), chap. 9.

44. Stratz, *Körperpflege der Frau*, 4ff., 189–95.

45. Schmersahl, *Medizin und Geschlecht*, 338.

46. Stratz, *Körperpflege der Frau*, 346–49.

47. Klara Ebert, "Die neue Frauenkleidung," *Vegetarische Warte* (1904): 57–60.

48. Klara Ebert, "Aufruf an alle vegetarischen Frauen," "An die vegetarischen Frauen," "Frauengruppe des deutschen Vegetarierbundes," *Vegetarische Warte* (1904): 169ff., 291–94, 465ff.

49. Otto Wenzel-Ekkehard, "Ist eine Frauenortsgruppe nötig? Bedenken eines Mannes," *Vegetarische Warte* (1905): 8ff.; Berta Wachsmann, "Verschwendete Kräfte. Pendant zum Bedenken eines Mannes," ibid., 108f.

50. Ebert, "Aufruf," "An die vegetarischen Frauen."

51. The proportion of women's membership in the vegetarian movement was relatively stable

through the years. Wolfgang R. Krabbe, *Gesellschaftsveränderung durch Lebensreform: Strukturmerkmale einer sozialreformerischen Bewegung im Deutschland der Industrialisierungsperiode* (Göttingen: Vandenhoek & Ruprecht, 1974), 141, cites 11 percent for the years 1877 and 1905.

52. "Dr. med. Anna Fischer-Dückelmann," *Vegetarische Warte* (1918): 7; Johanna Bleker, "Die ersten Ärztinnen und ihre Gesundheitsbücher für Frauen," in *Weibliche Ärzte: Die Durchsetzung des Berufsbildes in Deutschland*, ed. Eva Brinkschulte (Berlin: Hentrich, 1994), 75–78.

53. By 1896, women could attend lectures as guests at most German universities, but they were only admitted to the qualifying state exam in medicine in 1899. Baden was the first state to allow women to matriculate at universities without restrictions. Bavaria, Württemberg, and Saxony (1906) followed. The last state was Prussia, where women had to wait until 1908. See Claudia Huerkamp, "Frauen, Universitäten und Bildungsbürgertum: Zur Lage studierender Frauen," in *Bürgerliche Berufe: Zur Sozialgeschichte der freien und akademischen Berufe im internationalen Vergleich*, ed. Hannes Siegrist (Göttingen: Vandenhoek & Ruprecht, 1988), 200–204.

54. Anna Fischer-Dückelmann, *Die Frau als Hausärztin*, 2d ed. (Stuttgart: Süddeutsches Verlags-Institut, 1905), 6–10.

55. Ibid., 189.

56. Ibid., 132.

57. Ibid., 151ff.

58. Richard J. Evans, *The Feminist Movement in Germany, 1894–1933* (London: Sage, 1976), 115ff.

59. Fischer-Dückelmann, *Frau als Hausärztin*, 232f.; Anna Fischer-Dückelmann, *Das Geschlechtsleben des Weibes: Eine physiologisch-soziale Studie mit ärztlichen Ratschlägen* (Berlin: Bermühler, 1908), passim.

60. Fischer-Dückelmann, *Frau als Hausärztin*, 3.

61. Ibid., 185–88, quotation on 188 and plate 3.

62. Franz Schönenberger and Wilhelm Siegert, *Das Geschlechtsleben und seine Verirrungen: Was junge Leute davon wissen sollten und Eheleute wissen müßten*, 10th ed. (Berlin: Wilhelm Möller, 1902), 5.

63. Ibid., 102ff, 32–39.

64. Allan M. Brandt, *No Magic Bullet: A Social History of Venereal Disease in the United States Since 1880*, 2d ed. (Oxford: Oxford University Press, 1987), 16f.

65. Fischer-Dückelmann, *Geschlechtsleben*, 115f.

66. Ann Taylor Allen, "Feminism, Venereal Diseases, and the State in Germany, 1890–1918," *Journal of the History of Sexuality* 4 (1993): 27–50, esp. 39–43; Evans, *Feminist Movement*, 163f.

67. There are no reliable statistics on the incidence of venereal disease. But contemporary physicians and life reformers did their best to spread fear. For a thorough discussion of this issue, see Lutz Sauerteig, *Krankheit, Sexualität, Gesellschaft* (Stuttgart: Steiner, 1999), 75–88.

68. Nancy R. Reagin, "'A True Woman Can Take Care of Herself': The Debate on Prostitution in Hanover," *Central European History* 24 (1993): 347–80, esp. 35; Gerhard, *Unerhört*, 252f. Pappritz denounced the attitudes of promiscuous men as *Herrenmoral*. On prostitution in Germany, see Lynn Abrams, "Prostitutes in Imperial Germany, 1870–1918," in *Deviants and Outcasts in German History*, ed. Richard J. Evans (London: Routledge, 1988); Elisabeth Meyer-Renschhausen, "Die weibliche Ehre," in *Frauenkörper, Medizin, Sexualität*, ed. Johanna Geyer-Kordesch and Annette Kuhn (Düsseldorf: Schwann, 1986), 80–101; Vera Konieczka, "Arten zu sprechen, Arten zu schweigen. Sozialdemokratie und Prostitution im deutschen Kaiserreich," in *Frauenkörper*, ed. Geyer-Kordesch and Kuhn, 102–26; Regina Schulte, *Sperrbezirke, Tugendhaftigkeit und Prostitution in der bürgerlichen Welt* (Frankfurt: Syndikat, 1979).

69. Allen, "Venereal Diseases and the State," 37.

70. On the marketing, sale, and distribution of contraceptives during the empire and the moral concerns of the time see Bergmann, *Sexualität*, 163–98.

71. Schönenberger and Siegert, *Geschlechtsleben*, 192–96.

72. Ibid., 168ff.

73. Schmersahl, *Medizin und Geschlecht*, 72, 275. Freiherr Albrecht von Nothafft, for example, argued that an early and dominating sexual desire in women was abnormal, if not pathological, since women's "natural" sex drive was less pronounced. Von Nothafft, "Die krankhaften Äußerungen des Geschlechtstriebes," in *Mann und Weib*, ed. Koßmann and Weiß, 2:488–569, esp. 494.

74. Fischer-Dückelmann, *Geschlechtsleben*, 155f. This was also the argument of other contemporary feminists. Ann Taylor Allen, "German Radical Feminism and Eugenics," *German Studies Review* 11 (1988): 31–45, esp. 49ff.

75. Fischer-Dückelmann, *Frau als Hausärztin*, 225–28, 245–49.

76. Evans, *Feminist Movement*, 119f., 164.

77. Robby Koßmann, "Hygiene der Ehe," in *Mann und Weib*, ed. Koßmann and Weiß, 2:192–211, esp. 208.

78. Max von Gruber, *Hygiene des Geschlechtslebens*, 44th ed. (Stuttgart: Moritz, 1920), 51, 74–81.

79. Reinhold Gerling, *Das Goldene Buch des Weibes: Zehn Kapitel aus dem Intimsten Leben der Frau*, 3d ed. (Berlin: Pilz, 1906), 28–32.

80. Gerling, *Was muß der Mann*, 85.

81. Apparently, Gerling tailored his advice to the expectations of his audience and the economic realities that middle- and lower-middle-class families had to face. One has to remember that Gerling, who was not simply a very successful author but also a very popular speaker at meetings of natural healing associations, was in direct contact with his audience and therefore had the opportunity to adjust his message. In this sense, the prescriptions in his book were the products of a truly communicative process between author and audience. Gerling, *Wie das Weib am Manne leidet und der Mann am Weibe* (Oranienburg: Orania, 1912), 129f.; Gerling, *Was muß der Mann*, 85.

82. Bram Dijkstra, *Idols of Perversity: Fantasies of Feminine Evil in Fin de Siècle Culture* (Oxford: Oxford University Press, 1986).

83. Schönenberger and Siegert, *Geschlechtsleben*, 12.

84. Johanna Elberskirchen, "Das Geschlechtsleben des Weibes," in *Mann und Weib*, ed. Koßmann and Weiß, vol. 1, pt. 2, 187–230, 195–99, quotation on 199.

85. Bloch, *Sexualleben*, passim.

86. Ibid., 3–6, 104.

87. Ibid., 90–93.

88. The ideal advocated by Bloch here is very similiar to Helene Stöcker's "new morality." Both argued for women's right to sexual fulfillment. Gerhard, *Unerhört*, 265–75.

89. Bloch, *Sexualleben*, 195, 224f., 313–38.

90. Schönenberger and Siegert, *Geschlechtsleben*, 108–25. The contemporary cliché regarding innocent "fallen women" who had no choice but to become prostitutes for life was misleading. Many prostitutes seem to have drifted in and out of the profession; for some, prostitution was simply a way station and did not lead to a lifetime of stigmatization. Abrams, "Prostitutes in Imperial Germany," 194–97.

91. Willy Hellpach, "Kokotten- und Mätressenwesen," in *Mann und Weib*, ed. Koßmann and Weiß, 2:392–435, esp. 430–33.

92. Bloch, *Sexualleben*, 335–38.

93. Judith R. Walkowitz, *City of Dreadful Delight: Narratives of Sexual Danger in Late-Victorian London* (Chicago: University of Chicago Press, 1992), 45–52.

94. Hellpach, "Kokotten- und Mätressenwesen," 430–33. The outdooor activities of the youth movement, for example, allowed teenage girls and boys to mingle relatively freely with minimal adult supervision. Elisabeth Heineman, "Gender Identity in the Wandervogel Movement," *German Studies Review* 12 (1989): 249–70; Marion E. P. de Ras, *Körper, Eros und weibliche Kultur: Mädchen im Wandervogel* (Pfaffenweiler: Centaurus, 1988).

Chapter Four

1. F. König, ed., *Ratgeber in gesunden und in kranken Tagen*, 16th ed. (Leipzig: Karl Meyer, n.d.), 90, 123–31.

2. For a summary of the intellectual forerunners of racial theories, see Patrik von Zur Mühlen, *Rassenideologien: Geschichte und Hintergründe* (Berlin: Dietz, 1977); George Mosse, *Toward the Final Solution: A History of European Racism* (Madison: University of Wisconsin Press, 1985), esp. 17–34. On the intellectual history of racial theories in Europe, see also Leon Poliakov, *The Aryan Myth: A History of Racist and Nationalist Ideas in Europe* (London: Chatto, Heinemann, 1974).

3. Sander Gilman, *The Jew's Body* (New York: Routledge, 1991), 235.

4. On the intersection of racial and gender concepts, see Kimberlè Crenshaw, "Beyond Racism and Misogyny: Black Feminism and 2Live Crew," in *Words That Wound: Critical Race Theory, Assaultive Speech, and the First Amendment*, ed. Mai J. Matsuda and Kimberlè Crenshaw (Boulder: Westview, 1993), 111–32, esp. 116–f.

5. Zur Mühlen, *Rassenideologien*, 43ff. See also Bernd Herrmann, "Zur Entstehung und Wirkung ästhetischer Prinzipien in Der menschlichen Rassenkunde," in *Leib und Leben in der Geschichte der Neuzeit*, ed. Artur Imhof (Berlin: Duncker & Humblot, 1983), 165–75.

6. Benoit Massin, "From Virchow to Fischer," in *Volksgeist as Method and Ethic*, ed. George W. Stocking (Madison: University of Wisconsin Press, 1996), 79–154, esp. 106–14; Massin, "Anthropologie raciale et national-socialisme," in *La science sous le Troisième Reich: Victim ou Alliée du nazisme?* ed. Josiane Olff-Nathan (Paris: Seuil, 1993), 197–262, esp. 211ff.

7. Johannes Ranke, *Der Mensch* (Leipzig: Bibliographiches Institut, 1886),1:3f., 2:63–109, 231–36.

8. Nils Lösch, *Rasse als Konstrukt: Leben und Wirken Eugen Fischers* (Frankfurt: Lang, 1997), 27f. The cephalic index was first proposed by the Swedish anatomist Anders Retzius (1796–1860) in 1840.

9. Massin, "From Virchow to Fischer," 107ff.

10. On the Hammer movement, see Michael Bönisch, "Die 'Hammer'-Bewegung," in *Handbuch zur "Völkischen Bewegung,"* ed. Uwe Puschner, Walter Schmitz, and Justus H. Ulbricht (Munich: Saur, 1996), 341–65. See also Gunter Mann, "Biologie und der 'Neue Mensch,'" in *Medizin, Naturwissenschaften, Technik und das zweite Kaiserreich*, ed. Gunter Mann and Rolf Winau (Göttingen: Vandenhoek & Ruprecht, 1977), 172–88.

11. Giselher Spitzer, *Der deutsche Naturismus: Idee und Entwicklung einer volkserzieherischen Bewegung im Schnitt von Lebensreform, Sport und Politik* (Ahrensburg bei Hamburg: Czwalina, 1983).

12. Richard Ungewitter, *Nacktheit und Kultur,* 2d. ed. (Stuttgart: Ungewitter, 1913), 130–36.

13. Geoffrey G. Field, *Evangelist of Race: The Germanic Vision of Houston Stewart Chamberlain* (New York: Columbia University Press, 1981), 216–24.

14. Sander L. Gilman, *Freud, Race, and Gender* (Princeton: Princeton University Press, 1993), 42, 162.

15. Ibid., 104f.; George L. Mosse, "Max Nordau, Liberalism, and the New Jew," *Journal of Contemporary History* 27 (1992): 565–81. See also Michael Berkowitz, *Zionist Culture and West European Jewry: Before the First World War* (Cambridge: Cambridge University Press, 1993).

16. On the spread of anti-Semitism among the Bildungsbürgertum through the student subculture beginning in the 1880s, see Norbert Kampe, *Studenten- und "Judenfrage" im Deutschen Kaisserreich* (Göttingen: Vandenhoek & Ruprecht, 1988). See also Shulamit Volkov, "Antisemitism as a Cultural Code," *Leo Baeck Institut Year Book* 23 (1978): 25–46.

17. Carl Heinrich Stratz, *Was sind Juden? Eine ethnographisch-anthropologische Studie* (Vienna: F. Tempsky, 1903), 5.

18. Ibid., 8–11. Stratz was not the only one to claim Aryan origins for Jews; so did some Jewish intellectuals. Moritz Alsberg, for example, rejected arguments concerning the inferiority of Jews by claiming that some were of superior Aryan descent. Others, such as the Zionists Elias Auerbach and Ignaz Zollschan, appropriated contemporary racial discourse by claiming that Jews were a pure race separate from other Europeans. Racial theories provided them with an origin myth that served as a justification for Zionism. Annegret Kiefer, *Das Problem einer jüdischen Rasse: Eine Diskussion zwischen Wissenschaft und Ideologie* (Frankfurt: Lang, 1991), 60f., 66–80. See also Mitchell B. Hart, "Racial Science, Social Science, and the Politics of Jewish Assimilation," *Isis* 90 (1999): 268–97; Georg Lilienthal, "Die jüdischen 'Rassenmerkmale': Zur Geschichte der Anthropologie der Juden," *Medizinhistorisches Journal* 28 (1993): 173–98.

19. Stratz, *Was Sind Juden?* 19–30.

20. Reviews of his books appeared, for example, in the liberal daily *Frankfurter Zeitung,* as well as in art journals such as the *Monatsschrift über Kunst und Kunstwissenschaft.* For some of these reviews, see the final pages of Carl Heinrich Stratz, *Die Körperpflege der Frau: Physiologische und ästhetische Diätetik für das weibliche Geschlecht,* 5th ed. (Stuttgart: Enke, 1918); and Stratz, *Die Rassenschönheit des Weibes,* 5th ed. (Stuttgart: Enke, 1904).

21. See, e.g., the very favorable reviews of Stratz's *Rassenschönheit des Weibes* in *Blätter für Volksgesundheitspflege* 2 (1902): 207; Josef Kirchner, "Die Rassenschönheit des Weibes," *Die Schönheit* 1 (1904): 659–62. Life reform jounals even published his articles: Carl Heinrich Stratz, "Die normal-ideale Gestalt," *Kraft und Schönheit* 1 (1902): 7f.

22. On Dutch attempts to regulate sexual relations between European males and Indonesian women, see Ann Laura Stoler, "Carnal Knowledge and Imperial Power," in *Gender at the Crossroads of Knowledge,* ed. Micaela di Leonardo (Berkeley: University of California Press, 1991), 51–101.

23. Carl Heinrich Stratz, *Die Frauen auf Java: Eine gynäkologische Studie* (Stuttgart: Enke, 1897). He also published a book aabout Japanese women: *Die Körperformen in Kunst und Leben der Japaner,* 2d ed. (Stuttgart: Enke, 1904).

24. Stratz, *Rassenschönheit des Weibes,* 7f.

25. Ernst Grosse, *Kunstwissenschaftliche Studien* (Tübingen: Mohr, 1900), 115–66. On Grosse, see Herbert Ganslmeyr, "Ernst Carl Gustav Grosse," *Neue Deutsche Biographie* 7, 148f. Grosse's doctrine of the relation between race and cultural achievement also exerted considerable influence on the work of Eugen Fischer, the leading German anthropologist of the Weimar and

Nazi years. Fischer would become director of the Kaiser Wilhelm Institut für Anthropologie, menschliche Erblichkeitslehre und Eugenik in 1927. Lösch, *Rasse als Konstrukt*, 13, 144.

26. Stratz, *Rassenschönheit des Weibes*, 13–17.

27. Sierra Bruckner, "The Tingle-Tangle of Modernity: Popular Anthropology and the Cultural Politics of Identity in Imperial Germany" (Ph.D. diss., University of Iowa, 1999), 139–46, 264ff.

28. Stratz, *Rassenschönheit des Weibes*, 1–6, quotation on 46f.

29. On the different approaches in evolutionary morphology propagated by Gegenbaur, Hackel, and their students, see Lynn K. Nyhart, *Biology Takes Form: Animal Morphology and the German Universities* (Chicago: University of Chicago Press, 1996), esp. 243–77.

30. Stratz, *Rassenschönheit des Weibes*, 19–24.

31. Andrew Zimmerman, "Anthropology and the Place of Knowledge in Imperial Berlin" (Ph.D. diss., University of California, San Diego, 1998), 194–214.

32. In the case of a woman from the Sudan, Stratz commented that deviations from the Bantu racial type were the result of a weakening of the type due to mixture with whites. Stratz, *Rassenschönheit des Weibes*, 132–40, 151f.

33. Ibid., 156ff.

34. Ibid., 4f.

35. Carl Heinrich Stratz, *Die Schönheit des weiblichen Körpers*, 2d ed. (Stuttgart: Enke, 1899), 3.

36. Stratz, *Rassenschönheit des Weibes*, 2, 400. On the idealistic claims of the Bildungsbürgertum, see Rüdiger vom Bruch, "Kunst und Kulturkritik in führenden bildungsbürgerlichen Zeitschriften des Kaiserreichs," in *Ideengeschichte und Kunstwissenschaft*, ed. Mai Ekkehard, Stephan Waetzold, and Gerd Wolandt (Berlin: Mann, 1983), 320ff.; Gerhard Kratzsch, " 'Der Kunstwart' und die bürgerlich-soziale Bewegung," in *Ideengeschichte*, ed. Ekkehard, Waetzold, and Wolandt, 371ff. See also Karl Hutten's complaint about the materialistic corruption of aesthetics (below). As Linda Nead argues, the distinction between disinterestedness and aesthetics made by Immanuel Kant is one of the hallmarks of Western aesthetic theory: Nead, *The Female Nude: Art, Obscenity, and Sexuality* (London: Routledge, 1992), 23ff.

37. Stratz, *Rassenschönheit des Weibes*, 58, 85, 397. Other German physicians made similar arguments. According to Georg Buschan, the more highly a race was developed, the greater were the secondary sexual differences between men and women: European women had decidedly lighter bones than European men, a difference that was less pronounced in "lower" races, whereas sexual differences in the form of the skull were almost not discernible in the case of the latter. In keeping with contemporary German racist notions, Buschan argued that Jewish and Polish women had decidedly narrow pelvises, implying that feminized men and masculinized women were characteristic for both groups, but he also worried about the narrow pelvises of Teutonic women, which, when compared with those of Estonian women, showed why it was so difficult for the former to bear children. Georg Buschan, "Die beiden Geschlechter innerhalb der einzelnen Rassen," in *Mann und Weib*, ed. Koßmann and Weiß, 3:443–86, esp. 444f.

38. Stratz, *Rassenschönheit des Weibes*, 40–43, 113f., 228–34.

39. See chapter 3. According to Lynda Nead, the aesthetization of the female body in twentieth-century art criticism served to transform the body into pure artistic form devoid of any threatening sexuality or obscenity. Nead, *Female Nude*, 12–16.

40. Eduard Daelen, "Das Nackte in der Photographie," *Die Schönheit* 1 (1904): 154–61.

41. Joseph Kirchner, "Das Weib als Studienobjekt der Kunst," *Die Schönheit* 1 (1904): 396–404.

42. Ibid., quotations on 398ff., 402.

43. Stratz, *Rassenschönheit des Weibes*, 252f.

44. This cliché is a recurring topos in popular hygienic literature. See, e.g., Ungewitter, *Nacktheit und Kultur*, 104–10; Anna Fischer-Dückelmann, *Die Frau als Hausärztin* (Stuttgart: Süddeutsches Verlags-Institut, 1905), 144f., 151ff.; Paul Schultze-Naumburg, *Die Kultur des weiblichen Körpers als Grundlage der Frauenkleidung* (Jena: Diederichs, 1905), 21, 93, 99. Schultze-Naumburg condemned the French ideal of beauty as that of the masses.

45. Stratz, *Rassenschönheit des Weibes*, 320ff. Postcards depicting French and Hungarian "artist's models" were a popular form of erotic and pornographic photography in turn-of-the-century Germany. See Erwin J. Haeberle, "Der verbotene Akt: Unzüchtige Fotos von 1850 bis 1950," in *Das Aktfoto: Ansichten vom Körper im fotografischen Zeitalter*, ed. Michael Köhler and Gisela Barche (Munich: Bucher, 1985), 215; Michael Köhler, "Pikanterien, Pinups & Playmates," in *Das Aktfoto*, ed. Köhler and Barche, 249.

46. Julius Weiß, "Die Schönheit des Weibes," in *Mann und Weib*, ed. Koßmann and Weiß, vol. 1, pt. 2, 46–76, esp. 1:63–68.

47. Stratz, *Rassenschönheit des Weibes*, 373f.

48. Stratz, *Schönheit des weiblichen Körpers*, 48f.

49. Stratz, *Rassenschönheit des Weibes*, 107–14.

50. Ibid., 275ff., 365–68.

51. Ranke, *Mensch*, 2:77–80.

52. Bruckner, "Tingle-Tangle of Modernity," 282–92, 456–71.

53. Pierre Bourdieu, *Distinction: A Social Critique of the Judgment of Taste* (Cambridge: Harvard University Press, 1984), 68, 170–75, 474f.

54. Gilman, *Jew's Body*, 10–37.

55. Hugo Sellheim, *Die Reize der Frau und ihre Bedeutung für den Kulturfortschritt* (Stuttgart: Enke, 1909), 15–21.

56. See the very positive review of Stratz's *Racial Beauty of Women* in *Die Schönheit* 1 (1904): 659–62.

57. Karl Hutten, "Rasse und Schönheit," *Die Schönheit* 13 (1916): 545–59.

58. On Gobineau, see Zur Mühlen, *Rassenideologien*, 52–73.

59. Emil Schmidt, "Die Anthroplogie der Badener," *Die Umschau* 3 (1899): 950–53; Otto Ammon, "Anthropologie," *Die Umschau* 4 (1900): 51–53. The following quotations are all from this short article.

60. On Otto Ammon, see Hilkea Lichtsinn, *Otto Ammon und die Sozialanthropologie* (Frankfurt: Lang, 1987).

61. Notker Hammerstein, *Antisemitismus und deutsche Universitäten, 1871–1933* (Frankfurt: Campus, 1995), 40–44. In the 1870s, liberals loudly denounced the mass pilgrimages to the small village of Marpingen, where three small children had seen an apparition of the Virgin Mary in 1876. See David Blackbourn, *Marpingen: Apparitions of the Virgin Mary in Bismarckian Germany* (Oxford: Clarendon, 1995), 250–67.

62. Otto Ammon, *Die natürliche Auslese beim Menschen* (Jena: G. Fischer, 1893), 205–21, 252–56.

Chapter Five

1. Michael Hau, "The Holistic Gaze in German Medicine," *Bulletin of the History of Medicine* 74 (2000): 495–524.

2. *Kraft und Schönheit* 2 (1902): 15.

3. Gustav Fritsch, "Die Gestaltung des Menschen vom anthropologischen Standpunkt aus," *Kraft und Schönheit* 2 (1902), 53f.

4. Paul Weindling, *Health, Race, and German Politics Between National Unification and Nazism, 1870–1945* (Cambridge: Cambridge University Press, 1989), 170ff., 186f.

5. According to Krabbe and Regin, vitalism, in combination with a holistic conception of the human body, was the defining feature of the etiologic concepts of the natural therapy doctrines, which stood in contrast to the scientific medicine of the time. Wolfgang Krabbe, *Gesellschaftsveränderung durch Lebensreform* (Göttingen: Vandenhoek & Ruprecht, 1974), 79f.; Cornelia Regin, *Selbsthilfe und Gesundheitspolitik* (Stuttgart: Steiner, 1995), 100–106. Jütte argues that natural therapy in Germany emerged in part as a reaction against the localistic reductionism of modern scientific medicine. Robert Jütte, *Geschichte der Alternative Medizin* (Munich: Beck, 1996), 27ff.

6. On holism in modern medicine, psychology, and the life sciences, see Christopher Lawrence and George Weisz, eds., *Greater Than the Parts: Holism in Biomedicine, 1920–1950* (Oxford: Oxford University Press, 1998); Anne Harrington, *Reenchanted Science: Holism in German Culture from Wilhelm II to Hitler* (Princeton: Princeton University Press, 1996); Mitchell G. Ash, *Gestalt Psychology in German Culture, 1890–1967* (Cambridge: Cambridge University Press, 1995); Jonathan Harwood, *Styles of Scientific Thought: The German Genetics Community* (Chicago: University of Chicago Press, 1993).

7. Cornelia Regin describes the relation between scientific medicine and natural therapy as a struggle for the medical market between the two camps centering mainly around the issues of the effectiveness of orthodox or alternative therapies and the legitimacy of irregular healers. Regin, *Selbsthilfe und Gesundheitspolitik,* passim.

8. Ottomar Rosenbach, *Arzt c/a Bakteriologe* (Berlin: Urban & Schwarzenberg, 1903). Rosenbach, a Berlin clinician, was (besides the Munich hygienist Max von Pettenkofer) one of the earliest and most outspoken critics of Robert Koch and his school of bacteriology.

9. This chapter does not even come close to an exhaustive treatment of constitutional approaches within scientific medicine. I only discuss physicians who propagated holistic approaches aimed at a strengthening of the human constitution as a whole because only these approaches were similiar to disease models proposed by life reformers.

10. Gerhard Kloos, *Die Konstitutionslehre von Karl Gustav Carus mit besonderer Berücksichtigung der Physiognomik* (Basel: Karger, 1951), 45–50, 93.

11. Karl Eduard Rotschuh, *Naturheilbewegung, Reformbewegung, Alternativbewegung* (Stuttgart: Hippokrates, 1983), 20–24, 60–76. Rotschuh argues that the natural therapy movement emerged as a reaction against the dangerous heroic therapies used by regular physicians during the first half of the nineteenth century. Harmful or not, underlying both regular and irregular therapies was a holistic concept of the body.

12. The reevaluation of turn-of-the-century "outsider" physicians in the 1920s becomes evident, for example, in Louis. R. Grote, *Die Medizin der Gegenwart in Selbstdarstellungen* (Leipzig: Meiner, 1923–1928). For this work Grote elicited autobiographies from physicians who in his view had been especially influential in shaping trends within contemporary medicine. Included were Ferdinand Hueppe and Friedrich Martius, who had done all their major work before the war but who were considered most important in preparing the ground for the constitutionalist medicine of

the Weimar era. See also Isidor Fischer, *Biographisches Lexikon, der hervorragenden Ärzte der letzten fünfzig Jahre* (Berlin: Urban & Schwarzenberg, 1932), 521, 669, 1000, 1321ff., 1515, with positive assessments of the scientific contributions of the constitutionalists Gottstein, Hueppe, Martius, Rosenbach, and Stiller.

13. On the etiologic concepts of modern bacteriology, see Thomas Schlich, "Einführung," in *Strategien der Kausalität,* ed. Christoph Gradmann and Thomas Schlich (Pfaffenweiler: Centaurus, 1999), 3–28; John Andrew Mendelsohn, "Cultures of Bacteriology: Formation and Transformation of a Science in France and Germany, 1870–1914" (Ph.D. diss., Princeton University, 1996); Andrew Cunningham, "Transforming Plague: The Laboratory and the Identity of Infectious Disease," in *The Laboratory Revolution in Medicine,* ed. Andrew Cunningham and Perry Williams (Cambridge: Cambridge University Press, 1992), 209–44; K. Codell Carter, "The Emergence of Pasteur's Concept of Disease Causation," *Bulletin of the History of Medicine* 65 (1991), 528–48; K. Codell Carter, "Koch's Postulates in Relation to the Work of Jacob Henle and Edwin Klebs," *Medical History* 29 (1985), 353–74.

14. Rosenbach, *Arzt,* 30.

15. Ibid., 113, 191–206.

16. Ibid., 31f. With this Rosenbach anticipated the "intuitive gaze" of the constitutional physician, which in the view of his Weimar successors constituted the hallmark of the outstanding practitioner.

17. Dietrich von Engelhardt, "Kausalität und Konditionalität in der modernen Medizin," in *Pathogenese: Grundzüge und Perspektiven einer theoretischen Pathologie,* ed. Heinrich Schipperges (Berlin: Springer, 1985), 37ff.

18. Weindling, *Health, Race, and German Politics,* 171.

19. For some diseases such as measles, Flecktyphus, smallpox, bubonic plague, and syphilis, Gottstein conceded that exposure to the microorganisms was itself a sufficient cause for the disease and that the strength of the constitutions of affected persons did not really matter. Adolf Gottstein, *Allgemeine Epidemiologi*e (Leipzig: Wigand, 1897), 118f., 174f., 231f., 311–14.

20. Ibid., 426–38.

21. Michael Hubenstorf, "Die Genese der sozialen Medizin als universitäres Lehrfach in Österreich" (diss., Free University of Berlin, 1992), 299–324. Hubenstorf has shown how Hueppe reformulated Pettenkofer's concept of local-environmental predispositions according to which microorganisms had to mature in the soil before they could unfold their pathogenic effects through miasmas. Hueppe argued for acquired and inherited predispositions of the human body as the "soil" on which pathogenic microorganisms could thrive.

22. Ferdinand Hueppe, "Über die Ursachen der Gährungen und Infektionskrankheiten und deren Beziehungen zum Causalproblem und der Energetik," *Verhandlungen der Gesellschaft Deutscher Naturforscher und Ärzte* 65 (1895): pt. 1, 134–58, esp. 151ff. Hueppe argues that neither specific microorganisms nor specific tissues constitute the "ens morbi."

23. Ferdinand Hueppe, ed., *Handbuch der Hygiene* (Berlin: Hirschwald, 1899), 28f.

24. Ferdinand Hueppe, *Hygiene der Körperübungen,* 2d ed. (Leipzig: Hirzel, 1922), 14–20.

25. Ferdinand Hueppe, "Naturheilkunde und Schulmedizin," *Zeitschrift für soziale Medizin* 1 (1895): 65–87.

26. Hueppe, *Handbuch der Hygiene,* 417; Hueppe, *Hygiene der Körperübungen,* 4f.

27. *Kraft und Schönheit* 11 (1911): 161–69, 193–201.

28. Hueppe, *Handbuch der Hygiene*, 645ff.

29. See, e.g., the works of Adolf Gottstein, who claimed that orthodox medicine was superior to lay medicine because it had combined the most important aspects of natural therapy and orthodox therapies. Adolf Gottstein, *Die neue Gesundheitspflege* (Berlin: Siegismund, 1920), 22f.; Gottstein, *Das Heilwesen der Gegenwart: Gesundheitslehre und Gesundheitspolitik*, 2d ed. (Berlin: Deutsche Buch-Gemeinschaft, 1925), 310–17.

30. Christiane Brecht, "Das Publikum belehren—Wissenschaft zelebrieren," in *Strategien der Kausalität*, ed. Gradmann and Schlich, 53–76. On Lingner and Odol, see Büchi, "Schloßherr ohne Adelstitel—Lingner die Exzellenz," in *In aller Munde: Einhundert Jahre Odol*, ed. Martin Roth, Manfred Scheske, and Hans-Christian Täubrich (Stuttgart: Cantz, 1993), 73–83.

31. Günter Heidel, "Die I. Internationale Hygieneausstellung in Dresden und die Gründung des Deutschen Hygienemuseums," *Zeitschrift für die gesamte Hygiene* 33 (1987): 411–15;. Susanne Roeßiger, "In aller Munde—das Deutsche Hygiene-Museum," in *In aller Munde*, ed. Roth et al., 51–63. On the German Hygiene Museum see also Ulrich Schubert, "Vorgeschichte und Geschichte des deutschen Hygiene-Museums in Dresden, 1871–1931" (diss., Technical University, Dresden, 1986).

32. *Internationale Hygieneausstellung 1911* (Program); "Entstehung und Entwicklung der Internationalen Hygieneausstellung," *Hygiene* 2–3 (1911): 17–22; Max Gruber and Ernst Rüdin, *Fortpflanzung, Vererbung, Rassenhygiene*, 2d ed. (Munich, 1911).

33. *Katalog der Internationalen Hygieneausstellung Dresden* (Berlin, 1911), 375–400; *Der Mensch: Ausgewählte Gruppen aus der Internationalen Hygieneausstellung Dresden 1911* (Darmstadt, 1912), 42ff. This is the catalogue for the Darmstadt hygiene exhibition that was organized one year later using the Dresden materials. For a photo of the Popular Hall, the section with microscopes concerning people's diseases, see Deutsches Hygienemuseum, Bildsammlung, IHA 1911, No. 681, Bl. 51.

34. Deutsches Hygienemuseum, Bildsammlung, I. IHA 1911, 11/58, No. 1.

35. *Katalog 1911*, 398ff.

36. N. Zuntz, C. Brahm, and A. Mallwitz, *Sonderkatalog der Abteilung Sportausstellung* (Dresden, 1911), 6ff.

37. See, e.g., Franz Kleinschrod, "Die Naturheillehre," in *Die Neue Heilmethode*, ed. Moritz Platen (Berlin: Bong, 1907), 1:3–43, esp. 1:9–15.

38. Christoph Wilhelm Hufeland, *Makrobiotik, oder die Kunst das menschliche Leben zu verlängern* (Munich: Insel, 1984), esp. 34–52, 97–115. See also Eduard Seidler, "Christoph Wilhelm Hufelands 'Ideen über Pathogenie und Einfluß der Lebenskraft auf die Entstehung und Form der Krankheiten,'" in *Pathogenese*, ed. Schipperges, 83–90.

39. See, e.g., Eduard Baltzer, *Fünf Bücher vom wahren Menschenthume*, 2d ed. (Rudolstadt, 1882), 3ff. See also A. C. Fröhlich, "Makrobiotische Betrachtungen," *Vegetarische Rundschau* (1883): 133ff., 168ff.

40. Ruth Hubbard, *The Politics of Women's Biology* (New Brunswick: Rutgers University Press, 1990), 108.

41. Louis Kuhne, *Die Neue Heilwissenschaft oder die Lehre von der Einheit aller Krankheiten und deren darauf begründete, einheitliche, arzneilose und operationslose Heilung*, 35th ed. (Leipzig: Louis Kuhne, 1898), vf., 2f.

42. Ibid., 15–35.

43. Ibid., 65.

44. Ibid., 115ff.

45. *Vegetarische Rundschau* (1895), 230-35.

46. Regin, *Selbsthilfe und Gesundheitspolitik,* 27f. The notion of the healthy and beautiful human being as the result of a harmony of body, spirit, and soul is propagated, for example, in Reinhold Gerling, *Der vollendete Mensch,* 2d ed. (Oranienburg: Orania, 1906). But it can also be found in the work of regular physicians: F. König, ed., *Ratgeber in gesunden und in kranken Tagen,* 16th ed. (Leipzig: Karl Meyer, n.d.), 8f.

47. Denis C. Phillips, *Holistic Thought in Social Science* (Stanford: Stanford University Press, 1976), 29.

48. Heinrich Lahmann, *Die diätetische Blutentmischung (Dysämie) als Grundursache aller Krankheiten* (Leipzig: Spamer, 1892), 3-35, 62-66, 132ff.; Lahmann, *Die wichtigsten Kapitel der natürlichen (physikalisch-diätetischen) Heilweise,* 3d ed.(Stuttgart, 1897).

49. Kuhne, *Neue Heilwissenschaft,* vf.

50. See, e.g., Wilhelm Siegert, *Die Naturheilkunde in ihren Anwendungsformen und Wirkungen,* 6th ed. (Heidelberg: Arkana, 1985).

51. Friedrich Eduard Bilz, *Das neue Naturheilverfahren: Lehr- und Nachschlagebuch der naturgemaessen Heilweise und Gesundheitspflege,* 31st ed.(Leipzig: Bilz, n.d.).

52. Ibid., 713 for the causes of tuberculosis; for cholera, 158f.; for diphtheria, 190f.; for pneumonia, 705; for typhus, 1095.

53. None of the major studies of German eugenics has systematically examined the eugenic discourse within the alternative health movements of the time: Robert Proctor, *Racial Hygiene: Medicine Under the Nazis* (Cambridge: Harvard University Press, 1988); Weindling, *Health, Race, and German Politics;* Sheila Faith Weiss, "The Race Hygiene Movement in Germany, 1904–1945," in *Eugenics in Germany, France, Brazil, and Russia,* ed. Mark B. Adams (New York: Oxford University Press, 1990), 8–68; Weiss, *Race Hygiene and National Efficiency: The Eugenics of Wilhelm Schallmeyer* (Berkeley: University of California Press, 1987); Peter Weingart, Jürgen Kroll, and Kurt Bayertz, *Rasse, Blut und Gene: Geschichte der Eugenik und Rassenhygiene in Deutschland* (Frankfurt: Suhrkamp, 1992).

54. Weiss, "Race Hygiene Movement," 10ff., 23ff; Weingart, Kroll, and Bayertz, *Rasse, Blut und Gene,* 57f.

55. Weindling, *Health, Race, and German Politics,* 131, 158.

56. Paul Weindling, "Dissecting German Social Darwinism: Historicizing the Biology of the Organic State," *Science in Context* 11 (1998): 619–37, esp. 620f.

57. Reinhard Mocek, "The Program of Proletarian Rassenhygiene," *Science in Context* 11 (1998): 609–17.

58. Michael Schwartz, *Sozialistische Eugenik* (Bonn: Dietz, 1995); Michael Schwartz, "Sozialismus und Eugenik: Zur fälligen Revision eines Geschichtsbildes," *Internationale Wissenschaftliche Korrespondenz* 4 (1989): 465–89.

59. Weindling, *Health, Race, and German Politics,* 25.

60. Regin, *Selbsthilfe und Gesundheitspolitik,* 138, 176f. On the contemporary debate about the imperial epidemics law, see Richard J. Evans, *Death in Hamburg: Society and Politics in the Cholera Years, 1830–1910* (Oxford: Penguin, 1990), 494–502.

61. "Aus einem Colloquium beim Professor Schweninger: Das Gesetz gegen die Cholera," *Die Zukunft* 2 (1893), 318–21.

62. Max Haushofer, "Die Veredelung der menschlichen Rassen," *Neue Heilkunst* 13 (1901): 20.

63. Alfred Ploetz, *Die Tüchtigkeit unserer Rasse und der Schutz der Schwachen* (Berlin: Fischer, 1895).

64. Reinhold Gerling, "Wen darf ich heiraten?" *Neue Heilkunst* 8 (1896): 113f.

65. Weiss, "Race Hygiene Movement," 13–21.

66. Franz Schönenberger and Wilhelm Siegert, *Das Geschlechtsleben und seine Verirrungen: Was junge Leute davon wissen sollten und Eheleute wissen müßten*, 10th ed. (Berlin: Wilhelm Möller, 1902), 148–54, 223–37.

67. Rudolf Franck, "Die Philosophie Friedrich Nietzsches und der Vegetarismus," *Vegetarische Warte* (1904): 531ff.

68. Kurt Goldstein, *Über Rassenhygiene* (Berlin: Springer, 1913), 26–34.

69. Gustav Selß, "Mitleid," *Vegetarische Warte* (1910), 15f.

70. Karl Binding and Alfred Hoche, *Die Freigabe der Vernichtung lebensunwerten Lebens* (Leipzig: Meiner, 1920).

71. Michael Schwartz, " 'Euthanasie'—Debatten in Deutschland (1895–1945)," *Vierteljahreshefte für Zeitgeschichte* 46 (1998): 616–65.

72. Kuhne, *Neue Heilwissenschaft*, 369ff.

73. Klara Ebert, "Von dem Manne, den ich heute am höchsten verehre," *Vegetarische Warte* (1912): 205.

74. Klara Ebert, "An die vegetarischen Frauen," *Vegetarische Warte* (1904): 292.

75. Richard Ungewitter, *Nacktheit und Kultur*, 2d ed. (Stuttgart: Ungewitter, 1913), 122–30.

76. Sander L. Gilman, *Disease and Representation: Images of Illness from Madness to AIDS* (Ithaca: Cornell University Press, 1988), 1–17, esp. 4ff.

77. On turn-of-the-century utopian communities in general, see Ulrich Linse, ed., *Zurück, o Mensch, zur Mutter Erde: Landkommunen in Deutschland, 1890–1933* (Munich: dtv, 1983). On the vegetarian colony Eden, see Judith Baumgartner, *Ernährungsreform—Antwort auf Industrialisierung und Ernährungswandel* (Frankfurt: Lang, 1992).

78. Hugo Erdmann, "Neue städtische Gemeinden auf biologischer Grundlage," *Vegetarische Warte* (1917), 81ff.

Chapter Six

1. Robert Weldon Whalen, *Bitter Wounds: German Victims of the Great War, 1914–1939* (Ithaca: Cornell University Press, 1984), 40.

2. David Crew, "The Ambiguities of Modernity: Welfare and the German State from Wilhelm to Hitler," in *Society, Culture, and the State in Germany*, ed. Geoff Eley (Ann Arbor: University of Michigan Press, 1997), 325f.; Young-Son Hong, *Welfare, Modernity, and the Weimar State* (Princeton: Princeton University Press, 1998), esp. chaps. 3 and 4.

3. An excellent in-depth study of wartime rehabilitation efforts in Germany and France is Matthew Price, "Bodies and Souls: The Rehabilitation of Maimed Soldiers in France and Germany During the First World War" (Ph.D. diss., Stanford University, 1998), chap. 3 and pp. 229f.

4. On the interpretation of the Weimar period as a crisis of classical modernity, see Detlef J. K. Peukert, *The Weimar Republic: The Crisis of Classical Modernity*, trans. Richard Deveson (New York: Hill & Wang, 1993).

5. On the crisis of regular medicine, see Detlef Bothe, *Neue Deutsche Heilkunde, 1933–1945*

(Husum: Matthiesen, 1991), 16–37; Eva Maria Klasen, *Die Diskussion über eine Krise der Medizin in Deutschland zwischen 1925 und 1935* (diss., Mainz University, 1984).

6. Christiane Eisenberg, *"English Sports" und deutsche Bürger: Eine Gesellschaftsgeschichte, 1800–1939* (Schöningh: Paderborn, 1999), 330.

7. Arnd Krüger, "The German Way of Worker Sport," in *The Story of Worker Sport*, ed. Arnd Krüger and James Riordan (Champaign: Human Kinetics, 1996), 1–25; Herbert Dierker, *Arbeitersport im Spannungsfeld der Zwanziger Jahre* (Essen: Klartext, 1990). The Frankfurt Worker Olympics brought more than 100,000 people to Frankfurt. The Vienna spectacle was attended by 200,000 visitors. Franz Nitsch, " 'Wir erlebten wie Frieden sein kann': Die 1. Internationale Arbeiterolympiade 1925," in *Illustrierte Geschichte des Arbeitersports*, ed. Hans Joachim Teichler and Gerhard Hauk (Bonn: Dietz, 1987), 203–6; Reinhard Krammer, "Der ASKÖ und die Wiener Arbeiterolympiade 1931," in *Illustrierte Geschichte*, ed. Teichler and Hauk, 207–21.

8. Eisenberg, *"English Sports,"* 342–47.

9. Krabbe, *Gesellschaftsveränderung durch Lebensreform* (Göttingen: Vandenhoek & Ruprecht, 1974), 96; Cornelia Regin, *Selbsthilfe und Gesundheitspolitik* (Stuttgart: Steiner, 1995), 459f.

10. Gunnar Stollberg, "Die Naturheilvereine im deutschen Kaiserreich," *Archiv für Sozialgeschichte* 28 (1988): 289. There are no membership numbers available for 1930. See also Regin, *Selbsthilfe*, 459ff.

11. There can be no doubt that biochemical voluntary associations enjoyed a large membership during the Weimar years, but in my view there are no reliable data that independently confirm the biochemists' claims that their voluntary associations had as many as 200,000 members. The source for this claim is Walter Hayn, *Der Biochemische Bund Deutschlands und seine Einrichtungen im Lichte der Statistik* (Neubabelsberg: Bio-Verlag, 1930), 67. The author was the president of the Biochemical League of Germany. He tried to convince the public that the league was the largest and most important hygienic lay organization in Germany and was therefore to be taken seriously. His membership claims therefore ought to be regarded with suspicion, especially since Hayn liked to exaggerate the support that biochemistry enjoyed among the public. In a petition to President Ebert concerning the planned law for the fight against venereal diseases, he claimed in 1922 that the biochemical movement had six to seven hundred thousand supporters. BA Berlin-Lichterfelde, R 1501 No. 11892, Bl. 480f. The most accessible description of the biochemical movement is in Robert Jütte, *Geschichte der alternativen Medizin* (Munich: Beck, 1996), 221–28. See also Michael Dörter, "Die Naturheilbewegung in Deutschland zur Zeit der Weimarer Republik" (diss., Leipzig University, 1991), 31–37.

12. The central organization of homeopathic asociations, the Reichsbund für Homöopathie und Gesundheitspflege, had about 38,000 members by 1930 and 48,000 in 1936. Its predecessor had about 29,000 in 1912. Eberhard Wolff, *Gesundheitsverein und Medikalisierungsprozess* (Tübingen: Vereinigung für Volkskunde, 1989), 49. More traditional natural therapies (for example, cold water therapies) were also practiced in the so-called Kneipp-Vereine, substantially increasing their following during the Weimar republic (from about 9,000 to 45,000 members). The Kneipp movement (named after its Bavarian founder, the Catholic priest Sebastian Kneipp, 1821–1897) did not take an openly antagonistic position toward regular medicine but was viewed by many physicians with suspicion. Dörter, "Naturheilbewegung," 37–42. On the fragmentation of the medical reform movement, see Walter Wuttke-Groneberg, " 'Kraft im Schlagen, Kraft im Ertragen!' " in *Religions- und Geistesgeschichte der Weimarer Republik*, ed. Hubert Cancik (Düsseldorf: Patmos, 1982), 289–300. See also the list by the physician Erwin Liek, who wrote several books voicing the concerns of the rank and file of the regular medical profession. Erwin Liek, *Das Wunder in der Heilkunde* (Munich: Lehmann, 1930), 110ff. On Liek see Michael Kater, "Die Medizin im nationalsozialistischen Deutschland und Erwin Liek," *Geschichte und Gesellschaft* 16 (1990): 440–63.

13. There is almost no information about the social composition of vegetarian voluntary associations. Data from 1931 concerning the professions of the German Vegetarian League's leadership tells us that Weimar vegetarians continued to come from the middle class—teachers, merchants, or clerical employees (Kaufmänner) and civil servants. The membership of local associations also might have included people who were less solidly middle-class, however. *Vegetarische Warte* 64 (1931): 28. There were four teachers, four civil servants, two Kaufmänner, two physicians, one engineer, and one professor among members of the Federal Board and Federal Representation elected in 1931. All of them were male.

14. Wolff, *Gesundheitsverein und Medikalisierung*, 91–96.

15. The data on the Weimar membership are much less suggestive than the ones on the Wilhelmine period: In 1931 about 31 percent of the members were workers, 28 percent were economically independent *(Selbständige)*, 15 percent were civil servants, and 8 percent drew some type of pension. About 18 percent were women. Dörter, "Naturheilbewegung," 45.

16. BA Berlin-Lichterfelde, R 1501 No. 9371, Bl. 64f.; *Ärztliches Vereinsblatt* 49 (1922): 180, 216.

17. Neustätter to the Geheimrat Dr. Hamel in the Ministry of the Interior, 18 January 1921, BA Berlin-Lichterfelde, 1501 No. 9370, Bl. 257; see also Bl. 54f., 253ff., 258, 313–20. Neustätter propagated "defense through education" by the national committee instead of frontal attacks by professional organizations: Neustätter to Hamel, 20 June 1921, BA Berlin-Lichterfelde, R 1501 No. 9371, Bl. 20ff. Before the war Neustätter and Alexander, both prominent in the German Society for the Fight Against Quackery, had been among the most outspoken and ferocious critics of the natural therapy movement: Otto Neustätter, "Die sogenannte Naturheilkunde," in *Das Kurpfuschertum und seine Bekämpfung*, ed. Wilhelm Back (Straßburg, 1904), 45–90; Karl Alexander, *Wahre und falsche Heilkunde: Ein Wort der Aufklärung* (Berlin: Reimer, 1899); Regin, *Selbsthilfe und Gesundheitspolitik*, 443, 60.

18. Cornelia Regin, "Naturheilkundige und Naturheilbewegung im Deutschen Kaiserreich," *Medizin, Gesellschaft und Geschichte* 11 (1992): 175–200.

19. BA Berlin-Lichterfelde, 1501 No. 9371, p. 6. Friedrich Martius to the general secretary, 9 April 1921.

20. BA Berlin-Lichterfelde, 1501 No. 9370, Bl. 194, 202ff; No. 9371, Bl. 26ff., 64–69.

21. See BA Berlin-Lichterfelde, 1501 No. 9372, Bl. 19; No. 9375, Bl. 9ff. for a membership list of the national committee.

22. BA Berlin-Lichterfelde, 1501 No. 9374, Bl. 360–80; No. 9411, Bl. 106f; No. 9412, Bl. 11.

23. BA Berlin-Lichterfelde, 1501 No. 9413, 13 Feb. and 7 March 1926. Decision of the Ministry of the Interior in response to a complaint by the Natural Healing Association of Cologne that natural healing associations were not invited to conduct their own events within the framework of the RGW.

24. Paul Schirrmeister, "Die Reichsgesundheitswoche," *Naturarzt* 54 (1926): 87–92; Oskar Mummert, "Hygienemesse in Berlin," *Naturarzt* 54 (1926):168ff.

25. BA Berlin-Lichterfelde, R 1501 No. 11890, Bl. 262f.; Lutz Sauerteig, "Ethische Richtlinien: Patientenrechte und ärztliches Verhalten bei der Arzneimittelerprobung," *Medizinhistorisches Journal* 35 (2000): 325–30.

26. Petra Werner, "Zu den Auseinandersetzungen um die Institutionalisierung von Naturheilkunde und Homöopathie," *Medizin, Gesellschaft und Geschichte* 12 (1993): 205–19; *Vierzig Jahre Naturheilbewegung: Festschrift zum 40-jährigen Bestehen des Deutschen Bundes der Vereine für naturgemäße Lebens- und Heilweise (Naturheilkunde) E. V.* (Berlin, 1929): 77–84.

27. Eva Maria Klasen, "Die Diskussion über eine Krise der Medizin in Deutschland zwis-

chen 1925 und 1935" (diss., Mainz University, 1984), 32. On the divisions within regular medicine and the role of Liek as spokesperson for general practitioners, see Michael Hubenstorf, "Von der 'freien Arztwahl' zur Reichsärzteordnung," in *Medizin im "Dritten Reich,"* 2d ed., ed. Johanna Bleker (Cologne: Deutscher Ärzte-Verlag, 1993), 43–53, esp. 47.

28. Charles E. McClelland, *The German Experience of Professionalization* (Cambridge: Cambridge University Press, 1981), 180 ff.

29. Erwin Liek, *Der Arzt und seine Sendung,* 2d ed. (Munich: Lehmann, 1927), 45 ff., 135 ff.

30. Liek, *Wunder in der Heilkunde,* 192. Liek's emphasis on empathy as a source of healing was not unique for the time. Karl Jaspers, a former psychiatrist who taught philosophy and psychology in Heidelberg, also stressed the role of empathy in medical diagnosis and healing in his book on general psychopathology. Mitchell G. Ash, *Gestalt Psychology in German Culture, 1890–1967: Holism and the Quest for Objectivity* (Cambridge: Cambridge University Press, 1995), 289.

31. Liek, *Wunder in der Heilkunde,* 189–205.

32. Wolfgang Schmid, "Die Bedeutung Erwin Lieks für das Selbstverständnis der Medizin in der Weimarer Republik und Nationalsozialismus" (diss., University of Erlangen-Nürnberg, 1989), 107–12.

33. Oskar Mummert, "Der Arzt und seine Sendung," *Naturarzt* 55 (1927): 199–202.

34. Schmid, "Bedeutung Erwin Lieks," 116.

35. Bothe, *Neue Deutsche Heilkunde,* 20 ff., 32 f.; Schmid, "Bedeutung Erwin Lieks," 38–42.

36. Klasen, *Krise der Medizin,* 22–25.

37. Ibid., 76–83.

38. Oskar Mummert, "Eine Wandlung in der Krisis der Medizin," *Naturarzt* 59 (1932): 80 ff.

39. Martin Vogel, *Hygienische Volksbildung* (Berlin: Springer, 1925).

40. Martin Vogel and Rudolf Neubert, *Grundzüge der Alkoholfrage* (Dresden: Deutscher Verlag für Volkswohlfahrt, 1926). He made his case against meat consumption in a booklet that he wrote together with the chemist and nutritional reformer Ragnar Berg: Ragnar Berg and Martin Vogel, *Die Grundlagen einer richtigen Ernährung,* 5th ed. (Dresden: Deutscher Verlag für Volkswohlfahrt, 1928), 168–84.

41. Deutsches Hygienemuseum, Bildsammlung, No. K 1139; Fotoband Ausstellung: Richtige Ernährung, Leipzig 1928, Bl. 16. The display showed the result of ten long-distance contests held between 1908 and 1912. Of 965 participants, 80 were vegetarians; 32 vegetarians won prizes.

42. Oskar Mummert, "Naturheilkunde oder Medizin," *Naturarzt* 55 (1927): 134; Kapferer, "Eine Wandlung in der Medizin," *Naturarzt* 55 (1927):164 f.

43. "12. Bundesversammlung des Deutschen Bundes," *Naturarzt* 49 (1921): 105–9.

44. Schirrmacher, "Reichsgesundheitswoche," *Naturarzt* 54 (1926): 89.

45. Erwin Silber, "Wie weit ist der Naturheilgedanke in die medizinische Klinik eingedrungen," *Naturarzt* 57 (1929): 341–45.

46. BA Berlin-Lichterfelde, 1501 No. 11174, Bl. 3 ff. See also Nos. 11175, 11176.

47. Martin Vogel, "Das deutsche Hygienemuseum auf der Gesolei," in *GE-SO-LEI,* ed. Arthur Schloßmann and Martha Fraenkel (Düsseldorf: Schwann, 1927), 2:449–74, esp. 463–69.

48. Atina Grossmann, *Reforming Sex: The German Movement for Birth Control and Abortion Reform, 1920–1950* (Oxford: Oxford University Press, 1995); Peukert, *Weimarer Republik,* 132–43; Weindling, *Health, Race, and German Politics,* 399–439.

49. Weindling, *Health, Race, and German Politics,* 338–48, 430–39; Weiss, "Race Hygiene

Movement," 29–40. Eugenics was an important topic in all three of the hygienic exhibitions. In contrast, contemporary racial theories were not a prominent topic despite the popularity that such theories enjoyed during those years (see chapter 7).

50. Ernst Poensgen, "Die wirtschaftliche Bedeutung der Gesolei," in *GE-SO-LEI*, ed. Schlossmann and Fraenkel, 1:15ff.

51. Sebastian Fasbender, "Zwischen Arbeitersport und Arbeitssport: Werksport an Rhein und Ruhr, 1921–1938" (Ph.D. diss., Göttingen University, 1997), 82, 157–60.

52. Arthur Schloßmann, "Entwicklung, Wesen, Ziele und Erfolg der Gesolei," in *GE-SO-LEI*, ed. Schloßmann and Fraenkel, 43–48, esp. 44. Schloßmann, a pediatrician who had been close to Lingner, was the main organizer of the Gesolei.

53. Adolf Thiele, *Arbeitshygiene, Arbeiterschutz*, 2d ed. (Dresden: Deutscher Verlag für Volkswohlfahrt, 1929), 32–41.

54. Ernst Heinson, "Arbeits- und Gewerbehygiene; Unfallverhütung," in *GE-SO-LEI*, ed. Schloßmann and Fraenkel, 630–35; Fritz Rott, "Die Gesundheitsfürsorge," in ibid., 698ff. Psychotechnics was already developed before the war, but it only found a larger resonance in the context of the rationalization discourse of the Weimar era. On psychotechnics before the war, see Anson Rabinbach, *The Human Motor: Energy, Fatigue, and the Origins of Modernity* (New York: Basic, 1990), 262–80; Joan Campbell, *Joy in Work, German Work: The National Debate, 1800–1945* (Princeton: Princeton University Press, 1989), 74–83. On psychotechnics during the Weimar period, see Campbell, *Joy in Work*, 131–51; Alexandre Métraux, "Die angewandte Psychologie vor und nach 1933 in Deutschland," in *Psychologie im Nationalsozialismus*, ed. Carl Friedrich Graumann (Berlin: Springer, 1985), 222–62, esp. 230–45.

55. Mary Nolan, *Visions of Modernity: American Business and the Modernization of Germany* (Oxford: Oxford University Press, 1994), esp. 36–57, 60–70.

56. Ibid., 97f.

57. Adolf Halfeld, *Amerika und der Amerikanismus: Kritische Betrachtungen eines Deutschen und Europäers* (Jena: Diederichs, 1927), 5. From 1924 to 1929, Halfeld was a correspondent for the *Hamburger Fremdenblatt* and the *Münchner Neuesten Nachrichten* in New York City.

58. Halfeld, *Amerika*, 155.

59. The optimism is, for example, expressed in Schloßmann, "Entwicklung," and in an article by the mayor of Düsseldorf: Robert Lehr, "Die Gesolei, Düsseldorf wieder dem Licht entgegen," in *GE-SO-LEI*, ed. Schloßmann and Fraenkel, 18–22.

60. Lynn Abrams, *Workers' Culture in Imperial Germany: Leisure and Recreation in the Rhineland and Westphalia* (London: Routledge, 1992), 180–85; Dieter Langewiesche, "The Impact of the German Labour Movement on Workers' Culture," *Journal of Modern History* 59 (1987): 506–23.

61. Weindling, *Health, Race, and German Politics*, 411.

62. Nick Hopwood, "Producing a Socialist Popular Science in the Weimar Republic," *History Workshop Journal* 41 (1996), 117–53, esp. 124, 140. *Urania* had a circulation of twenty-five to thirty thousand copies.

63. Vogel, "Hygienemuseum auf der Gesolei," 449–74, esp. 456ff.

64. Martin Roth, "Menschenökonomie, oder der Mensch als technisches und künstlerisches Meisterwerk," in *Der gläserne Mensch—eine Sensation: Zur Kulturgeschichte eines Ausstellungsobjektes*, ed. Martin Roth and Rosmarie Beier (Stuttgart: Hatje, 1990), 39–67.

65. Walter Gehlen and Herbert Michael, "Der Mensch," in *Internationale Hygieneausstellung Dresden 1930: Amtlicher Führer* (Dresden, 1930), 178.

66. Michael Hau and Mitchell G.Ash, "Der normale Körper, seelisch erblickt," in *Gesichter der Weimarer Republik,* ed. Sander Gilman and Claudia Schmölders (Cologne: Dumont, 2000), 12f.

67. On the fusion of physiology and technology in Kahn's work, see Cornelius Borck, "Electricity as the Medium of Psychic Life: Psychotechnics, the Radio, and the Electroencephalogram in Weimar Germany" (Berlin: Max-Planck-Institut for the History of Science, 2000), Preprint 154.

68. Fritz Kahn, *Das Leben des Menschen: Eine volkstümliche Anatomie* (Stuttgart: Franckh'sche Verlagshandlung, 1927), vol. 3, plate 12.

69. Ibid., 4:307.

70. Ibid., 2:152: "Wer will was Lebend'ges erkennen und beschreiben, / Sucht zuerst den Geist herauszutreiben / Dann hat er die Teile in seiner Hand / Fehlt leider nur das geistige Band."

71. Ibid., vol. 3, plate 15.

72. Roth, "Menschenökonomie," 59; Karl August Lingner, *Der Mensch als Organisationsvorbild* (Bern: Drechsel, 1914), 10ff.

73. Hans Surén, *Surén-Atemgymnastik: Die Schule der Atmung für Körper und Geist für alle Leibesübungen und Berufe,* 36th ed. (Stuttgart: Dieck, 1929), table 2.

74. Schloßmann, "Entwicklung," 40.

75. Herbert Beschorner, *Tuberkulosebekämpfung, Tuberkulosefürsorge* (Dresden: Deutscher Verlag für Volkswohlfahrt, 1922), 7–23.

76. Ibid., 99.

77. Pierre Bourdieu, *Language and Symbolic Power* (Cambridge: Polity, 1991), 68f.

78. "Bericht über die Teilnahme an der Tagung der Deutschen Naturforscher und Ärzte," BA Berlin-Lichterfelde, R 86 No. 885, Gesolei. For a printed version of Sauerbruch's speech see Ferdinand Sauerbruch, "Heilkunst und Naturwissenschaft," *Die Naturwissenschaften* 48–49 (1926): 1081–90.

79. BA Berlin-Lichterfelde, R 1501 No. 26345, Internationale Hygieneausstellung Dresden 1930, Bl. 267.

80. Mitchell G. Ash, "Gestalt Psychology in Weimar Culture," *History of the Human Sciences* 4 (1991): 395–415, esp. 399f.

81. On Goethe's theory of color, see Felix Höpfner, *Wissenschaft wider die Zeit: Goethes Farbenlehre aus rezeptionsgeschichtlicher Sicht* (Heidelberg: Winter, 1990), 194–215. On Goethe's biological thought, see Gehlen and Michael, "Der Mensch"; Timothy Lenoir, "The Eternal Laws of Form," in *Goethe and the Sciences: A Reappraisal,* ed. Frederick Amrine, Francis J. Zucker, and Harvey Wheeler (Dordrecht: Reidel, 1987), 17–28.

82. Roderich von Engelhardt and Martin Vogel, "Was will der Mensch?" in *Der Mensch: Vom Werden und Wirken des menschlichen Organismus,* ed. Martin Vogel (Leipzig: Barth, 1930), ivf.; Roderich von Engelhardt, "Vom Menschen zum Menschen," in ibid., 1–9, quotation on 6.

83. On Klages, see Tomas Rohkrämer, *Eine andere Moderne? Zivilisationskritik, Natur und Technik in Deutschland, 1880–1930* (Paderborn: Schöningh, 1999), 162–211.

84. Roderich von Engelhardt, "Der Körper als Ganzes," in *Der Mensch,* ed. Vogel, 256f. (see also the discussion of Klages in chapter 2).

85. Ibid., 257f.

86. *Hygieneausstellung Dresden 1930*, 182f. On Fetscher, see Albrecht Scholz, "Eugenik und Rassenhygiene bei Rainer Fetscher: Höhen und Tiefen," in *Rainer Fetscher: Gedenkschrift aus Anlaß des 100. Geburtstags* (Dresden: Technical University, 1996), 31–42; Steffen Sachse, "Prof. Dr. Rainer Fetscher, 1895–1945" (diss., Technical University, Dresden, 1990). Fetscher also wrote two booklets on heredity and eugenics for the German Hygiene Museum: Rainer Fetscher, *Grundzüge der Erblichkeitslehre* (Dresden: Deutscher Verlag für Volkswohlfahrt, 1924); Fetscher, *Grundzüge der Eugenik*, 2d ed. (Dresden: Deutscher Verlag für Volkswohlfahrt, 1929).

87. See the section on "private eugenics" in Fetscher, *Grundzüge der Eugenik*, 66–73.

88. Ibid., 67f.

89. Rainer Fetscher, "Körper- und lebensgestaltende Faktoren," in *Der Mensch*, ed. Vogel, 355f.

90. Ibid., 340ff., 355f.

91. Weiss, "Race Hygiene Movement," 30–33.

92. Schwartz, "Sozialismus und Eugenik," 472f.; Weiss, "Race Hygiene Movement," 33–35.

93. Fetscher, *Grundzüge der Eugenik*, 5. It is also significant that the section about eugenics in the 1930 exhibition was titled "Heredity and Eugenics" and not "Doctrine of Heredity and Racial Hygiene," as the same section had been called during the Gesolei. Herbert Michael, "Vererbung und Eugenik," in *Hygieneausstellung Dresden 1930*, 182f.; *Gesolei: Amtlicher Katalog*, 87–88. See also Ludwig Stephan, "Das Dresdner Hygiene Museum in der Zeit des deutschen Faschismus (1933–1945)" (diss., Technical University, Dresden, 1986), 24ff., 397f., 486.

Chapter Seven

1. Fritz Lenz, quoted in Sheila Faith Weiss, "Race and Class in Fritz Lenz's Eugenics," *Medizinhistorisches Journal* 27 (1992): 5–25, quotation on 16.

2. Martin H. Geyer, *Verkehrte Welt: Revolution, Inflation und Moderne, München 1914–1924* (Göttingen: Vandenhoek & Ruprecht, 1999); Bernd Weisbrod, "The Crisis of Bourgeois Society in Interwar Germany," in *Fascist Italy and Nazi Germany: Comparisons and Contrasts*, ed. Richard Bessel (Cambridge: Cambridge University Press, 1996), 27–33; Gerald Feldman, *The Great Disorder: Politics, Economics and Society in the German Inflation* (New York: Oxford University Press, 1993), chap. 12.

3. Sander Gilman and Claudia Schmölders, eds., *Gesichter der Weimarer Republik* (Cologne: Dumont, 2000). For a cultural history of physiognomics, see Claudia Schmölders, *Das Vorurteil im Leibe: Eine Einführung in die Physiognomik* (Berlin: Akademie, 1995). There was even a phrenology of electrical responses of the brain, devised by the Ukranian physician Zacher Bissky, which caused a public sensation and was part of the cultural context for the development of the electroencephalograph by the psychiatrist Hans Berger. Cornelius Borck, "Electricity as the Medium of Psychic Life" (Berlin: Max Planck Institute for the History of Science), Preprint 154 (2000), 1–11.

4. Willibald Pschyrembel, *Klinisches Wörterbuch*, 47th ed. (Berlin: de Gruyter, 1942), 386.

5. Günther's book on the racial composition of the German people went through ten editions in the 1920s. On racial theories in the 1920s and 1930s, see Robert Proctor, *Racial Hygiene: Medicine Under the Nazis* (Cambridge: Harvard University Press, 1988); Robert Proctor, "From 'Anthropologie' to 'Rassenkunde' in the German Anthropological Tradition," in *Bones, Bodies, Behavior: Essays in Biological Anthropology*, ed. George W. Stocking (Wisconsin: University of Wisconsin Press, 1988), 138–79; Hans-Jürgen Lutzhöft, *Der nordische Gedanke in Deutschland, 1920–1940* (Stuttgart: Klett, 1971), 25.

6. Weisbrod, "Crisis of Bourgeois Society in Interwar Germany," 23–39; Konrad H. Jarausch, "Die Krise des deutschen Bildungsbürgertums," in *Bildungsbürgertum im 19. Jahrhundert,* ed. Jürgen Kocka (Stuttgart: Klett-Cotta, 1989), 180–205; Konrad H. Jarausch, *Deutsche Studenten, 1800–1970* (Frankfurt: Suhrkamp, 1984), 129f.

7. Hugo Iltis, *Volkstümliche Rassenkunde* (Jena: Urania, 1930), 6f. Iltis's assessment is confirmed by historians who attributed the popularity of racial thought among university students to such anxieties about success. Heide Ströle-Bühler, *Studentischer Antisemitismus in der Weimarer Republik* (Frankfurt: Lang, 1991), 117–20; Jarausch, *Deutsche Studenten,* 154f.

8. Fritz Herbst, "Rassenfrage und Deutsche Burschenschaft," *Burschenschaftliche Blätter* WS 1926/26, No. 5, 99–102.

9. This is remarkable because at the same time nationalist Germans were furious about the use of black troops during the French occupation of the Rhineland and denounced them as a dangerous source of pollution. Sally Marks, "Black Watch on the Rhine: A Study in Propaganda, Prejudice, and Prurience," *European Studies Review* 13 (1983): 297–334.

10. The scholar Wolfgang F. Haug has pointed out that the hereditarian assumptions in the works of Günther should not conceal the fact that Günther's racialism called for self-improvement on the part of the Bürger. Further, Haug makes a suggestive comparison between the work of Günther and that of the life reformer Reinhold Gerling. In Haug's view, both tried to resolve the basic contradiction between assumptions about the personal autonomy and potential for self-realization of the Bürger and the reality that bürgerliche Germans were usually not the masters of their fate. As Haug suggests, one should attempt to examine the racial theories of the Weimar period as a continuation of life reform concerns. Racial theorists tried to help members of the embattled middle sectors of the Bürgertum come to terms with such irresolvable contradictions of their existence such as their desires for upward mobility and the impossibility of fulfilling these desires in the postwar era. However, Haug's thesis is too simplistic in that it ignores social differences among the middle classes. Wolfgang F. Haug, *Die Faschisierung des bürgerlichen Subjekts* (Berlin: Argument, 1985).

11. Klaus-Dieter Thomann, "Dienst am Deutschtum—der medizinische Verlag J. F. Lehmanns und der Nationalsozialismus," in *Medizin im "Dritten Reich,"* 2d ed., Johanna Bleker (Cologne: Deutscher Ärzte-Verlag, 1993), 54–69; Lutzhöft, *Der nordische Gedanke,* 28ff. On the complicated story of Günther's appointment in Jena, see Uwe Hoßfeld, "Die Jenaer Jahre des 'Rasse-Günther' von 1930–1935," *Medizinhistorisches Journal* 34 (1999): 47–103.

12. Jarausch, "Krise des deutschen Bildungsbürgertums," 180–205.

13. Hans F. K. Günther, *Rassenkunde des deutschen Volkes* (Munich: Lehmann, 1922), 47, 76.

14. Ibid., 130–38.

15. Ibid., quotation on 138.

16. Ibid., 133, 139.

17. Ibid., 155f.

18. Thomas Childers, "The Social Language of Politics in Germany," *American Historical Review* 95 (1990): 331–58.

19. Günther, *Rassenkunde,* 151–56.

20. Ibid., 293ff.

21. Ibid., 32ff.

22. Hans F. K. Günther, *Rasse und Stil: Gedanken über ihre Beziehungen im Leben und in der Geistesgeschichte der europäischen Völker,* 2d ed. (Munich: Lehmann, 1926), 17f.

23. Günther, *Rassenkunde,* 70ff., 190, 233; Günther, *Rasse und Stil,* 14, 43, 66, 84.

24. Klaus Theweleit, *Männerphantasien* (Munich: dtv, 1995), 1:73, 2:31–39. On women's demonstrations and food riots during war and revolution, see Belinda Davis, "Reconsidering Habermas, Gender, and the Public Sphere, in *Society, Culture and the State,* ed. Geoff Eley (Ann Arbor: University of Michigan Press, 1997), 397–426, esp. 418–26.

25. Günther, *Rasse und Stil,* 18f.; Theweleit, *Männerphantasien,* esp. 2:206ff.

26. Cornelia Essner, " 'Im Irrgarten der Rassenlogik,' oder nordische Rassenlehre und nationale Frage (1919–1935)," *Historische Mitteilungen* 7 (1994): 81–101, esp. 87f.

27. Hoßfeld, "Jenaer Jahre des Rasse-Günther," 75.

28. Günther, *Rassenkunde,* 145–50.

29. Ibid., 369–73, 396–422. Günther clearly echoed here the stereotypes of *völkisch* anti-Semitism. A staple of the propaganda of the anti-Semitic German National Protection and Defense League *(Deutschvölkischer Schutz- und Trutzbund),* for example, was the accusation that during the war Jews had shirked front-line duty and exploited the German war effort as war profiteers. Helmut Berding, *Moderner Antisemitismus in Deutschland* (Frankfurt: Suhrkamp, 1988), 165–89.

30. Günther, *Rassenkunde,* 431–34.

31. Ibid., 186.

32. Ibid., 362ff.

33. Ibid., 1–12.

34. Ibid., 328f.

35. Gunter Mann, "Biologismus—Vorstufen und Elemente einer Medizin im Nationalsozialismus," in *Medizin im "Dritten Reich,"* ed. Bleker, 25–35.

36. Günther, *Rassenkunde,* 362f.

37. Proctor, "From 'Anthropologie' to 'Rassenkunde,'" 141f.

38. He wrote a very positive review of Günther's and Clauss's work: Paul Schultze-Naumburg, "Rassenforschung, Vererbungslehre und Rassenhygiene," *Die Umschau* 30 (1926): 386–89.

39. Willibald Sauerländer, "Vom Heimatschutz zur Rassenhygiene: Über Paul Schultze-Naumburg," in *Gesichter der Weimarer Republik,* ed. Gilman and Schmölders, 32–50.

40. Walter Gropius and Paul Schultze-Naumburg, "Who Is Right? Traditional Architecture or Building in New Forms," in *The Weimar Republic Source Book,* ed. Anton Kaes, Martin Jay, and Edward Dimendberg (Berkeley: University of California Press, 1994), 439–45.

41. Paul Schultze-Naumburg, *Kunst und Rasse* (Munich: Lehmann, 1928), 55–69.

42. Ibid., 1–28, 55.

43. Ibid., 86–100.

44. Mario-Andreas von Lüttichau, "Entartete Kunst, Munich 1937: A Reconstruction," in *"Degenerate Art": The Fate of the Avant-garde in Nazi Germany,* ed. Stephanie Barron (New York: Abrams, 1991), 46, 383–89.

45. Schultze-Naumburg, *Kunst und Rasse,* 112–27, quotation on 127.

46. On Clauss, see Peter Weingart, *Doppelleben: Ludwig Ferdinand Clauss: Zwischen Rassen-forschung und Widerstand* (Frankfurt: Campus, 1995), esp. 11–31.

47. Ludwig Ferdinand Clauss, *Von Seele und Antlitz, der Rassen und Völker: Eine Einführung in die vergleichende Ausdrucksforschung* (Munich: Lehmann, 1929), vii–xii.

48. Clauss conceived his racial style as analogous to architectural and artistic styles. There were Nordic farmers, merchants, and artists as there were Gothic cathedrals, houses, and department stores. Clauss, *Seele und Antlitz*, 94ff.

49. Ibid., 1–10.

50. Ibid., 10–15.

51. Ibid., 50–53.

52. Ernst Kretschmer, *Körperbau und Charakter: Untersuchungen zum Konstitutionsproblem und zur Lehre von den Temperamenten*, 8th ed. (Berlin: Springer, 1929), iv.

53. This distinction had already been made before the war by the psychiatrists Emil Kraepelin and Ernst Bleuler, both of whom had built on Kraepelin's concept of dementia praecox in their formulation of schizophrenia as a disease entity. Sander Gilman, *Disease and Representation: Images of Illness from Madness to AIDS* (Ithaca: Cornell University Press, 1988), 202–30.

54. Anne Harrington, "Interwar 'German' Psychobiology: Between Nationalism and the Irrational," *Science in Context* 4 (1991): 429–47.

55. Kretschmer, *Körperbau und Charakter*, 2.

56. Ibid., 7.

57. Ibid., 16–33.

58. Ibid., 21.

59. Rudie Trienes, "Type Concept Revisited: A Survey of German Idealistic Morphology," *History and Philosophy of the Life Sciences* 11 (1989): 23–42.

60. Kretschmer, *Körperbau und Charakter*, 31ff.

61. The house exhibition of the German Hygiene Museum devoted a section to Kretschmer's constitutional types: DHM, Bildsammlung, HA 1142 II, No. 1. Kretschmer's typology, for example, was frequently discussed in the popular scientific journal *Die Umschau*. On Kretschmer see Paul Rehfeldt, "Körperbau und Temperament, die Formelemente der Persönlichkeit," *Die Umschau* 32 (1928): 396–401; A. Dieminger, "Täuscht das Gesicht oder täuscht sich der Mensch, der daraus lesen will," *Die Umschau* 36 (1932): 344ff.

62. Kretschmer sometimes accounted for deviations from his constitutional-temperamental ideal types with a Mendelian theory of genetic crossing. In such cases an individual's constitution was expressed as a phenotype with an asthenic or athletic habitus and a zyklothyme predisposition and temperament, while the pyknic habitus and the schizophrenic predisposition and schizothyme temperament constituted the latent or recessive part of the entire constitution *(Gesamtkonstitution)*. A consistent Mendelism that maintained the independent heritability of separate characteristics could have undermined the constitutional paradigm, which depended on a meaningful interdependence and correlation between all characteristics of a human being. However, in Kretschmer's case, the invocation of Mendelism served to protect the constitutional concept against falsification. Kretschmer, *Körperbau und Charakter*, 95. This assessment also holds true for Julius Bauer, *Vorlesungen über Allgemeine Konstitutions-und Vererbungslehre* 2d ed. (Berlin: Springer, 1923), esp. 96. Bauer argues for the validity of the Mendelian laws of inheritance in human beings without addressing the issue of how Mendelism relates to constitutional typologies.

63. Ernst Kretschmer, *Geniale Menschen* (Berlin: Springer, 1929), 1–20, 71f.

64. Ibid., 111–24.

65. Weiss, "Race and Class in Fritz Lenz's Eugenics," esp. 14ff.

66. Kretschmer, *Geniale Menschen*, 73–106.

67. Claude Sigaud, *Les Origines de la Maladie* (Paris, 1906); Auguste Chaillou and Léon McAuliffe, *Morphologie Médicale: Etudes des quatre types humains, applications a la clinique et a la thérapeutique* (Paris: 1912).

68. Rainer Fetscher, "Körper- und lebensgestaltende Faktoren," in *Der Mensch*, ed. Martin Vogel (Leipzig: Barth, 1930), 344.

69. Ibid., 343ff. Kretschmer harshly criticized Sigaud's constitutional types. He maintained that the postulated relation between physical and psychological qualities was much too simple, because Sigaud's system was based on the proposition that thinkers needed to have a large head, eaters a beautiful belly, gymnasts powerful muscles, and runners large lungs. Kretschmer, *Körperbau und Charakter*, 12f.

70. According to Kretschmer, his types were also valid for women. Although women had the same psychopathological predispositions as men, however, Kretschmer categorically denied that women could have the same genius. Only so-called intersexed women, such as the poet Annette von Droste-Hülshoff, could create works of art of lasting importance, and only masculinized women such as Queen Elizabeth and Catherine the Great could play a role in history. True genius was limited to men. Ultimately women's genius lay in their sons. Kretschmer, *Geniale Menschen*, 125–28.

71. On Mathes see Fischer, *Biographisches Lexikon*, 1003.

72. Paul Mathes, *Der Infantilismus: Die Asthenie und deren Beziehungen zum Nervensystem* (Berlin: Karger, 1912).

73. Paul Mathes, "Die Konstitutionstypen des Weibes insbesondere der intersexuelle Typus," in *Biologie und Pathologie des Weibes: Ein Handbuch der Frauenheilkunde und Geburtshilfe*, ed. Josef Halban and Ludwig Seitz (Berlin: Urban & Schwarzenberg, 1924–1929), 3:1–122, esp. 109.

74. Ibid., 8f.

75. Ibid., 11f.

76. Ibid., 87–92.

77. Ibid., 14–22.

78. Ibid., 79.

79. Like Kretschmer, Mathes argued that the masculine psychology of some intersexual women enabled them to do extraordinary things; examples included the Italian poet Vittoria Colonna, who was the center of an intellectual circle that included the aging Michelangelo. Most intersexual women, however, would never achieve anything beyond the position of a teacher, secretary, or scientific assistant to men. Ibid., 78–84.

80. On the perception of a crisis of the moral order in postwar Germany, see Richard Bessel, *Germany After the First World War* (Oxford: Oxford University Press, 1993), 220–53. On the changing reproductive and sexual behavior of women see Atina Grossmann, *Reforming Sex: The German Movement for Birth Control and Abortion Reform, 1920–1950* (Oxford: Oxford University Press, 1995), 3–13; Cornelie Usborne, "The New Woman and Generational Conflict," in *Generations in Conflict: Youth Revolt and Generation Formation in Germany*, ed. Mark Roseman (Cambridge: Cambridge University Press, 1995), 137–63; Cornelie Usborne, *The Politics of the Body in Weimar Germany: Women's Reproductive Rights and Duties* (Ann Arbor: University of Michigan Press,

1992); Renate Bridenthal, Atina Grossmann, and Marion Kaplan, eds., *When Biology Became Destiny: Women in Weimar and Nazi Germany* (New York: Monthly Review Press, 1984).

81. Patrice Petro, *Joyless Streets: Women and Melodramatic Representation in Weimar Germany* (Princeton: Princeton University Press, 1989), 68ff.

82. Adolf Halfeld, *Amerika und der Amerikanismus: Kritische Betrachtungen eines Deutschen und Europäers*, 2d ed. (Jena: Diederichs, 1928), 189f., 209–27.

83. Lynne Frame, "Gretchen, Girl, Garionne? Weimar Science and Popular Culture in Search of the Ideal New Woman," in *Women in the Metropolis*, ed. Katharina von Ankum (Berkeley: University of California Press, 1997), 12–40, esp. 16.

Chapter Eight

1. Together, the voluntary associations of the sports movement, such as soccer clubs and traditional gymnastics clubs, had millions of members. Their organizational basis was therefore decidedly larger than that of the Freikörperkultur movement, although their formal membership figures say little about how many people actively participated in sports and physical exercise. Because of the loose organizational structure of the Freikörperkultur movement, estimates of its size are unreliable. For the early 1930s, rough estimates put the number of organized nudists at about twenty thousand. In 1929, the largest nudist umbrella organization, the Reichsverband für Freikörperkultur, had about sixty local associations. It is impossible to say how many people participated more or less regularly in such leisure activities. On the sports and gymnastics movements during the Weimar Republic, see Christiane Eisenberg, "Massensport in der Weimarer Republik: Ein statistischer Überblick," *Archiv für Sozialgeschichte* 33 (1993): 137–77; Martin L. Müller, "Turnen und Sport im sozialen Wandel: Körperkultur in Frankfurt am Main während des Kaiserreichs und der Weimarer Republik," *Archiv für Sozialgeschichte* 33 (1993): 107–36. For information on the organized memership of the nude culture movement, see Giselher Spitzer, *Der deutsche Naturismus: Idee und Entwicklung einer volkserzieherischen Bewegung im Schnitt von Lebensreform, Sport und Politik* (Ahrensburg bei Hamburg: Czwalina, 1983), 120; Michael Dörter, "Die Naturheilbewegung in Deutschland zur Zeit der Weimarer Republik" (diss., Leipzig University, 1991), 63; *Freikörperkultur und Lebensreform* (1929), 283f. The nudist Arno Vossen (alias Hermann Wilke) claimed that there were several hundred thousand unorganized nudists. Arno Vossen, *Sonnenmenschen: Sechs Jahrzehnte Freikörperkultur in Deutschland* (Hamburg: Großflottbek, 1956), 25.

2. Hans Surén, *Der Mensch und die Sonne*, 19th ed. (Berlin: Dieck, 1924), 93; Hans Surén, *Deutsche Gymnastik: Vorbereitende Übungen für den Sport, Frottierübungen, Atemgymnastik, Massage, Körperpflege, Verhalten im Licht-, Luft- und Sonnenbade*, 40th ed. (Oldenburg: Stalling, 1925), 40–45.

3. Franz Walter, Viola Denecke, and Cornelia Regin, *Sozialistische Gesundheits- und Lebensreformverbände* (Bonn: Dietz, 1991), 35–38, 49–52; Friedrich Wolf, *Die Natur als Arzt und Helfer* (Berlin: Deutsche Verlags-Anstalt, 1928), 309–13, 342–62; Nick Hopwood, "Producing a Socialist Popular Science in the Weimar Republic," *History Workshop Journal* 41 (1996): 136–40.

4. Adolf Koch, *Körperbildung Nacktkultur* (Leipzig: Oldenburg, 1924); Oliver König, *Nacktheit: Soziale Normierung und Moral* (Opladen: Westdeutscher Verlag, 1990), 153ff.; Spitzer, *Naturismus*, 141–50.

5. The founder of the league, Robert Laurer, was also the publisher of the most important nude culture journals of the period: *Die Freude, Lachendes Leben*, and *Lichtland*.

6. "Der Mitgliederzuwachs eines Großstadtbundes," *Lichtland* 9, no. 5 (1932): 12.

7. Modris Eksteins, *Rites of Spring: The Great War and the Birth of the Modern Age* (Boston: Houghton, 1989), 256ff.

8. Michael Hagner, "Verwundete Gesichter, verletzte Gehirne: Zur Deformation des Kopfes im Ersten Weltkrieg," in *Gesichter der Weimarer Republik: Eine physiognomische Kulturgeschichte,* ed. Sander Gilman and Claudia Schmölders (Cologne: Dumont, 2000), 78–95.

9. Jay Winter, *Sites of Memory, Sites of Mourning: The Great War in Cultural History* (Cambridge: Cambridge University Press, 1995), 161; Ernst Friedrich, *Das Anti-Kriegsmuseum* (Berlin, 1926), 22f.

10. K. Lichtner, "Schönheitskult und Freikörperkultur," *Lichtland* 9, no. 2 (1931): 2f.

11. *Wege zu Kraft und Schönheit,* Bundesarchiv-Filmarchiv Berlin. The movie was directed by Wilhelm Prager. The film archive has an English version titled *The Golden Road to Health and Beauty.* The movie was also discussed in the illustrated press: "Das Geheimnis der Lebensfrische: *Wege zu Kraft und Schönheit*—ein wahrhafter Kulturfilm," *Berliner Illustrierte Zeitung* 34 (1925), 349ff.

12. Wilhelm Hagen, *Sport und Körper* (Dresden: Deutscher Verlag für Volkswohlfahrt, 1926), 5ff., 55–70.

13. Ibid., 55–70; Karl Dohrn, *Gesundheitspflege im täglichen Leben* (Dresden: Deutscher Verlag für Volkswohlfahrt, 1925) 75–83, esp. 76.

14. Rudolf Neubert, *Freizeit* (Dresden: Deutscher Verlag für Volkswohlfahrt, 1927), 9–20, 34 ff. Ironically, the holistic cultivation of the personality was to be achieved by means of fragmentation of the human being. Leisure, as a residual time separated from work, provided the only opportunity for self-cultivation. The alienating experience of work contributed little to personal fulfillment and cultivation. On the debate about the alienating nature of work and the importance of leisure during the Weimar Republic, see Joan Campbell, *Joy in Work, German Work: The National Debate, 1800–1945* (Princeton: Princeton University Press, 1989), 228–42.

15. On aesthetic surgery during the period, see Sander Gilman, *Making the Body Beautiful: A Cultural History of Aesthetic Surgery* (Princeton: Princeton University Press, 1998).

16. "Schön sein oder wenigstens nicht unangenehm auffallen: Fortschritte in der Nasenplastik," *Berliner Illustrierte Zeitung* 37 (1928): 285f.

17. "Das Alter kann bekämpft werden," *Berliner Ilustrierte Zeitung* 40 (1931): 117f.

18. F. O. Hoppé, "Verrät ihre Nase Ihren Carakter?" *Berliner Illustrierte Zeitung* 37 (1928): 1069–71.

19. Klages's *Handschrift und Charakter* saw fifteen editions between 1917 and 1925 (see the discussion of Klages in chapter 2). Ludwig Klages, *Handschrift und Charakter: Gemeinverständlicher Abriss der graphologischen Technik,* in Klages, *Sämtliche Werke,* ed. Ernst Frauchiger et al. (Bonn: Bouvier, 1968), 7:285–40, esp. 309. Articles about graphology and other variations of a "physiognomy of movements" such as the "physiognomy of walking" also appeared in the contemporary illustrated press. See, e.g., Hermann Mauersberg, "Physiognomik," *Berliner Illustrierte Zeitung* 33 (1924): 1515–26; Bell, "Gang und Charakter," *Berliner Illustrierte Zeitung* 42 (1933): 1525.

20. Klages, *Handschrift und Charakter,* 485.

21. Ibid., 493, 507, 513.

22. Friedrich Wendenburg, *Gesunde Schönheitspflege* (Dresden: Deutscher Verlag für Volkswohlfahrt, 1926), esp. 42–49, quotation on 46.

23. Gertrud Pfister, "The Medical Discourse on Female Physical Culture in Germany in the 19th and Early 20th Century," *Journal of Sport History* 17 (1990): 191–97.

244 Notes to Pages 182–190

24. Wendenburg, *Gesunde Schönheitspflege*, 27.

25. Archive DHM, AS 1/1.

26. Bernd Wedemeyer, *Starke Männer, starke Frauen: Eine Kulturgeschichte des Bodybuildings* (Munich: Beck, 1996), 173f.

27. Archive DHM, AS 1/1.

28. Ibid.

29. Magnus Weidemann, "Zum Geleit," *Die Freude* 1 (1923): 1ff. On Weidemann see Spitzer, *Naturismus*, 122ff. Weidemann, born in 1880, had been a Protestant pastor from 1906 to 1920.

30. Häusser was one of the so-called *Inflationspropheten* of the early 1920s. See Ulrich Linse, *Barfüßige Propheten: Erlöser der zwanziger Jahre* (Berlin: Siedler, 1983); Hans F. K. Günther, *Rassenkunde des deutschen Volkes* (Munich: Lehmann, 1922), 363f.

31. Magnus Weidemann, "Mein Christusbekenntnis," *Die Freude* 1 (1923): 156–68, quotations on 168.

32. Jennifer Jenkins, "The Kitsch Collection and the 'Spirit of the Furniture': Cultural Reform and National Culture in Germany," *Social History* 21 (1996): 123–41. Weidemann was also a frequent contributor of nude photographs to the Bildungsbürger journal *Die Schönheit*. Prior to the war one of the most important journals directed at the Gebildeten among life reformers (see chapter 2), *Die Schönheit* lost much of its significance and readership during the Weimar years. Janos Frecot, "Die Schönheit: Mit Bildern geschmückte Zeitschrift für Kunst und Leben," *Fotogeschichte* 15 (1995): 37–46, esp. 44f.

33. Therese Mülhouse-Vogeler, "Robert Laurer der Werber für die Idee der Freikörperkultur," *Lachendes Leben* 8, no. 10 (1932): 12–16; Therese Mülhouse-Vogeler, "Egestorf, ein Freikörperkulturzentrum," *Lachendes Leben* 8, no. 11 (1932): 14–17.

34. Magnus Weidemann, "Kulturaufgaben," *Die Freude* 1 (1923): 99–106.

35. For a short biography of Surén, see Dietger Pforte, "Hans Surén—eine deutsche Karriere," in *"Wir sind nackt und nennen uns Du": Von Lichtfreunden und Sonnenkämpfern*, ed. Michael Andritzky and Thomas Rautenberger (Giessen: Anabas, 1989), 130–34.

36. Surén criticized Müller for living in London for several years and having his sons participate on the British side of the war. He was especially outraged that Müller was invited by German gymnastics associations to demonstrate his system after the war. Hans Surén, *Surén-Atemgymnastik: Die Schule der Atmung für Körper und Geist für alle Leibesübungen und Berufe*, 36th ed. (Stuttgart: Dieck, 1929), 51.

37. Pforte, *Surén*, 133f. Surén's opportunism is evident in the revisions to the 1936 edition of his *Der Mensch und die Sonne*. With a view toward the 1936 Olympics in Berlin, he claimed that his physical culture reflected an Aryan-Olympic spirit. Hans Surén, *Der Mensch und die Sonne: Arisch-Olympischer Geist*, 6th ed. (Berlin: Scherl, 1936). In contrast to Surén, the socialist Adolf Koch was thoroughly discredited in Nazi eyes because his school was tied to the working-class subculture. But as archival evidence suggests, Koch also tried to create a working relationship with the new rulers. He joined the Nazi Party in the spring of 1933 in an unsuccessful effort to prevent his school from being dissolved for political reasons. He stressed the value of his school for the health of the race and presented a letter to the Ministry of the Interior in which a *Standartenführer* of the SA (*Sturmabteilung*, or Storm Troopers) testified that Koch's work was important for the SA. BA Berlin-Lichterfelde, 15.01, No. 26337, Bl. 21f., 30ff.

38. Hans Surén, *Gymnastik im Bild: Körperschulung durch Gymnastik. Fünf Lehrtafeln für alle*, 4th ed. (Stuttgart: Dieck, 1923).

39. Ernst Gerhard Eder, "Sonnenanbeter und Wasserratten: Körperkultur und Freiluftbade-bewegung in Wiens Donaulandschaft," *Archiv für Sozialgeschichte* 33 (1993): 251ff.

40. Martin H. Geyer, *Verkehrte Welt: Revolution, Inflation und Moderne, München, 1914–1924* (Göttingen: Vandenhoek & Ruprecht, 1999), 162–66, 243–48; Adelheid von Saldern, "Massen-freizeitkultur im Visier. Ein Beitrag zu den Deutungs- und Einwirkungsversuchen während der Weimarer Republik," *Archiv für Sozialgeschichte* 33 (1993): 25.

41. Kopernikulus, "Das Müllerkorsett," *Lachendes Leben* 3, no. 1 (1927): 8f. The story featured one Mrs. Schieber, who vainly tried to control her ample girth with corsets.

42. Surén, *Mensch und Sonne*, 98.

43. Ibid., 72.

44. Ibid., 108.

45. Ibid., 91ff. Surén, *Deutsche Gymnastik*, 34ff.

46. Dora Menzler, *Die Schönheit deines Körpers: Das Ziel unserer gesundheitlich-künsterischen Körperschulung* (Stuttgart: Dieck, 1924).

47. Karl Toepfer, "Nudity and Modernity in German Modern Dance, 1910–1930," *Journal of the History of Sexuality* 3 (1992): 68ff.; Surén, *Deutsche Gymnastik*, 81f.

48. *Lachendes Leben* 3, no. 1 (1927): 23; Otto Ludwig Labus, "Für und Wider die Freikör-perkultur: Eine Betrachtung vom Standpunkte des Vorurteilslosen," *Lachendes Leben* 5, no. 3 (1929): 13–6; K. Wernecke, "Warum gemeinsames Sonnenbaden beider Geschlechter?" *Lichtland* 9, no. 6 (1932): 1.

49. H. Z., "Körperkeckheit," *Lichtland* 5, no. 20 (1928): 3f.

50. Therese Mülhouse-Vogeler, "Warum gemeinsames Nacktbaden der Geschlechter," *Lachendes Leben* 6, no. 7 (1930): 4f.

51. Hermann Brauns, "Freikörperkultur und Sexualmoral," *Lachendes Leben* 7, no. 12 (1931): 6–10.

52. For the argument that these social-cultural milieus had already started to disintegrate during the Weimar years, see Detlef Peukert, *The Weimar Republic: The Crisis of Classical Modernity* (New York: Hill & Wang, 1993), 147–56; Dieter Langewiesche, *Liberalismus in Deutschland* (Frankfurt: Suhrkamp, 1988), 240–51. On the illusion and appeal of the Volksgemeinschaft during the Nazi years see David Schoenbaum, *Hitler's Social Revolution: Class and Status in Nazi Germany, 1933–1939* (Garden City, N.Y.: Doubleday, 1967).

53. Mülhouse-Vogeler, "Warum gemeinsames Nacktbaden der Geschlechter," 4f.

54. Anton Schnitzinger, "Einfluß der Freikörperkultur auf die Angestellten und Arbeiter," *Lichtland* 7, no. 10 (1930): 1f.

55. Gotthard Jasper, *Die gescheiterte Zähmung: Wege zur Machtergreifung Hitlers* (Frankfurt: Suhrkamp, 1986), 175f.

56. Fedor Fuchs, "Nacktsportplatz 'Freisonnland,'" *Lachendes Leben* 2, no. 6 (1925–26): 15.

57. Gerhard Brock, "Gedanken über Grundlage und Idee der Freikörperkultur," *Lichtland* 7, no. 14 (1930): 4f.

58. Franz Walter and Cornelia Regin, "Vereine für Volksgesundheit," 35–38, 49–52.

59. Therese Mülhouse-Vogeler, "Weltfriedensidee und Freikörperkultur," *Lichtland* 8, no. 17 (1931): 2f.

60. Herbert Zeissig, "Pazifismus und Freikörperkultur," *Lichtland* 9, no. 3 (1932): 3f.

61. Therese Mülhouse-Vogeler, "Dürfen Nationalsozialisten Freikörperkultur treiben?" *Lichtland* 7, no. 21 (1930): 1 f.

62. Walter Heitsch, "Freikörperkultur und Nationalsozialismus," *Lichtland* 9, no. 12 (1932): 2 f.; Michelangelo Freiherr von Zois, "Das dritte Reich und die Freikörperkultur," *Lichtland* 9, no. 15 (1932): 1 f.

63. Therese Mülhouse-Vogeler, "Freikörperkultur und Rasse," *Lichtland* 8, no. 6 (1931): 2.

64. Karl Friedrich, "Körperkultur ein Schritt zum Völkerfrieden," *Lichtland* 5, no. 11 (1928): 3.

65. On Seitz see Spitzer, *Naturismus*, 92–97. The break with Ungewitter came about because of Ungewitter's intolerance of anything less than total abstinence from meat and alcohol consumption.

66. Josef Maria Seitz, *Die Nacktkulturbewegung: Ein Buch für Unwissende und Wissende* (Dresden: Verlag die Schönheit, 1923), 137. Ungewitter continued his agitation as a member of the radical anti-Semitic fringe: Richard Ungewitter, *Aus Judenknechtschaft zur Freiheit empor: Rettung oder Untergang des deutschen Volkes* (Stuttgart: Ungewitter, 1923).

67. Fidus, "Leibesbefreiung und Volksfreiheit" *Lichtland* 9, no. 14 (1932): 1 f. On Fidus, see Janos Frecot, Johann Friedrich Geist, and Diethardt Kerbs. *Fidus, 1868–1948: Zur ästhetischen Praxis bürgerlicher Fluchtbewegungen* (Munich: Rogner & Bernhard, 1972).

68. Walter Heitsch, *Freikörperkultur-Lebensfreude* (Egestorf: Laurer, 1932), 46 f. On the stereotype of the pronounced Jewish sex drive, see Sander Gilman, *The Case of Sigmund Freud: Medicine and Identity at the Fin de Siècle* (Baltimore: Johns Hopkins University Press, 1993), 176 ff.; Sander Gilman, *The Jew's Body* (New York: Routledge, 1991).

69. Saul Friedländer, *Nazi Germany and the Jews: The Years of Persecution, 1933–1939* (New York: HarperCollins, 1997), 122 f.

Conclusion

1. Michael Kater, *Studentenschaft und Rechtsradikalismus in Deutschland, 1918–1933* (Hamburg: Hoffmann & Campe, 1975), 180–97.

2. Thomas Childers, "The Middle Classes and National Socialism," in *The German Bourgeoisie: Essays on the Social History of the German Middle Classes from the Late Eighteenth to the Early Twentieth Century*, ed. David Blackbourn and Richard Evans (London: Routledge, 1991), 318–37.

3. Gotthard Jasper, *Die gescheiterte Zähmung: Wege zur Machtergreifung Hitlers* (Frankfurt: Suhrkamp, 1986), 172–76.

4. Peter Reichel, *Der schöne Schein des Dritten Reiches: Faszination und Gewalt des Faschismus* (Frankfurt: Fischer, 1993), 243–54.

5. Thomas Alkemeyer, *Körper, Kult, und Politik: Von der Muskelreligion Pierre de Coubertins zur Inszenierung von Macht in den Olympischen Spielen von 1936* (Frankfurt: Campus, 1996), 377–84.

6. Dietger Pforte, "Zur Freihörperkultur-Bewegung im nationalsozialistischen Deutschland," in *"Wir sind Nackt und nennen uns Du": Von Lichtfreunden und Sonnenkämpfern*, ed. Michael Andritzky and Thomas Rautenberger (Gießen: Anabas, 1989), 136–41. On the *Gleichschaltung* of life reform associations, see Wolfgang R. Krabbe, " 'Die Weltanschauung der deutschen Lebensreformbewegung ist der Nationalsozialismus': Zur Gleichschaltung einer Alternativströmung im Dritten Reich," *Archiv für Kulturgeschichte* 71 (1989): 431–61.

7. Sheila Faith Weiss, "Race and Class in Fritz Lenz's Eugenics," *Medizinhistorisches Journal* 27 (1992): 23. This is also evident in Nazi racial legislation. The infamous Nuremberg laws and their supplementary decrees prohibited marriage and sexual relations between Jews and non-Jews. They

did not address miscegenation between Nordics and "racially inferior" German non-Jews. Cornelia Essner, "Die Alchemie des Rassenbegriffs und die Nürnberger Gesetze," *Jahrbuch für Antisemitismusforschung* 4 (1995): 201–21; Saul Friedländer, *Nazi Germany and the Jews: The Years of Persecution, 1933–1939* (New York: HarperCollins, 1997), 141–55; Michael Burleigh and Wolfgang Wippermann, *The Racial State: Germany, 1933–1945* (Cambridge: Cambridge University Press, 1991).

8. Thomas Alkmeyer, "Politik mit dem Körper: Zur Aesthetik physischer Vollkommenheit in der öffentlichen-repräsentativen Szenerie des 'Dritten Reiches,'" in *Sportstadt Berlin in Geschichte und Gegenwart*, ed. Sportmuseum Berlin (Berlin: Sportmuseum Berlin, 1993): 146–59; Silke Wenk, "Volkskörper und Medienspiel," *Kunstforum International* 114 (1991): 226–35. See also Daniel Wildmann, *Begehrte Körper, Konstruktion und Inszenierung des "arischen" Männerkörpers im "Dritten Reich"* (Würzburg: Königshausen & Neumann, 1998), 39.

9. Klaus Wolbert, *Die Nackten und die Toten des "Dritten Reiches": Folgen einer politischen Geschichte des Körpers in der Plastik des deutschen Faschismus* (Gießen: Anabas, 1982).

10. Stephanie Barron, "1937: Modern Arts and Politics in Prewar Germany," in *"Degenerate Art": The Fate of the Avantgarde in Nazi Germany*, ed. Barron (New York: Abrams, 1991), 9–23; George Mosse, "Beauty Without Sensuality: The Exhibition 'Entartete Kunst,'" in ibid., 25–31; Kathrin Hoffmann-Curtius, "Die Kampagne 'Entartete Kunst': Die Nationalsozialisten und die moderne Kunst," in *Moderne Kunst*, ed. Monika Wagner (Reinbek bei Hamburg: Rowohlt, 1991), 467–90.

11. Michael Kater, *Doctors Under Hitler* (Chapel Hill: University of North Carolina Press, 1989); Robert Proctor, *Racial Hygiene: Medicine Under the Nazis* (Cambridge: Harvard University Press, 1988), 223–35.

12. Detlef Bothe, *Neue Deutsche Heilkunde, 1933–1945* (Husum: Matthiesen, 1991), 167–70, 290.

13. Proctor, *Racial Hygiene*, 237–41; Robert Proctor, *The Nazi War on Cancer* (Princeton: Princeton University Press, 1999), chap. 5.

14. Bothe, *Neue Deutsche Heilkunde*, chaps. 8, 11, and 13.

15. Ibid., 288.

16. Alfred Haug, *Die Reichsarbeitsgemeinschaft für eine neue deutsche Heilkunde, 1935/1936* (Husum: Matthiesen, 1985), 139.

17. Streicher's motto was "Die Impfung ist eine Rassenschande"; BA Berlin-Lichterfelde R 43 II/724, p. 51. On Streicher's support for alternative medicine, see Proctor, *Racial Hygiene*, 226–35.

18. Letter, Udny to Thomsen, BA Berlin-Lichterfelde R 43 II/724, pp. 14f.

19. Letter, Thomsen to Udny, ibid., p. 17.

20. Proctor, *Nazi War on Cancer*, 134–41.

21. BA Berlin-Lichterfelde R43 II/724, p.18.

22. "Gründe dafür liegen auf militärpolitischem Gebiet": Letter, Will to Thomsen, BA Berlin-Lichterfelde R 43 II/724, pp. 55f.

23. Response, Thomsen to Will, ibid., pp. 58f.

24. Letters, Reichenau to Frick, ibid., pp. 59f.

25. Bothe, *Neue Deutsche Heilkunde*, 96–103.

26. Memorandum, Ungewitter to Hitler and other Nazi leaders, BA Berlin-Lichterfelde, R 43II/725a, pp. 2–19.

Archival Sources

Bundesarchiv Berlin-Lichterfelde

Reichskanzlei R 43 II/724, 43 II/725a.

Reichsgesundheitsamt R 86, No. 885.

Reichsinnenministerium 1501, Nos. 9135–9136, 9370–9375, 9413, 10961–10962, 11174–11176, 11890–11895, 26345, 26337.

Bundesarchiv-Filmarchiv Berlin

Wege zu Kraft und Schönheit (The Golden Road to Health and Beauty), dir. Wilhelm Prager (1925).

German Hygiene Museum, Archive and Picture Collection DHM, IHA 1911, No. 681.

DHM, HA 1142 II, No. 1.

DHM Fotoband Ausstellung Richtige Ernährung, Leipzig 1928, No. K 1139.

DHM Strongfortismus, AS 1/1.

Primary Sources: Periodicals and Catalogues

Ärztliches Vereinsblatt für Deutschland: Organ des deutschen Ärztevereinsbundes 16 (1889)–59 (1932).

Berliner Illustrierte Zeitung 29 (1919)–43 (1933).

Blätter für Volksgesundheitspflege: Gemeinverständliche Zeitschrift: Organ des deutschen Vereins für Volkshygiene 1 (1900–1901)–19 (1919).

Burschenschaftliche Blätter WS 1926/26, No. 5.

Freikörperkultur und Lebensreform (1929).

Die Freude: Monatshefte für deutsche Innerlichkeit 1 (1923–24)–6 (1929).

Gesolei: Amtlicher Katalog. 2d ed. Düsseldorf, 1926.

Gruber, Max, and Ernst Rüdin. *Fortpflanzung, Vererbung, Rassenhygiene: Illustrierter Führer durch die Gruppe Rassenhygiene der internationalen Hygieneausstellung.* 2d ed. Munich, 1911.

Hygiene: Offizielle Monatsschrift der Internationalen Hygieneausstellung. Dresden, 1911.

Internationale Hygieneausstellung 1911. (Program)

Internationale Hygieneausstellung: Amtlicher Führer. Dresden, 1930.

Katalog der Internationalen Hygieneausstellung. Dresden, 1911.

Katalog Dr. Ziegelroth's Sanatorium Zehlendorf bei Berlin. Berlin, n.d.

Kraft und Schönheit: Illustrierte Zeitschrift des Vereins für vernünftige Leibeszucht 2 (1902–1903)–26 (1927).

Lachendes Leben 1925–1931.

Lichtland 5 (1928)–10 (1933).

Luftkurort und Sanatorium Bühlau bei Weißer Hirsch. Bühlau, n. d.

Der Mensch: Ausgewählte Gruppen aus der Internationalen Hygieneausstellung Dresden 1911. Darmstadt, 1912.

Die Neue Heilkunst: Familienblatt zur Beförderung der Volkswohlfahrt insbesondere durch die arzneilose und operationslose Heilweise und die naturgemäße Gesundheitspflege 1 (1889)–17 (1905).

Der Naturarzt: Zeitschrift des Deutschen Bundes der Vereine für Gesundheitspflege und für arzneilose Heilweise 17 (1889)–61 (1933).

Die Naturwissenschaften 48–49 (1926).

Die Schönheit 1 (1904)–15 (1918).

Sanatorium Franckenstein bei Rumburg: Physikalisch-diätetische Kuranstalt ersten Ranges. Rumburg, 1912.

Die Umschau: Übersicht über die Fortschritte und Bewegungen auf dem Gesamtgebiet der Wissenschaft, Technik, Literatur und Kunst 1 (1897)–36 (1932).

Vegetarische Rundschau: Monatsschrift für vernunftgemässe (naturgemässe) Lebensweise 1883–1896.

Vegetarische Warte: Zeitschrift für naturgemässe Lebensweise: Organ des Deutschen Vegetarierbundes 1895–1932.

Verhandlungen der Gesellschaft Deutscher Naturforscher und Ärzte 65 (1893).

Vierzig Jahre Naturheilbewegung: Festschrift zum 40-jährigen Bestehen des Deutschen Bundes der Vereine für naturgemäße Lebens- und Heilweise (Naturheilkunde) E. V. Berlin, 1929.

Zeitschrift für Morphologie und Anthropologie 1 (1899)–8 (1905).

Zeitschrift für soziale Medizin 1 (1895).

Die Zukunft 2 (1893).

Zuntz, N., C. Brahm, and A. Mallwitz. *Sonderkatalog der Abteilung Sportausstellung der Internationalen Hygieneausstellung.* Dresden, 1911.

Primary Literature

Alexander, Karl. *Wahre und falsche Heilkunde: Ein Wort der Aufklärung über den Wert der wissenschaftlichen Medizin gegenüber der Gemeingefährlichkeit der Kurpfuscherei.* Berlin: Reimer, 1899.

Ammon, Otto. D*ie natürliche Auslese beim Menschen*. Jena: G. Fischer, 1893.

Back, Wilhelm. *Das Kurpfuschertum und seine Bekämpfung*. Straßburg: Back, 1904.

Baltzer, Eduard. *Fünf Bücher vom wahren Menschenthume*. 2d ed. Rudolstadt, 1882.

Bauer, Julius. *Vorlesungen über allgemeine Konstitutions- und Vererbungslehre*. 2d ed. Berlin: Springer, 1923.

Berg, Ragnar, and Martin Vogel. *Die Grundlagen der richtigen Ernährung*. 5th ed. Dresden: Deutscher Verlag für Volkswohlfahrt, 1928.

Beschorner, Herbert. *Tuberkulosebekämpfung, Tuberkulosefürsorge*. Dresden: Deutscher Verlag für Volkswohlfahrt, 1922.

Bilz, Friedrich Eduard. *Das neue Naturheilverfahren: Lehr- und Nachschlagebuch der naturgemaessen Heilweise und Gesundheitspflege*. 31st ed. Leipzig: Bilz, n.d.

Binding, Karl, and Alfred Hoche. *Die Freigabe der Vernichtung lebensunwerten Lebens*. Leipzig: Meiner, 1920.

Bloch, Iwan. *Das Sexualleben unserer Zeit in seinen Beziehungen zur modernen Kultur*. 9th ed. Berlin: Louis Marcus, 1909.

Brücke, Ernst. *Schönheit und Fehler der menschlichen Gestalt*. Vienna: Braumüller, 1891.

Buschan, Georg. "Die beiden Geschlechter innerhalb der einzelnen Rassen." In *Mann und Weib*, ed. Koßmann and Weiß, 3:443–86.

Chaillou, Auguste, and Léon McAuliffe. *Morphologie Médicale: Etudes des quatre types humaines, applications a la clinique et a la thérapeutique*. Paris: Doin, 1912.

Clauss, Ludwig Ferdinand. *Von Seele und Antlitz der Rassen und Völker: Eine Einführung in die vergleichende Ausdrucksforschung*. Munich: Lehmann, 1929.

Dohrn, Karl. *Gesundheitspflege im täglichen Leben*. Dresden: Deutscher Verlag für Volkswohlfahrt, 1925.

Elberskirchen, Johanna. "Das Geschlechtsleben des Weibes." In *Mann und Weib*, ed. Koßmann and Weiss, vol. 1, pt. 2, 187–230.

Engelhardt, Roderich von. "Der Körper als Ganzes." In *Der Mensch*, ed. Vogel, 253–65.

———. "Vom Menschen zum Menschen." In *Der Mensch*, ed. Vogel, 1–9.

Erb, Wilhelm. *Über die wachsende Nervosität unserer Zeit*. Heidelberg: Hörning, 1893.

Fetscher, Rainer. "Körper- und lebensgestaltende Faktoren." In *Der Mensch*, ed. Vogel, 340–56.

———. *Grundzüge der Eugenik*, 2d ed. Dresden: Deutscher Verlag für Volkswohlfahrt, 1929.

———. *Grundzüge der Erblichkeitslehre*. Dresden: Deutscher Verlag für Volkswohlfahrt, 1924.

Fischer, Isidor. *Biographisches Lexikon der hervorragenden Ärzte der letzten fünfzig Jahre*. Vienna: Urban & Schwarzenberg, 1932.

Fischer-Dückelmann, Anna. *Das Geschlechtsleben des Weibes: Eine physiologisch-soziale Studie mit ärztlichen Ratschlägen*. Berlin: Bermühler, 1908.

———. *Die Frau als Hausärztin*. 2d special ed. Stuttgart: Süddeutsches Verlags-Institut, 1905.

Friedrich, Ernst. *Das Anti-Kriegsmuseum*. Berlin, 1926.

Fritsch, Gustav. *Die Gestalt des Menschen: Mit Benutzung der Werke von E. Harless und C. Schmidt für Künstler und Anthropologen dargestellt*. Stuttgart: Neff, 1899.

———. *Unsere Körperform im Lichte der modernen Kunst*. Berlin: Carl Habel, 1893.

Gehlen, Walter, and Herbert Michael. "Der Mensch," in *Internationale Hygieneausstellung Dresden 1930: Amtlicher Führer*. Dresden, 1930.

Gerling, Reinhold. *Wie das Weib am Manne leidet und der Mann am Weibe.* Oranienburg: Orania, 1912.

———. *Das Goldene Buch des Weibes: Zehn Kapitel aus dem intimsten Leben der Frau.* 3d ed. Berlin: Pilz, 1906.

———. *Der vollendete Mensch.* 2d ed. Oranienburg: Orania, 1906.

———. *Die Gymnastik des Willens: Praktische Anleitung zur Erhöhung der Energie und Selbstbeherrschung, Kräftigung von Gedächtnis und Arbeitslust durch Stärkung der Willenskraft ohne fremde Hilfe.* Berlin: Möller, 1905.

———. *Freie Liebe oder Bürgerliche Ehe?* Oranienburg: Orania, 1904.

———. *Was muß der Mann vor der Ehe von der Ehe wissen? Ein Ratgeber für Verlobte.* 4th ed. Oranienburg: Orania, 1904.

———, ed. *Praktische Menschenkenntnis.* Oranienburg: Orania, 1911.

Goldstein, Kurt. *Über Rassenhygiene.* Berlin: Springer, 1913.

Gottstein, Adolf. *Das Heilwesen der Gegenwart: Gesundheitslehre und Gesundheitspolitik.* 2d ed. Berlin: Deutsche Buch-Gemeinschaft, 1925.

———. *Die neue Gesundheitspflege.* Berlin: Siegismund, 1920.

———. *Allgemeine Epidemiologie* Leipzig: Wigand, 1897.

Gropius, Walter, and Paul Schultze-Naumburg. "Who Is Right? Traditional Architecture or Building in New Forms." In *Weimar Republic Source Book,* ed. Kaes et al., 439−45.

Grosse, Ernst. *Kunstwissenschaftliche Studien.* Tübingen: Mohr, 1900.

Großer, Otto. "Der menschliche Körperbau." In *Mann und Weib,* ed. Koßmann and Weiß, vol. 1, pt. 1, 41−51.

———. "Der Körperbau des Weibes (verglichen mit dem des Mannes)." In *Mann und Weib,* ed. Koßmann and Weiß, vol. 1, pt. 2, 1−43.

Grote, Louis R. *Die Medizin der Gegenwart in Selbstdarstellungen.* Leipzig: Meiner, 1923−1928.

Gruber, Max von. *Hygiene des Geschlechtslebens.* 44th ed. 1911; reprint, Stuttgart: Moritz, 1920.

Günther, Hans F. K. *Rasse und Stil: Gedanken über ihre Beziehungen im Leben und in der Geistesgeschichte der europäischen Völker, insbesondere des deutschen Volkes.* 2d ed. Munich: Lehmann, 1926.

———. *Rassenkunde des deutschen Volkes.* Munich: Lehmann, 1922.

Hagen, Wilhelm. *Sport und Körper.* Dresden: Deutscher Verlag für Volkswohlfahrt, 1926.

Halban, Josef, and Ludwig Seitz, eds. *Biologie und Pathologie des Weibes: Ein Handbuch der Frauenheilkunde und Geburtshilfe.* Vienna: Urban & Schwarzenberg, 1924−1929.

Halfeld, Adolf. *Amerika und der Amerikanismus: Kritische Betrachtungen eines Deutschen und Europäers.* 2d ed. Jena: Diederichs, 1928.

Hayn, Walter. *Der Biochemische Bund Deutschlands und seine Einrichtungen im Lichte der Statistik.* Neubabelsberg: Bio-Verlag, 1930.

Heinson, Ernst. "Arbeits- und Gewerbehygiene." In *GE-SO-Lei,* ed. Schloßmann and Fraenkel, 613−35.

Heitsch, Walter. *Freikörperkultur-Lebensfreude.* Egestorf: Laurer, 1932.

Hellpach, Willy. "Kokotten- und Mättressenwesen." In *Mann und Weib,* ed. Koßmann and Weiß, 2:392−435.

Hueppe, Ferdinand. *Hygiene der Körperübungen.* 2d ed. Leipzig: Hirzel, 1922.

————, ed. *Handbuch der Hygiene.* Berlin: Hirschwald, 1899.

Hufeland, Christoph Wilhelm. *Makrobiotik oder die Kunst das menschliche Leben zu verlängern.* 1796; reprint, Munich: Insel, 1984.

Iltis, Hugo. *Volkstümliche Rassenkunde.* Jena: Urania, 1930.

Kaes, Anton, Martin Jay, and Edward Dimendberg, eds. *The Weimar Republic Source Book.* Berkeley: University of California Press, 1994.

Kahn, Fritz. *Das Leben des Menschen: Eine volkstümliche Anatomie, Biologie, Physiologie und Entwicklungsgeschichte des Menschen.* Stuttgart: Frankhsche Verlagshandlung, 1926–1931.

Katz, [Dr. med.]. "Die Geschlechtskrankheiten und ihre Behandlung." In *Neue Heilmethode,* ed. Platen, 4:130–80.

Klages, Ludwig. *Sämtliche Werke,* ed. Ernst Frauchiger et al. Bonn: Bouvier, 1964–1971.

————. *Handschrift und Charakter: Gemeinverständlicher Abriss der graphologischen Technik.* In Klages, *Sämtliche Werke,* ed. Frauchiger et al., 7:285–540.

————. "Nachtrag zur Theorie des Schreibdrucks" (1903). In Klages, *Sämtliche Werke,* ed. Frauchiger et al., 8:128–30.

Kleinschrod, Franz. "Die Naturheillehre." In *Neue Heilmethode,* ed. Platen, 1:3–43.

Koch, Adolf. *Körperbildung Nacktkultur.* Leipzig: Oldenburg, 1924.

König, F., ed. *Ratgeber in gesunden und in kranken Tagen.* 16th ed. Leipzig: Karl Meyer, n.d.

Koßmann, Robby, and Julius Weiß, eds. *Mann und Weib: Ihre Beziehungen zueinander und zum Kulturleben der Gegenwart.* Stuttgart: Union Deutsche Verlags-Gesellschaft, 1907.

————. "Die Sonderung der Geschlechter." In *Mann und Weib,* ed. Koßmann and Weiß, vol. 1, pt. 1, 1–40.

————. "Hygiene der Ehe." In *Mann und Weib,* ed. Koßmann and Weiß, 2:192–211.

Kretschmer, Ernst. *Geniale Menschen.* Berlin: Springer, 1929.

————. *Körperbau und Charakter: Untersuchungen zum Konstitutionsproblem und zur Lehre von den Temperamenten.* 8th ed. Berlin: Springer, 1929.

Kühner, August. *Die Liebe, ihr Wesen und ihre Gesetze,* 3d ed. Berlin: Wilhelm Möller, 1903.

————. "Das Geschlechtsleben und seine Sörungen." In *Neue Heilmethode,* ed. Platen, 4:3–65.

Kuhne, Louis. *Gesichtsausdruckskunde: Lehrbuch einer neuen Untersuchungsart zur Erkennung der Krankheitszustände.* Leipzig: Louis Kuhne, [ca. 1904].

————. *Die neue Heilwissenschaft oder die Lehre von der Einheit aller Krankheiten und deren darauf begründete, einheitliche, arzneilose und operationslose Heilung.* 35th ed. Leipzig: Louis Kuhne, 1898.

Lahmann, Heinrich. *Die wichtigsten Kapitel der natürlichen (physikalisch-diätetischen) Heilweise.* 3d ed. Stuttgart, 1897.

————. *Die diätetische Blutentmischung (Dysämie) als Grundursache aller Krankheiten.* Leipzig: Spamer, 1892.

Lehr, Robert. "Die Gesolei, Düsseldorf wieder dem Licht entgegen." In *GE-SO-LEI,* ed. Schloßmann and Fraenkel, 18–22.

Liek, Erwin. *Das Wunder in der Heilkunde.* Munich: Lehmann, 1930.

————. *Der Arzt und seine Sendung.* 5th ed. Munich: Lehmnn, 1927.

Lingner, Karl August. *Der Mensch als Organisationsvorbild.* Bern: Drechsel, 1914.

Martius, Friedrich. *Über Nervosität.* Hamburg: Verlags Anstalt und Druckerei AG, 1894.

Mathes, Paul. "Die Konstitutionstypen des Weibes, insbesondere der intersexuelle Typus." In *Biologie und Pathologie des Weibes,* ed. Halban and Seitz, 3:1–122.

———. *Der Infantilismus, die Asthenie und deren Beziehungen zum Nervensystem.* Berlin: Karger, 1912.

Menzler, Dora. *Die Schönheit deines Körpers: Das Ziel unserer gesundheitlich-künstlerischen Körperschulung* Stuttgart: Dieck, 1924.

Möbius, Paul J. *Über den physiologischen Schwachsinn des Weibes,* 9th ed. Halle: Marhold, 1908.

———. *Über Entartung.* Wiesbaden: Bergmann, 1900.

———. *Über das Pathologische bei Goethe.* 1898; reprint, Munich: Matthes & Seitz, 1982.

Müller, J. P. *Mein System: 15 Minuten täglicher Arbeit für die Gesundheit.* 12th ed. Leipzig: Grethlein, n.d..

Neubert, Rudolf. *Freizeit.* Dresden: Deutscher Verlag für Volkswohlfahrt, 1927.

Neustätter, Otto. "Die sogenannte Naturheilkunde." In *Kurpfuschertum,* ed. Back, 45–90.

Nordau, Max. *Entartung.* 2d ed. Berlin: Duncker, 1893.

Nothafft, Albrecht von. "Die krankhaften Äußerungen des Geschlechtstriebes." In *Mann und Weib,* ed. Koßmann and Weiß, 2:488–569.

Platen, Moritz. "Das Weib als Gattungswesen." In *Die neue Heilmethode,* ed. Platen, 4:184–201.

———, ed. *Die neue Heilmethode: Lehrbuch der naturgemäßen Lebensweise, der Gesundheitspflege und der naturgemäßen Heilweise.* Berlin: Bong, 1907.

Ploetz, Alfred. *Die Tüchtigkeit unserer Rasse und der Schutz der Schwachen: Ein Versuch über Rassenhygiene und ihr Vehältnis zu den humanen Idealen besonders zum Socialismus.* Berlin: Fischer, 1895.

Poensgen, Ernst. "Die wirtschaftliche Beduetung der Gesolei." In *GE-SO-LEI,* ed. Schloßmann and Fraenkel, 1:15–17.

Pschyrembel, Willibald. *Klinisches Wörterbuch,* 47th ed. Berlin: de Gruyter, 1942.

Ranke, Johannes. *Der Mensch.* Leipzig: Bibliographisches Institut, 1886.

Reissig, Carl. *Medizinische Wissenschaft und Kurpfuscherei.* 2d ed. Leipzig: Vogel, 1901.

Rosenbach, Ottomar. *Arzt c/a Bakteriologe.* Vienna: Urban & Schwarzenberg, 1903.

Rott, Fritz. "Die Gesundheitsfürsorge." In *GE-SO-LEI,* ed. Schloßmann and Fraenkel, 668–720.

Schloßmann, Arthur. "Entwicklung, Wesen, Ziele und Erfolg der Gesolei." In *GE-SO-LEI,* ed. Schloßmann and Fraenkel, 1:43–48.

Schloßmann, Arthur, and Martha Fraenkel, eds. *GE-SO-LEI: Grosse Ausstellung Düsseldorf 1926 für Gesundheitspflege, Soziale Fürsorge und Leibesübungen.* Düsseldorf: Schwann, 1927.

Schönenberger, Franz, and Wilhelm Siegert. *Lebenskunst, Heilkunst: Ärztlicher Ratgeber für Gesunde und Kranke.* Zwickau: Förster & Borries, 1906.

———. *Das Geschlechtsleben und seine Verirrungen: Was junge Leute davon wissen sollten und Eheleute wissen müßten.* 10th ed. Berlin: Wilhelm Möller, 1902.

Schultze-Naumburg, Paul. *Kunst und Rasse.* Munich: Lehmann, 1928.

———. *Die Kultur des weiblichen Körpers als Grundlage der Frauenkleidung.* Jena: Diederichs, 1905.

Seitz, Josef Maria. *Die Nacktkulturbewegung: Ein Buch für Unwissende und Wissende.* Dresden: Verlag Die Schönheit, 1923.

Sellheim, Hugo. *Die Reize der Frau und ihre Bedeutung für den Kulturfortschritt.* Stuttgart: Enke, 1909.

Siegert, Wilhelm. *Die Naturheilkunde in ihren Anwendungsformen und Wirkungen.* 6th ed. 1899; reprint, Heidelberg: Arkana, 1985.

Sigaud, Claude. *Les Origines de la Maladie.* Paris, 1906.

Stratz, Carl Heinrich. *Die Körperpflege der Frau: Physiologische und ästhetische Diätetik für das weibliche Geschlecht.* 5th ed. Stuttgart: Enke, 1918.

———. *Die Körperformen in Kunst und Leben der Japaner.* Stuttgart: Enke, 1904.

———. *Die Rassenschönheit des Weibes.* 5th ed. Stuttgart: Enke, 1904.

———. *Was sind Juden? Eine ethnographisch-anthropologische Studie.* Vienna: F. Tempsky, 1903.

———. *Die Schönheit des weiblichen Körpers.* 2d ed. Stuttgart: Enke, 1899.

———. *Die Frauen auf Java: Eine gynäkologische Studie.* Stuttgart: Enke, 1897.

Surén, Hans. *Surén-Atemgymnastik: Die Schule der Atmung für Körper und Geist für alle Leibesübungen und Berufe.* 36th ed. Stuttgart: Dieck, 1929.

———. *Deutsche Gymnastik: Vorbereitende Übungen für den Sport, Frottierübungen, Atemgymnastik, Massage, Körperpflege, Verhalten im Licht-, Luft-, und Sonnenbade,* 40th ed. Oldenburg: Stalling, 1925.

———. *Der Mensch und die Sonne.* 19th ed. Stutgart: Dieck, 1924.

———. *Gymnastik im Bild: Körperschulung durch Gymnastik: Fünf Lehrtafeln für alle.* 4th ed. Stuttgart: Dieck, 1923.

Thiele, Adolf. *Arbeitshygiene, Arbeiterschutz.* 2d ed. Dresden: Deutscher Verein für Volkswohlfahrt, 1929.

Tränkner, Osmar. "Die Schönheitspflege vom hygienischen Standpunkt." In *Neue Heilmethode,* ed. Platen, 4:333–88.

Ungewitter, Richard. *Aus Judenknechtschaft zur Freiheit empor: Rettung oder Untergang des deutschen Volkes.* Stuttgart: Ungewitter, 1923.

———. *Nackt: Eine kritische Studie.* 1908; reprint, Stuttgart: Ungewitter, 1921.

———. *Die Nacktheit in entwicklungsgeschichtlicher, gesundheitlicher, moralischer und künstlerischer Beleuchtung.* 1905; reprint, Stuttgart: Ungewitter, 1920.

———. *Nacktheit und Kultur.* 2d ed. Stuttgart: Ungewitter, 1913.

———. *Diätetische Ketzereien: Die Eiweisstheorie mit ihren Folgen, als Krankheitsursache, und ihre wissenschaftlich begründete Verabschiedung.* Stuttgart: Ungewitter, 1908.

Vierath, Willy. "Die Physiognomik und ihre Bedeutung für die Erkennung von Krankheiten." In *Neue Heilmethode,* ed. Platen, 3:793–806.

———. "Die Körperformenkunde als Hilfsmittel zur Erkennung von Krankheiten und Krankheitsanlagen." In *Neue Heilmethode,* ed. Platen, 3:814–36.

Vogel, Martin. *Hygienische Volksbildung.* Berlin: Springer, 1925.

———. "Das Deutsche Hygienemuseum auf der Gesolei." In *GE-SO-LEI,* ed. Schloßmann and Fraenkel, 449–74.

Vogel, Martin, ed. *Der Mensch: Vom Werden und Wirken des menschlichen Organismus.* Leipzig: Barth, 1930.

Vogel, Martin, and Rudolf Neubert. *Grundzüge der Alkoholfrage.* Dresden: Deutscher Verlag für Volkswohlfahrt, 1926.

Weininger, Otto. *Geschlecht und Charakter.* Leipzig: Braumüller, 1903.

Weiß, Julius. "Das Gefühlsleben des Weibes." In *Mann und Weib,* ed. Koßmann and Weiß, vol. 1, pt. 2, 288–302.

———. "Die Schönheit des Weibes." In *Mann und Weib,* ed. Koßmann and Weiß, vol. 1, pt. 2, 46–76.

Wendenburg, Friedrich. *Gesunde Schönheitspflege.* Dresden: Deutscher Verlag für Volkswohlfahrt, 1927.

Wolf, Friedrich. *Die Natur als Arzt und Helfer.* Berlin: Deutsche Verlags-Anstalt, 1928.

Zahn, Friedrich. "Berufstätigkeit und Ehe." In *Mann und Weib,* ed. Koßmann and Weiß, 2:212–50.

Zeising, Adolf. *Neue Lehre von den Proportionen des menschlichen Körpers.* Leipzig: Weigel, 1854.

SECONDARY LITERATURE

Abrams, Lynn. *Workers' Culture in Imperial Germany: Leisure and Recreation in the Rhineland and Westphalia.* London: Routledge, 1992.

———. "Prostitutes in Imperial Germany, 1870–1918: Working Girls and Social Outcasts." In *Deviants and Outcasts in Imperial Germany,* ed. Evans, 189–209.

Adams, Carole Elizabeth. *Women Clerks in Wilhelmine Germany: Issues of Class and Gender.* Cambridge: Cambridge University Press, 1988.

Adams, Mark B. *The Wellborn Science: Eugenics in Germany, France, Brazil, and Russia.* New York: Oxford University Press, 1990.

Albisetti, James C. *Schooling German Girls and Women: Secondary and Higher Education in the Nineteenth Century.* Princeton: Princeton University Press, 1988.

Alkemeyer, Thomas. *Körper, Kult und Politik: Von der Muskelreligion Pierre de Coubertins zur Inszenierung von Macht in den Olympischen Spielen von 1936.* Frankfurt: Campus, 1996.

———. "Politik mit dem Körper: Zur Aesthetik physischer Vollkommenheit in der öffentlichen-repräsentativen Szene des 'Dritten Reiches.'" In *Sportstadt Berlin in Geschichte und Gegenwart,* ed. Sportmuseum Berlin, 146–59.

Allen, Ann Taylor. "Feminism, Venereal Diseases, and the State in Germany, 1890–1918." *Journal of the History of Sexuality* 4 (1993): 27–50.

———. *Feminism and Motherhood in Germany, 1800–1914.* New Brunswick: Rutgers University Press, 1991.

———. "German Radical Feminism and Eugenics, 1900–1908." *German Studies Review* 11 (1988): 31–56.

Amrine, Frederick, Francis J. Zucker, and Harvey Wheeler, eds. *Goethe and the Sciences: A Reappraisal.* Dordrecht: Reidel, 1987.

Andritzky, Michael. "Berlin—Urheimat der Nackten: Die Fkk-Bewegung in den zwanziger Jahren." In *"Wir sind nackt,"* ed. Andritzky and Rautenberger, 50–57.

Andritzky, Michael, and Thomas Rautenberger, eds. *"Wir sind nackt und nennen uns Du": Von Lichtfreunden und Sonnenkämpfern: Eine Geschichte der Freikörperkultur.* Gießen: Anabas, 1989.

Ankum, Katharina von, ed. *Women in the Metropolis: Gender and Modernity in Weimar Culture.* Berkeley: University of California Press, 1997.

Ash, Mithell G. *Gestalt Psychology in German Culture, 1890–1967: Holism and the Quest for Objectivity.* Cambridge: Cambridge University Press, 1995.

———. "Gestalt Psychology in Weimar Culture." *History of the Human Sciences* 4 (1991): 395–415.

Bakhtin, Mikhail. *The Dialogic Imagination,* ed. Michael Holquist and Caryl Emerson. Austin: University of Texas Press, 1981.

Barlösius, Eva. *Naturgemäße Lebensweise: Zur Geschichte der Lebensreform um die Jahrhundertwende.* Frankfurt: Campus, 1997.

Barron, Stephanie, ed. *"Degenerate Art": The Fate of the Avantgarde in Nazi Germany.* New York: Abrams, 1991.

———. "1937. Modern Arts and Politics in Prewar Germany." In *"Degenerate Art,"* ed. Barron, 9–23.

Baumgartner, Judith. *Ernährungsreform—Antwort auf Industrialisierung und Ernährungswandel. Ernährungsreform als Teil der Lebensreformbewegung am Beispiel der Siedlung und des Unternehmens Eden seit 1893.* Frankfurt: Lang, 1992.

Berding, Helmut. *Moderner Antisemitismus in Deutschland.* Frankfurt: Suhrkamp, 1988.

Bergmann, Anna. *Die verhütete Sexualität: Die medizinische Bemächtigung des Lebens.* Berlin: Aufbau, 1998.

Berkowitz, Michael. *Zionist Culture and West European Jewry Before the First World War.* Cambridge: Cambridge University Press, 1993.

Bessel, Richard, ed. *Fascist Italy and Nazi Germany: Comparisons and Contrasts.* Cambridge: Cambridge University Press, 1996.

———. *Germany After the First World War.* Oxford: Oxford University Press, 1993.

Blackbourn, David. *The Long Nineteenth Century: A History of Germany, 1780–1918.* Oxford: Oxford University Press, 1998.

———. *Marpingen: Apparitions of the Virgin Mary in Bismarckian Germany.* Oxford: Clarendon, 1995.

———. "Handwerker im Kaiserreich: Gewinner oder Verlierer?" In *Prekäre Selbständigkeit,* ed. Wengenroth, 7–21.

Blackbourn, David, and Richard Evans, eds. *The German Bourgeoisie. Essays on the Social History of the German Middle Classes from the Late Eighteenth to the Early Twentieth Century.* London: Routledge, 1991.

Bleker, Johanna. "Die ersten Ärztinnen und ihre Gesundheitsbücher für Frauen." In *Weibliche Ärzte,* ed. Brinkschulte, 65–83.

———. *Medizin im "Dritten Reich."* 2d ed. Cologne: Deutscher Ärzte-Verlag, 1993.

Bönisch, Michael. "Die 'Hammer-Bewegung.'" In *Handbuch zur "Völkischen Bewegung,"* ed. Puschner et al., 341–65.

Bonde, Hans. "I. P. Muller: Danish Apostle of Health." *International Journal of the History of Sport* 8 (1991): 346–69.

Borck, Cornelius. "Electricity as the Medium of Psychic Life: Psychotechnics, the Radio, and the Electroencephalogram in Weimar Germany." Berlin: Max Planck Institute for the History of Science, Preprint 154 (2000).

Borrmann, Norbert. *Paul Schultze-Naumburg, 1869–1949: Maler, Publizist, Architekt. Vom Kultureformer der Jahrhundertwende zum Kulturpolitiker im Dritten Reich.* Essen: Bacht, 1989.

Bothe, Detlef. *Neue Deutsche Heilkunde, 1933–1945.* Husum: Matthiesen, 1991.

Bourdieu, Pierre. *Language and Symbolic Power.* Cambridge: Harvard University Press, 1991.

———. *Distinction: A Social Critique of the Judgment of Taste.* Cambridge: Harvard University Press, 1984.

Brandt, Allen M. *No Magic Bullet: A Social History of Venereal Disease in the United States Since 1880,* 2d. ed. Oxford: Oxford University Press, 1987.

Brecht, Christiane. "Das Publikum belehren—Wissenschaft zelebrieren: Bakterien in der Ausstellung 'Volkskrankheiten und ihre Bekämpfung' von 1903." In *Strategien der Kausalität,* ed. Gradmann and Schlich, 53–76.

Bridenthal, Renate, Atina Grossmann, and Marion Kaplan, eds. *When Biology Became Destiny: Women in Weimar and Nazi Germany.* New York: Monthly Review Press, 1984.

Brinkschulte, Eva. *Weibliche Ärzte: Die Durchsetzung des Berufsbildes in Deutschland.* Berlin: Hentrich, 1994.

Bruch, Rüdiger vom. "Kunst und Kulturkritik in führenden bildungsbürgerlichen Zeitschriften des Kaiserreichs." In *Ideengeschichte und Kunstwissenschaft,* ed. Mai et al., 313–47.

Bruckner, Sierra Ann. "The Tingle-Tangle of Modernity: Popular Anthropology and the Cultural Politics of Identity in Imperial Germany." Ph.D. diss., University of Iowa, 1999.

Büchi, Walter A. "Schloßherr ohne Adelstitel—Lingner die Exzellenz." In *In Aller Munde,* ed. Roth et al., 73–83.

Burleigh, Michael, and Wolfgang Wippermann. *The Racial State: Germany, 1933–1945.* Cambridge: Cambridge University Press, 1991.

Campbell, Joan. *Joy in Work, German Work: The National Debate, 1800–1945.* Princeton: Princeton University Press, 1989.

Cancik, Hubert, ed. *Religions- und Geistesgeschichte der Weimarer Republik.* Düsseldorf: Patmos, 1982.

Carter, K. Codell. "The Emergence of Pasteur's Concept of Disease Causation and the Emergence of Specific Causes in Nineteenth Century Medicine." *Bulletin of the History of Medicine* 65 (1991): 528–48.

———. "Koch's Postulates in Relation to the Work of Jacob Henle and Edwin Klebs." *Medical History* 29 (1985): 353–74.

Chickering, Roger, ed. *Imperial Germany: A Historiographical Companion.* Westport: Greenwood, 1996.

Childers, Thomas. "The Middle Classes and National Socialism." In *German Bourgeoisie,* ed. Blackbourn and Evans, 318–37.

———. "The Social Language of Politics in Germany: The Sociology of Political Discourse in the Weimar Republic." *American Historical Review* 95 (1990): 331–58.

Conrad, Peter. "Medicalization and Social Control." *Annual Review of Sociology* 18 (1992): 209–32.

Conze, Werner, ed. *Sozialgeschichte der Familie in der Neuzeit Europas.* Stuttgart: Klett, 1976.

Crenshaw, Kimberlé. "Beyond Racism and Misogyny: Black Feminism and 2 Live Crew." In *Words That Wound,* ed. Matsuda and Crenshaw, 111–32.

Crew, David. "The Ambiguities of Modernity: Welfare and the German State from Wilhelm to Hitler." In *Society, Culture, and the State,* ed. Eley, 319–44.

Cunningham, Andrew. "Transforming Plague: The Laboratory and the Identity of Infectious Disease." In *Laboratory Revolution,* ed. Cunningham and Williams, 209–44.

Cunningham, Andrew, and Perry Williams, eds. *The Laboratory Revolution in Medicine.* Cambridge: Cambridge University Press, 1992.

Daum, Andreas W. *Wissenschaftspopularisierung im 19. Jahrhundert: Bürgerliche Kultur, naturwissenschaftliche Bildung und die deutsche Öffentlichkeit, 1848–1914.* Munich: Oldenbourg, 1998.

Davis, Belinda. "Reconsidering Habermas, Gender, and the Public Sphere: The Case of Wilhelmine Germany." In *Society, Culture, and the State,* ed. Eley, 397–426.

Dierker, Herbert. *Arbeitersport im Spannungsfeld der Zwanziger Jahre: Sportpolitik und Alltagserfahrungen auf internationaler, deutscher und Berliner Ebene.* Essen: Klartext, 1990.

Dijkstra, Bram. *Idols of Perversity: Fantasies of Feminine Evil in Fin de Siècle Culture.* Oxford: Oxford University Press, 1986.

Dörter, Michael. "Die Naturheilbewegung in Deutschland zur Zeit der Weimarer Republik." Diss., Leipzig University, 1991.

Eder, Ernst Gerhard. "Sonnenanbeter und Wasserratten: Körperkultur und Freiluftbadebewegung in Wiens Donaulandschaft 1900–1939." *Archiv für Sozialgeschichte* 33 (1993): 245–74.

Eisenberg, Christiane. *"English Sports" und deutsche Bürger: Eine Gesellschaftsgeschichte.* Paderborn: Schöningh, 1999.

———. "Massensport in der Weimarer Republik: Ein statistischer Überblick." *Archiv für Sozialgeschichte* 33 (1993): 137–77.

Eksteins, Modris. *Rites of Spring: The Great War and the Birth of the Modern Age.* Boston: Houghton, 1989.

Eley, Geoff, ed. *Society, Culture, and the State in Germany, 1870–1930.* Ann Arbor: University of Michigan Press, 1997.

———. *Reshaping the German Right: Radical Nationalism and Political Change After Bismarck.* 1980; reprint, Ann Arbor: University of Michigan Press, 1991.

Engelhardt, Dietrich von. "Kausalität und Konditionalität in der modernen Medizin." In *Pathogenese,* ed. Schipperges, 31–58.

Essner, Cornelia. "Die Alchemie des Rassenbegriffs und die Nürnberger Gesetze." *Jahrbuch für Antisemitismusforschung* 4 (1995): 201–21.

———. " 'Im Irrgarten der Rassenlogik' oder nordische Rassenlehre und nationale Frage (1919–1935)." *Historische Mitteilungen* 7 (1994): 81–101.

Evans, Richard J. *Death in Hamburg: Society and Politics in the Cholera Years, 1830–1910.* Oxford: Penguin, 1990.

———. *The Feminist Movement in Germany, 1894–1933.* London: Sage, 1976.

———, ed. *Deviants and Outcasts in German History.* London: Routledge, 1988.

Fasbender, Sebastian. "Zwischen Arbeitersport und Arbeitssport: Werksport an Rhein und Ruhr, 1921–1938." Ph.D. diss., University of Göttingen, 1997.

Feldman, Gerald. *The Great Disorder: Politics, Economics, and Society in the German Inflation, 1914–1924.* Oxford: Oxford University Press, 1993.

Field, Geoffrey G. *Evangelist of Race: The Germanic Vision of Houston Stewart Chamberlain.* New York: Columbia University Press, 1981.

Fischer-Homberger, Esther. "Krankheit Frau." In *Leib und Leben,* ed. Imhof, 215–29.

———. *The Birth of the Clinic: An Archaeology of Medical Perception,* New York: Vintage, 1973.

Fout, John C. "Sexual Politics in Wilhelmine Germany: The Male Gender Crisis, Moral Purity, and Homophobia." *Journal of the History of Sexuality* 2 (1992): 388–421.

Frame, Lynn. "Gretchen, Girl, Garçonne? Weimar Science and Popular Culture in Search of the Ideal New Woman." In *Women in the Metropolis,* ed. Ankum, 12–40.

Frecot, Janos. "Die Schönheit: Mit Bildern geschmückte Zeitschrift für Kunst und Leben." *Fotogeschichte* 15 (1995): 37–46.

———. "Die Lebensreformbewegung." In *Das wilhelminische Bildungsbürgertum*, ed. Vondung, 138–52.

———, Johann Friedrich Geist, and Diethardt Kerbs. *Fidus, 1868–1948: Zur ästhetischen Praxis bürgerlicher Fluchtbewegungen*. Munich: Rogner & Bernhard, 1972.

Frevert, Ute. *Ehrenmänner: Das Duell in der bürgerlichen Gesellschaft*. Munich: dtv, 1995.

———. *Frauen-Geschichte: Zwischen bürgerlicher Verbesserung und neuer Weiblichkeit*. Frankfurt: Suhrkamp, 1986.

———. *Krankheit als politisches Problem, 1770–1880: Soziale Unterschichten in Preussen zwischen medizinischer Polizei und staatlicher Sozialversicherung*. Göttingen: Vandenhoek & Ruprecht, 1984.

———, ed. *Bürgerinnen und Bürger: Geschlechterverhältnisse im 19. Jahrhundert*. Göttingen: Vandenhoek & Ruprecht, 1988.

Frey, Manuel. *Der reinliche Bürger: Entstehung und Verbreitung bürgerlicher Tugenden in Deutschland, 1760–1860*. Göttingen: Vandenhoek & Ruprecht, 1997.

Friedländer, Saul. *Nazi Germany and the Jews: The Years of Persecution, 1933–1939*. New York: HarperCollins, 1997.

Fuhs, Burkhard. *Mondäne Orte einer vornehmen Gesellschaft: Kultur und Geschichte der Kurstädte*. Hildesheim: Olms, 1992.

Ganslmeyr, Herbert. "Ernst Carl Gustav Grosse," in *Neue Deutsche Biographie* 7, 148–49.

Genschorek, Wolfgang. *Carl Gustav Carus: Arzt, Künstler, Naturforscher*. Leipzig: Hirzel, 1978.

Gerhard, Ute. *Unerhört: Die Geschichte der deutschen Frauenbewegung*. Reinbek bei Hamburg: Rowohlt, 1990.

Geyer, Martin H. *Verkehrte Welt: Revolution, Inflation und Moderne, München, 1914–1924*. Göttingen: Vandenhoek & Ruprecht, 1999.

Geyer-Kordesch, Johanna, and Annette Kuhn, eds. *Frauenkörper—Medizin—Sexualität: Auf dem Wege zu einer neuen Sexualmoral*. Düsseldorf: Schwann, 1986.

Giddens, Anthony. *Modernity and Self-Identity: Self and Society in the Late Modern Age*. Stanford: Stanford University Press, 1991.

Gilman, Sander. *Making the Body Beautiful: A Cultural History of Aesthetic Surgery*. Princeton: Princeton University Press, 1999.

———. *The Case of Sigmund Freud: Medicine and Identity at the Fin de Siècle*. Baltimore: Johns Hopkins University Press, 1993.

———. *Freud, Race, and Gender*. Princeton: Princeton University Press, 1993.

———. *The Jew's Body*. New York: Routledge, 1991.

———. *Disease and Representation: Images of Illness from Madness to AIDS*. Ithaca: Cornell University Press, 1988.

Gilman, Sander, and Claudia Schmölders, eds. *Gesichter der Weimarer Republik*. Cologne: Dumont, 2000.

Göckenjan, Gerd. "Medizin und Ärzte als Faktor der Disziplinierung der Unterschichten: Der Kassenarzt." In *Soziale Sicherheit und soziale Disziplinierung*, ed. Sachsse and Tennstedt, 286–303.

Goffmann, Erving. *The Presentation of Self in Everyday Life*. Garden City, N.Y.: Doubleday, 1959.

Goltermann, Svenja. *Körper der Nation: Habitusformierung und die Politik des Turnens, 1860–1890*. Göttingen: Vandenhoeck & Ruprecht, 1998.

Gradmann, Christoph, and Thomas Schlich, eds. *Strategien der Kausalität: Modelle und Institutionen ätiologischen Denkens in Medizin und Naturwissenschaft im 19. und 20. Jahrhundert.* Pfaffenweiler: Centaurus, 1999.

Graumann, Carl Friedrich, ed. *Psychologie im Nationalsozialismus.* Berlin: Springer, 1985.

Greven-Aschoff, Barbara. *Die bürgerliche Frauenbewegung in Deutschland, 1894–1933.* Göttingen: Vandenhoek & Ruprecht, 1981.

Grossmann, Atina. *Reforming Sex: The German Movement for Birth Control and Abortion Reform, 1920–1950.* Oxford: Oxford University Press, 1995.

Haeberle, Erwin J. "Der verbotene Akt: Unzüchtige Fotos von 1850 bis 1950." In *Das Aktfoto,* ed. Köhler and Barche, 212–24.

Hagner, Michael. "Verwundete Gesichter, verletzte Gehirne: Zur Deformation des Kopfes im Ersten Weltkrieg." In *Gesichter der Weimarer Republik,* ed. Gilman and Schmölders, 78–95.

Haltern, Utz. "Die Gesellschaft der Bürger." *Geschichte und Gesellschaft* 19 (1993): 100–134.

Hammerstein, Notker. *Antisemitismus und deutsche Universitäten, 1871–1933.* Frankfurt: Campus, 1995.

Harrington, Anne. *Reenchanted Science: Holism in German Culture from Wilhelm II to Hitler.* Princeton: Princeton University Press, 1996.

———. "Interwar 'German' Psychobiology: Between Nationalism and the Irrational." *Science in Context* 4 (1991): 429–47.

Hart, Mitchell B. "Racial Science, Social Science, and the Politics of Jewish Assimilation." *Isis* 90 (1999): 268–97.

Harwood, Jonathan. *Styles of Scientific Thought: The German Genetics Community.* Chicago: University of Chicago Press, 1993.

Hau, Michael. "The Holistic Gaze in German Medicine, 1890–1930." *Bulletin of the History of Medicine* 74 (2000), 495–524.

———. "Gender and Aesthetic Norms in Popular Hygienic Culture in Germany from 1900 to 1914." *Social History of Medicine* 12 (1999): 271–92.

Hau, Michael, and Mitchell G. Ash. "Der normale Körper, seelisch erblickt." In *Gesichter der Weimarer Republik,* ed. Gilman and Schmölders, 12–31.

Haug, Alfred. *Die Reichsarbeitsgemeinschaft für eine Neue Deutsche Heilkunde, 1935/1936.* Husum: Matthiesen, 1985.

Haug, Wolfgang F. *Die Faschisierung des bürgerlichen Subjects: Die Ideologie der gesunden Normalität und die Ausrottungspolitiken im deutschen Faschismus.* Berlin: Argument-Verlag, 1985.

Haupt, Heinz-Gerhard. "Männliche und weibliche Berufskarrieren im deutschen Bürgertum in der zweiten Hälfte des 19. Jahrhunderts: Zum Verhältnis von Klasse und Geschlecht." *Geschichte und Gesellschaft* 18 (1992): 143–60.

Hausen, Karin. "Die Polarisierung der 'Geschlechtscharaktere': Eine Spiegelung der Dissoziation von Erwerbs- und Familienleben." In *Sozialgeschichte der Familie,* ed. Conze, 363–93.

Heidel, Günther. "Die I. Internationale Hygieneausstellung in Dresden und die Gründung des deutschen Hygienemuseums." *Zeitschrift für die gesamte Hygiene* 33 (1987): 411–15.

Heineman, Elisabeth, "Gender Idenity in the Wandervogel Movement." *German Studies Review* 12 (1989): 249–70.

Herrmann, Bernd. "Zur Entstehung und Wirkung aesthetischer Prinzipien in der menschlichen Rassenkunde." In *Leib und Leben,* ed. Imhof, 165–75.

Herrmann, Bernhard. *Arbeiterschaft, Naturheilkunde und der Verband Volksgesundheit (1880–1918)*. Frankfurt: Lang, 1990.

Höpfner, Felix. *Wissenschaft wider die Zeit: Goethes Farbenlehre aus rezeptionsgeschichtlicher Sicht*. Heidelberg: Winter, 1990.

Hoffmann-Curtius, Kathrin. "Die Kampagne 'Entartete Kunst': Die Nationalsozialisten und die moderne Kunst." In *Modene Kunst*, ed. M. Wagner, 467–90.

Hohorst, Gerd, Jürgen Kocka, and Gerhard A. Ritter, eds. *Sozialgeschichtliches Arbeitsbuch: Materialien zur Statistik des Kaiserreichs, 1870–1914*. Munich: Beck, 1975.

Holz, Friedbert. "Ludwig Klages," in *Neue Deutsche Biographie* 11, 700–702.

Hong, Young-Son. *Welfare, Modernity, and the Weimar State, 1919–1933*. Princeton: Princeton University Press, 1998.

Hopwood, Nick. "Producing a Socialist Popular Science in the Weimar Republic." *History Workshop Journal* 41 (1996): 117–53.

Hoßfeld, Uwe. "Die Jenaer Jahre des 'Rasse-Günther' von 1930–1935: Zur Gründung des Lehrstuhls für Sozialanthropologie an der Universität Jena." *Medizinhistorisches Journal* 34 (1999): 47–103.

Hubbard, Ruth. *The Politics of Women's Biology*. New Brunswick: Rutgers University Press, 1990.

Hubenstorf, Michael. "Von der 'freien Arztwahl' zur Reichsärzteordnung: Ärztliche Standespolitik zwischen Liberalismus und Nationalsozialismus." In *Medizin im "Dritten Reich*," ed. Bleker, 43–53.

———. "Die Genese der sozialen Medizin als universitäres Lehrfach in Österreich: Ein Beitrag zum Problem der Disziplinbildung und wissenschaftlichen Innovation." Diss., Free University of Berlin, 1992.

Huerkamp, Claudia. "Ärzte und Patienten: Zum strukturellen Wandel der Arzt-Patient-Beziehung vom ausgehenden 18. bis zum frühen 20. Jahrhundert." In *Medizinische Deutungsmacht im sozialen Wandel*, ed. Labisch and Spree, 57–73.

———. "Frauen, Universitäten, Bildungsbürgertum: Zur Lage studierender Frauen 1900–1930." In *Bürgerliche Berufe*, ed. Siegrist, 200–222.

———. "Medizinische Lebensreform im späten 19. Jahrhundert: Die Naturheilbewegung in Deutschland als Protest gegen die naturwissenschaftliche Universitätsmedizin." *Vierteljahresschrift für Sozial- und Wirtschaftsgeschichte* 73 (1986): 158–82.

———. *Der Aufstieg der Ärzte im 19. Jahrhundert*. Göttingen: Vandenhoek & Ruprecht, 1985.

———. "The History of Smallpox Vaccination in Germany: A First Step in Medicalization of the General Public." *Journal of Contemporary History* 20 (1985): 617–35.

Imhof, Artur E., ed. *Leib und Leben in der Geschichte der Neuzeit*. Berlin: Duncker & Humblot, 1983.

Jarausch, Konrad H. "Die Krise des deutschen Bildungsbürgertums im ersten Drittel des 20. Jahrhunderts." In *Bildungsbürgertum im 19. Jahrhundert*, ed. Kocka, 180–205.

———. *Deutsche Studenten, 1800–1970*. Frankfurt: Suhrkamp, 1984.

———. *Students, Society, and Politics in Imperial Germany: The Rise of Academic Illiberalism*. Princeton: Princeton University Press, 1982.

Jasper, Gotthard. *Die gescheiterte Zähmung: Wege zur Machtergreifung Hitlers*. Frankfurt: Suhrkamp, 1986.

Jenkins, Jennifer. "The Kitsch Collection and the 'Spirit of the Furniture': Cultural Reform and National Culture in Germany." *Social History* 21 (1996): 123–41.

Jütte, Robert. *Geschichte der alternativen Medizin: Von der Volksmedizin zu den unkonventionellen Therapien von heute.* Munich: Beck, 1996.

Kampe, Norbert. *Studenten und "Judenfrage" im Deutschen Kaiserreich: Die Entstehung einer akademischen Trägerschicht des Antisemitismus.* Göttingen: Vandenhoek & Ruprecht, 1988.

Kaplan, Marion A. *The Making of the Jewish Middle Class: Women, Family, and Identity in Imperial Germany.* Oxford: Oxford University Press, 1991.

Kater, Michael. "Die Medizin im nationalsozialistischen Deutschland und Erwin Liek." *Geschichte und Gesellschaft* 16 (1990): 440–63.

———. *Doctors Under Hitler.* Chapel Hill: University of North Carolina Press, 1989.

———. *Studentenschaft und Rechtsradikalismus in Deutschland, 1918–1933.* Hamburg: Hoffmann & Campe, 1975.

Kerbs, Diethart, and Jürgen Reulecke, eds. *Handbuch der deutschen Reformbewegungen, 1880–1933.* Wuppertal: Hammer, 1998.

Kiefer, Annegret. *Das Problem einer jüdischen Rasse: Eine Diskussion zwischen Wissenschaft und Ideologie.* Frankfurt: Lang, 1991.

Klasen, Eva Maria. "Die Diskussion über eine Krise der Medizin in Deutschland zwischen 1925 und 1935." Diss., Mainz University, 1984.

Kloos, Gerhard. *Die Konstitutionslehre von Karl Gustav Carus mit besonderer Berücksichtigung der Physiognomik.* Basel: Karger, 1951.

Kocka, Jürgen. *Bildungsbürgertum im 19. Jahrhundert,* vol. 4: *Politischer Einfluss und gesellschaftliche Formation.* Stuttgart: Klett-Cotta, 1989.

———. "Bürgertum und bürgerliche Gesellschaft im 19. Jahrhundert: Europäische Entwicklungen und deutsche Eigenarten." In *Bürgertum im 19. Jahrhundert,* ed. Kocka, 1:11–76.

———. "Bürgertum und Bürgerlichkeit als Probleme der deutschen Geschichte vom späten 18. zum frühen 19. Jahrhundert." In *Bürger und Bürgerlichkeit im 19. Jahrhundert,* ed. Kocka, 21–63.

———. *Die Angestellten in der deutschen Geschichte, 1850–1890.* Göttingen: Vandenhoek & Ruprecht, 1981.

———, ed. *Bürgertum im 19 Jahrhundert: Deutschland im europäischen Vergleich.* Munich: dtv, 1988.

———. *Bürger und Bürgerlichkeit im 19. Jahrhundert.* Göttingen: Vandenhoek & Ruprecht, 1987.

Köhler, Michael. "Pikanterien, Pinups & Playmates: Zur Ästhetik und Geschichte des 'erotischen' Aktfotos." In *Das Aktfoto,* ed. Köhler and Barche, 245–52.

Köhler, Michael, and Gisela Barche, eds. *Das Aktfoto: Ansichten vom Körper im fotografischen Zeitalter.* Munich: Bucher, 1985.

König, Oliver. *Nacktheit: Soziale Normierung und Moral.* Opladen: Westdeutscher, 1990.

Konieczka, Vera. "Arten zu sprechen, Arten zu schweigen. Sozialdemokratie und Prostitution im deutschen Kaiserreich." In *Frauenkörper,* ed. Geyer-Kordesch and Kuhn, 102–26.

Krabbe, Wolfgang R. "'Die Weltanschauung der deutschen Lebensreformbewegung ist der Nationalsozialismus': Zur Gleichschaltung einer Alternativströmung im Dritten Reich." *Archiv für Kulturgeschichte* 71 (1989): 431–61.

————. *Gesellschaftsveränderung durch Lebensreform: Strukturmerkmale einer sozialreformerischen Bewegung im Deutschland der Industrialisierungsperiode.* Göttingen: Vandenhoek & Ruprecht, 1974.

Krammer, Reinhard. "Der ASKÖ und die Wiener Arbeiterolympiade 1931." In *Illustrierte Geschichte des Arbeitersports*, ed. Teichler and Hauk, 207‑31.

Kratzsch, Gerhard "'Der Kunstwart' und die bürgerlich-soziale Bewegung." In *Ideengeschichte und Kunstwissenschaft*, ed. Mai et al. 371–96.

Krüger, Arnd. "There Goes This Art of Manliness: Naturalism and Racial Hygiene in Germany." *Journal of Sport History* 18 (1991): 135–58.

————. "The German Way of Worker Sport." In *Story of Worker Sport*, ed. Krüger and Riordan, 1–25.

Krüger, Arnd, and James Riordan, eds. *The Story of Worker Sport.* Champaign: Human Kinetics, 1996.

Krüger, Michael. *Körperkultur und Nationsbildung: Die Geschichte des Turnens in der Reichsgründungsära—eine Detailstudie über die Deutschen.* Schorndorf: Hofmann, 1996.

Labisch, Alfons. "'Hygiene ist Moral—Moral ist Hygiene': Soziale Disziplinierung durch Ärzte und Medizin." In *Soziale Sicherheit und soziale Disziplinierung*, ed. Sachsse and Tennstedt, 265–85.

————. "Homo Hygienicus: Soziale Konstruktion von Gesundheit." In *Medizin: Momente der Veränderung*, ed. F. Wagner, 115–38.

Labisch, Alfons, and Reinhard Spree, eds. *Medizinische Deutungsmacht im sozialen Wandel des 19. und frühen 20. Jahrhunderts.* Bonn: Psychiatrie-Verlag, 1989.

Lachmund, Jens. *Der abgehorchte Körper: Zur historischen Soziologie der medizinischen Untersuchung.* Opladen: Leske & Budrich, 1997.

Lachmund, Jens, and Gunnar Stollberg. *Patientenwelten: Krankheit und Medizin vom späten 18. bis zum frühen 20. Jahrhundert im Spiegel von Autobiographien.* Opladen: Leske & Budrich, 1995.

Langewiesche, Dieter. "Bildungsbürgertum und Liberalismus im 19. Jahrhundert." In *Bildungsbürgertum im 19. Jahrhundert*, ed. Kocka, 95–113.

————. *Liberalismus in Deutschland.* Frankfurt: Suhrkamp, 1988.

————. "The Impact of the German Labour Movement on Workers' Culture." *Journal of Modern History* 59 (1987): 506–23.

Laqueur, Thomas. *Making Sex: Body and Gender from the Greeks to Freud.* Cambridge: Harvard University Press, 1990.

Lawrence, Christopher, and George Weisz. *Greater Than the Parts: Holism in Biomedicine, 1920–1950.* Oxford: Oxford University Press, 1998.

Lenman, Robin. *Die Kunst, die Macht und das Geld: Zur Kulturgeschichte des kaiserlichen Deutschland 1871–1981.* Frankfurt: Campus, 1994.

Lenoir, Timothy. "The Eternal Laws of Form: Morphotypes and the Conditions of Existence in Goethe's Biological Thought." In *Goethe and the Sciences*, ed. Amrine et al., 17‑28.

Leonardo, Micaela di, ed. *Gender at the Crossroads of Knowledge: Feminist Anthropology in the Postmodern Era.* Berkeley: University of California Press, 1991.

Lichtsinn, Hilkea. *Otto Ammon und die Sozialanthropologie.* Frankfurt: Lang, 1987.

Lidtke, Vernon L. "The Socialist Labor Movement." In *Imperial Germany*, ed. Chickering, 272–302.

Lilienthal, Georg. "Die jüdischen 'Rassemerkmale': Zur Geschichte der Anthropologie der Juden." *Medizinhistorisches Journal* 28 (1993): 173–98.

Linse, Ulrich. "Zeitbild Jahrhundertwende." In *"Wir sind nackt,"* ed. Andritzky and Rautenberger, 10–26.

———. *Zurück o Mensch zur Mutter Erde: Landkommunen in Deutschland, 1890–1933.* Munich: dtv, 1983.

———. *Barfüßige Propheten: Erlöser der zwanziger Jahre.* Berlin: Siedler, 1983.

———. "Die Lebensreformbewegung." *Archiv für Sozialgeschichte* 17 (1977): 538–43.

Lösch, Nils. *Rasse als Konstrukt: Leben und Wirken Eugen Fischers.* Frankfurt: Lang, 1997.

Lüttichau, Mario-Andreas von. "Entartete Kunst, Munich 1937: A Reconstruction." In *"Degenerate Art,"* ed. Barron, 45–81.

Lutzhöft, Hans-Jürgen. *Der nordische Gedanke in Deutschland, 1920–1940.* Stuttgart: Klett, 1971.

Mai, Ekkehard, Stephan Waetzold, and Gerd Wolandt, eds. *Ideengeschichte und Kunstwissenschaft: Philosophie und bildende Kunst im Kaiserreich.* Berlin: Mann, 1983.

Makela, Maria M. *The Munich Secession: Art and Artists in Turn-of-the-Century Munich.* Princeton: Princeton University Press, 1990.

Mann, Gunter. "Biologismus—Vorstufen und Elemente einer Medizin im Nationalsozialismus." In *Medizin im "Dritten Reich,"* ed. Bleker, 25–35.

———, and Rolf Winau, eds. *Medizin, Naturwissenschaft, Technik und das zweite Kaiserreich.* Göttingen: Vandenhoek & Ruprecht, 1977.

———. "Biologie und der 'Neue Mensch': Denkstufen und Pläne zur Menschenzucht im zweiten Kaiserreich." In *Medizin, Naturwissenschaft,* ed. Mann and Winau, 172–88.

Manning, Susan A. *Ecstasy and the Demon: Feminism and Nationalism in the Dance of Mary Wigman.* Berkeley: University of California Press, 1993.

Marchand, Suzanne L. *Down from Olympus: Archaeology and Philhellenism in Germany, 1750–1970.* Princeton: Princeton University Press, 1996.

Marks, Sally. "Black Watch on the Rhine: A Study in Propaganda, Prejudice, and Prurience." *European Studies Review* 13 (1983): 297–334.

Massin, Benoit. "From Virchow to Fischer: Physical Anthropology and 'Modern Race Theories' in Wilhelmine Germany." In *Volksgeist as Method and Ethic,* ed. Stocking, 79–154.

———. "Anthropologie raciale et national-socialisme: Heurs et malheurs du paradigme de la 'race.'" In *La science sous le Troisième Reich,* ed. Olff-Nathan, 197–262.

Matsuda, Mai J., and Kimberlè Crenshaw, eds. *Words That Wound: Critical Race Theory, Assaultive Speech, and the First Amendment.* Boulder: Westview, 1993.

McAleer, Kevin. *Dueling: The Cult of Honor in Fin de Siècle Germany.* Princeton: Princeton University Press, 1994.

McClelland, Charles E. *The German Experience of Professionalization: Modern Learned Professions and Their Organizations from the Early 19th Century to the Hitler Era.* Cambridge: Cambridge University Press, 1991.

Mendelsohn, John Andrew. "Cultures of Bacteriology: Formation and Transformation of a Science in France and Germany, 1870–1914." Ph.D.diss., Princeton University, 1996.

Métraux, Alexandre. "Die angewandte Psychologie vor und nach 1933 in Deutschland." In *Psychologie im Nationalsozialismus,* ed. Graumann, 222–62.

Meyer-Renschhausen, Elisabeth. "Die weibliche Ehre: Ein Kapitel aus dem Kampf von Frauen gegen Polizei und Ärzte." In *Frauenkörper*, ed. Geyer-Kordesch and Kuhn, 80–101.

Mocek, Reinhard. "The Program of Proletarian Rassenhygiene." *Science in Context* 11 (1998): 609–17.

Mosse, George L. "Max Nordau, Liberalism, and the New Jew." *Journal of Contemporary History* 27 (1992): 565–81.

———. "Beauty Without Sensuality: The Exhibition 'Entartete Kunst.'" In *"Degenerate Art,"* ed. Barron, 25–31.

———. *Toward the Final Solution: A History of European Racism.* Madison: University of Wisconsin Press, 1985.

Müller, Martin A. "Turnen und Sport im sozialen Wandel: Körperkultur in Frankfurt am Main während des Kaiserreichs und der Weimarer Republic." *Archiv für Sozialgeschichte* 33 (1993): 107–36.

Nead, Lynda. *The Female Nude: Art, Obscenity, and Sexuality.* London: Routledge, 1992.

Nipperdey, Thomas. *Deutsche Geschichte, 1866–1918*, vol. 1, *Arbeitswelt und Bürgergeist.* Munich: Beck, 1990.

Nitsch, Franz. "'Wir erlebten wie Frieden sein kann': Die 1. Internationale Arbeiterolympiade 1925." In *Illustrierte Geschichte des Arbeitersports*, ed. Teichler and Hauk, 203–6.

Nolan, Mary. *Visions of Modernity: American Business and the Modernization of Germany.* Oxford: Oxford University Press, 1994.

Nyhart, Lynn K. *Biology Takes Form: Animal Morphology and the German Universities.* Chicago: University of Chicago Press, 1996.

Olff-Nathan, Josiane, ed. *La science sous le Troisième Reich: Victim ou Alliée du Nazisme?* Paris: Seuil, 1993.

Paret, Peter. *The Berlin Secession: Modernism and Its Enemies in Imperial Germany.* Cambridge: Harvard University Press, 1980.

Petro, Patrice. *Joyless Streets: Women and Melodramatic Representation in Weimar Germany.* Princeton: Princeton University Press, 1989.

Peukert, Detlef J. K. *The Weimar Republic: The Crisis of Classical Modernity.* New York: Hill & Wang, 1993.

Pfister, Gertrud. "The Medical Discourse on Female Physical Culture in Germany in the 19th and Early 20th. Centuries." *Journal of Sport History* 17 (1990): 183–98.

Pforte, Dietger. "Hans Suren—eine deutsche FKK-Karriere." In *"Wir sind nackt,"* ed. Andritzky and Rautenberger, 130–35.

———. "Zur Freikörperkultur-Bewegung im nationalsozialistischen Deutschland." In *"Wir sind nackt,"* ed. Andritzky and Rautenberger, 136–41.

Phillips, Denis C. *Holistic Thought in Social Science.* Stanford: Stanford University Press, 1976.

Planert, Ute. *Antifeminismus im Kaiserreich: Diskurs, soziale Formation und politische Mentalität.* Göttingen: Vandenhoeck & Ruprecht, 1998.

Poliakov, Leon. *The Aryan Myth: A History of Racist and Nationalist Ideas in Europe.* London: Chatto, Heinemann, 1974.

Price, Matthew. "Bodies and Souls: The Rehbilitation of Maimed Soldiers in Germany and France During the First World War." Ph.D. diss., Stanford University, 1998.

Proctor, Robert N. *The Nazi War on Cancer.* Princeton: Princeton University Press, 1999.

————. *Racial Hygiene: Medicine Under the Nazis.* Cambridge: Harvard University Press, 1988.

————. "From 'Anthropologie' to 'Rassenkunde' in the German Anthropological Tradition." In *Bones, Bodies, Behavior,* ed. Stocking, 138–79.

Puschner, Uwe, Walter Schmitz, and Justus H. Ulbricht, eds. *Handbuch zur "Völkischen Bewegung,"* *1871–1918.* Munich: Saur, 1996.

Quataert, Jean. *Reluctant Feminists in German Social Democracy, 1885–1917.* Princeton: Princeton University Press, 1979.

Rabinbach, Anson. *The Human Motor: Energy, Fatigue, and the Origins of Modernity.* New York: Basic, 1990.

Radkau, Joachim. *Das Zeitalter der Nervosität: Deutschland zwischen Bismarck und Hitler.* Munich: Hanser, 1998.

————. "Die wilhelminische Ära als nervöses Zeitalter, oder: Die Nerven als Netz zwischen Tempo- und Körpergeschichte." *Geschichte und Gesellschaft* 20 (1994): 211–41.

Ras, Marion E. P. de. *Körper, Eros und weibliche Kultur: Mädchen im Wandervogel und in der bündischen Jugend, 1900–1933.* Pfaffenweiler: Centaurus, 1988.

Reagin, Nancy R. " 'A True Woman Can Take Care of Herself ': The Debate on Prostitution in Hanover," *Central European History* 24 (1993): 347–80.

Regin, Cornelia. *Selbsthilfe und Gesundheitspolitik: Die Naturheilbewegung im Kaiserreich (1889–1914).* Stuttgart: Steiner, 1995.

————. "Naturheilkundige und Naturheilbewegung im Deutschen Kaiserreich." *Medizin, Gesellschaft, und Geschichte* 11 (1992): 175–200.

Reichel, Peter. *Der schöne Schein des Dritten Reiches: Faszination und Gewalt des Faschismus.* Frankfurt: Fischer, 1993.

Reiser, Stanley. *Medicine and the Reign of Technology.* Cambridge: Cambridge University Press, 1977.

Ringer, Fritz K. *The Decline of the German Mandarins: The German Academic Community, 1890–1933.* 1969; reprint, Hanover: Wesleyan University Press, 1990.

Roberts, James S. *Drink, Temperance, and the Working Class in Nineteenth-Century Germany.* Boston: Allen & Unwin, 1984.

Roeßiger, Susanne. "In aller Munde—das Deutsche Hygienemuseum." In *In aller Munde,* ed. Roth, Scheske, and Täubrich, 51–63.

Rohkrämer, Thomas. *Eine andere Moderne? Zivilisationskritik, Natur und Technik in Deutschland, 1880–1930.* Paderborn: Schöningh, 1999.

————. *Der Militarismus der "kleinen Leute": Die Kriegervereine im deutschen Kaiserreich, 1871–1914.* Munich: Oldenbourg, 1990.

Roseman, Mark, ed. *Generations in Conflict: Youth Revolt and Generation Formation in Germany, 1770–1968.* Cambridge: Cambridge University Press, 1995.

Roth, Martin. "Menschenökonomie oder der Mensch als technisches und künstlerisches Meisterwerk." In *Der gläserne Mensch,* ed. Roth and Beier, 39–67.

Roth, Martin, and Rosmarie Beier, eds. *Der gläserne Mensch—eine Sensation: Zur Kulturgeschichte eines Ausstellungsobjektes.* Stuttgart: Hatje, 1990.

Roth, Martin, Manfred Scheske, and Hans Christian Täubrich, eds. *In aller Munde: Einhundert Jahre Odol.* Dresden: Cantz, 1993.

Rotschuh, Karl Eduard. *Naturheilbewegung, Reformbewegung, Alternativbewegung.* Stuttgart: Hippokrates, 1983.

Russett, Cynthia Eagle. *Sexual Science: The Victorian Construction of Womanhood.* Cambridge: Harvard University Press, 1989.

Sachse, Steffen. "Prof. Dr. Rainer Fetscher, 1895–1945." Diss., Technical University, Dresden, 1996.

Sachsse, Christoph, and Florian Tennstedt, eds. *Soziale Sicherheit und soziale Disziplinierung: Beiträge zu einer historischen Theorie der Sozialpolitik.* Frankfurt: Suhrkamp, 1986.

Saldern, Adelheid von. "Massenfreizeitkultur im Viser: Ein Beitrag zu den Deutungs- und Einwirkungsversuchen während der Weimarer Republik." *Archiv für Sozialgeschichte* 33 (1993): 21–58.

Sauerländer, Willibald. "Vom Heimatschutz zur Rassenhygiene: Über Paul Schultze-Naumburg." In *Gesichter der Weimarer Republik,* ed. Gilman and Schmölders, 32–50.

Sauerteig, Lutz. "Ethische Richtlinien, Patientenrechte und ärztliches Verhalten bei der Arzneimittelerprobung (1891–1931)." *Medizinhistorisches Journal* 35 (2000): 303–34

———. *Krankheit, Sexualität, Gesellschaft: Geschlechtskrankheiten und Gesundheitspolitik in Deutschland im 19. und frühen 20. Jahrhundert.* Stuttgart: Franz Steiner, 1999.

Schiebinger, Londa. *The Mind Has No Sex? Women in the Origins of Modern Science.* Cambridge: Harvard University Press, 1989.

Schiller, Francis. *A Möbius Strip: Fin de Siècle Neuropsychiatry and Paul Möbius.* Berkeley: University of California Press, 1982.

Schipperges, Heinrich, ed. *Pathogenese: Grundzüge und Perspektiven einer theoretischen Pathologie.* Berlin: Springer, 1985.

Schlich, Thomas. "Einführung: Die Kontrolle notwendiger Krankheitsursachen als Strategie der Krankheitsbeherrschung im 19. und 20. Jahrhundert." In *Strategien der Kausalität,* ed. Gradmann and Schlich, 3–28.

Schmersahl, Katrin. *Medizin und Geschlecht: Zur Konstruktion der Kategorie Geschlecht im medizinischen Diskurs des 19. Jahrhunderts.* Opladen: Leske & Budrich, 1998.

Schmid, Wolfgang. "Die Bedeutung Erwin Lieks für das Selbstverständnis der Medizin in der Weimarer Republik und Nationalsozialismus." Diss., Universty of Erlangen, 1989.

Schmölders, Claudia. *Das Vorurteil im Leibe: Eine Einführung in die Physiognomik.* Berlin: Akademie, 1995.

Schoenbaum, David. *Hitler's Social Revolution: Class and Status in Nazi Germany, 1933–1939.* Garden City, N.Y.: Doubleday, 1967.

Scholz, Albrecht. "Eugenik und Rassenhygiene bei Rainer Fetscher: Höhen und Tiefen." In *Rainer Fetscher: Gedenkschrift aus Anlaß des 100. Geburtstags.* Dresden: Technical University, 1990.

Schubert, Ulrich. "Vorgeschichte und Geschichte des deutschen Hygiene-Museums in Dresden (1871–1931)." Diss., Technical University, Dresden, 1986.

Schulte, Regina. *Sperrbezirke: Tugendhaftigkeit und Prostitution in der bürgerlichen Welt.* Frankfurt: Syndikat, 1979.

Schwartz, Michael. " 'Euthanasie'—Debatten in Deutschland (1895–1945)." *Vierteljahreshefte für Zeitgeschichte* 46 (1998): 616–65.

———. *Sozialistische Eugenik: Eugenische Sozialtechnologien in Debatten und Politik der deutschen Sozialdemokratie, 1890–1933.* Bonn: Dietz, 1995.

————. "Sozialismus und Eugenik: Zur fälligen Revision eines Geschichtbildes." *Internationale Wissenschaftliche Korrespondenz* 4 (1989): 465–89.

Seidler, Eduard. "Christoph Wilhelm Hufelands 'Ideen über Pathogenie und Einfluß der Lebenskraft auf die Entstehung und Form der Krankheiten.'" In *Pathogenese*, ed. Schipperges, 83–90.

Sengoopta, Chandak. *Otto Weininger: Sex, Science, and Self in Imperial Vienna.* Chicago: University of Chicago Press, 2000.

Shortland, Michael. "The Power of a Thousand Eyes: Johann Caspar Lavater's Science of Physiognomical Perception." *Criticism* 28 (1986): 379–408.

Siegrist, Hannes, ed. *Bürgerliche Berufe: Zur Sozialgeschichte der freien und akademischen Berufe im internationalen Vergleich.* Göttingen: Vandenhoek & Ruprecht, 1988.

Spitzer, Giselher. *Der deutsche Naturismus: Idee und Entwicklung einer volkserzieherischen Bewegung im Schnitt von Lebensreform, Sport und Politik.* Ahrensburg bei Hamburg: Czwalina, 1983.

Sportmuseum Berlin. *Sportstadt Berlin in Geschichte und Gegenwart.* Berlin: Sportmuseum Berlin, 1993.

Spree, Reinhard. *Soziale Ungleichheit vor Krankheit und Tod: Zur Sozialgeschichte des Gesundheitsbereichs im Deutschen Kaiserreich.* Göttingen: Vandenhoek & Ruprecht, 1981.

Sprondel, Walter M. "Kulturelle Modernisierung durch antimodernistischen Protest: Der lebensreformerische Vegetarismus." *Kölner Zeitschrift für Soziologie und Sozialpsychologie* supp. 27 (1986): 314–30.

Stafford, Barbara M. *Body Criticism: Imaging the Unseen in Enlightenment Art and Medicine.* Cambridge: MIT Press, 1991.

Stafford, Barbara M., John La Puma, and David L. Schiedermayer. "One Face of Beauty, One Picture of Health: The Hidden Aesthetic of Medical Practice." *Journal of Medicine and Philosophy* 14 (1989): 213–30.

Steck, Max. "Albrecht Dürer als Kunsttheoretiker: Die geistes- und problemgeschichtliche Stellung seiner Proportionslehre im Kunstraum der Renaissance." In Albrecht Dürer, *Vier Bücher von der menschlichen Proportion.* Dietikon-Zürich: Stocker, 1969.

Stephan, Ludwig. "Das Dresdner Hygienemuseum in der Zeit des deutschen Faschismus (1933–1945)." Diss., Technical University, Dresden, 1986.

Stern, Fritz. *Kulturpessimismus als politische Gefahr: Eine Analyse nationaler Ideologie in Deutschland.* 1961; reprint, Munich: dtv, 1986.

Stocking, George W., ed. *Volksgeist as Method and Ethic: Essays on Boasian Ethnography and the German Anthropological Tradition.* Wisconsin: University of Wisconsin Press, 1996.

————. *Bones, Bodies, Behavior: Essays in Biological Anthropology.* Madison: University of Wisconsin Press, 1988.

Stoler, Ann Laura. "Carnal Knowledge and Imperial Power: Gender, Race, and Morality in Colonial Asia." In *Gender at the Crossroads of Knowledge*, ed. Leonardo, 51–101.

Stollberg, Gunnar. "Health and Illness in German Workers' Autobiographies from the 19th and Early 20th Centuries." *Social History of Medicine* 6 (1993): 261–76.

————. "Die Naturheilvereine im deutschen Kaiserreich." *Archiv für Sozialgeschichte* 28 (1988): 287–305.

Ströle-Bühler, Heide. *Studentischer Antisemitismus in der Weimarer Republik: Eine Analyse der burschenschaftlichen Blätter.* Frankfurt: Lang, 1991.

Stürmer, Michael. *Das ruhelose Reich: Deutschland, 1866–1918*. Berlin: Severin & Siedler, 1983.

Teichler, Hans Joachim, and Gerhard Hauk, eds. *Illustrierte Geschichte des Arbeitersports*. Bonn: Dietz, 1987.

Teuteberg, Hans Jürgen. "Zur Sozialgeschichte des Vegetarismus." *Vierteljahresschrift für Sozial- und Wirtschaftsgeschichte* 81 (1994): 33–65.

Theweleit, Klaus. *Männerphantasien*. Munich: dtv, 1995.

Thomann, Dieter. "Dienst am Deutschtum: Der medizinische Verlag J. F. Lehmann und der Nationalsozialismus." In *Medizin im "Dritten Reich,"* ed. Bleker, 54–69.

Toepfer, Karl. *Empire of Ecstasy: Nudity and Movement in German Body Culture, 1910–1935*. Berkeley: University of California Press, 1997.

———. "Nudity and Modernity in German Modern Dance, 1910–1930." *Journal of the History of Sexuality* 3 (1992): 58–108.

Trienes, Rudie. "Type Concept Revisited: A Survey of German Idealistic Morphology in the First Half of the Twentieth Century." *History and Philosophy of the Life Sciences* 11 (1989): 23–42.

Usborne, Cornelie. "The New Woman and Generation Conflict: Perceptions of Young Women's Sexual Mores in the Weimar Republic." In *Generations in Conflict*, ed. Roseman, 137–63.

———. *The Politics of the Body in Weimar Germany: Women's Reproductive Rights and Duties*. Ann Arbor: University of Michigan Press, 1992.

Volkov, Shulamit. *The Rise of Popular Antimodernism in Germany: The Urban Master Artisans, 1873–1896*. Princeton: Princeton University Press, 1978.

———. "Antisemitism as a Cultural Code." *Leo Baeck Institute Year Book* 23 (1978): 25–46.

Vondung, Klaus. "Zur Lage der Gebildeten in der wilhelminischen Zeit." In *Bildungsbürgertum*, ed. Vondung, 20–33.

———, ed. *Das wilhelminische Bildungsbürgertum: Zur Sozialgeschichte seiner Ideen*. Göttingen: Vandenhoek & Ruprecht, 1976.

Vossen, Arno. *Sonnenmenschen: Sechs Jahrzehnte Freikörperkultur in Deutschland*. Hamburg: Großflottbek, 1956.

Wagner, Franz, ed. *Medizin. Momente der Veränderung*. Berlin: Springer, 1989.

Wagner, Monika, ed. *Moderne Kunst*. Reinbek bei Hamburg: Rowohlt, 1991.

Walkowitz, Judith R. *City of Dreadful Delight: Narratives of Sexual Danger in Late-Victorian London*. Chicago: University of Chicago Press, 1992.

Walter, Franz, Viola Deneke, and Cornelia Regin. *Sozialistische Gesundheits- und Lebensreformverbände*. Bonn: Dietz, 1991.

Walter, Franz, and Cornelia Regin. "Der Verband der Vereine für Volksgesundheit." In *Sozialistische Gesundheits- und Lebensreformverbände*, ed. Walter, Deneke, and Regin, 17–96.

Wecklein, N. "Adolf Zeising." *Allgemeine Deutsche Biographie* 55, 404–411.

Wedemeyer, Bernd. *Starke Männer, starke Frauen: Eine Kulturgeschichte des Bodybuildings*. Munich: Beck, 1996.

Wehler, Hans Ulrich. *Das deutsche Kaiserreich, 1871–1918*. 5th. ed. Göttingen: Vandenhoek & Ruprecht, 1983.

Weindling, Paul. "Dissecting German Social Darwinism: Historicizing the Biology of the Organic State." *Science in Context* 11 (1998): 619–37.

———. *Health, Race, and German Politics Between National Unification and Nazism, 1870–1945*. Cambridge: Cambridge University Press, 1989.

————. "Hygienepolitik als sozialintegrative Strategie im späten Deutschen Kaiserreich." In *Medizinische Deutungsmacht im sozialen Wandel*, ed. Labisch and Spree, 37–55.

Weingart, Peter. *Doppelleben: Ludwig Ferdinand Clauss: Zwischen Rassenforschung und Widerstand.* Frankfurt: Campus, 1995.

Weingart, Peter, Jürgen Kroll, and Kurt Bayertz. *Rasse, Blut und Gene: Geschichte der Eugenik und Rassenhygiene in Deutschland.* Frankfurt: Suhrkamp, 1992.

Weisbrod, Bernd. "The Crisis of Bourgeois Society in Interwar Germany." In *Fascist Italy and Nazi Germany*, ed. Bessel, 23–39.

Weiss, Sheila Faith. "Race and Class in Fritz Lenz's Eugenics." *Medizinhistorisches Journal* 27 (1992): 5–25.

————. "The Race Hygiene Movement in Germany, 1904–1945." In *Wellborn Science*, ed. Adams, 8–68.

————. *Race Hygiene and National Efficiency: The Eugenics of Wilhelm Schallmeyer.* Berkeley: University of California Press, 1987.

Wengenroth, Ulrich, ed. *Prekäre Selbständigkeit: Zur Standortbestimmung von Handwerk, Hausindustrie und Kleingewerbe im Industrialisierungsprozess.* Stuttgart: Steiner, 1989.

Wenk, Silke. "Volkskörper und Medienspiel." *Kunstforum International* 114 (1991): 226–36.

Werner, Petra. "Zu den Auseinandersetzungen um die Institutionalisierung von Naturheilkunde und Homöopathie an der Friedrich-Wilhelms-Universität zu Berlin zwischen 1919 und 1933." *Medizin, Gesellschaft und Geschichte* 12 (1993): 205–19.

Whalen, Robert Weldon. *Bitter Wounds: German Victims of the Great War, 1914–1939.* Ithaca: Cornell University Press, 1984.

Wildmann, Daniel. *Begehrte Körper: Konstruktion und Inszenierung des "arischen" Männerkörpers im Dritten Reich.* Würzburg: Königshausen & Neumann, 1998.

Winter, Jay. *Sites of Memory, Sites of Mourning: The Great War in Cultural History.* Cambridge: Cambridge University Press, 1995.

Wolbert, Klaus. *Die Nackten und die Toten des "Dritten Reiches": Folgen einer politischen Geschichte des Körpers in der Plastik des deutschen Faschismus.* Gießen: Anabas, 1982.

Wolff, Eberhard. *Gesundheitsverein und Medikalisierungsprozess: Der homöopathische Verein Heidenheim/Brenz zwischen 1886 und 1945.* Tübingen: Vereinigung für Volkskunde, 1989.

Wuttke-Groneberg, Walter. " 'Kraft im Schlagen—Kraft im Ertragen!' Medizinische Reformbewegung und Krise der Schulmedizin in der Weimarer Republik." In *Religions- und Geistesgeschichte der Weimarer Republik*, ed. Cancik, 277–300.

Ziegler, Ulf Erdmann. *Nackt unter Nackten: Utopien der Nacktkultur, 1906–1942.* Berlin: Nishen, 1990.

Zimmerman, Andrew. "Anthropology and the Place of Knowledge in Imperial Berlin." Ph.D. diss., University of California, San Diego, 1998.

Zur Mühlen, Patrick von. *Rassenideologien: Geschichte und Hintergründe.* Berlin: Dietz, 1977.

Made in the USA
Las Vegas, NV
19 March 2022

45946248R00173